D1282803

CASH & INVESTMENT MANAGEMENT FOR NONPROFIT ORGANIZATIONS

CASH & INVESTMENT MANAGEMENT FOR NONPROFIT ORGANIZATIONS

JOHN ZIETLOW

ALAN SEIDNER

JOHN WILEY & SONS, INC.

For general information on our other products and services, or technical support, please contact our Customer Care Department within the United States at 800-762-2974, outside the United States at 317-572-3993 or fax 317-572-4002.

Wiley also publishes its books in a variety of electronic formats. Some content that appears in print, however, may not be available in electronic books.

For more information about Wiley products, visit our Web site at http://www.wiley.com.

Library of Congress Cataloging-in-Publication Data:

ISBN: 978-0-471-74165-7

Printed in the United States of America.

10 9 8 7 6 5 4 3 2 1

CONTENTS

ABOUT THE AUTHORS

JOHN T. ZIETLOW, D.B.A., CTP, is a professor of finance at Malone College in Canton, Ohio, where he teaches corporate finance, investments, short-term financial management, personal finance, and macroeconomics. He previously taught at Lee University (Cleveland, TN) and Mount Vernon Nazarene University (Mount Vernon, OH). He is certified through the Association for Financial Professionals as a Certified Treasury Professional (CTP). Dr. Zietlow also serves as associate faculty member at Indiana University-Purdue University at Indianapolis (IUPUI), where he teaches graduate nonprofit financial management, and as an adjunct instructor for the University of Maryland University College, where he teaches graduate short-term financial management. He has done corporate training and consulting in the areas of cash management, treasury management, and investment management and portfolio performance evaluation. He holds membership in the Financial Management Association, Association for Financial Professionals, Association for Research on Nonprofit Organizations and Voluntary Action (ARNOVA), and the Financial Education Association. He also serves as a consultant/trainer for the Investment Management Consultants Association (IMCA). He may be reached via e-mail at: jzietlow@hotmail.com, and maintains a web site at: www.johnzietlow.com.

    ALAN G. SEIDNER was the founder of Seidner & Company of Pasadena, California, an investment management and consulting firm whose roster included high-net-worth investors, healthcare organizations, major corporations, nonprofit institutions, and municipalities. Mr. Seidner has written many financial reference works and is a frequent speaker on investment techniques and strategies. He has also provided testimony before federal government agencies on the performance of pension fund investments.

ACKNOWLEDGMENTS

John Zietlow acknowledges and is deeply grateful for the contributions of these individuals, who lent their expertise to specific areas of the book: Clara Miller, Mark Jones, Sandy Beigle, Mary Daciolas, Gregg Capin, Dan Busby, Nick Wallace, Bill Hopkins, Carolyn King, Wayne Kissinger, Georgette Cipolla, William Michels, Kathleen Kavanagh, David Minei, Dave Wechter, and Eric Lane. He also thanks administrative assistant Gretchen Sudar, student assistant Dan Yard, and financial intern Matthew Toppin, all of Malone College, for their clerical and research assistance.

Special appreciation goes to Lilly Endowment, Inc., for initiating a major study of the financial management of faith-based organizations by providing grant money to Indiana State University while I was on the finance faculty there. The individuals responsible for evaluating and guiding the grant process were Fred Hofheinz and Jim Hudnut-Beumler. Members of the advisory panel assembled as part of that grant project were invaluable in shaping the research project that underlies several of the significant findings presented in this book. They believed, as we do, that proficient financial management can greatly aid in the accomplishment of charitable missions. I am particularly thankful to the 288 financial managers who took part in the exhaustive survey covering financial management practices employed by their organizations. Thanks also for research input and critiques provided by Dr. Raj Aggarwal and Dr. Kathleen Eisenhardt.

We are particularly grateful to Susan McDermott, senior editor at John Wiley & Sons, who was instrumental in directing the project from inception to publication. Thanks also go to Natasha Andrews-Noel for her work as the production editor. Our sincere appreciation also goes to Marla Bobowick, who first made it possible to publish with Wiley.

Finally, we thank our families for bearing with us in the arduous process of putting this guide together. My contribution is dedicated to my parents, Harold and Miriam Zietlow, for their continual encouragement, support, and prayers.

Alan Seidner wishes to thank former professional staff members of Seidner & Company, Investment Management, for their help in researching and completing some of the material in this publication. Specifically, special thanks go to Joan West, Leah Romero, Sandee Glickman, Joe Flores, and Lina Macias. I am also very appreciative to Malone College for a summer research grant that helped me complete the research and writing for this project.

PREFACE

This book addresses two management issues that came up often in the nonprofit arena. One challenge that most nonprofits face is cash flow management. A second dilemma is how, amidst all of the other management tasks, to build and then effectively steward investment assets. We provide information that should prove useful to financial managers and staff, the CEO/ED, board members, foundations and other grantmakers, and educators and trainers working to provide focused help for those carrying out the nonprofit treasury function.

Anyone who has worked for or served on the board of a financially stressed organization knows how challenging cash flow problems can be. Often, this stress comes from being undercapitalized even from start-up; at other times, the underlying cause is an inadequate cash and liquidity position. Financial stress is compounded when cash inflows and outflows are uneven (maybe due to overly high expenses), unsynchronized, or unpredictable. We develop an understanding of these problems, tools to monitor cash flow dynamics and the cash position, and cash forecasting methods.

Investable assets may come from purposeful actions or unforeseen events. Your organization may deliberately "save" five or even ten percent of its revenues each year in order to build up operating or maintenance expense reserves. It may solicit capital campaign or endowment fund gifts. Proceeds from a loan or bond issue may be invested prior to the disbursement of these funds. Or, your organization may unexpectedly receive a bequest or gift of appreciated stock, or receive a large grant or contract thought previously to be a long shot at best. Regardless, investment dollars are now available to your organization, and you wish to be an effective steward of those funds.

Our presentation assumes that basic financial management policies and procedures are already in place at your organization. Should you wish to review your core financial management policies in such areas as accounting, budgeting, reporting and scorecards, risk management, financial aspects of human resource or information technology management, long-term debt, capital project analysis, social enterprise evaluation, and strategic and long-range financial planning, please consult our companion book entitled *Financial Management for Nonprofit Organizations: Policies and Practices* (Hoboken, NJ: John Wiley & Sons, 2007).

We begin our presentation with a look inside the "typical" finance office in a nonprofit organization as part of our first chapter. We develop the primary financial objective, which is target liquidity (including cash and items that can provide cash within a reasonable period of time). We address the steps you may follow to set your organization's target liquidity.

In Chapter 2 we delve into the all-important cash planning process and the measures that you can use to monitor and manage your organization's liquidity. We introduce the basic elements of managing cash flow.

Chapter 3 details the objective and methods for bringing in cash and positioning cash and liquidity. The U.S. payments system and all of the major methods used to remit cash by your donors, grantors, customers, and contractors are covered. We have a special focus on electronic collections through direct payment. The basics of international cash collections and positioning are also profiled.

Cash disbursements are the subject of Chapter 4. Value may be created for your organization based on payment method and timing. Your organization's financial integrity is preserved through appropriate internal controls and several bank services such as positive pay, imaging, and account reconciliation. We provide coverage of checks, drafts, and electronic disbursement methods, including card payments. Our inclusion of controlled disbursement and zero balance accounts will assist you in fine-tuning your organization's disbursement system.

Your greatest potential ally in managing cash is your banking partner. Banking relationship management comprises our Chapter 5 material. We not only give you a banker's perspective on your account, but also profile the bank's availability schedule for making funds available to your organization as well as the bank's account analysis statement. We explain how banks may be compensated via balances or service fees for the services they provide your organization. We also give counsel on how best to select your organization's primary bank.

One source of cash for organizations temporarily short of funds is borrowing. Debt management, with a special focus on short-term loans, is the topic developed in Chapter 6. Included here are bank perspectives on a nonprofit loan request and several debt management metrics and benchmarks.

Our attention turns to investments and investment management in our final two chapters. Chapter 7 provides the principles and procedures you will need for managing shorter-term investments that form your organization's operating and strategic reserves. Included here are standard operating investment procedures and an introduction to investment operations. For organizations wishing to earn enhanced returns, risk-return perspectives are provided in this chapter.

Finally, Chapter 8 offers investment principles and procedures for longer-term investments appropriate for endowments, self-insurance, and pensions. The primary focus is on endowment management and the reasons for using outside investment advisors.

We trust that you will find this guide helpful in establishing or revising your policies for cash and investment management. We are confident that many of the tools and techniques presented, including the case studies and examples of nonprofits' practices, will prove instrumental in improving and benchmarking your organization's practices. Please direct any feedback to John Zietlow (jzietlow@hotmail.com).

CASH FLOW AND YOUR CASH POSITION

Your organization's primary financial objective is to ensure that financial resources are available when needed (timing), as needed (amount), and at reasonable cost (cost-effectiveness), and that once mobilized, these resources are protected from impairment and spent according to mission and donor purposes. The goal of this book is to enable you and your organization to achieve this primary financial objective. The reality of many nonprofit organizations is quite different: recurrent cash crunches representing a mismatch in timing or amount, or worse—perhaps an unsolvable cash crisis that leads to high-cost fundraising, asset sale, or borrowing episodes. For others, fraud or mismanagement lead to misspending of funds, and the organization falls short of doing all it could in reaching its mission or complying with donors' intent.

Surveys of chief executive officers and executive directors (CEOs/EDs) indicate that financial management is one of the areas that these managers find most challenging.[1] Many managers, including those who are held responsible for the financial management of the organizations—whom we shall refer to as chief financial officers (CFOs) even though their actual titles vary widely—lack the necessary time, training, and aptitudes for properly managing the finance function. This book should prove helpful for the latter two issues. Furthermore, after "develop, communicate, and execute strategic plans," the three "musts" for effective finance leaders in the business sector for the twenty-first century are (1) inspire other groups to get behind overall financial goals, (2) educate colleagues on financial implications of business decisions, and (3) improve core function efficiency to assume expanded responsibilities.[2] Similar objectives apply to nonprofit financial leaders, and you will find the information presented here to be valuable for all three purposes.

This book will guide you on many facets of cash and investment management in order for your organization to achieve and maintain financial strength. We believe this is accomplished only by financial management proficiency. Proficient financial management includes using the best available methods and tools to achieve the primary financial objective. Our road map toward financial management proficiency includes practical help with:

- Defining the appropriate financial target for your organization
- Cash planning
- Tapping sources of cash to improve your cash flow
- Setting liquidity policies, including those for cash reserves, operating reserves, and strategic reserves
- Gathering cash efficiently
- Mobilizing and controlling cash
- Disbursing cash efficiently while averting fraud
- Managing your bank relationship
- Borrowing for short-term needs
- Investing for the short-term
- Investing for the medium-term
- Investing for endowments, annuity accounts, and retirement accounts
- Harnessing information technology (IT) to better accomplish cash and investment management

We start our journey in this chapter by setting the context for nonprofit financial management. Then we profile the primary financial objective of the nonprofit: achieving a liquidity target. Next we list the metrics and financial ratios that may be used to evaluate the organization's liquidity and indicate how to set your organization's target liquidity. Finally we show how improved cash management and investment management facilitate your achievement of targeted liquidity.

1.1 LIFE IN THE NONPROFIT FINANCE OFFICE

We see two common maladies in the financial practices of nonprofits. Fortunately, these operating modes are easily improved.

Operating Mode #1: "I'll Fly by the Seat of My Pants." Translation: Why bother setting a targeted cash position or targeted liquidity level? Most nonprofits operate in this operating mode. These organizations use either a break-even financial target (revenues equal to expenses each year, or a "balanced budget"), or what is somewhat better, a small profit ("net surplus") target. The former nonprofits believe they are scrupulously carrying out their mandate—"after all, we're a nonprofit organization"—and should therefore be congratulated. The latter know that growth in programs and services and funding new facilities or improved future salaries and benefits require the organization to earn revenues in excess of expenses. However, an organization can have a cash crunch or cash crisis when pursuing either break-even or a small net profit, and may not properly manage its investments or borrowing if not pursuing a liquidity target. We shall have more to say about this shortly.

Operating Mode #2: "Your Guess Is as Good as Mine." Translation: Why bother forecasting the organization's cash flow and cash position? Managers in most organizations really don't get it when it comes to doing these projections. Some of them argue: "But we project the remainder of the year as far as staying within the budget—isn't that good enough?" That's a great practice, but no, it really isn't sufficient. Your revenues and expenses are done on an accrual basis, meaning they may not reflect when cash is coming in or going out. Put another way, your operating budget is not the same as a cash budget. We will illustrate this point by using an actual organization's operating results for two recent years, as captured by its year-end Statement of Activity report. You can think of the Statement of Activity as an "income statement." Although slightly different from your operating budget, the Statement of Activity shows your organization's revenues and expenses (whether included in your budget or not) for the period just ended. It does include the results of some nonoperating activities—such as unrealized investment gains and losses that you may not have included in your budget. For our purposes, though, it will give us a good idea of why changes in your cash position can vary greatly from your operating results and especially from your reported change in net assets. Here are two recent years' actual data from the Leukemia and Lymphoma Society; we show the amount by which revenues exceed expenses ("change in net assets") as well as the cash actually provided (used) by the organization's operations that year. Notice in the last row the difference we calculated in these amounts for the two years.

	YEAR 1	YEAR 2
Change in net assets	$ 6,136,000	$ 8,481,000
Net cash provided by operating activities	$10,636,000	$12,046,000
Difference (amount of additional cash)	$ 4,500,000	$ 3,565,000

In this case, the Society brought in between $3.5 and $4.5 million in additional cash from its operations, over and above what its "income statement" reported. For the Society this is great news, in that the cash position is higher than what one would have expected from looking at revenues and expenses; in other years, or for other organizations, though, the difference could be negative—and the organization could be thrust into a cash crunch or cash crisis.

No doubt some readers will wonder "But what if my organization is accounting for things on a cash basis—wouldn't that eliminate the need to forecast cash?" Again, the answer is emphatically "No!" The two activities that drive a wedge between changes in your operating results and your cash position changes are investing activities and financing activities. Let's compare the Society's change in net assets with the change in its cash position for the same two years:

	YEAR 1	YEAR 2
Change in net assets	$ 6,136,000	$8,481,000
Net (decrease) increase in cash and cash equivalents	$22,066,000	($8,991,000)
Difference (amount of additional cash)	$15,930,000	$−17,472,000

The differences between the reported "net revenue" and the actual change in the Society's cash position are very large in both years. In year 2, had the Society just assumed that its cash position would change in the same amount as its operating results, it would have had a $17 million surprise. Worse yet, what if management had assumed that cash would increase more than net revenues, as it had in year 1? Unfortunately, we are constantly told by nonprofit managers and staffers that they do not construct a cash forecast. The single best way to ensure that your organization sees the importance of a cash forecast is to adopt the appropriate primary financial objective: a targeted liquidity level.

1.2 TARGET LIQUIDITY AS THE PRIMARY FINANCIAL OBJECTIVE

Let's recap: We are striving "to ensure that financial resources are available when needed (timing), as needed (amount), and at reasonable cost (cost-effectiveness), and that once mobilized, these resources are protected from impairment and spent according to mission and donor purposes." The best way to ensure that we accomplish this goal is to restate the organization's primary financial objective as "achievement of a target liquidity level." We will expand on liquidity and what that means later, but for now we make this operational by restating our primary financial objective this way: "Manage cash flow to ensure that the organization achieves its target cash position." "Keeping your eye on the ball" means you will have two focuses: cash flow and cash position. Well-run businesses recognize that cash is the lifeblood of the business and the engine of value for shareholders; we recognize that cash and cash flow are even more vital for nonprofits, in that some of the financing sources available to businesses are unavailable or available in smaller amounts to nonprofits. Nonprofits do not have the ability to issue stock to raise capital, and short-term borrowing and long-term bonds are restricted by organization policy and/or lender credit standards. Correspondingly, these lending sources may not lend to nonprofits or may lend smaller amounts, and possibly charge higher interest rates. This is less true for nonprofits that are in the education or healthcare fields, although private elementary and secondary schools often have difficulty in borrowing. There are two key points here: (1) Internal generation of cash is preeminent; and (2) once your cash position is impaired, it is often quite difficult to regain your footing.

(a) WHAT IS LIQUIDITY?　Liquidity, broadly defined, includes solvency, liquidity as traditionally defined, and financial flexibility. Liquidity, solvency, and financial flexibility are related concepts but are easily confused.

(i) Narrow Definition of Liquidity.　Liquidity, as traditionally defined, is what we were defining earlier when we spoke of having enough financial resources to pay obligations without incurring excessive cost. It entails the resources we have stored up (cash and short-term investments), the resources we have available from the bank (credit line amounts not already drawn down), and incoming cash resources (cash revenues in excess of cash expenses in the forthcoming months). Notice, then, that it encompasses the stock of liquid resources as well as the incoming cash flow. It considers how long it takes to convert an asset into cash or how close a liability is to being paid as well as the cost at which added funds may be obtained.

(ii) Solvency.　By contrast, solvency is the degree to which our near-term assets exceed our near-term liabilities—as measured on the balance sheet or the statement of financial position. It focuses solely on the stock, or stored-up amount, of "current assets:" cash, uncollected credit sales or uncollected legally enforceable pledges that we expect within one year, grant or contract receipts we expect within one year, inventories, and prepaid expenses. The total of these is then compared to the stock of near-term or current liabilities: bills such as invoices for supplies that we owe within one year but have not yet written a check for. Nowhere is the speed of asset conversion to cash or nearness of payables due dates measured in the computation of solvency. A common measure of solvency is the current ratio, which simply divides current liabilities into current assets. Another common solvency measure is net working capital, which is the difference between current assets and current liabilities.

　　Both current ratio and net working capital are poor ratios for indicating how liquid an organization is: If an organization has obsolete and unsalable inventories and uncollectible pledges or other receivables, most of which are financed by long-term financing (past years' net revenues, let's say), it would report a high current ratio and large positive net working capital but very little liquidity. In general, solvency measures are deficient measures of the organization's cash resources and cash demands, both because of the failure to reflect how soon assets or liabilities add to or subtract from our cash position and also because they view the organization as about to be liquidated (we will sell off current assets, pay off current liabilities) rather than as it really is, a going concern (both current assets and current liabilities will be replaced by newly arising current assets and liabilities, possibly of larger amounts than those we have today). Note again, the flow of cash is not captured by solvency measures. To get at that, one must know how soon the various current assets will turn to cash and how soon the various current liabilities must be paid. This critical difference between solvency and liquidity means you or your banker might under- or overestimate the liquidity of your organization if only solvency measures are considered. It is important to calculate and monitor liquidity measures and not rely solely on solvency measures. We shall return to specific measures later in this chapter.

(iii) Financial Flexibility.   Finally, we need to understand *financial flexibility*. One way to define financial flexibility is "the ability of the firm to augment its future cash flows to cover any unforeseen needs or to take advantage of any unforeseen opportunities."[3] Thinking also about an organization's financial plans for the future, we suggest that financial flexibility includes *strategic liquidity*—the ability to tap liquid funds, including those made available by foundations, grantors, or arranged borrowing, to fund strategic initiatives such as program expansion, geographical expansion, new hires, mergers and acquisitions, social enterprises, and collaborative ventures. In fact, one measure of financial flexibility—sustainable growth rate—implicitly incorporates strategic liquidity by addressing whether an organization's financial policies are consistent with its growth plans.[4] Finally, a "financially strong organization"— one with a high degree of liquidity *and* a low degree of debt financing—would tend to have greater financial flexibility, all other things being equal. That strength is further enhanced by an organization that (1) could augment its revenue because it has a very good reputation among present and potential donors, grant or contract sources, and (if a commercial nonprofit such as a college or hospital) present and potential customers or clients; and (2) could reduce its expenses because it has mostly contract workers instead of permanent full-time employees or has other discretionary expenses that it could reduce at short notice and still maintain the same level of service provision.

(iv) Broad Definition of Liquidity.   The relationship between these different liquidity of solvency concepts can be confusing, so we offer Exhibit 1.1 to show the relationships. Liquidity broadly defined encompasses financial flexibility, narrow liquidity (liquidity as traditionally defined), solvency and financial flexibility. Narrow liquidity, in turn, includes solvency. Your organization should determine the appropriate target for liquidity, as traditionally defined, but also include in its planning model the financial flexibility concept. In this way, its financial function will best support mission achievement, the reason why your organization exists as a nonprofit entity.

(b) WHY IS ACHIEVING TARGET LIQUIDITY THE PREFERRED OPERATIONAL PRIMARY FINANCIAL OBJECTIVE?   Setting and attaining your target liquidity level should be your primary financial objective for at least seven reasons.

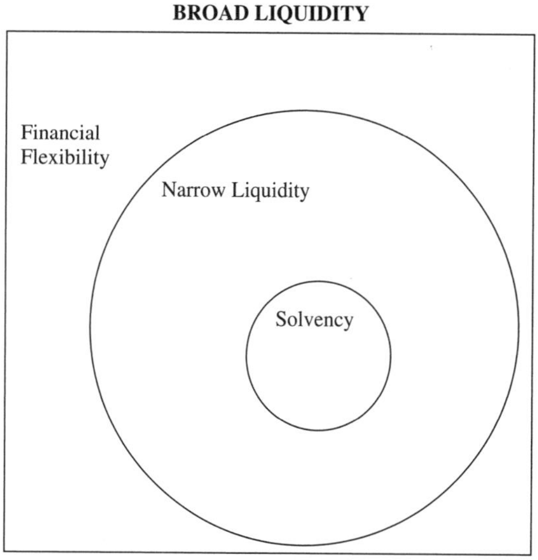

BROAD LIQUIDITY

Financial
Flexibility

Narrow Liquidity

Solvency

EXHIBIT 1.1 RELATIONSHIP OF BROAD LIQUIDITY TO SOLVENCY, NARROW LIQUIDITY, AND FINANCIAL FLEXIBILITY

First, it is too complex to try to juggle multiple financial objectives simultaneously. We understand the importance of achieving a net surplus—revenues greater than expenses—for many organizations, for example. In a nonprofit organization, however, profits are not a measure of success, and there may be periods during which the organization will incur expenses greater than revenues. Furthermore, in an organization that is properly accounting for depreciation—and setting aside cash to maintain or replace deteriorating assets—and not growing, revenues may not need to exceed expenses for the organization to maintain its financial health. At bottom, the organization's need to generate a surplus serves the organization's need to achieve a certain level of liquidity, not vice versa. Correspondingly, we recommend that the financial manager focuses on the liquidity position and then secondarily on the net revenue target since that may constitute one of the means to enable the organization to build toward its liquidity target.

We also understand the desire to reduce or minimize financial risk—another of the financial objectives we hear articulated by nonprofit CFOs. Let's say that your organization has three primary financial objectives: Achieve its target liquidity, earn $50,000 in net revenue, and minimize financial risk. It is far easier to measure and monitor target liquidity and consider the effects of net revenue and financial risk on tomorrow's liquidity position than to try to gauge every programmatic alternative's effect on all three objectives simultaneously. It is also easier to communicate to program managers the need to cut expenses in order to maintain the organization's financial strength than to say something like: "We should pare expenses because that will have a 10 percent effect on financial strength, a 20 percent effect on net revenue, and a 7 percent effect on financial risk."

Second, targeting liquidity frees the organization to run surpluses or deficits in some years in support of the mission and the organization's programs, as long as the organization does not veer outside its targeted liquidity range. For example, consider an organization that has just altered its policy and is now targeting $100,000 to $350,000 in liquidity, but is running above that range and projects that the next fiscal year will end with $450,000 in liquidity. Its board may approve a budget with a $100,000 deficit—or even larger. Relatively few nonprofit boards purposefully run an operating deficit, partly because they are targeting the wrong objective—financial break-even or perhaps a net surplus. This slows the growth of some nonprofits and causes others to fall short of meeting large one-time needs in their service populations. Other organizations are very "cash poor" and desperately need to run very large surpluses for several years to address their lack of liquidity. A mindless "financial break-even" or $X surplus primary financial objective unnecessarily handicaps organizations.

Third, liquidity targeting supersedes cost minimization as the primary financial objective. Those organizations that indicate cost minimization is their primary financial objective run several risks. They may not invest in technology, because that is seldom the least costly way of accomplishing something. For example, online banking may cause the organization to incur cost, but the speed of fraud detection, the closer-to-real-time balance information that becomes available 24/7/365, the ability to transfer funds or pay off purchase card balances quickly, and the rapid detection of cash forecast misses that combine to make this an effective financial management tool. Organizations may underinvest in training as well, causing losses in organizational effectiveness, greater personnel turnover, and less effective provision of the nonprofit's services by these employees. "Penny-wise and pound-foolish" tactics such as underinvesting in fundraising—one of the more common maladies of donation-dependent nonprofits—also arise from a cost minimization approach. True, there's no sense overpaying for supplies, products, and services—but let's not focus on cost minimization as our primary financial objective. That said, there are times in which a cash crunch or cash crisis will force a cost minimization and cost deferral mode on the nonprofit.

Fourth, the most commonly espoused primary financial objectives—earning a surplus or breaking even financially—are ambiguous at best and misleading at worst. They are not cash-based, unless the organization operates on a cash basis during the year and has an accountant convert them to an accrual basis of accounting at year-end. Even if the organization operates on a cash basis, not keeping track of receivables and payables, it can land in a cash crunch or cash crisis. It may incur obligations that are not reflected in its financial statements and then not have cash on hand to pay those obligations when they come due. Accrued wages, salaries, interest, and taxes may come due and payable, as may amounts owed to clients (deferred revenues), suppliers (accounts payable), or other organizations (grants payable). An organization would have to develop and use a comprehensive and accurate cash forecasting system to avoid such an occurrence. Even then, an operating surplus or operating break-even mind-set may lead to a cash shortfall. At times this happens because a large amount of cash comes in that is temporarily or permanently restricted, but not properly segregated and spent on current operating expenses. This happens most often when certain operating items are left out of the cash forecast or when nonoperating items are significant. Nonoperating items are items that fall under either investing cash flows or financing cash flows categories. For example, an organization may purchase a van or bus but it has not yet received pledges or grant monies to pay for the vehicle. Or it may have a balloon payment on a note or loan that comes due after 10 years, but because the organization does not have a liquidity target, it has not adequately planned its cash position for this event. Organizations targeting liquidity are aware of all drivers of cash flow, including accrual-based accounting entries, investing inflows and outflows, and financing inflows and outflows.

Our fifth reason is a positive one: Targeting liquidity keeps the focus on the cash position and cash flows—and the effects of cash flows on the cash position. The chances of being thrust into a cash crunch or cash crisis are much lower, and if either would occur, it would most likely have been anticipated. When you see a cash crunch coming, you may be able to arrange for additional grants, donations, or a bank loan to cover the shortfall.

Sixth, targeting liquidity as the primary financial objective enforces a necessary discipline on the organization's board, managers, and employees. This discipline includes the need to replenish the liquidity position if it is reduced for an urgent need. This discipline is thus a valuable proactive and proficiency-enhancing safeguard for the organization. In the event that the organization builds liquidity above its target range, having the target as the primary financial objective forces the board and management team to determine how and when to burn off the excess.

Seventh and finally, this objective of liquidity targeting leads to the right managerial actions. To generate cash flow to maintain or build the liquidity position, an organization is incented to increase revenues (perhaps fundraising, grants, and contracts) and decrease expenses, while keeping an eye on the cash effects of these activities rather than the net revenue effects. The organization will naturally want to increase revenues and decrease expenses in order to maximize its mission attainment and still reach its cash target. Its cash target is a range and is managed intertemporally, or across time. The organization may move up and down within its liquidity range without major concern. It is thus able to operate with maximum flexibility in its mission outreach, all the while conserving financial strength within some range deemed appropriate.

In summary, achieving an approximate liquidity target is the most appropriate primary financial objective. This primary financial objective best supports mission attainment. The operational primary financial objective linked to this approximate liquidity target objective is: Manage your cash position and your cash flow. This restatement puts "approximate liquidity target" into operational terms. Reviewing yesterday's financial results and statements, making today's decisions, and planning for tomorrow's initiatives are all best done while focusing on cash flow and the resultant cash position.

(c) WHY DO SO FEW NONPROFITS STRIVE FOR AND ACHIEVE TARGET LIQUIDITY?   A growing number of nonprofits strive for cash flow and liquidity objectives. There are several reasons why other organizations still target financial break-even, a net surplus, or some other primary financial objective. The good news is that more and more nonprofits *are* striving for and beginning to achieve a target liquidity level.

First, we note that many healthcare and educational organizations are really "businesses in disguise." These "commercial nonprofits" price their services or products much like a for-profit business would. And, yes, other nonprofits cloak their business orientation behind their nonprofit status-many of the nonprofit credit counseling organizations were exposed by the IRS because of their abusive practices:

> Over the last few years, the IRS has seen an increasing number of credit counseling organizations become mere sellers of debt-management plans. They appear motivated primarily by profit, and offer little or no counseling or education. In many cases the credit counseling organizations also appear to serve the private interests of related for-profit businesses, officers, and directors. ... As a result, the IRS has revoked, terminated or proposed revoking the exemptions of credit counseling organizations representing 41 percent of the revenue in the industry, based on the latest available IRS filing data. The IRS also halted the growth of abusive credit counseling organizations. Of 110 applications reviewed, only 3 met the requirements for tax-exempt status; 95 were not approved and the remaining 12 are pending.[5]

Commercially oriented nonprofits, especially hospitals and other healthcare organizations that are considering a future conversion to for-profit status, may favor a primary financial objective of net revenue maximization (also called profit maximization). Liquidity targeting may then serve as a secondary objective.

Second, numerous nonprofits have run with the "received wisdom" of past generations that, since they are legally nonprofit, they should not make a profit. What to do then? Striving for financial break-even became the default primary financial objective. Organizations such as Yale University made front-page news because they did not save up for maintenance and renovation of their crumbling buildings. Cash flow concerns and liquidity concerns were swept under the carpet and just considered to be part of the nonprofit landscape. Many nonprofits, established with ideals and wonderful missions but little financial understanding, went belly-up.

Third, on a positive note, we see more organizations that *are* becoming aware of the importance of cash flow and the cash position, leading a number of them to strive for target liquidity.

Illustrating from one of the field studies we conducted in the early 1990s, we found that a top-performing human services agency, Peoria Rescue Ministries, managed overtly toward a cash position target. After studying its cash position and cash flow patterns over a period of several years, management determined the amount of liquidity it would need to hold in cash and short-term investments after its peak donation season (ending about at Christmas). Management determined that this "stockpile" would last it through the dry late summer season, and afterward the donation stream would enable rebuilding the liquidity position.

In a more broadly based survey of 29 faith-based organizations holding membership in the Evangelical Fellowship of Mission Agencies, we asked member organizations' CFOs what the primary financial objective was. We found that 35.7 percent stated this as "break even financially," which is a traditional response that seems to be tied to the notion that the identity as a nonprofit dictates this sort of an objective. Positively, we found that 21.4 percent of the CFOs articulated "maintain a targeted level of cash reserves and financial flexibility" as the primary financial objective, and an additional 14.3 percent selected "maximize cash flow." Summarizing, we note that 35.7 percent (21.4 + 14.3) are focusing, now, on cash flow and cash position—or "liquidity management."[6]

The growing recognition that many nonprofits are undercapitalized is also seen in the behavior of private foundations, as they increasingly focus on grantee organization capacity. A prime example is the Kellogg Foundation initiative launched midyear 2006, which provided $9.3 million to enable Fieldstone Alliance and the Nonprofit Finance Fund to jointly consult, train, and otherwise build organizational and financial capacity in the 800-plus Kellogg grantee organizations.

In past nonprofit financial management, the bean counters have predominated, but true treasurers are coming to the fore. Let's explain this by looking at the treasury function versus the controllership function.

The treasury function includes cash management, credit management, financial input to inventory management, arranging short-term borrowing, making short-term investments, arranging long-term borrowing and mortgage borrowing, pension fund management, financial aspects of benefit administration, banking relationship management, and the financial aspects of fundraising evaluation. The controllership function, however, is concerned with accounting, taxes, financial reporting, adhering to regulations, budgets, and audits. It may also include mechanical aspects of payables and receivables. In our experience, the controllership function, because it must be completed to satisfy your grant agencies, donors, the IRS, and your audit firm, takes precedence over the treasury function in most nonprofits. We commonly hear that nonprofits spend a tremendous amount of time on their financial compliance and reporting. As many nonprofits have limited financial staff, something has to give—and that something is proficient management of the treasury function.

Fourth, it has been difficult to set the appropriate target liquidity level. There is some disagreement as to what is "enough liquidity" versus "too much liquidity." Three months to six months of expenses constitute a partial answer to how much liquidity to hold, but at best this simply buffers your organization against cash inflow and cash outflow mismatches and the seasonality of your organization's funds flows. Typically organizations need to hold more funds than that in order to buffer against emergencies and to pre-fund large investment amounts, such as capital expenditures or program expansion. This is especially so when the organization does not have a credit line at a financial institution or has drawn down most or all of the line.

Fifth, the best time to set policy and get a handle on target liquidity is at start-up. Nonprofits can learn from businesses, and the businesses nonprofits are most comparable to are small businesses. The primary reason for the failure of a small business is that it is undercapitalized. This means that the founders of the organization did not fully anticipate just how much money it would take to launch the organization successfully. We see the same thing with nonprofits. It also happens that, even if the organization was properly capitalized at start-up, liquidity erodes and is not replenished.

1.3 SETTING YOUR LIQUIDITY TARGET

(a) STARTING POINTS.   Setting your organization's target liquidity is not a simple process. There is some hard work to do before your management team can first agree and your board can then agree on what the appropriate target liquidity is.

First, study the failure rates in your industry. What organizations have failed and had to be acquired by other organizations, or went bankrupt and had to be shut down? Why did these organizations fail? What could have been done to prevent them from failing? Did they start out undercapitalized? Did they fail to set an appropriate liquidity target, once the organization had gotten started up? Did they draw down funds from this liquidity level and fail to replenish them? Or was it due to the loss of a key funding source or some new competition?

Second, study bond ratings of nonprofits similar to yours. A.M. Best Company, Inc., Dominion Bond Rating Service Ltd., Fitch, Inc., Moody's Investors Service, and the Standard & Poor's Division of the McGraw Hill Companies Inc. are all bond rating organizations that are nationally recognized in the United States. One or more of these rating agencies will evaluate the financial position and creditworthiness of large healthcare and educational organizations. Within healthcare, hospitals, nursing homes, and comprehensive care organizations are rated. Within education, public universities, private colleges, and some large elementary and secondary private schools are rated. Some large human service organizations are also rated. More important than the actual rating assigned is the reasoning behind that rating. For example, if a hospital received a triple-B rating, what financial attributes of that hospital led to that rating being assigned? Specifically, how was liquidity measured by the rating agency, and how did it score the level of liquidity that was measured? If you go to the Web site of any of these rating organizations, search for its "ratings criteria." Within the ratings criteria, search for liquidity. Try to determine how important liquidity is for the rating organization and the exact way in which liquidity is measured.

Third, ask your banker or ask bank calling officers about liquidity and how much liquidity to hold when they try to sell you on their services. Ask them about organizations that they are aware of that have failed and the reasons for those failures. Church lending practices are a great example here. When a bank considers a building loan proposal, it will offer better terms or a larger loan amount when a church has a larger dollar amount of cash and short-term investments. Or a bank may allow a higher level of debt service (principal plus interest) as a percentage of normal monthly giving if the church is holding a higher level of liquidity.

Fourth, do some networking to check around for practices within your industry. Determine, for your industry, the highest amount, the lowest amount, and the median amount of each of these values:

- Cash and cash equivalents
- Short-term investments
- Amount of cash that is unrestricted
- Size of credit line, if any
- Average usage of credit line, if any (not just the year-end amount, though)
- From the previous two items, calculate the unused portion of the credit line (total size of credit line minus average usage of credit line)

Fifth, study your organization's seasonality and cyclicality of cash flow. Has there been any financial crisis in the past? What are the causes of any financial crisis your organization may have experienced? What corrections have been taken or could be taken to prevent future a recurrence? What information can you glean from this data that would help you to set your cash position?

Sixth, assess your organization's vulnerability to a cash crunch or cash crisis. Does most of your revenue come from a single source? Is the marketplace becoming crowded with similar organizations? Is donor fatigue an issue with your donor base? Are expenses such as energy costs and benefit costs rising rapidly, while your revenues increase only slowly? Any of these scenarios suggest holding a higher level of liquidity. You will also want to project your operating cash flow, investing cash flow, and financing cash flow, as we show later.

Seventh, total up your "standbys." That is, what are some of the sources of funds that you could access quickly in an emergency? These might include the unused portion of your credit line, accounts receivable that you could factor (sell to a third party, receiving an advance), gifts from board members, or even your own personal funds. List all such sources and the amount that you could most likely receive from them within, say, a two-month time frame. The greater the amount and the more reliable your standbys, the less liquidity you may have to hold on an ongoing basis.

(b) CALCULATE KEY RATIOS.   Your job of comparing your solvency, liquidity, and financial flexibility to previous years as well as to peer organizations in your industry will be much easier once you calculate some key ratios. Be careful when doing peer comparisons: Other organizations may use a different approach to valuing assets or estimating future obligations, given the latitude offered by generally accepted accounting principles (GAAP). We offer some ratios in each category. You may wish to calculate two or three from each category both for your organization and for a similar organization, then place the numbers in a chart or table to facilitate your management and board discussions. For more on these and similar ratios, as well as calculation and interpretation examples, see Chapter 7 and the appendixes to that chapter in our companion book, *Financial Management for Nonprofit Organizations* (John Wiley & Sons, 2007).

(i) Solvency Ratios.   We present four solvency ratios to assist you in assessing your organization's solvency. Calculating and analyzing more than one provides you with a composite measure of solvency. One ratio in isolation should never be relied on to provide an adequate perspective on solvency.

CASH RATIO.
The cash ratio is calculated as:

Cash and cash equivalents / Current liabilities

All data is taken from the balance sheet (or statement of financial position). Use unrestricted and temporarily restricted cash and cash equivalents in any case in which a portion of the organization's cash and equivalents is permanently restricted. The more cash the organization has relative to near-term bills coming due, the more solvent the organization is. Low cash ratios signal high risk of not being able to make upcoming payments. Recognize that this perspective is incomplete, as some bills are not recorded on the balance sheet but paid out when invoices are received (if due and payable when received) or payroll dates roll around.

CASH RESERVE RATIO.
The cash reserve ratio is calculated as:

Cash and cash equivalents / Total expenses

The cash amount is taken from the balance sheet (or statement of financial position) and total expenses are from the same year's statement of activity. Use unrestricted and temporarily restricted cash and cash equivalents in any case in which a portion of the organization's cash and equivalents is permanently restricted. The ratio value shows how long the organization could maintain its spending if no revenues came in and it had to rely on its cash to pay the bills. The more cash the organization has relative to total annual expenses, the more solvent the organization is. Low cash reserve ratios signal high risk of not being able to make ongoing payments. This ratio may give overly optimistic signals of solvency when expenses are clustered in one or a few months rather than evenly spread out. The cash held may not be able to cover these high-expense months if revenues are not also coming in at higher-than-normal rates during these months.

NET LIQUID BALANCE.
The net liquid balance (NLB) is calculated by starting with cash and equivalents plus short-term investments and then subtracting short-term arranged borrowing (such as bank loans).

TARGET LIQUIDITY LEVEL.
We believe that the primary financial objective of a noncommercial nonprofit, expressed in its simplest form, is to achieve a target liquidity level. The target liquidity level is calculated by taking cash and short-term investments, adding the total amount of your credit line, then subtracting the amount of the credit line currently used (or "drawn down"). Check the notes accompanying the financial statements for the total amount of the credit line.

LIQUID FUNDS INDICATOR.
The liquid funds indicator is calculated as:

$$\text{Liquid funds indicator} = \frac{([\text{Net assets} - \text{Permanently restricted net assets} - \text{Land, buildings, and equipment}] \times 12)}{\text{Total expenses}}$$

The numerator gives us yet another look at the resources from which we can pay our expenses. Note that the denominator is the same as that of the cash reserve ratio.

WORKING CAPITAL RATIO.
Charity Navigator (www.charitynavigator.org) publishes comparative ratio values of the working capital ratio for several types of nonprofits. The working capital ratio is calculated by taking these items in the numerator:

Numerator: (Cash and equivalents + Savings accounts + Pledges receivable
+ Grants receivable) − (Accounts payable + Grants payable
+ Accrued expenses)

And then dividing this numerator by total expenses, with affiliate payments (if any) added in the denominator:

Denominator: Total expenses, including payments to affiliates

The numerator can be thought of as "net liquid assets," similar to the NLB but accounting for more than just financial current assets and financial current liabilities. The ratio value indicates, as with the cash reserve ratio, how long the organization could maintain its spending if no new revenues came in. Once again, as with the other solvency ratios, higher values show greater solvency and numbers of one or less signal potentially serious solvency problems.

(ii) Liquidity Ratios. Think about liquidity as having three basic ingredients: time, amount, and cost.[7] The more quickly an asset such as a pledge receivable may be converted into cash, the more liquid it is. The longer it takes for a liability such as an account payable to be disbursed, the more liquid the organization is as a result. The amount of resources the organization has to cover outflows, when greater, signals higher liquidity. If an asset may be converted to cash quickly at minimal cost, it is considered liquid.

Liquidity measures take into account solvency but also view the flow of resources and provide more accurate readings based on the time it takes current assets or current liabilities to add to or drain cash, respectively.

We propose eight different liquidity measures from which you may select to best gauge your organization's liquidity. Calculating and analyzing more than one ratio provides you with a composite measure of liquidity. One ratio in isolation should never be relied on to provide an adequate perspective on liquidity.

LAMBDA.
Lambda is a measure that simultaneously takes into account your "liquid reserve" (cash, short-term investments, and unused credit line), next-period operating cash flow (forecasted), and the uncertainty of your organization's operating cash flows (usually estimated using historical data). We believe that lambda is the single best measure of liquidity because it includes actual and potential cash, includes aspects of solvency in the liquid reserve, and accounts for the riskiness of the organization's operating cash flows. In fact, lambda actually incorporates some aspects of solvency, narrow liquidity, and financial flexibility, qualifying it as a "broad liquidity" measure. We will show how this measure is calculated, but in a modified form, in our later presentation of target liquidity level lambda. In-depth coverage of lambda is available elsewhere.[8]

HISTORICAL LAMBDA.
When looking back in time, operating cash flow is no longer a forecast but is an actual, historical value. Furthermore, one may use several years of historical operating cash flows to calculate the uncertainty of operating cash flows, by

either measuring the standard deviation of those flows or estimating that number by taking the range of operating cash flows and dividing by 6.[9]

TARGET LIQUIDITY LEVEL LAMBDA.

The target liquidity level lambda takes the insights we gain from lambda and couples them with the primary financial target, target liquidity level, to provide a valuable measure of your organization's liquidity. Here is the formula for target liquidity level lambda.

$$\text{Target liquidity level lambda (TLLL)} = \frac{\text{Target liquidity level} + \text{Projected OCF}}{\text{Uncertainty of OCF}}$$

Where:

Target Liquidity Level = (Cash and cash equivalents + short-term investments + total amount of credit line – short-term loans)

Projected OCF (operating cash flow) is the operating cash flow amount you predict for the next year

Uncertainty of OCF is the standard deviation of the organization's historical operating cash flows for at least the past three years

Notice that two estimates are required here to calculate TLLL:[10]

1. Someone must forecast your organization's OCF. You may wish to look at last year's statement of cash flows to see what the OCF amount was and perhaps plug that in as a naïve forecast. Or perhaps reduce that amount by some arbitrary amount (say, 25 percent) for a more conservative estimate. A third option is to take the average of your organization's past three years of OCFs. A fourth option, if your organization has been growing, is to project a somewhat higher level of OCF. (But be careful: Often growth causes higher investment levels in receivables and perhaps in inventories or prepaid expenses, so OCF will not grow as much as revenues and may actually decline somewhat.) Careful study of the relationship between past years' changes in net assets and OCF is very helpful here.

2. The uncertainty of OCF reflects the financial vulnerability your organization faces. It only makes sense if your organization has large fluctuations in its cash revenues and/or cash expenses, to need a higher level of liquidity. Placing risk of your operating cash flows in the denominator, TLLL indicates through the resulting lower calculated value (quotient) that you have less liquidity. There are two ways to estimate this uncertainty: Calculate the standard deviation of the past 7 to 10 years of OCFs, perhaps using the STDEV function built into Microsoft Excel™; or take the highest OCF in the past 7 to 10 years, subtract from it the lowest OCF in that same time frame, then divide that amount by 6. The latter is an approximation of the standard deviation of your organization's OCFs, based on

the idea that there are six standard deviations of numerical values in an entire range (or distribution) of numbers.[11]

Calculating TLLL is extremely helpful to your analysis for three reasons:

1. It demonstrates to your policy-making team that steady, dependable cash flows require holding less liquidity and that highly risky cash flows may be offset by having more cash and equivalents, more short-term (unrestricted) investments, a higher unborrowed credit line, the ability to borrow quickly for working capital on an as-needed basis (rare for nonprofits), or a positive and high inflow of funds over the upcoming period. (But watch for seasonality—if yours is a donative organization, much of that is likely to materialize between Thanksgiving and Christmas, when a very high percentage of cash donations are made.)

2. If your calculated number turns out too low for comfort (see #3 below)—meaning it is below your financial policy for target liquidity, as discussed in Chapter 2—you can plug in different numbers for credit line amounts or short-term investment amounts and then see the impact. Doing this helps you to know how much is enough for liquidity-filling investing or borrowing actions.

3. Used with a standard normal table (or the Excel NORMDIST function), the TLLL tells you the probability of running short of cash over the forecast period. A particular value for TLLL is associated with a 5 percent chance of running out of cash, a different value for TLL matches to a 1 percent chance, and so on. No other liquidity measure provides decision makers with this type of information.

Our next three measures are forecasts of the three major components of your organization's statement of cash flows. The rationale for projecting these is that, just as this period's cash flow is the sum total of operating, investing, and financing cash flows, so too next year's and the following year's net cash flow will be the combined result of these three distinct cash flow engines.

PROJECTED OCF IN THE FORMAT OF THE STATEMENT OF CASH FLOWS.
Larger operating cash flows coming in to the organization's cash till may cover a multitude of low-solvency sins. Make sure the forecast is reliable; too many nonprofits have run into trouble because their revenue, especially funds raised, forecasts are too rosy.

PROJECTED INVESTING CASH FLOW IN THE FORMAT OF THE STATEMENT OF CASH FLOWS.
Larger projected investing outflows necessitate higher solvency positions and/or larger incoming operating cash flows for the same period. A measure that you could calculate here is the capital expenditure ratio:

$$\text{Capital expenditure ratio} = \text{OCF} / \text{Capital expenditures}$$

This ratio separates out from investing cash flows the line item representing additional investment in property, plant, and equipment. Put it into the formula as a positive number, assuming the organization is making additional capital expenditures during the year you are evaluating. If the ratio value is greater than 1.0, the organization has enough cash to cover all capital expenditures and has money left over to meet debt obligations.

PROJECTED FINANCING CASH FLOW IN THE FORMAT OF THE STATEMENT OF CASH FLOWS. Unlike a business, you need not worry about two typical business "financing" section outflows, cash dividends and share repurchases. However, look ahead at principal repayments on bank loans, other notes, and bonds. These will necessitate planning ahead; otherwise, you could be facing a cash crunch with little ability to tide the organization over until revenues pick up again.

CASH CONVERSION PERIOD.
This measure captures the amount of time that elapses from when you pay for your goods or supplies to the time when you get spendable funds from the sale of your final product or service. This measure fits healthcare organizations the best, followed by educational institutions and then other nonprofits. You want to be out of pocket for a shorter time, necessitating less cash to be tied up in your operations. Money tied up in operations must be financed through short-term borrowing, or reduces your investable balances, reducing your interest income. However, resist the temptation to stretch payables—to place money in your pocket by taking it out of your suppliers' pockets—unless of course they agree ahead of time to new terms through a negotiation process. We show the calculation of the cash conversion period in Appendix 2B.

CURRENT LIQUIDITY INDEX.
The current liquidity index (CLI) reflects on your organization's ability to cover its fixed, financing-related obligations. Higher ratio values are better as they reflect a greater ability to cover those obligations. Notice in the denominator that both bank loans and principal payments due within the next year for long-term debt (such as term loans and bonds) are brought into the picture. Both represent arranged outside financing, as opposed to spontaneous short-term financing arising from accrued expenses or accounts payable.

$$\text{CLI} = \frac{(\text{Cash and equivalents} + \text{Short-term investments} + \text{Projected OCF})}{(\text{Short-term notes payable} + \text{Current portion of long-term debt})}$$

(iii) Financial Flexibility Ratios.

PROJECTED LAMBDA.
This technique was developed by William Beyer, who applied it in his forecasting work at Portland Cement. Essentially the idea is to see how lambda changes as

the operating cash flow forecast, operating cash flow uncertainty, and amount of unused credit line are changed in value. One can do worst-case, most likely case, and best-case analyses with this method.[12]

SUSTAINABLE GROWTH RATE.

The idea here is to see how rapidly your organization can grow given its present "profitability," asset intensity, and use of debt. Full coverage is beyond our scope, but the nonprofit model of sustainable growth rate developed by Marc Jegers may be accessed in Chapter 9 of our companion book, *Financial Management for Nonprofit Organizations: Policies and Practices* (John Wiley & Sons, 2007.).

SHOCK TESTING.

You could calculate the value-at-risk (VaR) for your investments, which shows the predicted worst-case loss at, say, a 5 percent "confidence interval," on the investment portfolio within the next year.[13] The VaR measure allows one to consistently monitor market risk over time, and see how the portfolio's diversification affects the risk being borne.

STRATEGIC LIQUIDITY.

Gordon Donaldson developed a framework for strategic liquidity in his classic 1963 *Harvard Business Review* article.[14] Donaldson conceptualized the key risk factors that would affect an organization's financial position a year or more into the future. Since the key distinction between operating liquidity and strategic liquidity is the timeframe (operating measures are mostly focused on intrayear or one-year ahead horizons), you will need to incorporate multi-year forecasts to determine whether your liquidity will change dramatically in the long-term. Ideally, you will want to customize Donaldson's model so that you may determine the amount of strategic liquidity that your organization needs.

(c) EVALUATE YOUR RATIOS IN LIGHT OF YOUR STARTING POINTS.   Evaluating your ratio values in isolation could be very misleading. Here are three pointers:

1. Always evaluate a particular ratio's values in the context of what the other ratios are telling you.
2. Make sure to include more than one year of ratio values before drawing any conclusions.
3. Of greatest importance here, evaluate the ratio values in part B above ("Calculate key ratios") in light of the information that you discovered in the starting points analysis in part A ("Starting points"). For example, if each of the starting points indicators in part A suggests that you should have a larger level of liquidity, then you would want to have higher values for the solvency, liquidity, and financial flexibility indicators in part B.

1.4 HOW DO PROFICIENT CASH MANAGEMENT AND INVESTMENT MANAGEMENT ENABLE YOUR ORGANIZATION TO ACHIEVE ITS LIQUIDITY TARGET?

(a) CASH MANAGEMENT.   The chances of your organization hitting its liquidity target and maintaining that liquidity target are much higher if it has optimal policies and procedures in several treasury management areas. These areas are cash collections and concentration, cash disbursements, banking relationship management, information technology, short-term borrowing, and fraud/misappropriation deterrence.

The effect of cash collections helps because you receive the money you are owed on time without paying too much to do so. The more quickly you can bring in cash, the less financial stress your organization will face. And if you can get monies out of small accounts spread all over the globe and pool them in one central location that will give you the funds for your disbursements or to increase your investments or pay down your borrowings. Put another way, having your liquidity target monies all in one account in one location will keep these reserves usable. Or you could maintain a smaller liquidity target as a result of concentration. Disbursements also help: For example, don't pay invoices before they are due unless you receive a cash discount for doing so. That keeps the monies invested or keeps your short-term credit line balance lower.

Banking relationship management, in turn, includes pooling/mobilizing funds, availability schedule issues, funding your disbursement account, investing any surplus on perhaps an overnight basis, and paying down your credit line.

Information technology should facilitate having accurate real-time or close to real-time information on funds balances in your depository and concentration accounts.

Short-term borrowing measures include having a standby credit line and paying a minimal interest rate on amounts borrowed. Related to the latter, your organization should strive to minimize its net interest income; the technique to enable you do this is available elsewhere.[15]

Deterring fraud and misappropriation of funds is an objective that covers multiple treasury management functions. The primary one is disbursements, but fraud also occurs in collections (in any retail environment, employees may pilfer funds from the cash register; in a church setting, funds may be siphoned from the offering plate). Concentration is also a vulnerable area, as any time large amounts of funds are moved there is always the possibility that an employee will misdirect the funds to his or her own account, possibly abroad. Information technology and your banking system are key components to fraud prevention. Much of the more advanced fraud prevention methodology is part of your information technology. Your banker is a great ally in preventing fraud as well. Positive pay systems, which involve sending an information file of checks issued to your bank, which the bank will then matches to checks when they are presented, is the best way to prevent or reduce check fraud.

Thus, cash collections and concentration, cash disbursements, your banking system, information technology, short-term borrowing, and fraud prevention techniques enable your organization to better achieve its liquidity target, your primary financial objective.

(b) INVESTMENT MANAGEMENT.   The effective management of short-term, medium-term, and long-term investments also enables the organization to better achieve its liquidity target. Consider the purposes for which these investments are held as a way of clarifying why they would enable you to be more proficient in your financial management.

Short-term investments are actually part of your liquidity target. They provide you with a pool of funds to tap in the event of an emergency need or a mismatch between cash receipts and cash disbursements. One way of thinking about your short-term investments is to view them as cash reserves that you know you will not need immediately and on which you wish to earn interest. And because monies invested in short-term investments are monies unavailable for program accomplishment, you want to manage them effectively to earn interest while keeping those monies safe.

Medium-term and long-term investments serve a multitude of purposes. They may be used to fund pensions, to self-insure your organization against risks it faces, as a strategic reserve (perhaps to prefund capital expenditures or maintenance expenditures), or for endowment purposes. A great example of a strategic reserve is that held by the Salvation Army. This organization holds over $1 billion in a strategic reserve in the event it may be needed quickly or to provide monies for necessary capital expenditures for maintenance costs.

We recognize that you may run into resistance by donors, grant agencies, and possibly even your board members if you hold more than some minimal level of operating reserves. An effective way to help your donors and others understand your strategic reserve is to hold the monies in your strategic reserve in the form of a quasi-endowment. Although money in a quasi-endowment must be held in what are called unrestricted funds, it signals to your donors and grant agencies that this money is not able to be spent for any particular need that may arise.

Your organization may also decide to have an endowment. This money is permanently restricted. Generally, the intent here is to generate a stream of income from the endowment that will be used to supplement other revenue sources. A second advantage, however, is that this money is also there in case your organization ever gets into deep financial trouble. Resist the temptation to "cut down the trees" when you face only a temporary shortfall of funds, however. The board should set a spending policy that is consistent with inflation and the maintenance of purchasing power on the endowment principal. In this way your endowment will help you to generate income to help fund your operations, while assuring long-term stability and survival for your nonprofit organization.

Risk management is another area related to cash and investment management. It deserves separate attention. Yes, it does include fraud prevention, but it goes beyond this to consider all risks faced by the organization and how they will be managed. Think broadly here: Anything that could impair your liquidity anytime in the future is something that you should think about in terms of risk management. Let's say that salaries for trained counselors were to double in the next 10 years. Possibly your revenues with double as well, but if not, you may need to tap some of your liquidity in order to survive this change. The thought process to engage in now is to ask, "Is there anything we could do ahead of time proactively in order to keep from reducing our liquidity if this event in fact occurs?"

1.5 SUMMARY

This chapter has provided the context for proficient treasury management in the nonprofit organization. We looked inside the nonprofit finance office and found two common maladies in there: Either the organization has not set a target liquidity level, or it is not engaging in cash forecasting and so cannot effectively manage that cash position. In either case, the organization is financially handicapped. More important than whether your organization runs a surplus or breaks even financially, has it established and is it monitoring and managing a liquidity target? To do this, the organization's management team and board must determine an appropriate cash position and also manage its cash flows carefully. A number of reasons were provided why target liquidity is the appropriate operational financial objective for a nonprofit. We then looked at why many organizations do not set a liquidity target or do not manage toward that target. Guidance was then provided regarding how to go about setting the liquidity target, including background information that serves as a starting point and relevant financial ratios. We find three ratios—the net liquid balance, lambda, and the cash conversion period—to be especially valuable measures. After presenting more detail on liquidity management in Chapter 2, in Appendix 2 C we present a hypothetical case study on setting the liquidity target. We concluded our chapter by looking at how proficient cash management, investment management, and risk management assist your organization in meeting its liquidity target. Chapter 2 provides assistance in improving your organization's liquidity management and projecting its cash position.

Notes

1. Kirsten A. Grønbjerg and Richard M. Clerkin, *Indiana Nonprofits: Financial and Human Resource Challenges* (Bloomington, IN: Indiana University School of Public and Environmental Affairs, August 2004). Copies of this report are available on the Indiana Nonprofit Sector Web site (www.indiana.edu/~nonprof).

2. Based on a survey of 439 business financial executives and published in "Nurturing the Creative Spirit: The 2005 T&RM/ Citigroup Financial Leadership Survey of Executives," *Treasury & Risk Management* 9 (October 2005): 71–75.

3. David R. Campbell, James M. Johnson, and Leonard M. Savoie, "Cash Flow, Liquidity, and Financial Flexibility," *Financial Executive* 52, no.8 (1984): 14–17. Also see the presentation on financial flexibility in Terry S. Maness and John T. Zietlow, *Short-Term Financial Management*, 3rd ed. (Cincinnati: South-Western, 2005), 31–32, 41–43.

4. This is developed for businesses in Maness and Zietlow, *Short-Term Financial Management*, pp. 41–43, and for nonprofits in Chapter 9 of John Zietlow, Jo Ann Hankin, and Alan Seidner, *Financial Management for Nonprofit Organizations: Policies and Practices* (Hoboken, NJ: John Wiley & Sons, 2007). The latter presentation is based on the adaptation of sustainable growth modeling to nonprofits by Marc Jegers.

5. IRS, "Executive Summary: Credit Counseling Compliance Project," May 15, 2006. Located online at: www.irs.gov/pub/irs-tege/cc_executive_summary.pdf. Accessed: 6/27/06.

6. The remainder of the responses were as follows: 7.1 percent selected "Minimize costs," 7.1 percent selected "Maximize net revenue," 7.1 percent selected "Maximize net donations," 7.1 percent selected "Make a small surplus," and no one (0.0 percent) selected "Avoid financial risk."

7. Maness and Zietlow, *Short-Term Financial Management*, p. 31.

8. Id., Chapter 2. Lambda was developed by Kenneth Cogger and Gary Emery; further information and interpretation of this measure are provided in the referenced chapter.

9. This range approach to estimating standard deviation assumes a normal distribution, or the familiar bell-shaped curve, for your organization's operating cash flows. Since your cash flows are most likely not normally distributed, this estimate must be viewed as a rough approximation.

10. This presentation is from our companion book, *Financial Management for Nonprofit Organizations: Policies and Practices*. In Chapter 7 you will find a numerical example illustrating the calculation of this ratio.

11. Again, this range approach to estimating standard deviation assumes a normal distribution, or the familiar bell-shaped curve, for your organization's operating cash flows. Since your cash flows are most likely not normally distributed, this estimate must be viewed as a rough approximation.

12. Willliam E. Beyer, "Liquidity Measurement in Corporate Forecasting," *Journal of Cash Management* 8, no. 6 (1988): 14–16.

13. For more on the VaR measure, see Karen Luprypa, "Short-Term Volatility Does Matter," *Canadian Investment Review* (Summer 2002), p. 17.

14. Gordon Donaldson, "Strategy for Financial Emergencies," *Harvard Business Review* (November/December 1969): 67–79.

15. Maness and Zietlow, *Short-Term Financial Management*, Chapter 13.

CASH PLANNING AND LIQUIDITY

If there's one thing that seems to characterize nonprofits when it comes to finances, it would be that they are "cash poor." In this chapter, we discover the difference between a cash crunch and a cash crisis, ways to bridge these cash gaps, expand on the difference between solvency liquidity and financial flexibility, and get our first look at some of the key issues and tools to be used in cash management.

 Your organization's primary financial objective is to ensure that financial resources are available when needed (timing), as needed (amount), and at reasonable cost (cost-effectiveness), and that once mobilized, these resources are protected from impairment and spent according to mission and donor purposes. The best starting place as you work to achieve that objective is to gain understanding of the cash flow characteristics of nonprofits.

2.1 CASH FLOW CHARACTERISTICS OF NONPROFITS

For a business, the *operating cycle* is the elapsed time from when the business purchases raw materials until it sells and then collects on its credit sales for its final product. The business is not out of pocket for cash this entire time. It typically pays for its inventories after a time period called the credit period elapses. The amount of time for which the business is out of pocket for cash, then, is the operating cycle minus the credit period—or the *cash conversion cycle*. The credit period is often called days payable outstanding, assuming the organization pays on or before the invoice date. Nonprofits that rely on grants and gifts must raise those funds when they are most available, as opposed to when they are most needed. Funds are then invested or used to pay down borrowings by these "donative nonprofits" until monies are distributed or transformed into products or services. Businesses and "commercial nonprofits"—hospitals and educational institutions—that sell products or services experience a closer time match between revenues and expenses. Consider the differences in these two measures, or metrics, depending on whether a nonprofit is a donative nonprofit or a commercial nonprofit:

- The operating cycle and cash conversion cycle for donative nonprofits may start with the year's initial funding—maybe from the previous year's Thanksgiving-to-Christmas fund drive—followed by cash outflows for payroll and other operating expenses, and then end-of-year replenishment of the liquidity stockpile. There are often other spikes of revenue (annual fund drive, or Easter collections) and perhaps long periods over which inflows are negligible ("the summer slump").
- The operating cycle and cash conversion cycle for commercial nonprofits is typically more synchronized, as revenues come at least quarterly, or even monthly (although many schools have the two tuition spikes at the beginning of the fall and spring semesters), and disbursements remain pretty steady over the entire year. However, many times government contracts are paid out slowly, and your organization may have expended funds for a month or more before being reimbursed.

Before even beginning your liquidity analysis, make sure you have the proper internal controls and documentation in place for your treasury function. Although that is not our purpose here, we provide in Appendix 2A a template you may use for a checklist of required validations. The whole area of enterprise risk management (ERM) is an important one for your treasury function. Enterprise risk management may be defined as:

> ...a process, effected by an entity's board of directors, management and other personnel, applied in strategy setting and across the enterprise, designed to identify potential events that may affect the entity, and manage risk to be within its risk appetite in order to provide reasonable assurance regarding the achievement of entity objectives.[1]

ERM should be adopted as a core value within your organization, and overseen by your organization's board of directors. Regardless of whether others in your organization see the importance of an integrated risk evaluation, the finance function should assess all factors that presently and potentially may affect the organization's cash position and liquidity target, and move proactively to monitor and possibly protect against those effects.[2]

2.2 CASH SHORTFALLS AND WHAT TO DO ABOUT THEM

Cash shortfalls may be short term or long term. Knowing whether a cash shortfall is a cash crunch or a cash crisis makes all the difference in knowing what to do about it.

- *Cash crunch.* A cash crunch is a temporary imbalance of cash receipts in cash disbursements. It may self-correct, but over a long period of time.
- *Cash crisis* A cash crisis is a long-term imbalance between cash coming in and cash going out. It normally does not self-correct. You have heard the stories of operas, ballets, and symphonies that have had to close their doors because of cash crises that are seemingly unsolvable.

The University of Hartford's experience provides an instructive example here. The University had its bonds downgraded in the 1990s to a lower credit-worthiness rating based on the following factors:[3]

- The review of its just-completed fiscal year audit and the amounts it had budgeted for the forthcoming year;
- Severe and persistent historical deficits which had reduced net assets and drained liquidity;
- The inability of its current cash flow to cover debt service (principal and interest payments), as illustrated by its recent drawdown of liquid assets to pay debt service; and
- Enrollment sensitivity to deteriorating local and regional economic factors.

Clearly, this was not a temporary situation that could be expected to self-correct, but an ongoing mismatch of revenues and expenses that could be expected to deplete the University's liquidity for some years to come. Such a cash crisis is a serious threat to an organization. Fortunately, the University of Hartford took decisive action and saw their bonds upgraded less than four years later. The upgrade to "investment grade" came because of three consecutive years of balanced budgets, higher net revenue arising from tuition, and a lower debt burden based on the fact that the University did not issue any new bonds.[4]

Once you have identified whether a cash imbalance is a cash crunch or a cash crisis, you're ready to consider two menus of choices from which to choose your response.

Filling the Gap—Cash Crunch

- Defer payments to the extent possible, within ethical bounds.
- Accelerate collections of donations, grants, or receipts from sales.
- Tap your bank credit line.
- Sell off some short-term investments.
- Tap your bank account.
- Conduct a fundraising appeal.
- Sell off unneeded assets.
- Cut expenses.
- Get a grant (operating grants are rare).

Filling the Gap—Cash Crisis

- Make sure you're working capital management processes—cash collections, cash concentration/positioning, cash disbursements, receivables management, inventory management, payables management, and short-term borrowing and investing—are as efficient as possible.
- Cut back the scale of your operations.[5]
- Permanently cut your overhead expenses (salaries, grant, interest expense, utilities, mortgage payment, and benefits).
- Increase your revenue stream while keeping expenses stable, perhaps through an earned income venture.

Three cautions are in order here. First, "soft-money" grants are not an ideal revenue source. You cannot rely on soft-money grants to cover your expenses for the foreseeable future. Second, your organization should be vigilant to turn away resources that would divert attention from its core mission—what it is passionate about and the best in the world at—and that might hamper its ability to attract buy-in from employees, volunteers, and potential supporters.[6] Third, earned income ventures may prove to be a drag on your financial position for quite a while as you build a customer base. For example, if a museum opens a gift shop, it must first disburse funds to stock the shelves of that shop. And then it will have to advertise the fact that it has a gift shop, involving yet another outlay. The point is, there are cash outflows to absorb prior to beginning to receive cash inflows. The museum's chief financial officer (CFO) is responsible for pointing these cash flow issues out to operating and program managers. Yes, in a very real sense, the CFO is the "policeman" for the organization's financial position. The financial viability of the organization is especially the CFO's domain. Maintaining financial viability through cash crunches and cash crises is assisted by an understanding of the tiers of liquidity and the spectrum of liquidity.

2.3 TIERS OF LIQUIDITY AND THE SPECTRUM OF LIQUIDITY

We can think about liquidity management and operational terms by conceiving of "tiers of liquidity."[7] In this framework, the organization's liquidity is ordered in tiers of decreasing liquidity, with six layers of liquidity:

- Tier 1: Cash flow, cash balances, and the investment portfolio.
  - Comment: Most liquid.
- Tier 2: Short-term credit.
  - Comment: This, more so than cash balances and short-term investments, provides the majority of the liquidity reserve for businesses.
- Tier 3: Management of cash flows.
  - Comment: Examples are to delay payments, offer services at lower prices, offer easier credit terms, or alter inventory positions.
- Tier 4: Renegotiation of debt contracts.
  - Comment: Some lenders are more flexible than others.
- Tier 5: Asset sales.
  - Comment: The organization is beginning to liquidate valuable assets simply to provide cash to stay afloat.
- Tier 6: Bankruptcy.
  - Comment: The purpose of bankruptcy is to buy time to reorganize by protecting the organization from creditors. Bankruptcy may culminate in reorganization or liquidation. A nonprofit's asset will be placed with a similar organization.

One caution here: Stretching payables is not viewed as an ethical business practice. If you know you will be unable to pay an invoice, be sure to contact the supplier and work it out with the supplier first.

Another useful framework for considering liquidity management has been developed by Edgar Norton.[8] Norton orders liquidity using a timeline. At the beginning of the timeline is cash. As one moves out in time along the spectrum, one gets to asset sales, stock issues for businesses, and bond issues. A proactive CFO or treasurer is always thinking down the road toward future sources of liquidity.

2.4 MEASURING AND MANAGING SOLVENCY, LIQUIDITY, AND FINANCIAL FLEXIBILITY

(a) MEASURING AND MANAGING SOLVENCY. An organization is said to be *insolvent* when its assets are insufficient to cover its liabilities. From a short-run perspective, insolvency arises when current assets are insufficient to cover current liabilities. Current assets include:

- Cash and cash equivalents
- Other items that will turn into cash within one year

- ○ Short-term investments
- ○ Receivables
- ○ Accounts receivable
- ○ Pledges receivable
- ○ Inventories
- ○ Prepaid expenses

Current liabilities include bills owed but not yet paid, such as accounts payable and accrued expenses.

The best measure of solvency is the net liquid balance (NLB). A formula for net liquid balance is:

NLB = (Cash & Cash Equivalents + Short-Term Investments − Notes Payable)

For example, let's say that your nonprofit has cash and cash equivalents of $100, short-term investments of $50, and notes payable (bank loan owed) of $25. Your organization's net liquid balance would equal $125 ($100 plus $50 minus $25).

Other measures of solvency include: current ratio, cash ratio, the asset ratio, and the working capital ratio. The *current ratio* is defined as current assets divided by current liabilities. The current ratio measures your ability to cover near-term bills with cash and items that will turn into cash within one year. Current assets are also called working capital. (A closely related measure called net working capital equals current assets minus current liabilities.) The cash ratio is defined as cash divided by current liabilities. On a balance sheet, cash is often called cash and cash equivalents. The *cash ratio* measures your ability to cover bills due within one year by the cash and cash equivalents that you have right now. Recognize that some of the cash may be restricted. The *asset ratio* equals current assets divided by total assets. This ratio measures solvency by showing how much of the total asset investment is in a more liquid form. Notice a common element in all of these ratios: All of the data for numerator and denominator in each ratio comes from the balance sheet. The *working capital ratio* compares relatively more liquid current assets to relatively more liquid current liabilities. The numerator equals cash and cash equivalents plus savings accounts, or short-term investments, plus pledges receivable plus grants receivable. The denominator equals accounts payable, plus grants payable, plus accrued expenses. The advantage of calculating the working capital ratio is that you can compare the calculated value for your organization with an average calculated by Charity Navigator. Again, it represents the ability of the organization to cover near-term bills payable. Think of solvency ratios as balance sheet–based ratios. Also notice a common shortcoming of each of these ratios: None of the ratios shows how long it takes for an asset to turn into cash or a liability to drain your cash account. Because of this shortcoming, focus on the ratios that include cash and cash equivalents as one element in the ratio. If you forget this, think about the definition of an asset's liquidity. An asset is truly liquid if it is already in the form of cash or will very soon turn into cash. Obviously, cash is already in the form of cash, and so is the truly liquid asset in every sense of the word. Anything other than cash, and listed on the balance sheet, may take awhile to turn into cash or, if a liability, to drain your cash account. The net liquid balance ratio, focusing as it does on cash and cash equivalents, as adjusted by short-term investments net of short-term borrowing (which could augment your cash account quickly), is therefore the best solvency ratio. The reason we net out short-term borrowing in this ratio is that you have already exhausted this potential amount of added liquidity.

(b) MEASURING AND MANAGING LIQUIDITY.   Recall from Chapter 1 that liquidity, narrowly defined, means having enough financial resources to pay obligations without incurring excessive cost. It includes the cash sources that we show in our solvency measures as well as unused short-term borrowing (similar to the amount of your credit card's credit limit that you have not spent at the moment). Additionally, liquidity measures focus on how long an asset takes to turn to cash or how long before a liability results in a drain to your cash account. In this section we look at two types of liquidity measures. The first set of measures monitor the flow of cash. The second set of measures attempts to determine how much liquidity the organization should hold.

The simplest and most direct flow of cash measure comes straight from the statement of cash flows. It is the "operating cash flow." *Operating cash flow* is the subtotal for the first category of cash flows shown on the statement of cash flows. You want this amount to be positive, showing that operations added cash to your organization's cash position for the period. If negative, operations were a drain on your cash flow for the period. When we say "operations," we are referring to the cash flows arising from the services your organization provides. We are *not* referring to cash from, say, selling off some of your short-term securities. A more complex measure of the flow of cash is called the *cash conversion period*. The cash conversion period is constructed by taking the operating cycle (the time cash is tied up in receivables plus the time cash is tied up in inventories, if any) and then subtracting the days payable outstanding. It measures the amount of time that elapses from when you make payment for inventories (cash outflow) until your customers pay you (cash inflow). To finance this elapsed time, your organization either has to sell off some short-term investments or draw down its line of credit. In either case, there is a cost to your organization: either interest income lost or interest expense paid. For more on the cash conversion period and how to calculate it, see Appendix 2B.

How much liquidity should my organization hold? Two measures attempt to answer this question. The first measure is called the *current liquidity index*. It starts with cash and cash equivalents plus short-term investments at the beginning of a period. But in addition, since we are now talking about liquidity (not solvency) measures, it adds in a flow measure. The flow measure is the cash flow from operations for that particular time period. So we have beginning cash and cash equivalents, plus operating cash flow. Then, in the denominator, we have short-term notes payable and current portion of any long-term debt. Both of these items should be located under current liabilities on the organization's balance sheet.

The single best liquidity measure is called *lambda*. Lambda starts with the organization's liquid reserve. The liquid reserve consists of cash and cash equivalents plus short-term investments plus any *unused* short-term borrowing capacity. Unused short-term borrowing capacity equals the amount of credit line the organization has arranged with its bank or banks, less any portion of the currently being used (drawn down). Think of unused short-term borrowing capacity in a personal context: the amount of your credit card credit limit that is currently not charged. The numerator of lambda also includes the operating cash flow for that period. Putting all of this together, the numerator has the beginning-of-period liquid reserve, added to the operating cash flow that comes in during the period. The denominator is a bit more complex. It is the uncertainty of your organization's operating cash flows. There are two ways you may calculate this uncertainty. One is to take the range of operating cash flows and to divide this by 6. The other way to calculate uncertainty is to calculate the statistic called standard deviation. This is easily done in Microsoft Excel.

Lambda actually captures two elements of financial flexibility, our next topic. First, it incorporates unused short-term debt capacity. Debt capacity, short term and long term, is invaluable for your organization. Second, by including the upcoming year's operating cash flow and the uncertainty of all years' operating cash flows, it turns our attention to upcoming funding needs. Both debt capacity and upcoming funding needs are integral to the evaluation of financial flexibility.

(c) MEASURING AND MANAGING FINANCIAL FLEXIBILITY. Measuring financial flexibility is more subjective than measuring solvency or liquidity evaluation, and is usually done qualitatively. The key issue here is: Does your organization have adequate financial resources to fund its growth plan, including growth of buildings, growth of programs, and growth of staffing? In other words, are your financial policies consistent with your program and strategic objectives?

Although some organizations try, there really is no way adequately to assess financial flexibility unless your organization is constructing a long-run financial plan. This plan projects the asset requirements of your program as well as financial requirements related to staffing growth and assesses whether you will have enough financing in place to fund those assets. Ideally, someone in your organization should construct a long-run financial plan each year, with five years worth of financial projections included. This allows enough time to arrange adequate financing in cases where normal net revenues (revenues exceeding expenses) are inadequate to fund this growth and you do not have strategic liquidity reserves built up to fund these needs.

An excellent illustration of build-up and subsequent tapping of financial flexibility is provided by Legacy Health Systems. Legacy willingly gave up one notch in its bond rating as it drew down some of its liquidity to fund a new building. Its days' cash on hand (as a percent of its daily expenses) fell to 148 days from 254 days over a two-year period.[9] We believe well-managed organizations build cash in advance of major outlays, and willingly draw that cash down to fund new projects or expansion. Like Legacy, they will have to keep expense coverage up in order to maintain and rebuild their financial strength.

Businesses use a measure called the *sustainable growth rate* to assess their financial flexibility. However, this measure must be adapted to nonprofits, because sales and asset growth are not as closely linked for most nonprofits. Marc Jegers has adapted the sustainable growth rate model so that you can determine whether your program or service growth rate is consistent with your funding. Further development of this model is beyond our present scope.[10]

(d) BROAD LIQUIDITY: AN ALL-ENCOMPASSING VIEW.   Liquidity, properly defined, includes solvency, liquidity as defined earlier, and financial flexibility. Your organization may be viewed as *liquid* if it can pay its upcoming bills on time without straining itself and without undue cost. Signs that your organization may be *illiquid* include paying suppliers late, missing payroll, intrafund fund borrowing, engaging in nonmortgage borrowing from a bank or other source during all periods of the year, or having no short-term investments. Recall your organization's primary financial objective: "To ensure that financial resources are available when needed (timing), as needed (amount), and at reasonable cost (cost-effectiveness), and that once mobilized these resources are protected from impairment and spent according to mission and donor purposes." Your organization has failed to meet its primary financial objective if insufficient financial resources are available at the point needed or in the amount needed or if you have to pay too much in order to procure those resources. As the CFO or as the treasurer of your organization's board of directors, you have a primary responsibility to ensure that the organization reaches its primary financial objective. You enable this by managing cash flow and the organization's cash position. Visualize an organization that never has to delay payments, can always make payroll, gives raises each year to its employees, does not have to slow its expansion, has funds for its program requirements, and is able to maintain its plant and equipment. This is a liquid organization. Proficient financial management enables mission accomplishment. "Keeping your eye on the ball" as a proficient financial manager means proactively planning for liquidity and ensuring that proper liquidity is there when needed. In the remainder of this book, when we use the term "liquidity," we mean by that broad liquidity. Broad liquidity includes all facets of solvency, narrow liquidity, and financial flexibility.

2.5   MANAGING CASH FLOW

(a) CASH AND DEMANDS FOR CASH.   There are two keys to managing cash flow. The first key is to understand what amount of "cash" is spendable. The second key is to understand what items increase or decrease your cash position.

How much money can your organization spend right now? Your organization can only spend the amount of unrestricted cash held as available funds in its bank account right now. A common confusion is for someone to say that the amount that can be spent right now is the amount shown as "unrestricted net assets" in the statement of net assets (also called the balance sheet). However, much of the amount shown as unrestricted net assets has been deployed in assets other than cash—receivables, inventories, or even plant and equipment, such as the building that houses your organization's headquarters. Another common error is to focus on the checkbook balance for cash instead of the bank balance for cash. The checkbook balance differs from the bank account balance because of deposits that are showing as ledger account balances, but not yet spendable, as well as checks written and not yet presented to the bank.

There are many demands on your organization's cash. Let's disregard cash demands related to restricted purposes for the moment. Upcoming cash outflows include payments to suppliers, payments for utilities, payments for gasoline and other incidental expenses, payments for wages salaries and benefits, payments for rent or for your mortgage payment, and other payments related to the type of nonprofit.

Then there are outflows related to the passage of time or expenditures for a specific purpose. These outflows come from restricted cash amounts, such as amounts that came in to your organization from contracts or grants.

Well-managed organizations have planned for these outflows. The best way to plan for these outflows is by constructing a cash budget, also called a cash forecast. Before doing a cash forecast, however, you will need to determine what the different categories of cash inflows and outflows are. You will also need to think about other cash movements, called cash mobilization flows. Sometimes these cash mobilization flows are called cash concentration flows. For example, you may wish to move funds to a central or master account from which you will make a cash disbursements or move monies into an investment account. If your organization has been running a balance in its line of credit (or other short-term borrowing account), you will want to move as much in unrestricted funds as possible in order to pay down the amount borrowed.

(b) CASH AND VALUE FOR LIQUIDITY.   Cash has more value for your organization in these situations:

- Its cash inflows and cash outflows do not occur at the same time (they are unsynchronized).
- It is grant- or contract-dependent and must disburse funds prior to receiving cash from the grantor or contractor.
- It has either a very unpredictable cash inflows or cash outflows.
- It must periodically make large investments in either new programs for new or refurbished buildings or equipment.

- Its creditworthiness is not perceived favorably by banks.
- It is able to borrow but faces high interest rates for borrowing.
- It faces intense competition from other service providers.
- It has few or no short-term investments.
- It may face a very large and sudden need for its services.

Some organizations possess two or three of these characteristics; a few organizations even more. The latter organizations are especially advised to hold larger amounts of cash. Were these organizations stockholder-owned organizations, stockholders would reward the larger cash holdings with a higher stock price.

(c) CASH COLLECTIONS. There are four key objectives for your cash collections:

1. Bring the money in quickly.
2. Bring the money in cost-effectively.
3. Bring the money in electronically, if possible.
4. Maintain control by receiving information about incoming money quickly and accurately.

We expand on cash collections in Chapter 3.

(d) CASH CONCENTRATION/POSITIONING. There are four key objectives for your cash concentration/positioning:

1. Pool monies in one or very few locations.
2. Move monies quickly.
3. Move monies inexpensively.
4. Maintain control of monies through accurate, real-time or close to real-time information

We expand on cash concentration/positioning in Chapter 3.

(e) CASH DISBURSEMENTS. There are four key objectives for your cash disbursements:

1. Disburse monies inexpensively.
2. Prevent fraud.
3. Disburse monies electronically, if possible.
4. Maintain control of monies through accurate real-time or close to real-time information.

We expand on cash disbursements in Chapter 4.

At times these objectives will conflict. For example, disbursing monies inexpensively may be at odds with preventing fraud. The "killer product" for preventing fraud is the positive pay system. You may have to pay your bank a monthly fee in order to have and use a positive pay system. We discuss banking system products in Chapter 5.

2.6 CASH BUDGETING

The cash budget shows anticipated cash inflows, cash outflows, and the amount and duration of cash shortages or surpluses for a certain future time horizon, usually the next 12 months. The cash budget's primary value is spotlighting the periods of imbalance between cash receipts and cash disbursements, so that you can take early action to proactively manage your organization's cash position. In a corporate sector study of 167 financial managers, those managers in smaller organizations selected "improve cash flow forecasting" as the top action item to improve their organizations' treasury and cash management.[11] It is not difficult to understand why—improving cash forecasting would better enable these organizations to achieve their top three goals: reduce costs, improve investment returns, and improve working capital (managing current assets and current liabilities).

(a) **CASH BUDGET.**   Techniques for preparing the cash budget are demonstrated next. When actual cash receipts are different from forecasted cash receipts, or actual cash disbursements are different from forecasted cash disbursements, it is very important to analyze the reasons why. You may check the accuracy of your year-earlier forecast for this year, as well as determine if seasonal or trend patterns emerge in the actual cash flows that occurred. You should also see in which months your forecast was furthest off and the reasons for your forecast miss. Use that information to guide your development of the next year's cash budget. Most important, decide whether the target liquidity should be adjusted based on the past year variance. Remember, your organization's target liquidity includes an amount for cash flow imbalances, for emergency needs, as well as for anticipated major expenditures in the future.

When an actual amount is different from a forecasted amount, we call that a variance. Let's further analyze the two cases of positive and negative variances in the net cash flow, which we define as:

$$\text{Net cash flow} = \text{cash receipts} - \text{cash disbursements}$$

Case 1: Net cash flow comes in above the amount forecasted in your cash budget. In this case, the cash position is growing. (Perhaps the trend was spotted earlier in the year and additional expenses incurred or assets purchased. In this case, the cash position would not be growing.) If your cash position continues to grow, as cash receipts exceed cash disbursements, then perhaps the liquidity target should be adjusted downward, but whether you do so depends on several considerations. Here are some of the factors you should consider:

- If the upward trend in your cash position is temporary (possibly because of special situations, such as one-time undesignated gifts to the organization) and is about to be reversed, do not revise the liquidity target, because your cash position will soon return to its normal level. If some of the cash receipts were simply proceeds from borrowing,[12] the amount will be repaid, bringing the cash position back to its normal level.

- If the upward trend is expected to last some time, and your organization does not anticipate increasing its level of service provision or making any major capital expenditures, you may reduce the amount of liquidity because your operations bring in revenues more than adequate to cover expenses, and your organization does not have to prefund major expenditures.
- If you are unsure regarding the cause or permanence of the change in its cash position, you may choose to gain interest income and retain flexibility by parking some of the cash buildup in longer-term securities, say with one-year or two-year maturities, making sure to choose those that are readily marketable (liquid).
- If your organization is expanding rapidly, hang onto the higher level of liquidity until you have a better idea of how much liquidity the organization needs.

Case 2: Net cash flow comes in below the amount projected in your cash budget. In this case, cash expenses are exceeding cash revenues, and you will have less cash at the end of the year than you originally anticipated. This may come as a surprise to some in your organization, as it may be "on budget" as far as the operating budget goes. However, not all revenues and expenses are cash revenues and cash expenses, and sometimes cash expenses exceed cash revenues in early months of the fiscal year, even though by the end of the year cash revenues catch up.

Possibly, your organization will go out and borrow some money to meet the shortfall. To the extent possible, you will want to rebuild the drained cash reserves and pay back any borrowings. Cash disbursements may be deferred where possible and cash expenses cut. If this is insufficient, you will need to consider increased fundraising activity to meet that target. In some cases, taking the flip side of the list we just looked at, the change is temporary and possibly self-correcting. More often than not, nonprofit executives and board members blithely assume that such events will self-correct, but you should take this situation seriously. It may be that your organization is heading for chronic cash deficits and a rapidly eroding cash position. Your organization may also need to make changes in its programming, if fees are part of the revenue base, or engage in earned income ventures to supplement donations. Cash deterioration often is compounded in rapidly growing organizations, because funds are disbursed to finance the growth before the donor base or other funding source responds to the increased outreach.

(b) HOW TO CONSTRUCT A CASH BUDGET. If your organization does its accounting on a cash basis, its operating statement or operating budget provides the basic background information for the cash budget. The cash budget differs in purpose from the operating budget, in that the cash budget highlights the cash available to the organization at various points in the future. The cash budget is very revealing for your organization's personnel, especially the first time it is constructed. Nonfinancial managers typically are unaware of just how unsynchronized cash inflows and cash outflows are until they see a cash projection. Grant- or contract-based organizations often find that they must expend cash before cash comes in from their funding source.

(i) Cash Budget and Its Purposes.   The cash budget shows the timing of cash inflows and outflows, usually on a monthly basis for the next 12 months. It is sometimes called a cash plan or cash forecast. Exhibit 2.1 shows the value of a cash budget. The cash budget has five major purposes. It shows the:

1. Unsynchronized nature of inflows and outflows (e.g., see October figures in illustrative historical cash flow table in Exhibit 2.2).
2. Seasonality of cash flows (e.g., donations run high around Easter and especially high between Thanksgiving and Christmas).
3. Degree of mismatch (amount of surplus or shortfall).
4. Duration of these surpluses or shortfalls (how long they last, in months).
5. Necessary inputs for planning your short-term investments or short-term borrowing (together the degree and duration of receipt-disbursement

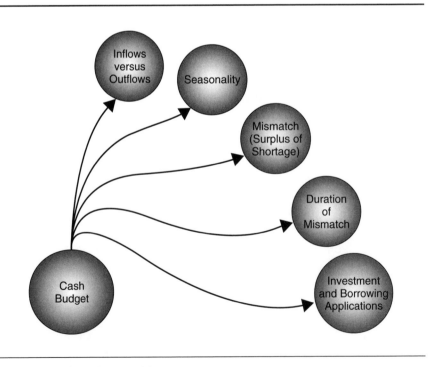

EXHIBIT 2.1   CASH BUDGET: USES

Month	Oct.	Nov.	Dec.	Jan.	Feb.	Mar.	Apr.	June	July	Aug.	Sep.
Line item: Cash Receipts (Total Deposits)	$1,373,317.26	$1,495,458.64	$2,296,298.05	$1,600,345.48	$1,585,68234	$1,455,742.97	$1,474,501.30	$1,528,613.80	$2,872,784.74	$1,928,010.02	$1,405,515.21
−Cash Disbursements (Total Payments/withdrawals)	1,866,433.15	1,358,838.60	2,191,922.40	1,826,944.39	1,598,544.96	1,516,459.75	1,417,947.23	1,469,020.89	3,064,544.94	1,715,130.63	1,459,922.01
Net cash Flow	($ 493,115.89)	$ 136,620.04	$ 104,375.65	($ 226,598.91)	($ 12,862.62)	($ 60,716.78)	$ 56,554.07	$ 59,592.91	($ 191,760.20)	$ 212,879.39	($ 54,406.80)
+Beginning cash (Beginning Balance)	$ 626,414.41	$ 133,298.52	$ 269,918.56	$ 374,294.21	$ 147,69530	$ 134,832.68	$ 74,115.90	$ 180,601.06	$ 240,193.97	$ 48,433.77	$ 261,313.16
=Ending Cash (Ending Balance or New Balance)	$ 133,298.52	$ 269,918.56	$ 374,294.21	$ 147,695.30	$ 134,832.68	$ 74,115.90	$ 130,669.97	$ 240,193.97	$ 48,433.77	$ 261,313.16	$ 206,906.36

EXHIBIT 2.2 COLLECTING HISTORICAL INFORMATION

39

mismatch provide this information, with the output of the planning process being the amounts and maturities of short-term investments or borrowing).

The four steps in developing a cash budget are:

1. Determine which measure of cash to manage and forecast.
   - General ledger cash balance (checkbook balance if that's your only accounting)
   - Bank balance (preferred)
2. Decide on presentation format.
3. Collect historical information (see Exhibit 2.2 for an actual nonprofit's prior year cash flows).
4. Develop cash forecast.

(ii) Forecasting Your Cash Position. Your cash budget may follow one of several formats. Because you probably are already developing a statement of cash flows (SCF), one alternative is to use the SCF format. You would then show projections for cash from/(to) operating activities, cash from/(to) investing activities, and cash from/(to) financing activities. This works well for an annual consolidated projection but is unnatural for monthly or daily projections.

An alternate format, which you may decide to use for your daily or monthly projections, is the cash receipts and disbursements method shown in Exhibit 2.3.

To implement this method, we need the necessary detail for each category of cash flow and for the minimum necessary cash:

- Categories of cash inflows
- Categories of cash outflows
- Needed minimum cash

Basically, all we are doing here is looking back to see sources of our cash inflows and outflows in the past and before deciding how much detail to show for each category.

	August	September
Beginning Cash	$350	$325
+ Cash receipts	150	
− Cash disbursements	325	
= Ending cash	$175	
− Minimum cash	200	
= Cash surplus	—	
OR		
Cash shortage	($ 25)	

EXHIBIT 2.3 BASIC CASH BUDGETING/ FORECASTING TEMPLATE

Let's look more closely at projecting cash receipts, and then we'll comment on cash disbursements.

Determine Cash Receipts. The determination of cash receipts proceeds in a straightforward fashion.

- The operating budget is your starting point.
- An accrual versus cash basis adjustment may need to be made (if numbers are already on cash basis, don't worry about adjustments).
- Watch out for these common oversights:
  - Don't forget prearranged financing inflows, such as loan repayments or bond interest.
  - Don't forget (formerly) restricted net assets, such as deferred giving or time-restricted or purpose-restricted prior-period gifts that will become unrestricted this period.
- Calendarization:
  - Study historical data to see seasonal patterns.
- Anticipate changes in the forthcoming 12 months.
- Show quarterly totals to provide one check-and-balance of your accuracy of yearly totals and to provide data for comparison purposes as the year unfolds.

Determine Cash Disbursements. Again, the operating budget expenses are the starting point. Because of unpaid bills listed as "accounts payable," you may have to make an accrual-to-cash basis adjustment.

One of the other key items to watch out for is the amount shown for capital budget outlays; many organizations forget to include these outflows in the cash budget.

Then calendarize the cash outlays correctly, recognizing seasonal or other ups and downs. Pull together quarterly subtotals to use down the road for comparisons with actual cash flows.

Putting It All Together. Now we are ready to bring the cash receipts and disbursements together to find the difference ("net cash flow") for each month. Once we have the net cash flow amount, we will add it to beginning cash to arrive at ending cash. We then compare ending cash to minimum cash required (by subtracting the latter) and see if we have a cash surplus anticipated for the month's end or a cash shortage. Be careful to deduct any restricted cash from the amount shown, which is best done by including any restricted cash as part of the "minimum cash required."

This procedure gives a three-step sequence that you should carry out at least monthly and probably weekly or, for large organizations, even daily. This sequence may be termed "compute/analyze/recommend."

- Compute NCF (= Cash inflows − Cash outflows), ending position, cash surplus/(shortfall) for each month.

- Analyze pattern(s)—Are there distinct seasonal highs or lows for either cash receipts or cash disbursements? How will this feed back into our cash planning (i.e., building up larger reserves) or fundraising appeal timing?
- Make recommendations with regard to both cash reserve buildup (How does the sum of the forecasted amounts of cash, cash equivalents, and short-term investments compare to our target liquidity level?) and fundraising campaign timing or frequency, as well as for short-term investments (amount and maturity of securities) and short-term borrowing (amount and anticipated maturity of any short-term borrowing, if our financial policy allows for such borrowing).

The cash forecasting exercise is valuable in assisting with your organization's implementation of financial policies, particularly your target liquidity level, and with carrying out your financial management processes.

(c) USING THE CASH BUDGET TO HELP SET THE TARGET LIQUIDITY LEVEL.
For background on our discussion of how much liquidity an organization should have, you may wish to refer to our discussion of the target liquidity level in Chapter 1. Here are some pointers on the optimal liquidity level. As for the optimal level of target liquidity, you will have to do the analysis yourself; no technique will provide that specific target level for you.

As a starting point, take a look at the cash position low point in your fiscal year, which for many nonprofits is late September or early October. Set a liquidity level for your peak season, probably early January, that is sufficient to cover your organization through the dry season. This is where your end-of-year annual cash budget reevaluation is so helpful. Study past cash flow patterns carefully to see when the cash crunches came as well as how much liquidity should have been held earlier in the year to prevent each cash crunch.

The degree of flexibility your organization has in quickly increasing revenues or quickly reducing expenses will also help you determine the size of your "safety buffer" of liquidity.

In addition, consult Exhibit 2.4, which provides you with a road map to determine whether your organization has too little liquidity. Work through it carefully, providing answers to the probe areas listed. Notice that the key indicators or signals of inadequate liquidity are: slow growth, missed opportunities, risky financial posture, small or zero net interest income (investments income less interest paid on borrowed funds), wage/salary freezes or very small increases, loans turned down or received on unattractive terms, recurrent cash crunches (or cash crises), late invoice payments (or lateness on other amounts paid), and ongoing stringency in your organization's financial posture despite successful fundraising campaigns. Once you have worked through these diagnostic questions in order to evaluate illiquidity, consider the flip side of each factor in order to determine whether your organization might have too much liquidity. Readjust your target liquidity level according to your answers. For a closer look at the processes

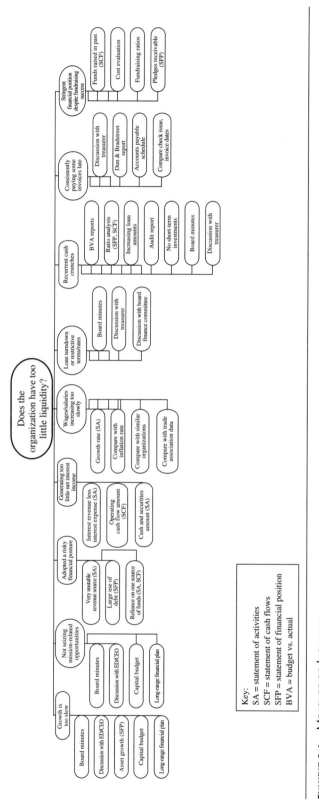

EXHIBIT 2.4 MEASURE OF LIQUIDITY

Key:
SA = statement of activities
SCF = statement of cash flows
SFP = statement of financial position
BVA = budget vs. actual

43

involved in setting the target liquidity level, consult the hypothetical case study in Appendix 2 C.

(i) Cash Position.   As your cash position changes, you will be in the position of advising management and the board of the seriousness of the change and what corrective actions, if any, are needed. You will want to do this each quarter and, if warranted, more often. Some organizations take a new look at the liquidity each week or even daily. As treasurer or cash manager of the organization, assuming you have enough cash to make it worth your while, each day you will look at the checking account balance to determine whether and how much to transfer to overnight or longer investments.

Now that we have an idea of the role of analysis and reports in utilizing the cash budget effectively, we turn to some ways in which you might cope with financial difficulties. Or you may wish to look at these as ways to fine-tune your already healthy financial position.

(ii) Responses to Financial Difficulties.   First, many organizations within and outside of the nonprofit sector are engaging in reengineering. This happens when service delivery and internal management processes are opened up for radical redesign instead of just incremental improvements. The approach is much like zero-based review or zero-base budgeting, except it is applied to efficiency of service delivery and internal management processes.

Second, some organizations are noting the difficulties that peer organizations are getting into and are moving proactively to build an endowment or cash reserves as "money for the rainy days." Similarly, financial managers are planning ahead for the overhaul of aging plant and equipment so as not to be caught short when the time comes for refurbishment or replacement. Organizations such as residential colleges, churches, and museums must be especially careful to anticipate the fixed asset needs for which they will have to plan internal funding or arrange funding. Other organizations are noting the need for pension funding or benefits funding.

But what if it's too late to plan ahead? Common responses to financial shortfalls are:

- Quickly eliminate deficit spending.
- Quickly increase internal control.
- Quickly increase the role and prominence of the finance department (it sounds self-serving, but this elevation of the finance function has been instrumental in helping organizations that have gotten into financial distress).
- Quickly reorient the organization to a slowed pace of program expansion (whether new programs or expansion of existing ones).
  - o "Managed growth," which means a measured, manageable rate of growth (practiced by Cedarville University, Cedarville, OH)

   ○ Sustainable growth rate[13]
   ○ Internal growth rate[14]

In addition to these stopgap measures, you can take some internal and external measures to stem a long-term decline.

INTERNAL MEASURES.
There are seven major financial strategies to embark on within your organization to prevent or contend with financial decline. Briefly, they are:

1. Better information available more quickly. Treasury and cash management improvements are very predictable: First comes more visibility/transparency of cash flow and related data (which implies clear assignments for who is to do cash account reconciliation and who the account owners are), followed by cleaner, real-time data, culminating in better decision making.[15] Weak working capital/liquidity management decision-making and inadequate financial reporting practices were listed as two of the top four internal inefficiencies hindering optimization of treasury and cash management by financial executives at 167 businesses.[16] The same shortfalls handcuff nonprofit financial staff.

2. New emphasis on cash forecasting with shorter horizon (month) and interval (weekly). "Inability to forecast company cash flows" is the number 1 internal inefficiency hampering treasury and cash management, according to surveyed financial executives in the business sector.[17] Your organization may wish to adopt 3 M's forecasting policy: Accurately forecast cash sources and uses and take whatever actions are deemed appropriate so that adequate cash is on hand at all times and so that daily and long-term liquidity needs are met at the best price. Consult Appendix 2D for statistical tools that should prove helpful in your cash forecasting.

3. Asset sales: This may involve a "strategic disposition," in which noncore assets or organizational units are shed, and/or renewed focus on core businesses] (that is[are] central to the mission)

4. Expansion strategy: This may include land purchase or a sale to builder/leaseback to the nonprofit organization. This strategy enables the builder to utilize the depreciation (40-year) expense deduction against income taxes, whereas the nonprofit would be unable to because it is tax-exempt.

5. Asset redeployment: This typically implies putting scarce labor and volunteer resources in the most critical areas.

6. Cost reduction/containment: This is an attempt to become more efficient, often in the form of automation or outsourcing, resulting in reduced employee headcount (the "downsizing" or "rightsizing" we hear so much about).

7. Treasury strategies: Many of the strategies here involve revising your treasury management approach and operations based on benchmarking. We provide techniques in Chapters 3 and 4 and benchmarks to begin using to gauge your treasury operation in Chapter 5.

EXTERNAL MEASURES.

External measures that organizations may take to cope with financial problems fall into three major categories:

1. Fundraising: Increase the intensity and focus of your fundraising efforts. Because so many donors now restrict their donations to a certain cause or purpose, about one in three nonprofits are attempting to cover operating expenses by seeking additional foundation grants, about one in three organizations are pursuing non-grant revenue sources for the same purpose, and about one in seven organizations are seeking government grants to offset a portion of operating expenses.[18]

2. Bank borrowing: Document future improvements to merit short-term financing to bridge the gap until more cash inflows will be received. Be aware that many banks are leery of lending to nonprofits, both because of insufficient planning practices and because of lack of collateral with which to secure the loan (see Chapter 6 for more on short-term loans).

3. Merger/acquisition partner or strategic alliance: Join hands with a partner that has deep (or deeper) pockets. Summit Christian College in Fort Wayne, Indiana, did just this in the mid-1990s, being acquired by Taylor University, a private college about 60 miles away, and becoming Taylor University-Fort Wayne as a result.

Cash budgeting and liquidity management practices are most valuable when they are well planned, carefully executed, and include the types of control and follow-up we have discussed.

2.7 SUMMARY

In this chapter, we have profiled liquidity analysis, liquidity measurement, and cash planning practices. Because your cash position and your net cash flow are so critically important as part of your organization's financial management, begin now to implement or improve your organization's cash budgeting (cash forecasting) process. Not only will you maintain an improved level financial control, but you will experience fewer cash crunches and cash crises and improve on the amount of interest income earned or reduce the amount of interest expense paid. Improved cash management will reduce the number of cash crunches and occasionally even prevent a cash crisis. We also note that there are a number of other internal and external steps that you can take to prevent or stem a cash crisis.

Appendix 2A provides you with a Sarbanes-Oxley compliance checklist that will help you assess your internal controls and processes (even though most non-profits are not presently required to comply with this legislation, some states are considering similar legislation for nonprofits operating in those states). Appendix 2B gives further guidance on calculating and interpreting the cash conversion period. In Appendix 2C we offer a case study to give you some practice in formulating an organization's target liquidity level. Appendix 2D briefly profiles some statistical tools that you may find helpful in forecasting cash receipts or cash disbursements.

Now that we understand the context of liquidity management, the primary financial objective of the nonprofit organization, the measures used for assessing liquidity, and the techniques of projecting future liquidity, we are ready to delve into the methods of cash management and banking relationship management. We turn next to a consideration of cash collections and cash positioning in Chapter 3.

Notes

1. The Committee of Sponsoring Organizations of the Treadway Commission (COSO), *Enterprise Risk Management—Integrated Framework*, September 2004.

2. For more on risk management principles and procedures, see Chapter 14, "Managing Risk, Legal Issues, and Human Resources," in John Zietlow, Jo Ann Hankin, and Alan Seidner, *Financial Management for Nonprofit Organizations: Policies and Practices* (Hoboken, NJ: John Wiley & Sons, 2007); Chapter 18, "Managing Financial Risk with Derivatives," in Terry S. Maness and John T. Zietlow, *Short-Term Financial Management: Text and Cases* (Cincinnati, OH: Thomson/South-Western, 2005); and Melanie L. Herman, George L. Head, Peggy M. Jackson, and Toni E. Fogarty, *Managing Risk in Nonprofit Organizations: A Comprehensive Guide* (Hoboken, NJ: John Wiley & Sons, 2004).

3. "Moody's downgrades the University of Hartford's debt to Ba2 from Baa3; $74.5 million of debt affected," BUSINESS WIRE, January 8, 1997, 4:57 PM EST.

4. Martin Van Der Werf, *Chronicle of Higher Education*; 47 (February 16, 2001), p.A37.

5. Cutback strategies are covered in more detail in Zietlow, Hankin, and Seider, *Financial Management for Nonprofit Organizations: Policies and Practices* (Wiley 2007), pp. 55-60.

6. This is conceptualized in the Hedgehog Concept by Jim Collins in *Good to Great and the Social Sectors* (Author, 2005), pp. 17-23.

7. Jarl Kallberg and Kenneth Parkinson, *Corporate Liquidity: Management and Measurement* (Homewood, IL: Richard D. Irwin, 1993), pp. 17–19.

8. Personal communication.

9. Cinda Becker, "Proceed With Caution," *Modern Healthcare* 36 (July 31, 2006), p.17.

10. The sustainable growth model for nonprofits is developed in our companion guide, *Financial Management for Nonprofit Organizations: Policies and Practices*, pp. 322-325.

11. Aberdeen Group, *Setting PACE in Treasury and Cash Management: Benchmark Report* (April 2006), at www.aberdeen.com/summary/report/benchmark/RA_PaceTCM_LM_2863.asp. Accessed: 12/28/06.

12. This should not be the case if you followed the recommended format offered later in this chapter (Exhibit 2.3). In that format, each month gives a cash surplus (if positive) or cash shortage (if negative), with the cash shortage reflecting the cumulative shortfall and therefore the borrowed balance at that point in time. The loan amount never appears in cash receipts.

13. For information on the sustainable growth rate, see Terry S. Maness and John T. Zietlow, *Short-Term Financial Management: Text and Cases* (Cincinnati, OH: Thomson/South-Western, 2005), Chapter 2.

14. The internal growth rate is profiled in most introductory corporate finance texts.

15. Aberdeen Group, *Setting PACE in Treasury and Cash Management: Benchmark Report*.

16. Id.

17. Id.

18. "Blackbaud Survey: Restricted Gifts on the Rise—New Funding Challenges for Non-profits," October 12, 2005, at www.blackbaud.com. Accessed 12/16/2006.

SARBANES-OXLEY COMPLIANCE CHECKLIST

Financial Statement	Area of Significance	Financial Statement Element	Policy	Required	Status			Notes
					Unknown/ Not started	Partially complete (needs updating)	Approved	
Balance Sheet								
	Assets							
		Cash & Cash Equivalents						
			Cash receipts					
			Bank account reconciliations					
			Banking policy and relationships					
			Cash disbursements/manual checks					
			Check signing requirements					
			Outstanding checks					
			General cash					

This checklist has been reprinted with permission from Protiviti's KnowledgeLeader - *www.knowledgeleader.com*. KnowledgeLeader is a subscription-based website that provides resources and best practices to help internal auditors and risk management professionals save time, manage risk, and add value. Free 30-day trials available.

Financial Statement	Area of Significance	Financial Statement Element	Policy	Required	Unknown/ Not started	Partially complete (needs updating)	Approved	Notes
		Cash & Cash Equivalents cont.	Petty cash					
			Deposits					
		Investments/ Foreign Exchange	Investment responsibility					
			Foreign currency translation					
			Fair value of financial instruments					
			Derivatives policy					
			Investments in associated companies					
			Functional currency					
			Hedging guidelines					
			Investment portfolio composition					
		Accounts Receivable	General accounts receivable					
			Credit memos					
			Allowance for doubtful accounts/credit risk					
			Credit risk					
			Credit balances					
			Customer deposits					

Financial Statement	Area of Significance	Financial Statement Element	Policy	Required	Unknown/ Not started	Status Partially complete (needs updating)	Approved	Notes
			Records maintenance					
			Invoice billings					
		Property and Equipment						
			AFE's					
			Acquisitions and dispositions					
			Assets of discontinued operations					
			Disposals					
			Asset retirement obligations					
			Reconciliations					
			Physical asset security					
			General property and equipment					
			Inventory					
		Other Assets						
			Inventory accounting					
			Physical inventory procedures					
			Multi-client library					
			Goodwill and intangible assets					
			Other long-lived assets					
			Other current assets (pre-paid expenses,					

Financial Statement	Area of Significance	Financial Statement Element	Policy	Required	Status			Notes
					Unknown/ Not started	Partially complete (needs updating)	Approved	
		Other Assets, cont.	inventory, spares, deferred costs, advances					
			Software costs					
			General other assets					
	Liabilities							
		Accounts Payable						
			Accounts payable					
			Competitive bids					
			Request for proposal					
			Purchase requisitions					
			Purchase orders					
			Contracts					
			Purchasing procedures					
			Vendor selections					
			Vendor file maintenance					
			Equipment rentals					
		Other Liabilities						
			General					
			Accrued expenses (employee benefits, debt restrictions, vessel					

Financial Statement	Area of Significance	Financial Statement Element	Policy	Required	Unknown/ Not started	Partially complete (needs updating)	Approved	Notes
			operations, interest, severance, advances)					
			Deferred revenue					
			Allowance for bad debts					
			Bank overdrafts					
			Income taxes					
			Accrued employee compensation					
			Deferred taxes					
			Warranties					
		Debt	General					
			Long-term debt (Approval, debt issuance cost, accounting for current maturities)					
			Subsidiaries with separate debt					
			Operating and capital lease obligations					
			Short-term debt					
		Stockholders' Equity						
			Capital stock					
			Stock transactions					

53

Financial Statement	Area of Significance	Financial Statement Element	Policy	Required	Status			Notes
					Unknown/ Not started	Partially complete (needs updating)	Approved	
Income Statement								
	Revenues							
			Revenue recognition					
			Revenue reporting					
	Expenses							
			Cost of sales					
			Third party reimbursable expenses					
			Payroll					
			Operating income (expense)					
			Capitalization					
			Depreciation and amortization					
			Research and development					
			Selling, general and administrative costs					
			Travel and entertainment					
			Impairment of long-lived assets					
			Steaming and mobilization					
			Income (loss) from associated companies					
			Interest expense/income					

Financial Statement	Area of Significance	Financial Statement Element	Policy	Required	Status			Notes
					Unknown/ Not started	Partially complete (needs updating)	Approved	
			Minority expense					
			Results of discontinued operations					
			Insurance					
			Other expenses					
			Fiscal adjustments					
General								
	Financial Management							
			Chart of accounts					
			Consolidation					
			Segment reporting and disclosures					
			Reporting packages					
			Business combinations					
			Period-end financial reporting					
			Month-end closing procedures					
			Reconciliations					
			Inter-company allocations					
			Variable interest entities					
			Commitments and contingencies					
			Related parties					
			Disclosures					

Financial Statement	Area of Significance	Financial Statement Element	Policy	Required	Status			Notes
					Unknown/ Not started	Partially complete (needs updating)	Approved	
	Financial Management, cont.		Process change control					
			Unusual transactions					
			Budgeting and forecasts					
			Release of financial/confidential information					
			Journal entry					
	Human Resources		Employment (hiring, promotion) policies					
			Employee benefits					
			Compensation/Payroll					
			Termination					
			Performance appraisals					
			Executive compensation					
			Incentive compensation					
			Employee handbook					
			Attendance, holidays, vacation, sick leave					
			Relocation payments					
			Internal transfers					

Financial Statement	Area of Significance	Financial Statement Element	Policy	Required	Unknown/ Not started	Status Partially complete (needs updating)	Approved	Notes
			Family & medical leave					
			Americans with Disabilities Act					
			Share-based compensation plans					
			Fair employment practices					
			Orientation and training					
			Employment verifications/background check					
			Equal opportunity					
			Sexual harassment/other harassment					
			New employee processing					
			Hiring of consultants/contractors					
			Personnel files and records					
	IT		Information security					
			Systems change policy					
			Software licensing					
			Electronic information (e-mail) systems					
	Other		Trade shows					
			Workplace rules, safety and health					

Financial Statement	Area of Significance	Financial Statement Element	Policy	Required	Unknown/ Not started	Partially complete (needs updating)	Approved	Notes
	Other, cont.		Disaster management/business resumption					
			Corporate credit cards					
			Use of company vehicles					
			Magazine subscriptions					
	Corporate Governance	General						
			Record retention, storage and disposal					
			Ethics hotline and policy on handling of complaints					
			US Antitrust Law Compliance					
			Delegation of authority					
			Code of Conduct					
			Entertainment and gifts					
			Insider trading					
			Related party transactions					
			Conflict of interest					
			Foreign Corrupt Practices Act					

Financial Statement	Area of Significance	Financial Statement Element	Policy	Required	Status			Notes
					Unknown/ Not started	Partially complete (needs updating)	Approved	
		Board of Directors	Personal loans to directors and executive officers					
			Corporate governance guidelines					
			Audit committee charter					
			Remuneration committee charter					
		Internal Audit	Internal audit charter					
			Pre-approval of audit and non-audit services					

CASH CONVERSION PERIOD

In this appendix, we briefly cover average collection period (ACP), inventory conversion period (ICP), average payment period (APP), operating cycle (OC), and the cash conversion period (CCP).[1] These techniques are most helpful for an organization that buys inventory on credit, processes it or merchandises it, and sells on credit. Regardless of whether your organization does all these things, the thought behind the CCP is very helpful. Essentially, what we are measuring is the elapsed period for which our organization is "out of pocket" for cash as part of its normal operating cycle. For most businesses, that period is the time between payments for their materials (when they pay on their accounts payable) until cash is collected on credit sales. Over that period, external financing must be arranged (or lower short-term investments held), which is costly. We consider the CCP to be the single best narrow liquidity measure. For more details, see Maness and Zietlow (2005).[2]

ICP (also called days inventory held, or DIH), measures the length of time it takes to convert your inventory into sales. Again, shorter is better, because inventories also tie up your cash. Good marketing and not overstocking slow-moving inventory are the keys to keeping the ICP down. The denominator has cost of goods sold, not sales, because inventories are accounted for at cost. Using sales there would also distort the measurement because it includes the markup added to your cost.

$$ICP = (Inventory \times 365)/Cost\ of\ goods\ sold$$

ACP (also called day sales outstanding, or DSO) measures the length of time it takes to collect credit sales. You want this to be as close to your offered credit period (commonly 30 days) as possible, as higher numbers tie up more of your cash. Aggressive collections and careful evaluation of which customers receive credit and in what amounts are the keys to keeping the ACP close to terms.

$$ACP = (Accounts\ receivable \times 365)/Total\ sales$$

Your operating cycle (OC) is the sum of the elapsed times for converting inventories to sales and then collecting on those sales (so that you once again have cash):

$$OC = ICP + ACP$$

Fortunately, you are not out of pocket for cash for the entire length of the operating cycle, normally. This is because you generally buy inventories on credit. We adjust for this by first calculating the average payment period (APP), then subtracting that from the operating cycle to get the cash conversion period.

APP (also called days payable outstanding or DPO) measures the length of time it takes to pay for your credit purchases. You want this to be as close to your suppliers' offered credit periods (commonly 30 days) as possible, but some businesses stretch payables unethically because higher numbers tie up less of their cash as it ties up more of their suppliers' cash. If your organization is truly cash-starved at a point in time, contacting your suppliers and explaining the situation and appealing for more time is the appropriate course of action.

$$APP = (Accounts\ payable \times 365)/Total\ purchases$$

Many times purchases data are not available to an external analyst, and cost of goods sold is used in the denominator instead.

We may now calculate the cash conversion period (CCP), which shows us for how long the organization has its cash tied up in its operations:

$$CCP = OC - APP$$

Or

$$CCP = ICP + ACP - APP$$

Illustrating, if ICP is 70 days, ACP is 45 days, and APP is 30 days, CCP would be:

$$CCP = 70 + 45 - 30$$

$$CCP = 85\ days$$

We can use this information to estimate minimum operating cash (MOC) for an organization. First, we calculate cash turnover (CT), which measures how many times per year cash cycles through the organization:

$$CT = 365/CCP$$

In our example, since CCP = 85 days:

$$CT = 365/85$$

$$CT = 4.29$$

Think of this as similar to inventory turnover, but the turnover is in your inventory of cash.

Some organizations estimate their minimum cash by taking some percent of their sales (for example, if set to 8% of sales, and sales are $2 million annually, minimum cash = $160,000 (= .08 × $2,000,000)). Our CT data, coupled with annual cash expenses, gives us another way to estimate minimum operations-related cash, or MOC. (You would hold cash for other reasons, as well, as noted in Chapter 2.)

$$MOC = \text{Annual cash expenses}/CT$$

If annual cash expenses are $1,600,000, using our CT of 4.29, we get MOC:

$$MOC = \$1,600,000/4.29$$

$$MOC = \$372,960.37$$

To express the effect of this level of "frozen cash" on your annual interest expense, multiply MOC by your annual cost of capital. Assuming your cost of funds, or what you would have to pay to get the funds from outside sources,[3] is 10 percent, or 0.10 in decimal form, we calculate that our organization would incur an annual interest expense of $37,296 related to our cash conversion period:

$$\text{Annual interest expense of MOC} = MOC \times \text{annual cost of capital}$$

$$\text{Annual interest expense of MOC} = \$372,960.37 \times 0.10$$

$$\text{Annual interest expense of MOC} = \$37,296$$

If we could convert our inventories more quickly, collect our receivables more quickly, or renegotiate more favorable payment terms, we could reduce our CCP, increase our CT, reduce our MOC, and thereby reduce the interest expense related to our operating cycle. When the CCP increases, we get the opposite effect, as shown in the chain reaction diagram (see Exhibit 2B.1).

What if our organization has no inventories and does not make credit sales? We still benefit from looking at the APP and how that allows assets to be financed without paying a bank or other party an explicit interest expense. (Not taking credit terms when offered is unwise, in that suppliers have built the cost of the credit extension into the price of the product or service.) Furthermore, there are other receivables that our organization may be working with, such as short-term

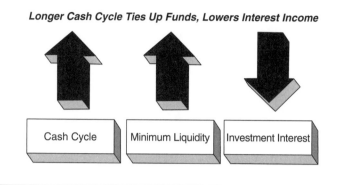

EXHIBIT 2B.1 CHAIN REACTION

pledges receivable, dues receivable, or grants/contracts receivable. Every day that elapses without cash coming in on these receivables represents one more day for which we must fund this amount through short-term borrowings or reduced short-term investments. The CCP enables us to see the effects of this on our organization's liquidity—something we would not be able to accurately evaluate if we merely calculate the current ratio (current assets/current liabilities) or net working capital (current assets minus current liabilities).

Notes

1. This material is drawn from our companion book, *Financial Management for Non-profit Organizations: Policies and Practices* (Hoboken, NJ: John Wiley & Sons, 2007), Appendix 7B.

2. Terry S. Maness and John T. Zietlow, *Short-Term Financial Management* (Cincinnati: Thomson/South-Western, 2005).

3. Technically, one should use the organization's weighted-average cost of capital (WACC) for the cost of funds. On how to arrive at an appropriate cost of funds, see *Financial Management for Nonprofit Organizations: Policies and Practices*, pp. 359–360.

HYPOTHETICAL CASE STUDY FOR SETTING TARGET LIQUIDITY

Matt Toppin, the Midsouth Symphony Orchestra (MSO)[1] chief financial officer, is persuaded that his organization should reprioritize its financial objectives to strive for a target liquidity level. In the past, the focus has been on trying to balance the budget, but cash flow problems seem to recur even after balanced budget years. He has assembled some ratios and other data in preparation for determining whether MSO's liquidity level is adequate, and if not, what level MSO should target.

BACKGROUND INFORMATION

SYMPHONY FAILURES   Failure rates for symphonies are relatively high, and many surviving symphonies seem to have ongoing financial struggles. Issues raised by failing symphonies include management-performer conflicts over extra performances, increasing salaries and benefits for performers, flat or declining ticket revenues, lack of appreciation in the local community for traditional symphony fare, difficulty in getting donations, competition in the local market with not only other arts organizations but also other entertainment outlets, and growing consumer preference for home entertainment. Most symphonies only cover about half of their expenses with earned income, necessitating that private or corporate contributions be raised and possibly government grants be received to make up the difference.

CULTURAL INSTITUTION BOND RATINGS   Matt also found that few symphonies are rated by the chief bond rating agencies, Moody's and Standard & Poor's. From materials published by the raters, he has made some interesting discoveries regarding the way in which objective and knowledgeable outsiders view symphony finances. When cultural organizations such as symphonies garner most of their revenue from visitor revenue (i.e., tickets in the case of a symphony), only barely cover expenses with revenues, or face a widely fluctuating customer demand, they are required to hold more liquidity to get a high rating (indicating creditworthiness) by Moody's.[2] Further complicating the financial management task for symphonies, a significant number of their employees are represented by collective bargaining units. Highly-rated organizations are characterized by an "expendable financial resources to operations" ratio value of 1.95 times in 20XX, the most recent year.[3]

Moody's analyzes five different factors in determining its creditworthiness rating for an organizations: market position, financial resources, operating performance, debt position and legal structure of borrowing, and strategy and management.

To be assigned one of its two highest ratings for creditworthiness (which indicates significant financial strength and stability), Moody's requires the organization to hold a relatively high level of reserves (cash and short-term investments) in order to cushion the organization through an extended period of negative net revenues. Moody's also requires the organization to have a strong market position, measured by such factors as volunteer involvement, subscription revenue as a percent of total ticket revenue, and reputation in the local community as well as nationally.

Matt has also read somewhere that performing arts organizations normally "earn" significantly less than their expenses in most fiscal years, necessitating a search for unearned income to meet this "earnings gap." Earned income, as defined by this source, includes investment income. As a percentage of total revenue, classical music organizations earned about 54% of their total revenues according to one study.[4] Subtracting investment income from their earnings, these organizations "earned" 45% of their total revenues. Matt recalls that MSO's ratio of earned income to revenue is near 43%, and after subtracting investment income approximately 42% for the most recent fiscal year.

BANK PERSPECTIVE   The bank with which MSO has its credit line continually emphasizes cash flow. The relationship manager at the bank, with whom Matt has the most contact, periodically reminds him that the Symphony has no collateralizable assets, because it leases its office space and the performance hall that it owns has few it any potential buyers in the community were it to be put up for sale (in the event of a loan default, a case in which the lending bank would sell off the collateral to pay off most of the loan remaining outstanding). Predictable and growing cash flows are what rings his banker's bell, Matt concludes.

PEER ORGANIZATIONS' LIQUIDITY   Matt pulls up some other symphonies' Form 990s to find cash, savings, and investments numbers. He finds five symphonies to which he decides to compare (benchmark against) MSO, due to size and similarity of programming. For these five symphonies, the cash plus savings (Lines 45, Cash – non-interest bearing; Line 46, Savings and temporary cash investments) average amount is $1,651,250. The investments numbers are tough to interpret, since they include long-term investments such as endowments. The average amount in investments (Line 56, Investments – other) is $67,534,106. Of the latter, almost all amounts are long-term investments, and the short-term investments are normally all held in the endowment fund of these organizations – and as part of the endowment fund, considered to be permanently restricted. Matt is unable to determine the unused portion of other symphonies' credit lines from the Form 990 data.

MSO FINANCIAL DATA   Matt compiled this data as an aid to setting MSO's target liquidity level. All data is for Year 20XX.

Program Expense Ratio	80.0%
Support Services:	
Administration Expense Ratio	12.8%
Fundraising Expense Ratio	7.2%
Revenue Growth[a]	−1.1%
Program Growth[a]	0.1%
Working Capital Ratio[b]	−0.01 years
Total Revenue[c]	$6,550,000
Total Expenses[d]	$6,975,000
Net Assets	$4,625,000
Market Value of Endowment	$500,000
Visitor Revenue as a % of Total Revenue	88%
Liquid Funds Indicator	0.45
Amount of Credit Line	$150,000
Amount of Credit Line Presently Used	$145,000
Amount of Cash and Cash Equivalents	$7,750
Amount of Short-Term Unrestricted Investments	$11,450
Projected Operating Cash Flow for Next 12 Months	−$225,000
Standard Deviation of Past 5 Years' Operating Cash Flows	$343,730
Cash Conversion Period (Days)	145

[a]Average annual growth, or compound annual growth, of the primary revenue source ("revenue growth") and of program expenses ("program growth"). No deferred gifts were received, and no capital campaign is presently ongoing.
[b]Calculated as [(cash and equivalents + savings accounts + pledges receivable + grants receivable)–(accounts payable + grants payable + accrued expenses)]/total expenses. For items not applicable to MSO, Matt plugs in a 0. MSO's numerator is slightly negative and the denominator (as expected) is positive.
[c]Includes unrestricted, temporarily restricted, and permanently restricted revenues for Year 20XX. Revenue from the endowment to support operations was $25,000 in Year 20XX.
[d]Total expenses do include depreciation expense but do not include any amount to serve as a contingency reserve. Some nonprofits, in their operating budgets, build in a contingency reserve as some percent of revenues or of expenses.

QUESTIONS

1. Calculate all relevant financial ratios, given the data that Matt has collected. What advice do you have for Matt as he advises the board of directors and chief executive officer/executive director (CEO/ED) on the target liquidity level, based on your analysis?
2. Using the Internet or library resources, see what comparative data you can locate on your ratios in #1 as well as ratio values given in the case. How does MSO compare to other symphonies or performing arts organizations (or cultural organizations, if you cannot find data on the former)? Based on this comparison, what advice might you give Matt as he advises the board of directors and CEO/ED?
3. MSO has no immediate plans to issue any bonds. Why should it still use the insights Matt gained from reading about cultural institution bond ratings? Based on the ratings information he gathered, what advice could you give Matt as he advises the board of directors and CEO/ED?
4. Are the insights Matt gleaned from his banker generally favorable or unfavorable regarding symphony creditworthiness? Given your conclusion here, should Matt be advised to recommend a larger or smaller target liquidity level as he advises the board of directors and CEO/ED?
5. The Liquid Funds Indicator value for Year 20XX for cultural institutions is 0.80. What light does this cast on MSO's present liquidity position? On MSO's target liquidity level?
6. Based on items #1 to #5, what is your final recommendation to Matt regarding MSO's target liquidity level?
7. What additional information should Matt collect before determining his final target liquidity level recommendation to take to the CEO/ED and the board of directors?

Notes

1. This organization and chief financial officer are fictitious, although the issues and concerns raised in this case are very real to an actual symphony.
2. Moody's Investor Service, "Moody's Rating Approach for Not-for-Profit Cultural Institutions," (New York: Author, 2004), p. 5.
3. Id. Expendable financial resources are equal to total unrestricted net assets plus temporarily restricted net assets minus net investment in plant. "Operations" equals total operating expenses. The ratio takes expendable financial resources and divides it by operations.
4. Based on U.S. Census Bureau Data for 1997, and reported in Kevin F. McCarthy, Arthur Brooks, Julia Lowell, and Laura Zakaras, *The Performing Arts in a New Era,* (Santa Monica, CA: RAND Institute, 2001), p. 83. For more information on this study, visit www.rand.org/pubs/monograph_reports/MR1367/.

CASH FORECASTING METHODS

In this appendix we cover some advanced forecasting methods that you will find helpful in your liquidity planning. Our primary focus is on regression analysis, as we view it as the single most helpful forecasting technique involving statistical analysis.

FORECASTING METHODS

Examples of quantitative (statistical) and qualitative (judgmental) forecasting methods can be found in Exhibit 2D.1. We will focus on the "Causal or regression" category primarily in this appendix. Regression has been shown to be one of the most powerful statistical tools available to the forecaster.

REGRESSION ANALYSIS

Regression analysis involves forecasting the future values of an item of interest based on known values of that same items or known or forecasted values for related items. For example, it is logical to forecast inventories based on one's sales forecasts.

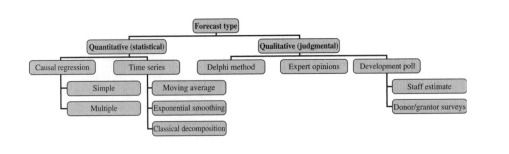

EXHIBIT 2D.1 FORECASTING METHODS

The regression model for simple regression follows this format:

$$Y = a + b(X)$$

Where Y is the "dependent" variable, the one being forecasted, X is the "independent" or "predictor" variable that has some logical connection to Y, b is how many units Y changes for a one-unit change in X, and a is the base value that characterizes that variable regardless of what value X takes on.

Let's construct a simple regression example. Let's say that your organizations' donations are predictably related to the disposable income (income less taxes) of people living in your geographic area. You collect data from the past ten years and find donations and disposable income to be:

Year	Donations	Disposable Income (mils)
1	$450,310	$735
2	$485,770	775
3	$514,990	817
4	$572,000	899
5	$650,000	1,045
6	$722,000	1,142
7	$852,000	1,359
8	$920,000	1,452
9	$938,400	1,466
10	$910,240	1,415

You may wish to graph this data first to get a visual check on how close of a relationship exists between donations and disposable income. Notice that we have a simple regression model here, in that only one predictor variable, disposable income, is being used to forecast the variable of interest, donations. If we had a second predictor variable, say the percentage increase in a stock market index for the year, our model would be a multiple regression model—more than one data variable would be used to predict donations.

After entering this data into Microsoft Excel™, and selecting Tools/Add-ins/ Analysis ToolPak, run the regression analysis on this data by selecting Tools/Data Analysis/Regression. After highlighting the column of Donations data for the Y values and the column of Disposable Income for the X values (including the top of the column, in which the words "Donations" and "Disposable Income" appear), check the Labels box and type a name for the results of the regression in the "New Worksheet Ply" menu box. Then click OK. The results then appear in the new worksheet. Here is what you will see (we selected from the results screen):

SUMMARY OUTPUT

Regression Statistics

Multiple R	0.999250736
R Square	0.998502034
Adjusted R Square	0.998314789
Standard Error	7912.38255
Observations	10

ANOVA

	df
Regression	1
Residual	8
Total	9

Coefficients	
Intercept	−21621.47133
DispIncome	651.2314015

The R Square tells us we have a very close relationship between disposable income and our organization's donations. The highest possible R Square value is 1.0. Recognize that there is no guarantee that this lock-step relationship will persist into the future, however. For one thing, we have only ten years of data. Secondly, other variables certainly affect donations, and they will not always move in concert with disposable income.

We will assume that this close relationship between disposable income and donations continues into the future as we do our forecast for Year 11. The Coefficients are really the key part of the output, assuming that we have a good fit between the disposable income and our donations. The coefficients are −21,621.47133 and 651.2314015. This gives us a formula for predicting next year's or any future year's donations:

$$\text{Donations} = -21{,}621.47133 + 651.2314015 \text{ (DispIncome)}$$

where "DispIncome" is our abbreviation for Disposable Income in millions of dollars. Be careful to keep your units consistent as you take numbers from the worksheet regression output.

To do a forecast with our regression model, we first need to make or get a forecast for disposable income. The Chamber of Commerce may know of a good source, or you may wish to check with your state's Commerce Department. There may be private sector forecasts of the disposable income for your metropolitan area, depending on it size. In our case, let's say that the following number is forecasted:

$$Year\ 11\ Disposable\ Income\ Forecast = \$1,489\ million$$

Plug this number into the formula to get the donation forecast:

$$Donations = -21,621.47133 + 651.2314015\ (\$1,489)$$
$$= \$948,062$$

Your judgment and that of others with relevant expertise comes in at this point. If you know one of your donors has already promised a six-figure gift next year, by far the largest your organization has ever received, you will override your forecast to bump up the numbers by some amount. Two cautions are germane here: many nonprofits like to use a conservative revenue forecast, so do not over-adjust, and statistical forecasts have been shown in many cases to be more accurate than even the most seasoned expert's judgmental forecast. Put another way, we turn out to be worse at forecasting than we think we will be.

OTHER STATISTICAL METHODS

Referring back to Exhibit 2D.1, notice the other category of statistical forecasting methods, under the "Time Series" caption. Here, the passage of time brings with it a predictable change in the variable you wish to forecast. Though this sounds very naïve, in reality the passage of time coincides closely enough with the natural progression of the true underlying causal variables—those that in fact cause your forecasted value to change. In a sense, time "proxies" for the variables that drive your forecast variable higher or lower.

The three primary time series methods are moving averages, exponential smoothing, and classical decomposition. We briefly present the first two methods, following closely the presentation of these in Maness and Zietlow (2005); you may consult this and other sources for more on these methods and on classical decomposition.[1]

The basic idea behind time series methods is to project ahead, or extrapolate, the past numerical values of your forecast variable. The simplest method for doing this is the moving average.

A moving average uses the mean, or average, of the most recent values of the variable you wish to forecast. For example, you might calculate a 3-month, 3-year, or 7-year moving average. Once calculated, this average takes on the meaning of a "most likely outcome," and thus serves as your best guess forecast for the next period. The longer the period over which you calculate the average, the less influence a very recent value will have on the average. This is a real advantage when you just experienced an abnormal year for the item you are forecasting—perhaps the dramatic drop of donations for many nonprofits following the tsunami and hurricanes in 2005 would best illustrate this phenomenon.

Illustrating, if your last 5 years saw expenses of $450, $475, $440, $455, and $490, the five-year moving average would be:

$$5\text{-year moving average} = (\$450 + \$475 + \$440 + \$455 + \$490)/5$$
$$= \$2,310/5 = \$462.$$

This value of $462 is then your forecast for next year's expenses. Notice that the average will not change immediately as the historical values upon which it is based begin to change in trend. This is a disadvantage because your forecast is not recognizing the new trend for several years, giving inaccurate forecasts.

Exponential smoothing overcomes this slowed trend recognition by permitting a greater weighting for your most recent values. This technique begins with a base forecast for the next period, and then adjusts that base up or down depending on the error made in the most recent period's forecast. Essentially, it is a forecasting model that learns from its errors. The exponential smoothing model is a formula:

$$F_{t+1} = F_t + \alpha(A_t - F_t)$$

Where:

F_{t+1} is the forecasted value for next period

In other words, this is your new forecast.

F_t is the forecast you made last period for this (present) period

α is the smoothing constant ($0 \leq \alpha \leq 1$)

A_t is the actual value for this (present) period

If you missed by a large amount this period on your forecast (which you made last period), you will make a larger revision to this period's forecast to come up with next period's forecast. Notice also that the larger the smoothing constant α, the larger the revision, regardless of the amount of the forecast error just experienced. The actual values from the distant past are weighted less than recent values, regardless of what value of α you use (except in the very special case in which $\alpha = 0$). Changes in trend, or effects of new seasons when doing monthly or quarterly forecasts, have a delayed effect on the forecast in the exponential smoothing model.

Regardless of whether you use statistical techniques in assisting with your cash forecasting, be aware that having accurate data upon which to construct your forecasts is essential. Getting timely and accurate data is the greatest challenge you will face in forecasting. Beyond that, finding out what drives each major cash flow type (segregate out your disbursements into smaller categories, and do the same with your receipts) will prove most valuable in honing your forecasting methods to achieve greater accuracy.

Notes

1. For more on time series methods, see Terry S. Maness and John T. Zietlow, *Short-Term Financial Management*, 3rd edition (Cincinnati: Thomson/South-Western, 2005), pp. 445-450.

CASH COLLECTIONS AND POSITIONING

3.1 INTRODUCTION

The U.S. cash management environment is one in which check usage and the cost of information technology are on the decline and interest rates and the use of electronic payments are on the upswing. Add in the phenomenal opportunities to harness the Internet for banking and other finance tasks, and you have a recipe for remarkable improvements in nonprofit cash management.

According to one recent survey of nonprofits, the four main causes of cash flow problems cited by nonprofits are all at least partly related to cash coming into the organization. In 2003, 50.2 percent of surveyed nonprofits indicated that they experienced cash flow problems. The reasons given for these problems are "(1) delays in government payments, (2) normal business cycles, (3) unmet fundraising goals, and (4) a prior-year deficit."[1] Improving your management of cash inflows will help directly with items 1 and 2 and partly offset items 3 and 4. In her path breaking case studies of four nonprofits' revenue cycles, Kirsten Grønbjerg discovered that each experienced wide fluctuations in their cash receipts, primarily because of delayed payments of vouchers: United Way payments came in as quickly as within two days, but some state agencies delayed payments for 22 weeks—forcing the nonprofits to get bank loans.[2]

Best-in-class nonprofits with regard to cash management are ones that generally follow certain guidelines and pay attention to organizational issues. First, they attend to the primary financial objective first, last, and in between: to ensure that financial resources are available when needed (timing), as needed (amount), and at reasonable cost (cost-effectiveness), and that once mobilized, these resources are protected from impairment and spent according to mission and donor purposes. Second, they attend to organizational issues that may help or hinder effective cash and treasury management. These organizational issues apply to cash collections, cash mobilization or positioning, and cash disbursements (see Chapter 4). Some best practices that we notice in organizations of all sizes include:

- Policies are in place for cash management, who is authorized to do what (with dollar limits), short-term investments, and long-term investments.
- Board has someone(s) with financial expertise and has a functioning and effective finance committee and audit committee.
- The chief financial officer (CFO)/treasurer has financial education, training, a heart for the mission, ability to say no persuasively, and (ideally) nonprofit experience.
- The organization taps service provider expertise:
  - Bank or credit union
  - Auditor
  - Information system provider
- The organization uses volunteers and college interns effectively.
- The organization taps the power of Microsoft Excel for financial reports and modeling.

We begin this chapter with a discussion of the objectives of cash collections and cash positioning systems. We then set the stage for a discussion of receivables and cash collections by talking about the "order-to-cash" cycle. This leads naturally to a discussion of receivables management, including receivables from contracts or sales (if any), pledges, and grants. A key piece of this is collecting on receivables. We then move to a discussion of the payments system, as this is a vital part of understanding how payments will be made to your organization. We present information about coins and currency, checks, card payments, and electronic payments. Of special interest here are whether your organization should even accept credit card or debit card payments and the increasing use of direct payments and Internet-based payments. Our presentation then moves to how to mobilize cash, including global issues that may be involved if your organization deals at more than one country. Finally, we discuss the four hot-button issues facing nonprofit financial managers today: fraud, imaging, outsourcing, and benchmarking.

3.2 OBJECTIVES OF CASH COLLECTIONS AND POSITIONING SYSTEMS

Cash collection systems include all processes and tools used to bring cash into the organization. Positioning (traditionally known as concentration) systems include all processes and tools used to mobilize cash into a central location so that it may be used for investments, to pay down borrowing, or to fund disbursements.

A key measure to keep in mind here is the idea of *collection float*. Think of collection float as a measure of the efficiency of your collections function. Collection float includes mail float, processing float, and availability float. Each of these flows represents a delay incurred in receiving expendable funds. Consider mailed checks. *Mail float* refers to how long in mail time it takes for a check to arrive at its destination.[3] This delay is related to how distant the two points are (from where the check was mailed to where the check is received), and such factors as whether a holiday or weekend intervened, how efficient the postal system is, and even the weather. Mail float might be two to five days for domestic mailings. *Processing float* starts when a check is received by the addressee and ends when the check is dropped off at the bank as a deposit. Processing float may be less than half a day or extend to one or two days. Finally, *availability float* refers to the "hold time" that the bank imposes before you can spend the funds. This might be a matter of hours or, in special situations, one or more days. According to a piece of federal legislation called Regulation CC, local checks may be held for two days and distant checks as many as five days.[4]

Although cash collections and cash positioning overlap, we consider objectives for them separately.

The primary objective for cash collections is to bring cash in quickly and accurately in a cost-effective manner. Identifying the source of cash collections also suggests other secondary objectives:

- Donations and dues: Collect electronically if possible.
- Loans and advances: Don't allow delays in related payments.
- Service fees and sales revenue: be assertive, do not allow buyers to "stretch payables."
- Use bank/third-party and/or internal treasury information services as an ally to verify inflow amounts and timing.

When it comes to mobilizing or positioning cash, organizational activities are aimed at pooling, employing, protecting, amassing, and monitoring funds. Brief explanations of each of these objectives follow.

- Pools funds: does not allow small balances to remain in multiple accounts
- Employs funds: puts "funds awaiting investment" to work
- Protects funds: watches for and guards against foreign exchange risk and interest rate risk
- Amasses funds: there is some controversy here.

  - Exercises collective faith (collective expression of the organizational members': faith for faith-based organizations) proactively (build now) rather than reactively (scramble once in crisis) to assemble needed cash reserves[5]
  - Three to six months of expenses in operating reserves for emergencies, rainy-day fund, missed forecasts, unforeseen opportunities
  - As much as one to two years of expenses in prefunding account or sub-account for planned needs, such as loan repayments, capital expenditures, program expansion, earned income venture launch, and so on. The exact amount to hold for prefunding is driven by the organization's inability to issue stock and/or inability or unwillingness to use various forms of debt financing.

- Monitors funds: uses bank/third-party and/or internal treasury information services as an ally to help control fund balances

Businesses asked about what processes represent the greatest potential for improving their organizations' cash management selected the order-to-cash process and cash pooling (concentration) behind only cash forecasting in importance. Exhibit 3.1 profiles these responses. This chapter provides ideas you can use immediately to improve your order-to-cash (or appeal-to-cash) and cash positioning processes.

Before we can discuss cash collections and cash concentration in greater detail, we have to back up to the front end of the collections process. Before there is cash to collect, there must be some generation of revenue. Oftentimes that revenue is not immediately collected as cash, because it first materializes in the form of a receivable. Be very careful here to distinguish between the collections of receivable process and cash collections. Before there can be cash

WHICH PROCESSES REPRESENT THE HIGHEST POTENTIAL FOR IMPROVING CASH
MANAGEMENT?

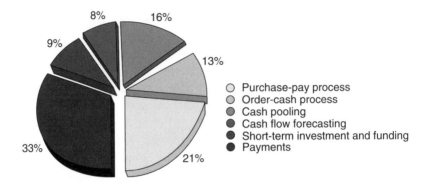

○ Purchase-pay process
○ Order-cash process
● Cash pooling
● Cash flow forecasting
● Short-term investment and funding
● Payments

Precentage of total responses (corporate respondents were asked to choose two processes)

Source: CAPGENT, gtnews.com, Corporate Trends in Cash Management, June
20, 2006, in association with Skandinaviska Enskilda Banken AB, www.gtnews.
com/feature/134.cfm. Used by permission.

EXHIBIT 3.1   NET REVENUE POSSIBILITIES FROM BETTER CASH MANAGEMENT

collections, there must be the triggering of the payment of a receivable. For
organizations that have a credit department, the collections process is negatively
construed. However, it is actually a very important and very critical part of the
entire receivables management function.

3.3 FRONT END OF COLLECTIONS: RECEIVABLES MANAGEMENT

"You can't pay your payroll with accounts receivable." This truism, often repeated
in the business world, applies equally well to the different forms of nonprofit
receivables. Let's start out with your organization's revenue cycle so that you can
better see how collecting your receivables fits into your "order-to-cash" cycle.

(a) YOUR ORGANIZATION'S REVENUE CYCLE.   Your organization's revenue
cycle begins when someone orders or contracts for something (or decides to
use one of your services); followed by order entry; scheduling; service delivery
or inventory release; coding; invoicing or billing; dispute resolution; follow-up
contacts, if necessary; customer or client payment authorization; payment transmission; payment receipt; cash application; and ongoing customer or donor
relationship management processes. All of these activities make up your
"order-to-cash processes." Managed well, they will all contribute to your cash
position on an ongoing basis.

According to the Healthcare Financial Management Association 2004 Revenue Cycle Survey,[6] which reflected the views of 254 respondents, there are

three major environmental issues impacting the revenue cycle in healthcare: unpaid care (including write-offs and bad debt), regulatory and policy issues, and delays in payments for services. The most important measures of revenue cycle performance, according to the respondents, include: cash flow, days' sales outstanding (or days in receivables), bad debt write-offs, reimbursement under-payments, and performance by payer measured as contract performance. It is interesting to note that managing accounts receivable today is viewed broadly as managing the entire revenue cycle, including staff training and development and more information capture and publicity. One healthcare organization found tremendous improvement in cash collections once it started publicizing internally each unit's cash collections. Increased point-of-service collections and projects targeted at reducing denials and underpayments also lead to improvement in collections.

(b) METRICS TO REDUCE YOUR ORGANIZATION'S RISK. Operational risk is defined as "the risk of monetary losses resulting from the inadequate or failed internal processes from external events."[7] Specific to the revenue cycle are two metrics: days between payments and invoices produced on time.[8] *Days between payments,* when increasing, may signal malfunctioning billing systems or customer disaffection with your organization's products or services. *Invoices produced on time* reveals the number of invoices going out on a timely basis and with complete accuracy.

(c) ACCOUNTS RECEIVABLE. If your organization sells on credit, it includes all uncollected credit sales in an account called accounts receivable. Every aspect of your organization's credit policy is important in managing your accounts receivable. Your credit standards, defining the marginal customer that is minimally acceptable for credit extension, result in lost sales if set too high and uncollectible sales if set too low. Your credit period results in lost sales if set too short; if it is set too long, it results in you banking your customers for too long of a period.[9] If competitors offer a cash discount, normally you will have to offer one as well. The best advice for small nonprofit organizations? Do not offer credit. Most likely your cash position does not allow you the flexibility to sell on credit.

(d) GRANTS OR CONTRACTS RECEIVABLE. Government receivables are sometimes very difficult to collect. The prerequisites for effectively dealing with government receivables include: mastering the laws/regulations that govern payment practices, understanding definitions and interpretations of those laws, and comprehending the requirements involved with your contracts.[10] Read and understand contracts before signing them, asking questions, if necessary. Do not sign contracts that have built-in automatic payment delays. Make sure to correctly address invoices, including, if necessary: an individual's name, office symbol, code for the department, room number, purchase order number, and any additional identifying characters to ensure proper routing of your invoice. In accordance with what the government calls a "good and proper invoice," a Department of Defense contract using form DD1155 includes a "mail invoice to" in Block 13. For federal government contracts, the Prompt Payment Act stipulates that bills for most items must be paid within 30 days of receipt and acceptance of material and/or services. However, recognize that if a proper receipt is not received by that time, the federal government has 30 days after receipt of the proper invoice. So "invoicing float" will delay your collections from the federal government. Some items are not covered under the Prompt Payment Act. These include cost plus contracts, cost reimbursable contracts, progress payments, and advances.

The 30-day clock for the federal government is based on the date the invoice is actually received or the seventh day after your services are completed or your product is delivered (this is termed "constructive acceptance"). Small-dollar purchases are paid through a VISA card program. Small businesses and disadvantaged businesses may be paid more quickly than 30 days as well. You may also collect interest on late payments from the federal government. Check with your state or local government for payment practices for state or local government–related payments.

(e) CONTRIBUTIONS AND PLEDGES RECEIVABLE.   Contributions and pledges receivable are a delicate issue for nonprofit managers. Part of the difficulty is estimating which pledges are truly uncollectible and should be included in your "allowance for doubtful accounts" in your accounting system. Your organization's historical experiences, as well as the experiences of peer organizations, provide the best guidelines. For example, evangelical Protestant missions agencies surveyed in our Lilly study indicated that 95 percent of their pledges would be received.[11] A very different picture is seen from an archdiocese, which established a $2.7 million allowance for uncollectible amounts, from its total of $6.9 million amount for pledges. A more difficult issue is how the archdiocese or any other organization might press for payment of pledges. Although these pledges are "unconditional," few organizations are willing to take legal action to collect on them. Yet if your organization is facing an operating deficit, aggressive collection of contributions and pledges receivable is very important.

(f) COLLECTIONS FUNCTION.   Delays in collecting amounts owed are a major issue. One study in the United Kingdom found that late payments were the major reason for business failures, with the greatest incidence being in the small-business arena. One survey of Fortune 1000 financial managers in the United States indicated that speeding collection of accounts receivable is the single most important activity in all of corporate short-term financial management practices.[12] Collections are important for nonprofits as well, as they need to bring in the cash, while not harming a strong relationship with donors, grantors, or customers in the case of nonprofits also selling products or services.

Four principles of collections[13] are:

1. Collect the money.
2. Maintain a systematic follow-up.
3. Get the customer to discuss the account.
4. Preserve goodwill.

Determining how to collect from a particular delinquent payer depends on the amount owed, how long the item has been unpaid, whether there has been a partial payment or effort on the part of the payer to settle the debt, how long one has been dealing with the payer, and previous dealings with the customer, especially in regard to commitments made in the past. In the event of a temporary cash flow problem on the part of the payer, insist that a renegotiated payment schedule be adhered to. Be very sure that any payments in the past have been applied to the account, any disputes have not already been resolved. Billing questions have been taken care of, the credits that had been given in the past had been applied to the account, and any special arrangements are being adhered to.

Bill promptly, and make sure your invoice clearly states your terms, including when and how much to pay and where to mail the check or make the electronic payment.

Make sure your first contact to a delinquent payer occurs after no more than 10 days (many organizations make that contact within three to five days of the due date), and your second contact in the 11- to 20-day period of delinquency. Your chance of collecting is about 90 percent within the first 60 days, 50 percent in the over-90 day period, 20 percent over 180 days, and negligible if payment is one year overdue.[14] The best way to collect is in person, although that may not be possible. Telephoning is usually the most cost-effective collection method. Follow-up letters should be addressed to a specific individual, be certain and to the point, be serious and firm, and worded as if the message is being spoken to the customer.[15] Referral to a collection agency or an attorney is a last resort.

3.4 U.S. PAYMENTS SYSTEM

The United States is currently migrating away from a system that relies largely on checks for payments to one that relies on electronic media. Notice in Exhibit 3.2, which reflects the most recent periodic Federal Reserve study, the rapid transformation that is going on toward debit cards and credit cards, as well as the usage of electronic benefits transfer (EBT). In 2005, only 33% of in-store payments were made by cash and 11% by check, according to Dove Consulting.[16] Dove Consulting projects that as few as 20 percent of noncash payments will be made by check in the year 2010. The Federal Reserve has reduced its check processing locations from 45 in 2003 to 18 by year-end 2007.

The key consideration for you as a manager when considering the ways in which you will collect funds is, "How will my customers or donors wish to pay me?" The answer to that question is not as simple as it may seem. Yes, it is

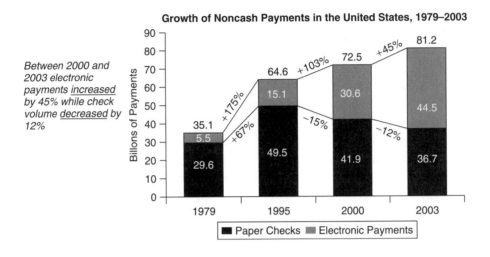

EXHIBIT 3.2 INCREASING USAGE OF ELECTRONIC PAYMENTS IN U.S.

true that older Americans still prefer checks for many of their payments, but it is also surprisingly true that many 18- to 34-year-olds like to use checks extensively. To help you in assessing your customer or donor base, consult Exhibit 3.3. Yes, you may be charged a fee from 1.5 percent to 5 percent to accept a credit card payment or donation. However, would you want to do without that donation?

Each payment method comes with a set of benefits and costs. Let's consider coins and currency, checks, card payments, electronic payments using the automated clearinghouse (ACH) system, and wire transfers for very large dollar payments.

(a) COINS AND CURRENCY. Consumer usage of coins and currency is on the decline. Consider these survey findings: (1) more consumers are opting to use credit and debit cards (including the new contactless cards) and using less cash as a result—62 percent report using cash less often in their purchases; (2) nearly half of consumers (49 percent) carry less cash than they did five years ago, with 60 percent carrying $20 or less cash, and 75 percent believe that carrying large amounts of cash is no longer necessary.[17] Nevertheless there are still an estimated 15 billion cash transactions in the United States per year, or about 6 out of 10 transactions.[18]

Cash is still used predominantly on two purchase occasions: entertainment and quick-service restaurants. Performing arts organizations and organizations with a snack shop or gift shop still have to have cash-handling procedures and

When consumers are profiled according to overall payment behavior, they tend to cluster into distinct segments. The following are some of the most significant clusters.

YOUNG, DEBIT-ORIENTED CONSUMERS

These younger consumers use debit and cash to make purchases at the point of sale, checks to pay bills, and ATMs and debit cash back to obtain cash.

RICH, YOUNG, HEAVY TRANSACTORS

These consumers are the most affluent cluster in the survey, make the most payments, and use the broadest array of payment methods. These are the users of electronic bill payment; they pay almost 60% of their bill payments via the Internet, phone, and/or cards. At the point of sale, they use everything but checks.

OLDER TRADITIONALISTS

These consumers use the traditional payment methods: cash at the point of sale (and some credit card); checks for bill payment; and the branch (and some ATM withdrawals) for accessing cash. They do not use debit cards, obtain debit cash back, or pay bills electronically. They are older, affluent, and more likely to be retired.

"MIDDLE AMERICA" CHECK USERS

These consumers use checks for all types of transactions. They pay for almost 60% of their POS purchases with checks, the highest level of check usage at the point of sale. Almost 40% of the time, they obtain cash through check cash back. As might be expected, these consumers pay bills almost exclusively by check.

UNBANKED, HEAVY CASH USERS

Over 80% of consumers in this cluster are unbanked. They use cash exclusively for POS purchases, and cash and money orders exclusively for bill payments.

Source: Steve Ledford, Tim Mills, and Tom Murphy, "Your Depositors Aren't 'Average'," *Banking Strategies* 81 (January/February 2005): 41–52). Used by permission.

EXHIBIT 3.3 PAYMENT BEHAVIOR CLUSTERS

cash control policies. Private colleges and elementary and secondary schools may have extensive cash handling related to events, cafeterias, and product sales.

Cash is advantageous because it is the most liquid of all payments—you don't have a "hold" placed on cash you deposit at the bank. Nonprofits are normally cash-constrained, as we noted in Chapters 1 and 2, and prefer to receive monies as quickly as possible. The downsides are that cash is risky and costly. The risk is in losing and having the cash stolen (bonding cash handlers is a good idea), and the cost is in counting, storing (including the cost of a good safe on the premises), transporting the cash to the depository institution, and then being charged for the bank to handle the cash as part of your deposit. National averages for small-business charges include: a branch night drop deposit service cost $4.54 a month; branch daytime deposits, including envelopes, cost $4.75 a month; main office deposits including envelopes cost $1.28 per month.[19]

(b) CHECKS.   While 80 to 90 percent of business-to-business payments are made by check, a declining proportion of individual-to-business payments are made by check, as noted. For the first time ever, in 2003 businesses and consumers as a whole made more electronic payments (including card payments) than check payments. This was due to a tripling of electronic payments from the mid-1990s to 2003. Some donors still prefer to make their donations by check, considering the returned cancelled check or, more commonly today, the image of the check that comes in their monthly statement to be the best proof for tax purposes. Donor education is key here: The best evidence of a donation is the statement that comes back from the charity to the donor. Donations of $250 or more must be evidenced by a statement from the charity in order for the deduction to be tax-deductible. Collection float is the highest on check payments, especially when the checks are mailed from a distant location and must be processed back to a different Federal Reserve district because they're drawn on a bank in that district.

Let's trace the path of a check for a ticket purchase written from a baseball fan in St. Louis and mailed to the Chicago Cubs ticket office in Chicago (Exhibit 3.4). The Cubs office then mails the tickets out and deposits the check in its bank in Chicago. The Chicago bank must then decide how best to clear the check. It may transport this check and many others to the Federal Reserve Bank in Chicago, which will then transport the check to the Federal Reserve Bank in St. Louis. Noticing the bank on which the check is drawn (the drawee bank), the

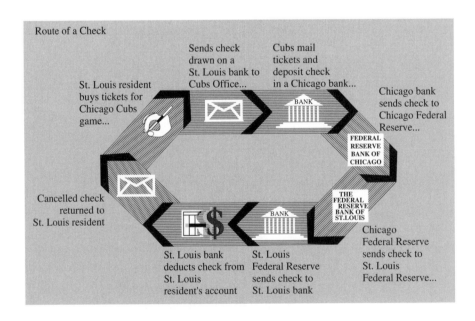

Source: http://ecedweb.unomaha.edu/ve/library/WWAW.PDF, pp. 11, 12.

EXHIBIT 3.4   CHECK CLEARING PROCESS

St. Louis Fed then transports the check to that bank by using a courier service. This is called *presentment*. Shortly thereafter, the St. Louis bank will deduct the amount for which the check was written from the check writer's account. Within the month, the monthly account activity statement is mailed, and either the cancelled check or now, more commonly, an image of that check is returned to the check writer. Online banking services allow the check writer to view the front and back images of that check shortly after it has been presented to the bank.

Because checks are such an important way of receiving payment for goods delivered or donations, our next section is devoted to determining how best to expedite check collections. Notice in Exhibit 3.3 that "Older Traditionalists" as well as "'Middle America' Check Users" use checks extensively. These two groups may form a disproportionate part of your donor population.

In 2003 new legislation was passed and signed into law allowing for "substitute checks" or "image replacement documents" to be used in lieu of the original checks. This "Check Clearing for the 21st Century Act" is normally just called Check 21.

The purpose of check 21 was to facilitate check truncation (image replacing original check, normally by the bank of first deposit) and electronic check presentment. *Electronic check presentment* happens when a bank creates an electronic entry from the MICR line of a check that is "suitable for posting to a customer's account" and transmits that entry to the drawee bank. This transmission of the data from the bottom line of the check may have paper checks included, but normally is either a stand-alone electronic data transmission or one that is transmitted electronically with the accompanying check images.[20] The MICR line is the magnetic ink character recognition area at the bottom of a check. The numbers that appear there are machine readable to enable automated processing and include the bank on which the check is drawn, the account number of the check writer, and, once deposited, the amount of the check.

According to the National Automated Clearing House Association (NACHA), a substitute check is a paper reproduction of the original check that:

- Contains an image of the front and back of the original check;
- Bears a MICR line containing all the information appearing on the MICR line of the original check, except as provided under generally applicable industry standards for substitute checks to facilitate the processing of substitute checks (regulations may contain exceptions);
- Conforms, in paper stock, dimension, and otherwise, with generally applicable industry standards for substitute checks; and
- Is suitable for automated processing in the same manner as the original check.[21]

The key implication of Check 21 is that checks are beginning to be presented more quickly, reducing collection float. Do not assume that banks will

---

- How will account agreements change for depository customers?
- Can the bank handle check image deposits?
- If the bank offers check image deposit capabilities, what will the requirements for quality be?
- If the bank offers image deposit capabilities, will the bank offer a later deadline for deposits?
- If the depository bank clears checks electronically through a combination of image exchange and substitute checks, will the bank require depository customers to assume liability for disputes arising from substitute checks and image presentments?
- If the depository bank accepts electronic check deposits from a company, what legal liabilities will the company assume for image quality, double posting, and fraud prevention?
- What are the bank's policies and procedures for responding to expedited recredit claims? How will these policies affect depository customers receiving payments from consumers?
- How will changes in the bank's check processing operations affect the returns process? Will the bank send returns to the depository customer as electronic images or as substitute checks?
- Will cutoff times for check deposits change? How? When?

Source: Association for Financial Professionals, "Frequently Asked Questions About Check 21 and Its Impact on Corporate Treasury," October 2004, pp. 25–26. Used by permission.

EXHIBIT 3.5   QUESTIONS TO ASK YOUR BANK RELATED TO IMAGE EXCHANGE AND CHECK 21

automatically pass on to your organization improved availability of collected funds; you will need to negotiate that with your banks. While the impact will be felt progressively, not immediately, donation-based organizations will benefit significantly in upcoming years, especially from reductions in check transportation costs and processing float. There are several issues you need to discuss with your bank or other depository institution right now, however, as profiled in Exhibit 3.5.

(c) CARD PAYMENTS.   For many nonprofits, the biggest question regarding collection systems is whether to accept payment for products or services or receive donations in the form of debit card or credit card payments. Many consumers now like to use their credit cards for almost all purchases in order to earn the rebates of up to 5 percent offered by some issuing banks (for MasterCard or VISA) or by Discover or American Express. Credit card amounts are usually received one to two business days later, and debit card amounts are usually received two to three business days later.

Nonprofits may be following the lead of quick-service restaurants, which resisted the idea but finally have agreed to accept credit card and in some cases debit card payments. Accepting all four card types may be beneficial: When the Christian Children's Fund (CCF; Richmond, VA) accepted giving by American Express and Discover credit cards in addition to VISA and Master Card acceptance, credit card giving increased by 65 percent. Additionally, overall credit card giving to CCF increased by 25 percent each year in 2001 and 2002 as more donors seized this new giving medium opportunity.

Mark Jones and Mary Daciolas of the Evangelical Christian Credit Union (Brea, CA) observe these trends regarding credit and debit cards and how nonprofits should view them:

1. Card spending (including the use of debit cards) is outpacing that using checks and cash.
2. Credit card use is more valued by the younger generation.
3. Credit cards enable the use of other payment channels, including the telephone and the web.
4. Segmenting donors is an organizational "best practice," which we alluded to earlier in Exhibit 3.3.[22]

A key benefit from taking card payments is the possibility of getting more funds through new donors or larger gifts from existing donors. Dan Busby, who writes a newsletter called *Faithful Finances*, notes that the emphasis from the nonprofit's standpoint is not on "how" donors are giving but "that" they are giving.

Opposing this benefit are the costs of card payments: Credit cards may cost up to 5 percent to process, which the merchant bank charges as a "discount" to the organization receiving the payment. Our next payment medium, electronic payments using debits to donors' checking accounts, may cost only 5 cents each to process.

(d) ELECTRONIC PAYMENTS USING THE ACH SYSTEM.   It would seem that the best of all worlds for both a donor and an organization would be if the bank account of the donor is automatically debited each month for the amount of the donor's recurring donations. Not only does the donor avoid the time and expense of writing out a check and mailing it, but the organization receives the money reliably, quickly, and without any holds being attached to that dollar amount. Furthermore, if the organization is "on account," it is charged less for being paid electronically than for being paid with a check.[23]

There are two types of ACH transfers.[24] If you are initiating or originating the transfer and want to pay someone else, you have your bank do an *ACH credit*. In other words, you are telling the bank to credit someone else's account. If you signed an authorization form that enables an organization to debit your account, or charge it, this is called an *ACH debit*. Again, this is from the perspective of the party who is initiating the transaction. The organization in this case is telling the bank to debit the individual's account.

We share the process for an ACH debit in Exhibit 3.6. In this case, a consumer purchases something and the seller initiates an ACH debit to get paid. About 80 percent of all ACH transactions are carried through a Federal Reserve operator. Electronic instructions simply tell which account at which bank is to be debited and which account in which bank is to be credited. These transactions actually settle in one or two business days, but we are moving toward same-day settlement. Although you will pay a monthly fee in order to have an organizational ACH payment set up at your bank, the per item fee will be $0.20 or less.

(e) WIRE TRANSFERS.   There are occasions when you'll want to move large amounts of money for immediate settlement. Real estate closings are a perfect example.

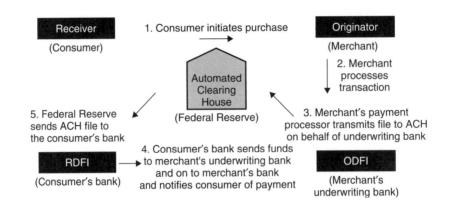

Source: www.veruscs.com/Products/ACHProcessing.aspx

EXHIBIT 3.6 ACH Processing Flowchart

Although you will be charged $10 or more to send or receive a wire transfer, the immediacy—such transactions often are completed within half an hour and the finality of such a transfer are key advantages. International money movements are often accomplished through wire transfers, which may cost $30 to consummate. If two units of your organization are the sending and receiving parties, you will pay two charges.

3.5 EXPEDITING CHECK COLLECTIONS

For the foreseeable future, we will be living with check payments and donations by checks. We need to consider how best to work with check payments.[25]

The first key to expediting check collections is to get the checks out of the inbox. Too many nonprofits allow time to elapse from the point when donors or clients mail the checks and when those checks are deposited and become spendable funds at the bank. Prolonged mail and processing float are very detrimental to the cash position of your organization.

The good news here for all organization is that check truncation (related both to Check 21 legislation implemented in October 2004 and to bank-to-bank bilateral image exchange) and check conversion (point-of-sale conversion of a check to an electronic ACH debit, which is being used by some healthcare organizations, and lockbox accounts receivable conversion "ARC" conversions of mailed checks to ACH electronic debits—both of which result in what are often called e-checks) are cutting the processing delay as well as the availability delay in having spendable funds. The effects on the depositor's funds availability of Check 21, which allows check images to be transmitted and then replaced with image prints called substitute checks (or image replacement documents), may not be as dramatic or immediate as you hear in the press, however, according to Carolyn King, vice-president of Treasury Management, Fifth Third Bank

(Columbus, OH)[26] and Wayne Kissinger, group vice-president, Central Region, SunTrust Bank (Atlanta).[27] Also, once new truncation and conversion procedures are implemented and reduce check float, will banks pass all the float gains on to their clients? Maybe not immediately, as they try to recoup some of the infrastructure investments they have made to implement the new clearing processes.

(a) REMOTE CAPTURE.   Image capture of checks at remote locations is something every nonprofit should be learning about. You can feed checks into a scannerlike device attached to your PC and convert the checks to images. You can then transmit the images as an electronic deposit to your bank from the location and at the time you choose. "Electronic depositing augments the migration toward paperless banking, using remote capture technology to process images as opposed to the actual paper checks," explains Georgette Cipolla, vice president of Product Development and Product Management at Fifth Third Bank. She continues, "Whether our customers receive checks by mail, in a drop box, or over the counter, they can deposit them from the security of their own office, significantly reducing the time, effort, and resources expended on remittance processing."[28] You may also be able to deposit items later in the day—Wells Fargo allows customers to electronically deposit as late as 7:00 p.m. Pacific Time.

(b) PRE-ENCODING DEPOSITS.   Many areas in cash management represent make-or-buy decisions for your organization.[29] Normally, after you drop your checks and deposit slip off to the bank, one of the steps the bank must perform is to encode on the MICR line the amount of the check. *Pre-encoding deposits* at your site before transporting them to the bank, by imprinting the dollar amount of the checks on them in magnetic ink, makes sense for organizations having at least 4,000 or 5,000 checks in their monthly deposits, according to William Michels, assistant vice president of Global Treasury Management Sales for Key-Bank (Cleveland, OH).[30] Doing this gets the organization reduced fees or better availability.

(c) LOCKBOX SYSTEMS.   There are two types of lockbox systems, an in-house system (or company processing center) and a bank or third-party system.

(i) *In-House System.*   Some large nonprofits, such as Campus Crusade for Christ (Orlando, FL), receive so many mailed checks that it is worthwhile to set up an in-house processing center. Essentially this is a lockbox run by the company itself. The availability of volunteer labor is a great asset that might be tapped in such a case.

(ii) *Bank or Third-Party System.*   Many other large nonprofits tap bank or other third-party lockbox services, in which donors' checks are received at a dedicated post office box, avoiding at least one sort because the checks get routed to a unique zip code assigned to the lockbox bank or third-party provider at the area distribution center or sectional center facility so that banks can immediately gain access to them.[31] This box is emptied by processor couriers as often as 15 to 21 times a day and then items are taken to a specialized check-processing operations center for automated document and check processing. Organizations may get reductions in mail float (although sometimes there is some additional mail float because of the location of the lockbox facility) and assured reductions in processing float and availability float in return for the monthly fee the processor charges. Organizations may also get microfilmed or imaged checks and the transmission of remittance information after that day's deposits are processed.

SunTrust and some other banks offer a lockbox service for organizations that have high check deposit volumes twice a year during fundraising campaigns; a minimal maintenance lockbox fee is assessed during the months in which the service is not being used. Your organization may also elect to use a lockbox service during its capital campaign. Large organizations ($50 million in annual revenues and above) will want to investigate "electronic lockbox" services that merge data streams, including remittance details, from the traditional lockbox, credit card payments, incoming wire transfers, and ACH remittances, allowing auto-posting to your receivables system.

If you cannot or do not wish to improve your check collection processes on your own, enlist the help of another organization or a financial institution. Christian Children's Fund (CCF), an international relief and development agency located in Richmond, VA, is a superb example of this. Treasurer Bill Hopkins located a nonbank company that had worked to expedite check collections in-house and had excess capacity. Now CCF authorizes the processing company to pick up checks received at CCF's post office boxes, pre-encode the checks with the dollar amounts and image those checks for later retrieval, and make the check deposits at CCF's bank. CCF receives some checks at its offices, and scans and images those checks for internal purposes; it then delivers the check deposits to its bank that same day. It is now discussing with its bank the possibility of "remote capture"—providing the bank images of checks handled by its processor as well as those processed in-house instead of providing to the bank the physical checks, in order to save costs and gain better availability.

3.6 ACCEPTING CARD PAYMENTS

(a) DEBIT CARDS. About three-fourths of all individuals with checking accounts have a debit card, but perhaps only half use them in a given two- or three-week period. About one in five individuals are using their debit cards to make at least one bill payment per month.[32] In 2003 the number of debit card transactions surpassed the number of credit card transactions in the United States for the first time. Some consumers who cannot qualify for a credit card can still get a debit card.

Expect to pay an interchange fee of about 1.6 percent for debit card transactions that are "off-line," meaning no PIN (personal identification number) was entered by the customer. You should pay somewhat less than this for PIN-based transactions.

(b) CREDIT CARDS. About three-fourths of all Americans have at least one credit card. Quick-service restaurants and other outlets that formerly did not accept credit cards now do so in recognition of the changing culture and payment preference of consumers. Many nonprofits are aware of this trend and are also accepting credit card payments.

A standard interchange fee of 2 percent plus a per-transaction charge of about $0.10 is typical in credit card transactions. Most of the interchange fee goes to the issuing bank (the customer's bank), with the remainder going to the merchant bank (the seller's bank).[33]

3.7 ACCEPTING ELECTRONIC PAYMENTS

Collecting money electronically is fast, inexpensive, and typically recorded very accurately. Individual giving after Hurricane Katrina was commonly done through the Internet—one estimate placed it at over 50 percent.[34] One charity received 100,000 new contributions on the Internet in 2005 and found that its proportional fundraising costs declined significantly as a result.[35]

Recurring collections of sales revenue or donations may be done with preauthorization through electronic debits, as may one-time collections from customers or donors.

(a) DIRECT PAYMENTS. Once a donor or customer signs a preauthorization form, your organization may collect recurring amounts from that party until the party cancels or amends the authorization. The party's checking account is then debited on or around the 15th of the month, for example, for the same dollar amount. These transfers are very inexpensive as far as bank charges go, especially if you already are using ACH services for direct deposit of payroll or to pay suppliers. For annual campaigns, donors on "direct payments" tend to renew at a higher rate than those who write checks each month. Direct payments also are convenient for donors and save them the cost of checks and postage. From a cash flow perspective, this method of being paid will help to eliminate the summer slump (no one forgets to write out a check while on vacation), enables you to more accurately forecast when funds are coming in, and some donors will allow you to send them contribution receipts by e-mail.

Consumers are becoming increasingly comfortable with direct payment. For example, Christian Children's Fund now receives approximately $1 million monthly in ACH donations versus approximately $2 million monthly in credit and debit card donations (overwhelmingly credit).

Advantages to electronically drawing money from your customers' or donors' accounts include:[36]

- More rapid funds collection as manual processing is replaced by electronic processing
- Receivables postings may be auto-applied (crediting accounts for accounts receivable or pledges receivable)

- Funds availability is more rapid (no availability or processing float after the due date)
- More rapid return of "bounced" electronic payments relative to check return timing
- Bank account reconciliation is simpler
- There is a direct cost savings in the form of lower bank charges

Appendix 3A provides valuable guidance as you begin to implement ACH direct payments for collecting revenues from various parties.

(b) TEL AND INTERNET PAYMENTS.   Credit card companies now collect many late customer payments through one-time authorized payments authorized through phone calls. Telephone-Initiated Entry (TEL) payments are a simple method of making one-time electronic debits to consumers' accounts using the ACH system. Unfortunately, a few telemarketers are using this system fraudulently—perhaps by debiting an account without the consumer's authorization or by cold-calling customers with which there is no existing relationship and then selling them merchandise and debiting their accounts—which may hurt all organizations attempting to utilize the TEL system. Guidelines for using the TEL system are contained in Exhibit 3.7.

You may have donated to disaster relief by going to a charity's Web site and authorizing a one-time draft to your checking account. This is known as a WEB ACH transaction type. It involves a debit entry to a consumer transaction account. For example, a college may collect fees from its students using these Internet-generated payments. The interchange fees are higher for telephone-initiated or Internet-initiated payments, which are called card not present payments. The risk is higher to the issuing bank.

3.8 COMPARISON OF ALTERNATIVE COLLECTION SYSTEMS

Let's step outside all the details of these various payment methods and collection systems for just a moment. How will your organization know which system or systems work best for it? Here's a brief checklist for you to consider. For each payment method or collection system, consider how it rates in each of these categories:

(a) TIMING AND EFFECT ON CASH POSITION.   How long will your mail, processing, and availability float be? Watch out for early cut-off times. Let's say that a bank gives you one-day availability but your checks must be to the bank's operations center by 12 noon. If your checks get there at 12:15, you missed the cut-off time and so do not get one day availability. Put another way, the clock starts tomorrow, and you really have two-day availability from today for checks getting to the bank's operations center at 12:15.

(b) ONE-TIME, MONTHLY, AND PER-PAYMENT COSTS.   There are one-time setup fees for remote capture hardware and software. If you decide to accept credit

THE TEL ENTRY APPLICATION

A Telephone-Initiated (TEL) Entry is a single entry (one-time) debit to a consumer Receiver's account, initiated pursuant to an authorization that was obtained from the Receiver orally via the telephone. Originators may use TEL entries only when the following criteria have been met:

- There must be an existing relationship between the Originator and the consumer. That is, there must be a written agreement in place between the Originator and the consumer for the provision of goods or services (e.g., when the consumer has an insurance policy with the Originator), or the consumer must have purchased goods or services from the Originator within the past two years.

OR

- When no relationship exists between the Originator and the consumer, the consumer must be the one to place the telephone call to the Originator.

TEL entries may *not* be used in circumstances where:

- No relationship exists between the Originator and the consumer, and the Originator has initiated the telephone call (i.e., the Originator has "cold-called" the consumer). In such cases, the Originator must provide the consumer with a *written* authorization that is signed or similarly authenticated and initiate a PPD or a WEB entry.
- There is a standing authorization provided by the consumer to the Originator for the transmission of multiple but nonrecurring ACH debit entries to the consumer's account, as in the example when the consumer has provided a written authorization to a brokerage firm to debit the consumer for occasional securities purchases. While the written authorization may contain language permitting the initiation of a debit via a telephone instruction, this type of entry must be transmitted as a PPD debit.

AUTHORIZATION REQUIREMENTS

Originators of TEL entries must obtain the consumer's explicit oral authorization, via the telephone, prior to initiating a debit entry to the consumer's account. Because TEL entries are single-entry (i.e., one-time) debits, a separate and distinct oral authorization must be obtained from the consumer for each TEL entry to be initiated to the consumer's account. The *NACHA Operating Rules* require that the Originator (1) clearly state during the telephone call with the consumer that the consumer is authorizing an ACH debit to his account, and (2) express the terms of the authorization in a clear manner.

The authorization must include:

- The date on or after which the consumer's account will be debited;
- The amount of the debit entry to the consumer's account;
- The consumer's name;
- A telephone number that is available to the consumer and answered during normal business hours for customer inquiries;
- The date of the consumer's oral authorization; and
- A statement by the Originator that the consumer's authorization will be used to originate an ACH debit to the consumer's account.

The *Rules* further require the Originator to tape-record the consumer's oral authorization or to provide written notice to the consumer, prior to the settlement date of the TEL entry, confirming the terms of the oral authorization (including the information specified above). A copy of the

(continues)

EXHIBIT 3.7 RULES FOR INITIATING TEL ONE-TIME ACH DEBITS

> tape-recorded authorization or written notice must be retained for two years from the date of the authorization.
>
> Voice response units (VRUs) may be used by the Originator during the telephone call to prompt consumers to key enter data and to respond to questions. However, key-entry responses by the consumer do not qualify as an oral authorization for purposes of TEL entries. Originators must understand that the actual authorization by the consumer and disclosure of the information noted above must be provided orally.

Source: *"Telephone-Initiated (TEL) Entries,"* NACHA Operations Bulletin, (September 19, 2002). Used by permission.

EXHIBIT 3.7   (*continued*)

card payments, you will have to buy or lease hardware and also pay per-month and per-transaction fees. Check with other organizations to learn about their fee experiences and any unforeseen charges they have incurred.

(c) CONTROL/STEWARDSHIP/ACCURACY.   Will you be able to do your donor receipting properly and on a timely basis? Will you be able to segregate funds as needed, particularly those received through a capital campaign? If payments are for goods or services rendered, will the data feed include enough information so that you can credit customers' accounts?

(d) DONOR MARKETING.   Some payment methods lend themselves better than others to good donor marketing. An Internet Web site is an effective way to market your organization as well as collect Internet-based payments. Some organizations are more effective than others at promoting their cause when they send out mail solicitations. The grace period built into credit card billing cycles allows people to give this month and not pay for it until next month.

(e) OTHER FACTORS.   Banks and other third-party providers are happy to let you know some of the other considerations that you should be considering in this purchase decision.

3.9 CASH POSITIONING

Recall that positioning systems (or what are traditionally known as concentration systems) include all processes and tools used to mobilize cash into a central location so that it may be used for investments, to pay down borrowing, or to fund disbursements.

(a) MOBILIZING CASH.   Cash positioning means moving cash, as necessary, to get it into the right account in the right amount. Often this means moving money into one master or concentration account. This fits with the trend in treasury management to centralize activities to gain economies of scale, reduce costs, and maintain control.

(b) OBJECTIVES OF CASH POSITIONING SYSTEMS.   We noted earlier that objectives for a cash positioning system include pooling, employing, protecting, amassing, and monitoring funds. While doing these things, your organization will want to maintain "cash visibility," which means knowledge of the amounts and their status (ledger balance but not yet available, versus available balance) as exactly as possible. "It doesn't do you any good to have it if you don't know you have it" is a pretty accurate statement.

(c) POOLING/NETTING/OVERLAY. Cash pooling means getting the money out of outlying accounts, where it is not gaining interest (or at least significant interest, since some of this may be in negotiable order of withdrawal (NOW) interest-bearing checking accounts), and moving it into a central concentration or master account. The idea behind pooling may also be to use the positive balance in one or more accounts to offset what would have been a negative or deficit balance in another account(s), across different business entities, or across national borders.

(d) ESTABLISHING YOUR BANKING NETWORK. Your key decisions in doing cash positioning well are selecting banks (which, where, how many) and accounts (number, type, at which banks). Even some relatively small organizations may benefit from the principles of cash positioning. For example, consider this standard positioning, or concentration, system that one bank, Cass Commercial Bank (St. Louis), offers to churches and other nonprofits that have two or more accounts:

CASH CONCENTRATION—Providing your church or ministry with a way to move funds from your non-Cass account to your Cass account.

- Funds can be moved electronically using Cass Internet Banking or with paper checks
- Funds moved electronically using Cass Internet Banking require minimal effort
- Transfers made only with your authorization
- Transfers can be initiated by you or a Cass staff member, including via a touch-tone phone on a 24-hour/7-day basis for transfers between different Cass accounts
- Transfer funds from your non-Cass account to your Cass account via the ACH module. Can be used to move funds from most bank accounts located in the United States
- Concentration of funds in one account ensures that all available funds are used to offset service charges
- Well suited for churches & ministries located outside of the St. Louis metropolitan area; a toll-free number ensures non-local users can access account information and services without paying long-distance fees
- Compensating balances may be used to offset fees[37]

The types of accounts with which you should be familiar include checking ("demand deposit" or NOW accounts), zero balance accounts, and concentration accounts.

Checking accounts do not pay any interest and may not charge any fees or have any minimum balance. For now we simply observe that "free checking" is anything but "free" (there is an opportunity lost by leaving significant balances in the account because of what you could have earned elsewhere). We return to some of the particulars of selecting and managing checking accounts in Chapter 5.

NOW accounts are allowable for nonprofits, even though some bank personnel are not properly trained and will tell you that they are only for individuals. The advantage of these "negotiable order of withdrawal" accounts is that they pay a modest interest rate on average balances. In our investment chapter, we will show how sizable balances warrant moving money out of deposit accounts to gain a better interest rate. A few banks offer sweeps out of an interest-bearing checking (NOW) account, but the average balance you must leave in the NOW account may be relatively high (e.g., $75,000).

A very small organization really has no need for a concentration system. If all of its cash receipts and cash disbursements go to and from one account, that account is in reality a concentration account for all practical purposes. As your organization grows in size, expands geographically, and adds new divisions, multiple accounts and careful account configuration are essential.

(i) Zero Balance Accounts.   Zero balance accounts (ZBAs) are another account structure to become familiar with. These allow your deposits in various locations to get transferred via bookkeeping entries to a master account (also known as concentration account) at the same bank that same day without individual transfer fees. Think of it as an autopilot system whereby any amount in an account over $0 gets transferred out to another designated account at the end of the business day (or at some other interval). You don't have to initiate ACH credits or debits to move money from account to account. Notice that the accounts must be held with the same bank, although possibly at many locations. Using a ZBA structure, your organization avoids transfer fees as well as multiple investment sweep fees (discussed in Chapter 7). ZBAs are also useful for disbursement accounts, as we shall see in Chapter 4.

(ii) Concentration Account.   Sometimes called a master account, this is the central account at which an organization tries to position its funds on a regular basis. Larger organizations will move monies daily to this account. They could move the money with a ZBA or deposit concentration setup (discussed later) or initiate ACH transfers (normally debits initiated by headquarters or the concentration bank) or wire transfers. Wires are used for large dollar amounts when immediate value transfer is cost-effective. The minimum dollar amount for which one should utilize a wire transfer can be determined if one knows the cost of a wire, the cost of an ACH transfer, the difference in funds availability, an earnings credit rate (your bank may "give you a credit against fees" for average balances you hold in the account, if they are collected balances), and the interest rate earned on avail-

able funds. The calculation of the minimum cost-effective amount for choosing a wire transfer over an ACH transfer is based on Equation 3.1:

$$\text{MINIMUM BALANCE FOR WIRE} = \frac{\text{Additional cost for wire transfer}}{(DS/365) \times [y - \{ecr \times (1 - rr)\}]} \quad (3.1)$$

Where:

Additional cost for wire transfer = per item wire cost minus per-item ACH transfer cost

DS = days saved awaiting available funds when using a wire transfer versus an ACH transfer

y = investment yield that could be earned (annual rate) on freed-up funds

ecr = earnings credit rate (use 0 if bank does not give you credit against fees for average balances)

rr = reserve requirement (currently 10 percent, so 0.10; set by the Federal Reserve Board)

The rr item is a reserve requirement that the Federal Reserve Board imposes on banks; they cannot lend out $1 for $1 of new deposits, but must keep 0.10 × $1 = $0.10 on reserve as vault cash or as a deposit at the nearest Federal Reserve district or branch bank. As you would expect, banks then drop their earnings credit rate (also called an earnings allowance rate) by that 10 percent factor; our formula adjusts for that correction.

Illustrating, if a wire costs $20, and ACH transaction costs $0.15, you will have available funds one day earlier by using a wire, you can earn 4.00 percent on your short-term investments, and the earnings credit rate is 2.00 percent, we find the minimum amount for a wire concentration transfer to be:

$$\text{MINIMUM BALANCE FOR WIRE} = \frac{(\$20.00 - \$0.15)}{(1/365) \times [0.04 - \{0.02 \times (1 - 0.10)\}]}$$

$$\text{MINIMUM BALANCE FOR WIRE} = \frac{(\$19.85)}{(1/365) \times [0.04 - \{0.02 \times (0.90)\}]}$$

$$\text{MINIMUM BALANCE FOR WIRE} = \frac{(\$19.85)}{(0.00274) \times [0.04 - 0.018]}$$

$$\text{MINIMUM BALANCE FOR WIRE} = \frac{\$19.85}{0.00006028}$$

$$\text{MINIMUM BALANCE FOR WIRE} = \$329,296.62$$

Because of the low interest rates in our example, the significant cost difference between a wire and an ACH transfer implies that your organization would have to be transferring almost $330,000 to make the one-day pickup in availability worthwhile. If the wire cost was negotiated down to $15.00, the minimum balance would fall to \$246,375; you may verify this by replacing the numerator above with (\$15.00 − \$0.15). Also, notice that if your organization does not get earnings credits from its bank for available (or collected) balances left on account at the bank, *ecr* becomes 0, and the organization earns the full 4 percent on freed-up funds; this gives a minimum balance for doing a wire of only \$181,113.14 (assuming our original \$20 wire fee).

(iii) Deposit Concentration.   Banks also have deposit reconciliation services, allowing special deposit tickets to cause your deposits from various branches in a geographic region to get deposited into one account. This gives you automatic funds concentration without initiating costly and time-consuming transfers, as well as providing location-by-location accounting.

(iv) Effect of Nationwide Banking.   With the consolidation underway in U.S. banking, more and more checks become "on-us" items (written by another account holder at the bank at which they are deposited and at which your organization banks), reducing float time and reducing the number of different banks or accounts that your organization will need to maintain to get optimal cash collection and positioning results.

(v) Importance of TWS or Bank Information System.   A Treasury Workstation (TWS) software package, for very large nonprofits, and online banking through your bank's web portal, for all organizations, give the visibility into bank account positions and funds availability that organizations need. We cannot overemphasize the importance of web access to account data and previous-day activity for cash positioning. The Internet is the "great leveler" in cash management, offering even the smallest organization the ability to view account activity, initiate account activity, and provide greater control through imaging of checks deposited or written.

3.10 INTERNATIONAL CASH COLLECTIONS AND CONCENTRATION

As you begin to do business abroad, there are payment and banking differences, new ACH rules (even for transfers to or from Canada or Mexico), netting and pooling structures, remittance issues and risks, and varying balance information access capabilities with which you will want to be aware.

(a) DIFFERENCES IN FOREIGN PAYMENT SYSTEMS.   Foreign payment systems and banking systems may be much different from those in the United States.[38] Many countries have already migrated to direct debits and credits, largely ridding the payment system of checks. Many other countries have banks offering interest on positive balances and charging (higher rates of) interest on negative balances, allowing one to reduce transfers into and out of investments or credit lines. Different customs, legal and regulatory systems, accounting standards, time zones, banking practices, governmental role, and payment clearing systems imply the need to study the country or region before doing business there. Many times your bank can network with its correspondent bank(s) to find a bank already in the area that can brief you on the key differences. Most important, do not blithely assume that what works here will work there.

(b) CROSS-BORDER ACH.   As with domestic ACH payments, significant cost savings and more rapid funds availability come with moving money across borders with an automated clearing house transfer. NACHA estimates for the savings relative to checks and international wires using the SWIFT system are shown in Exhibit 3.8. U.S. organizations use cross-border ACH primarily to move money to and from Canada, but they increasingly make or receive payments from Mexico as well.[39]

(c) POOLING/NETTING/OVERLAY.   Transactions costs and interest expense may be reduced with the right account structures and bank services related to using those structures efficiently. One objective organizations pursue is minimizing interest expense. No organization wants to pay a bank interest to borrow when it has small amounts scattered in various bank accounts elsewhere in the same country, in nearby countries, or globally. Pooling, done in various ways, helps an organization reduce its borrowing or increase its investing by offsetting deficit account balances with positive balances held in other accounts at the same bank.

Additionally, organizations wish to reduce the number of foreign exchange transactions they must engage in, due to the expense of these transactions (mainly due to paying more when you buy than the amount you would get in selling the same currency at the exact same time—known technically as the bid-ask spread). Related ways of accomplishing these two objectives are netting, pooling, and overlay account structures.

Netting involves a system by which two domestic subsidiaries' intracompany receivables are netted out and only the difference in those amounts is transferred. In a multinational organization, a netting system is in operation when "receipts denominated in a currency are netted against expenses due to be paid in the same currency in order to reduce the total volume of foreign currency transactions."[40] When organizations do not have a netting system, they may

Cost of current marketplace options with respect to international payments:

Payment Type	Average Cost	Clearing Time
Check/Cheque	$3–$15	3–15 days
Wire (SWIFT)	$15–$30	Up to 6 days
International ACH	$1.25–$3.00	1–3 days

Source: "Cross Border Payments User Guide," NACHA, October 2001, p. 12. Used by permission.

EXHIBIT 3.8   COST SAVINGS USING CROSS-BORDER ACH

decide not to engage in as many transactions, but this adds another layer of complexity: foreign exchange risk until the transactions are conducted.

Pooling in non-U.S. countries is similar to the cash positioning or concentration accounts we discussed earlier. Essentially, banks look at all of the organization's accounts as one aggregate balance and pay interest on that balance if it is positive and charge interest if that balance is negative (remember that overdrafts are legal outside the United States, in general). Two types of pooling are physical pooling and notional pooling.[41]

Physical pooling entails currency by currency "zero balancing," in which each division or subsidiary has its own accounts. These subsidiary accounts are usually subaccounts linked to a master account. All funds in the divisional or subsidiary accounts are actually (physically) transferred to the master account at the end of each business day. The master account may be a regional subsidiary or the parent organization. Then the net amount of funds in the master account is invested or, if negative, funded from a central credit line. The organization "books" the money movements to and from the subsidiary or divisional accounts as intercompany loans unless these organizational units all belong to the same legal entity. Changes to information systems and the advent of the euro and the Eurozone have popularized physical pooling. In the United States, it is usually called cash concentration or zero balancing.

Notional pooling is

> the offset of consolidated cash surpluses and deficits that result from the varying positions in separate bank accounts. ...Each company participating in the pool [and sharing a common parent company] maintains its own account or accounts in the currencies being pooled. The bank then creates a shadow or notional position from all the participant accounts reflecting the consolidated cash position...[which] is the position on which interest is paid or charged....There was no movement of funds to calculate this position.[42]

Notional pooling is very common in the United Kingdom, the Netherlands, and Belgium, and is especially attractive in Brazil, which levies a tax on cash payments from bank accounts.

Notional pooling can handle currency-by-currency netting of amounts or be done on a multiple currency basis. In Europe, notional pooling is commonly practiced on a regional scale. Notional pooling is prohibited in Germany and by IRS regulations in the United States, as it is considered a commingling of funds.

(d) CROSS-BORDER POOLING.   Doing notional pooling on a cross-border basis in the same currency is tough enough, but when multiple currencies are involved, the difficulties mount. Multiple currencies must be brought to a common currency to calculate the pooling and interest offset. This may be done with a short-dated swap or through a bookkeeping conversion that is later adjusted through the interest rate charged or paid in each of the currencies involved.

If funds have to be transferred from the local in-country bank account to another overlay bank's in-country account to "handle collections or disbursements outside the pool," this is termed an *overlay*.[43] The downside there is that one now has more bank accounts and more fees for those accounts.

(e) BRINGING FUNDS BACK TO THE UNITED STATES.   Checks may take four to six weeks to clear, as they must clear back to the home country of the currency in which they are denominated. So, even if you could get foreign buyers, grantors, governments, or donors to agree to "cash in advance," it may be awhile before you are paid. Many times sales abroad are made with a letter of credit (L/C), in which a bank obliges itself to pay, as long as the seller is in compliance with the L/C's terms and conditions.[44]

A documentary draft may be in the form of a *sight draft*. A sight draft is sent with the bill of lading or air waybill (either of which is endorsed at this point by the shipper since the shipper has shipped the merchandise) by the shipper's bank to either the buyer's bank or another designated third party. This and other documents (such as an insurance certificate) allow the bank to notify the buyer. Once the amount of the draft has been paid, the bill of lading is released to the buyer by its bank, and the buyer can take possession of the shipment. Another form of documentary draft, called a *time draft*, is also a credit extension to the buyer (payment is not due until maybe 30 days after the buyer "accepts" the draft and receives the shipped goods). Once accepted, it is termed a trade acceptance, and as the seller you can sell it to a bank at some amount less than the face value to get funds immediately.

(f) FOREIGN EXCHANGE RISK.   When you agree to a contract and fix a price in a certain currency other than your own currency, you are at risk of an unfavorable change in the value of that currency relative to your currency. This risk, foreign exchange (FX) risk, can have a significant impact on your future cash flows if it is related to a receivable or payable due in the future. Your organization may wish to hedge this risk. If not, recognize that the risk is being borne and the possible need to hold a higher level of liquidity to buffer your organization against financial crisis should the foreign exchange rate move adversely. For example, if you have 100,000 Euros due in 90 days, and the euro depreciates relative to the dollar over those 90 days, those 100,000 Euros will buy fewer dollars when converted at the end of the 90 days.

(g) REAL-TIME BALANCE INFORMATION.   As bank information systems improve, negotiate for more rapid availability of information. The closer to "real time" your reports are, the better your understanding of your organization's cash position at home and abroad.

3.11 FRAUD ISSUES

Fraud is not merely a payables and disbursements issue. Skimming of cash coming in, endorsing a check for one's personal use, redirecting restricted funds to a cause other than the purpose for which the funds were given and remitted, and theft of credit card numbers or checking account numbers for later fraudulent use are all collections/receipts fraud issues. Proper controls and oversight are important for fraud prevention and control.

A fraud policy, separate from your ethics or conduct code, is helpful here. It should include:

- A statement of fairness and honesty as organizational goals. This includes a commitment on the part of the organization to deter, detect, and correct acts of fraud or dishonesty.
- A statement of purpose, namely the communication of organizational policy for deterring and investigating suspected dishonesty, and of what will be done in such cases.
- This organization's definitions of dishonesty and misconduct.
- Responsibilities for reporting incidents when one suspects misconduct.
- The responsibilities of this organization's supervisors to deter and detect misconduct.
- How investigations of incidents will be carried out.
- Who should be contacted if there are questions about the policy.
- Notation that the policy has been approved by the CEO/executive director and board of directors.[45]

3.12 IMAGING

Imaging checks and other payment media, remittance documents, and related correspondence are all great ways to improve your treasury function. American Productivity & Quality Center (APQC), a resource for benchmarking studies of process and performance improvement, finds significant differences between high and low performers when it comes to managing receivables and cash collections.[46] Integrating your operational systems with your billing systems is one key to improving collections experience and receiving incoming cash more quickly with fewer errors in transactions or cash application. Imaging checks and remittances is very cost beneficial, and it also has been shown to notably improve quality and cycle time. Average remittance error rates dropped to 5 percent, compared with an average error rate of 11 percent for those not imaging. Even more interesting, organizations that used imaging had average collection periods 15 days shorter than other organizations. We address imaging further in Chapters 4 and 5.

3.13 BENCHMARKING AND OUTSOURCING

One final word as we conclude with a brief discussion of benchmarking and outsourcing: Enlist the help of your allies. You may learn from other nonprofits and from financial service providers what benchmarks to strive for and what services are best outsourced for an organization of your size and type.

A number of financial institutions now have dedicated nonprofit departments or groups, and their specialization may be a significant advantage for your organization. For example, the Evangelical Christian Credit Union (Brea, CA) and the Bank of the West specialize in making loans to nonprofits. Union Bank of

California, SunTrust, Mellon Financial, JP MorganChase, Fifth Third, KeyBank, Riggs Bank, Wainwright Bank & Trust, and others have nonprofit departments (beware, though—sometimes the names are not indicative of this focus: Sun-Trust calls its group "I & G" for "Institutional & Governmental" in its Atlanta and Nashville offices). Perhaps the most creative and unique initiative is Fifth Third's "Community Belief Banking" office in Columbus, OH. This office offers a nifty bundle of services to faith-based organizations and their membership. These services include depository services for both the organization and individual members, working capital loans not collateralized by inventory or receivables, payroll services, direct payments by which member checking accounts are electronically debited so members can give without writing a check and can honor pledge obligations over a number of months in a convenient manner, trust and other investment services, and free financial seminars for members.

What about outsourcing? Wayne Kissinger, group vice-president, Central Region, SunTrust Bank (Atlanta), notes two guidelines you may use as you determine to do things in-house or outsource them:[47] "For any bank product your organization is considering, ask yourself two questions: (1) Will this product make me more productive by taking activity and time commitment out of my back office and allowing me to focus on work that is more essential to my organization; and (2) Will this product give me valuable information, such as whether to honor a check that has been presented to my account that was not in my original check issue file?"

Finally, networking with other treasury professionals and attending treasury management conferences is vital for keeping up with new developments and learning from colleagues. You can do both by attending the Association for Financial Professionals annual conferences. The conferences have many informative treasury management sessions (AFP conference link: www.afponline.org/pub/conf/ed.html), and you can network with others working for nonprofit organizations at the nonprofit industry roundtable breakfast meeting that is held one morning at the conference www.afponline.org/pub/conf/networking.html).

Improving your organization's cash collections and positioning systems will enable it to better ensure that financial resources are available when needed (timing), as needed (amount), and at reasonable cost (cost-effectiveness), and that once mobilized, these resources are protected from impairment and spent according to mission and donor purposes. Appendix 3A will further assist your organization as it improves its efficiency and speed of receipt-to-cash conversion via ACH direct payments.

Notes

1. Illinois Facilities Fund and Donors Forum of Chicago, "Getting It Right: How Illinois Nonprofits Manage for Success," 2004,3p. 2.
2. Kirsten Grønbjerg "Managing Grants and Contracts: The Case of Four Nonprofit Social Service Organizations," *Nonprofit and Voluntary Sector Quarterly* 20 (1991):

5–24. See also Kirsten Grønbjerg, *Understanding Nonprofit Funding: Managing Revenues in Social Services and Community Development Organizations* (San Francisco: Jossey-Bass, 1993).

3. This section draws heavily from the presentation in Terry S. Maness and John T. Zietlow, *Short-Term Financial Management*, 3rd ed. (Cincinnati: South-Western, 2005), p. 321.

4. Local checks are defined as those processed within a certain Federal Reserve District, and distant checks are defined as those coming from outside of a certain Federal Reserve District.

5. Faith-based organizations would apply the scriptural admonition from Proverbs 21:20 (KJV): "There is treasure to be desired and oil in the dwelling of the wise; but a foolish man spendeth it up."

6. HFMA, "Strategies for Improving the Revenue Cycle: Industry Views," downloaded from www.hfma.org. Accessed 8/25/06.

7. Bruce Lind, "Operational Risk: Are You Prepared?"*AFP Exchange* 26 (July/August 2006): 40–45.

8. Id.

9. There are many factors that influenced terms of sale, which include credit period and whether a cash discount is offered. These include competition, market and product characteristics (how long your customers operating cycle is, whether the product is basic materials as opposed intermediate for finished goods), perishability, seasonal demand, consumer acceptance (are the goods protected by trademarks?), cost, type of customer, and profitability. These items are explained in The Credit Research Foundation, "Logistics of Payment Terms," *An Occasional Paper* (November 2002).

10. Credit Research Foundation, "Collecting from the Federal Government," downloaded from www.crfonline.org/orc/cro/CRO-6.html. Accessed: 8/25/06. This section draws heavily on that document.

11. John Zietlow, "Organizational Goals and Financial Management in Donative Nonprofit Organizations," (Terre Haute, IN: Indiana State University, 1992–1994). This research project covering 288 faith-based organizations of various types was sponsored by Lilly Endowment, Indianapolis, IN.

12. Keith V. Smith and Brian Belt, "Working Capital Management and Practice: An Update," Krannert School of Management (Purdue University), *Working Paper 951* (March 1989).

13. Credit Research Foundation, "Principles and Methods of Collections," downloaded from www.crfonline.org/orc/cro//cro-5.html. Accessed 8/25/06.

14. Id.

15. Id.

16. American Bankers Association/Dove Consulting, "Consumer Payment Preferences: Understanding Choice," 2005. Available at www.doveconsulting.com. Accessed 12/30/06.

17. Andy Williams, "One Year after Nationwide Launches, Big Three U.S. Payment Card Brands Remain Bullish on Contactless," CR80News, August 23 2006. Located online at:www.cr80news.com/library/2006/08/23/one-year-after-nationwide-launches-big-three-us-payment-card-brands-remain-bullish-on-contactless/. Accessed: 9/21/06.

18. This estimate comes from Global Concepts, a subsidiary of McKinsey & Company, and is quoted in David Stewart, "Cash Today, Debit Tomorrow—How Banks Can Benefit," *Payments Strategies* (September/October 2006).

19. Informa Research Services, Inc., "Bank Pricing Data Level 1: Small-Business Company National," 2005. www.afponline.org/mbr/res/brm/bpd/lvl1_sm_nt.html. Accessed: 9/21/2006.

20. NACHA, Check 21 Resource Document (March 2004): 13.

21. Id., 6.

22. Personal correspondence, December 12, 2002.

23. The size threshold varies by bank, though once an organization keeps $50,000 or more in its checking account on an ongoing basis, it may well be placed "on account." This means it will be charged per check deposited, per check written, and for other bank services that it uses, with the fees assessed on a monthly basis. Amounts left in the account go to offset those fees through the use of what is called an earnings credit rate. We return to this issue in Chapter 5.

24. This entire section draws heavily from Maness and Zietlow, *Short-Term Financial Management*.

25. This section is taken from our companion guide, John Zietlow, Jo Ann Hankin, and Alan Seidner, *Financial Management for Nonprofit Organizations: Policies and Practices* (Hoboken, NJ: John Wiley & Sons, 2007).

26. Personal communication.

27. Personal communication.

28. Personal communication.

29. This and following sections draw heaving from Maness and Zietlow, *Short-Term Financial Management*.

30. Personal communication.

31. For more on the post office handling of lockbox mail, see Richard Richardson, "Understanding, Establishing, and Maintaining a Lockbox System," available online at: www.crfonline.org/orc/cro/cro-1.html.

32. This estimate comes from Global Concepts, a subsidiary of McKinsey & Company, and is quoted in Stewart, "Cash Today, Debit Tomorrow."

33. Douglas Akers, Jay Golter, Brian Lamm, and Martha Solt, "Overview of Recent Developments in the Credit Card Industry," *FDIC Banking Review* (November 2005).

34. Estimate made by Trent Stamp, executive director of Charity Navigator. Quoted in Jane Lampmen, "Much Has Been Given, Much Is Still to Be Done," *Christian Science Monitor*, November 21, 2005, pp. 11–12.

35. Id. The charity quoted is Save the Children.

36. These advantages are adapted from those provided in Joseph D. Tinucci, "Business Case for Consumer Direct Deposit/Direct Payment," 2001. Available from: www.nacha.org. Accessed: 9/26/2006.

37. Downloaded from: www.cassinfo.com/cassbank/prod_church.html#zba. Accessed: 9/26/2006.

38. This section draws from Maness and Zietlow, *Short-Term Financial Management*.

39. See the Fed's Fed ACH International Mexico Service Implementation Manual for more on U.S.-Mexico ACH procedures. Available at the time of this writing online at: www.frbservices.org/Retail/pdf/FedACHiMxManual.pdf#search=%22cross-border%20ACH%20with%20Mexico%22.

40. Maness and Zietlow, *Short-Term Financial Management*, p. 688.

41. Our discussion of notional and physical pooling is closely based on Treasury Alliance Group LLC, "Cash Pooling: Improving the Balance Sheet," n.d.

42. Id., p. 4.

43. Id., p. 5.

44. Credit Research Foundation, "How to Get Paid When Selling Overseas," n.d.

45. John B. Duncan, "Fraud Detection and Prevention," *CPA Letter/Business & Industry* (November 2003): D2.

46. APQC, "F&A Benchmarking," April 4, 2006.

47. Personal communication, July 20, 2005.

DIRECT PAYMENT IMPLEMENTATION PLAN

IMPLEMENTATION CHECKLIST

The following checklist will help you seamlessly plan, implement, and execute your Direct Payment plan. Be sure to refer to electronicpayments.org for more information on how to get started using Direct Payment and other forms of electronic payments

INTERNAL PLANNING AND COMMUNICATION

☐ Announce your plan to managers and encourage support.
☐ Develop authorization form.
☐ Define program sign-up and billing procedures.
☐ Develop promotional materials
☐ Create employee training materials for Direct Payment procedures.
☐ Begin collection of customer authorizations.
☐ Advise employees just prior to first live Direct Payment collection.

EXTERNAL PROMOTION AND CUSTOMER EDUCATION

☐ Send billing insert with authorization form to customers offering enrollment.
☐ Encourage employees to promote Direct Payment when receiving customer calls.
☐ Send press releases to media—both as an initial announcement and again later, to emphasize participation.
☐ Schedule ongoing Direct Payment promotion efforts.

PROCESSING PROCEDURES

☐ Develop programming for Direct Payment file creation.
☐ Test file formatting with financial institution or processor for possible reject errors.

☐ Load customer routing and account information for pilot group test data.
☐ Financial institution tests Direct Payment formatted file with test data.
☐ Make any necessary corrections advised by your financial institution
☐ Continue to load customer routing and account information.
☐ Create and send first pre-notification (non-value transaction) file to financial institution for processing.
☐ Financial institution processes pre-notification file and responds with necessary changes.
☐ Make corrections from pre-notification responses and send corrected pre-notifications as needed.
☐ Create live Direct Payment file.
☐ Deliver live Direct Payment file to financial institution.
☐ First Direct Payment transactions processed electronically.
☐ Funds are credited to company's account.

Source: www.electronicpayments.org. Used by permission.

CASH DISBURSEMENTS

4.1 INTRODUCTION

Surveyed corporate accounts payable managers' preeminent goals for their disbursements and payables processes are to: (1) initiate or increase usage of electronic data interchange (structured, formatted computer-to-computer transmission of payment coupled with the associated remittance information), evaluated receipt settlement (no-invoice pay process in which your receipt of goods auto-triggers payment) and electronic invoicing, and (2) initiate or increase usage of electronic payments. These two goals are among six primary goals these managers state:

1. Install or increase the use of electronic data interchange (EDI), evaluated receipt settlement (ERS), and electronic invoicing.
2. Improve efficiency, timeliness, and processes.
3. Install or increase the use of imaging.
4. Improve customer service.
5. Install or increase the use of electronic payments.
6. Clean up the vendor (supplier) file.[1]

Nonprofits can utilize each of these goals to enhance their payables and disbursements efficiency. Recall that your organization's primary financial objective is to ensure that financial resources are available when needed (timing), as needed (amount), and at reasonable cost (cost-effectiveness), and that once mobilized, these resources are protected from impairment and spent according to mission and donor purposes. Notice that funding payroll and payables targets the "as needed" part of this objective, and that the cost of your disbursements system relative to what it accomplishes for your organization are also in view in this objective. Part of the target liquidity level that you establish for your organization is there to fund ongoing disbursements, and another part is there to meet unexpected disbursements—such as when a collaborative venture or grant funding require immediate payments.

A *disbursement policy* indicates which payment mechanism to use for a given disbursement type or supplier and when to pay a given invoice, and sets up guidelines for the disbursement system (including which bank[s] might be involved).[2] Your organization's disbursement policy may be an informal strategy or it may be formalized in a written document.

There are six primary drivers of organizational disbursement policy. The payment systems in the economies in which the organization operates represent the one influence that is outside the control of the organization. The remaining five factors are mostly under your control: the organization's philosophy, its reporting and responsibility structure, its banks, its information technology (IT), and the amount and dependability of its daily net cash flow, on average.

The financial management philosophy of most nonprofits relative to its payables and disbursements is to be a good steward and to honor all of their financial obligations in a timely manner. This philosophy implies that they will not "stretch payables," seeing this as unethical for two reasons. First, to do so violates a contract—the nonprofit agreed to pay according to the supplier's terms when first beginning to do business using credit terms with the supplier. Second, a purchaser stretching payables beyond due dates is basically doing additional borrowing from suppliers without them knowing about it or authorizing it.

Reporting and responsibility structures may be centralized or decentralized. Most consultants recommend a centralized structure, primarily for control and investment income purposes. *Centralized disbursing* allows the corporate headquarters' staff to oversee each disbursement and possibly also initiate each disbursement, and offers these advantages:[3]

- Centralized control is a great way to make sure you have enough funds in your disbursement account, in that the cash manager at headquarters has better visibility into the organization's cash position than divisional or service unit personnel.
- Centralized data gives a quicker and more accurate picture of disbursement timing and amounts, in turn enabling a more accurate cash position forecast and better decisions about ability to take a cash discount and the dollar amount needing to be transferred to "fund" the organization's disbursement account.
- Disbursement float is higher, on average, when disbursing centrally rather than having local operating units pay nearby firms from nearby banks.
- Elimination of extra disbursement accounts diminishes your disbursement system cost at the same time as it deters fraud—fewer people have access to payment media and requisite authority.
- If disbursement services are bundled with credit services, the greater size of centralized balances should enable the manager to negotiate lower total (credit and noncredit service) banking costs.

Small and recently formed nonprofits as well as those operating at only one location are by nature centralized and tend to deal with only one bank. Because of the control and interest revenue possibilities, quite a few larger organizations are working to centralize disbursing as well—using a central disbursement account, at a minimum.

Decentralized disbursing involves payments being made by divisional offices or individual service sites, generally from accounts at nearby banks. These advantages emerge from decentralized disbursing:

- Organizations with operations spread throughout multiple locations or even in more than one country tend to be decentralized because of the need to pay wages and local bills or to disburse from an overseas subsidiary or other operating unit.
- Although decentralization may improve relationships with suppliers, who receive both payment and available funds more rapidly, on the downside, decentralized disbursing may hurt the control and efficiency desired for disbursement accounts. As well, less desirable investment opportunities may result.

Some organizations couple features from centralized systems with those of decentralized systems: Payments may be issued and accounts reconciled at outlying operating units, but they are drawn on a single central disbursement account. The nonprofit's central headquarters staff selects the bank(s) and funds the disbursement account.

Your banks must be equipped to provide the right services in the right locations at the right prices to give your organization proficient disbursing. Your disbursing banks' capabilities influence the flexibility and cost of your organization's disbursement system. Fraud prevention methods such as "positive pay" are an integral component of those capabilities. We have more to say about the importance of a positive pay service later in the chapter. Altering your organization's use of banking services and/or banks typically brings the greatest reductions in cost. Consult Appendix 4A to see representative bank prices for various services, as compiled by Phoenix-Hecht. Also, for larger organizations, the bank's electronic data interchange capability, or whether it is "EDI-capable," is essential. The EDI-capable bank has the ability to send "dollars and data" together so that the payment and invoice information do not have to be reattached by the payee, and the payee's receivables function can automatically process the payment and credit the payer's account. When combining collections, positioning, and disbursements, by far the biggest interest and use of bank products is for Internet applications.

The capabilities of the organization's information technology are another limiting factor on an organization's disbursement systems. Organizations vary widely in the degree to which their payables and disbursements processes are automated. Payables systems in businesses are more highly automated than any other cash management area; payroll is automated for many nonprofits, but vendor payments tend to be manually processed. Automated systems ensure that organizations pay bills (1) on time, (2) without manual processing, and (3) with tremendous cost savings. PC-based systems facilitate account reconciliation, electronic initiation and tracking of orders, and initiation of electronic payments (PC-initiated automated clearinghouse [ACH] payments or wire transfers). Your cash manager may use PC systems using the same platform, often your bank's web portal, to access account balances at concentration and outlying banks as well as to initiate investment of excess balances or borrowing under existing credit agreements.

Your organization's cash flows are unsynchronized, uneven, and uncertain—that is a given. Where your organization may vary is in how predictable those cash flows are and whether you spend most of the year in a cash-rich or cash-poor position. Most nonprofits are typically cash-poor, with the possible exception of the five weeks between Thanksgiving and calendar year-end.

Relatively small and/or predictable flows reduce the need for advanced disbursement accounts with their correspondingly higher fees. An organization with fairly predictable cash flows that is cash-rich should opt for a disbursement system in which excess cash balances are inexpensively and easily moved into interest-bearing investments. The organization might select banks having the most advantageous sweep accounts, in which amounts above compensating balance requirements (or all positive amounts) are automatically moved into overnight or other short-term investments. Typically cash-poor organizations, especially those with very unpredictable cash flows, should prefer banks that link disbursement accounts and services to credit facilities, such as a "credit sweep" that pays down the credit line balance when funds become available. Larger organizations should also bargain for volume-based pricing when contracting with disbursement banks.

Guided by the foregoing considerations, the disbursement policy should reflect the application of five principal objectives.

4.2 OBJECTIVES OF CASH DISBURSEMENT SYSTEMS

Here are the five principal objectives that should guide your disbursements systems management:[4]

1. *Maximize value through payment timing.* Payments should be timed to add the maximum value to the organization. Three observations help us see how to implement this principle.

   a. This is basically the same as minimizing costs—especially for the cash-starved organization that is typically in a net borrowed (illiquid) position—by paying on terms but not before. If the invoice is "net 30," time the payment so the recipient receives the check on Day 30. Credit periods for healthcare providers are not very generous, as a rule: days payable outstanding (average number of days from purchase to payment) for six organizations ranged from 3.7 days (UnitedHealth) to 27.6 days (Omnicare), with a median of 12.2 days.[5]

   b. This principle implies that an organization should take cash discounts when advantageous. If your organization passes on a "2%/10, net 30" cash discount, it is in effect borrowing from the supplier at roughly 37 percent per year. We know of very few organizations that borrow from banks' at an interest rate higher than 37 percent, so unless policy forbids using short-term borrowing, organizations are advantaged by tapping their credit line to take a cash discount if they do not have enough in their payment account to do so otherwise.

   c. Within ethical, legal, and practical constraints, an organization should avail itself of float offered by disbursement banks. Some nonprofits, as well as this book's publisher, John Wiley & Sons, disburse from a controlled disbursement account located in Ashland, OH, for example. Nonprofit organizations pay most bills with mailed checks. From the time when you mail out the check, there come three delays that together make up disbursement float: mail float, followed by processing float, and finally clearance (availability and clearing slippage) float. The locations of the mail origination and destination points, how long it takes the recipient to internally process it prior to depositing it at the bank, and which clearing method is used determine the length of the total disbursement float.

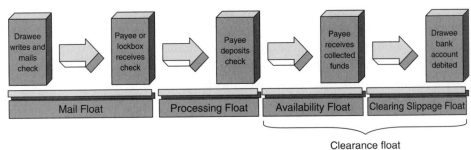

EXHIBIT 4.1 DISBURSEMENT FLOAT AND ITS COMPONENTS

Exhibit 4.1 illustrates mail, processing, and clearance float. Mail float varies from 1 to 5 calendar days, processing float varies from 1 to 3 calendar days, and clearance float ranges from 0 (e.g., "on-us" checks or checks drawn on the U.S. Treasury) to 3 business days. The Federal Reserve System has eliminated much of the clearing slippage, or "Fed float," which is the difference between the availability float experienced by the payee (when the Fed grants the collecting bank availability, which is pretty close to when you get use of your funds) and the presentment float experienced by the one writing the check (based on when the Fed charges the paying bank's account, which in turn drives the timing of the debit to your checking account).

Some organizations unethically extend float by remote mailing, mailing to the wrong address intentionally (usually to headquarters instead of to the "mail to" address on the invoice), or altering the check to prevent it from being handled by machine processing. The check writer's float gains come solely from a bank's or payee's pocket. Abuses of float are considered unethical and poor business practice, because the payee and collecting bank(s) are damaged by it.

2. *Optimize the accuracy and timeliness of information.* Accuracy and timeliness of information are key attributes of disbursement systems. Optimizing an organization's configuration of disbursement systems occurs only when your organization is getting accurate information in a timely manner without incurring excessive costs. Accurate funds balance information received early in the day adds value through access to investments with higher interest rates or better credit quality.

3. *Minimize balances in disbursement accounts.* Although some demand deposit balances may be necessary to support disbursements, as a rule these balances should be minimized. There are three possible exceptions to this principle.

a. Nonprofit organizations are permitted to have interest-bearing checking accounts, and those with low average balances may not lose much interest by leaving funds in the disbursement account.

b. When your organization contracts with its bank(s) for a bundled package of services, a holistic approach may negate this principle. The holistic approach involves considering the total cost and reliability of bank services instead of negotiating the price for each service individually. For banks that have adequate cost accounting systems and will bundle services (sell services as a group), significant cost savings may be possible for the customer. The appropriate focal point is the organization's overall banking costs, not the cost of each individual service.

c. If you have a loan and your bank requires a certain level of balances ("compensating balances") to support the loan, this minimum balance requirement may limit how far an organization can go in reducing disbursement account balances.

4. *Prevent fraud.* One of the fastest-growing crimes in the United States is check fraud. Fraud prevention and detection techniques as well as greater use of electronic payments are disbursement system essentials.

5. *Improve the purchase-to-pay processing cycle.* The purchase-to-pay cycle or procurement-to-pay (P2P) cycle encompasses more than just disbursements. This broader view helps you to see what other related processes can help your organization in payables and disbursements management. Consult Exhibit 4.2 to see two different takes on what is included in this important cycle.

Once you have this cycle in mind, it is time to diagnose your specific purchasing and disbursements issues. To assist you in this diagnosis, we include Exhibit 4.3, which presents the red flags that show you a worsening purchasing area situation. One or more of these indicators gives you early warning of a potentially serious situation that may be unfolding.

Finally, what may be done constructively to improve your P2P processes? Study Exhibit 4.4, which gives some of the best ways that companies and non-profits have significantly enhanced their purchasing and disbursements activities. Surely two or three of these ideas can bring value to your organization's performance.

4.3 DISBURSEMENTS POLICY

In today's Sarbanes-Oxley environment in which organizations work—even though much of this law does not specifically apply to nonprofits—controls, documentation, and policy are invaluable tools for treasury management. Informal policies and processes should be formalized in a written document. If your organization has not already crafted a formal disbursements policy, begin to craft one now.

The Procure-to-Pay Process

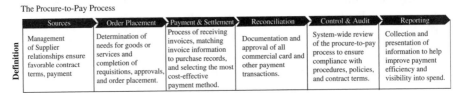

	Sources	Order Placement	Payment & Settlement	Reconciliation	Control & Audit	Reporting
Definition	Management of Supplier relationships ensure favorable contract terms, payment	Determination of needs for goods or services and completion of requisitions, approvals, and order placement.	Process of receiving invoices, matching invoice information to purchase records, and selecting the most cost-effective payment method.	Documentation and approval of all commercial card and other payment transactions.	System-wide review of the procure-to-pay process to ensure compliance with procedures, policies, and contract terms.	Collection and presentation of information to help improve payment efficiency and visibility into spend.

Source: VISA Commercial Solutions, "Procure-to-Pay Best Practices,"
Commercial Perpectives (February 2006): 2. Used by permission.

EXPENDITURE MANAGEMENT

Source: REL Consultancy Group, "Improving Shareholder Value Through Total Working Capital^SM Management." Downloaded from www.cshpi.com/docs/White-Paper-Improving-Shareholder-Value-Through-TWCM.pdf. Used by permission.

EXHIBIT 4.2   TWO LOOKS AT THE PROCUREMENT-TO-PAY OR PURCHASE-TO-PAY PROCESS

Some of the issues to address in your disbursements policy include authorized payment methods, when these should be used, who authorizes payments, exception occasions, security measures, and board of director approvals (see Exhibit 4.5).

A well-defined disbursement policy is a great first step toward fraud prevention and control. This has been a very weak area for many nonprofits, including faith-based organizations, over the past several decades.

Before addressing the best way to configure your disbursements system, we first discuss the primary disbursement methods: checks and drafts, card payments, and other electronic payments.

4.4 CHECKS AND DRAFTS

You may recall from Chapter 3 that consumers are using more and more card-based and other electronic transactions. This same trend is emerging, but much more slowly, in the business/organizational payments arena. Between 80

WARNING SIGNS: PURCHASE TO PAY[SM]

- Interest payments to suppliers are increasing.
- The company is logging more payment disputes.
- The company has a payment run every day.
- The supplier list is expanding rapidly.
- The same supplier delivers to different sites on different terms.
- There is no payment term "floor" representing the minimum terms the purchasing department should obtain.
- The company does not have an authorization procedure that demands approval for nonstandard terms.
- Credit sanctions have been imposed on the company.
- A majority of non–cost-of-goods purchases are made outside the formal purchasing system.
- The company's discount line seems to get lost while pressure to pay increases.

Source: REL Consultancy Group, "Improving Shareholder Value Through Total Working Capital[SM] Management." Downloaded from www.cshpi.com/docs/White-Paper-Improving-Shareholder-Value-Through-TWCM.pdf. Used by permission.

EXHIBIT 4.3 WARNING SIGNS IN YOUR PURCHASING PROCESSES

PURCHASE TO PAY[SM]

Arbitrarily holding invoices until they are past due is not a long-term solution to inflated levels of working capital. Suppliers do notice—and inevitably reflect the increased costs they are being asked to absorb in their pricing and service. Better solutions:

- Consolidate spending among fewer suppliers.
- Differentiate among suppliers. Categorize them according to their risk and profit impact (the risk they present to the company if they should perform poorly or disappear, and the extent to which they impact profitability).
- Concentrate on optimizing relationships with the high-risk, high-profit-impact suppliers by providing them with open access to information, developing common processes, and sharing efficiency benefits.
- Automate purchases from low-risk, low-profit-impact suppliers, perhaps through the use of P-cards.
- Search for new or alternative supply options in cases where suppliers present high risk but have a low profit impact.
- Negotiate favorable payment terms under customized contracts or blanket purchase orders, especially for strategic, high-volume products.
- Implement controls to prevent payments in advance of negotiated terms.
- Integrate spending approvals into the purchase process, thereby avoiding multiple, time-consuming sign-offs at the end of the process and enabling use of early payment discounts.

Source: REL Consultancy Group, "Improving Shareholder Value Through Total Working Capital[SM] Management." www.cshpi.com/docs/White-Paper-Improving-Shareholder-Value-Through-TWCM.pdf. Used by permission.

EXHIBIT 4.4 IMPROVING YOUR ORGANIZATION'S PURCHASE-TO-PAY PERFORMANCE

As your organization considers formulating a written policy for outgoing payments, perhaps as you are now making web-based or e-marketplace purchases, utilize these suggested elements for inclusion from the Association for Financial Professionals' Payments Advisory Group:

☑ Which payment methods are authorized?
☑ What are the circumstances under which each of these payment methods should be used?
☑ Who is responsible for approving payments?
☑ What procedures may be used for unusual or urgent situations?
☑ What is the organization's position on the security, efficiency, and cost-effectiveness of each payment method?
☑ Is the treasury department designated by the board of directors and/or senior management as the department responsible for cash, banking relationships, and the control of credit facilities?

Source: Adapted from the Report of the AFP Payments Advisory Group, "Payments Pitfalls II: Learn the Truth and Avoid the Consequences," October 15, 2001, pp. 4–5. Used by permission.

EXHIBIT 4.5 WHAT SHOULD BE IN YOUR DISBURSEMENTS POLICY?

and 85 percent of business-to-business payments are made by check. Consider these survey findings of corporate accounts payable managers:

> With most organizations (69–75 percent) printing them daily, checks are still the predominant mechanism for disbursing payment, despite the increasing electronic options available. Most organizations are using ACH, FEDI [Financial EDI] and/or Direct Deposit at some level though. E-commerce appears to be in its infancy in the corporate world. Based upon information obtained elsewhere, a small but growing number of very large companies are beginning to explore the use of e-commerce payment mechanisms.[6]

(a) CHECK UTILIZATION.   Nonprofits, like businesses, make most of their payments by check. Why are checks still so popular for businesses and nonprofits as they select how to pay their bills? Consulting firm Phoenix-Hecht suggests it is because "checks are widely accepted, relatively inexpensive, easy to produce, and provide a good audit trail. They also provide the additional benefit of float."[7] Marketing research conducted by The Clearing House documents ten reasons for sticking with checks and not originating electronic payments:

1. The seller does not disseminate account information required to make electronic payments (e.g., invoices do not contain an electronic payment remittance address).

2. The buyer accounts payable/banking system cannot create electronic payments (ACH or wire). Many PC-based small and medium-size business accounting software packages do not have electronic payment initiation or receipt capabilities.

3. Businesses and nonprofits believe there is a loss of float with electronic payments.

4. The buyer cannot provide electronic remittance information.

5. The beneficiary accounts receivable system is unable to handle electronic payments with remittance information.

6. There are conflicting, multiple message formats and a lack of minimum remittance information standards.

7. Cash management systems that are available to small and medium-size businesses have either poor electronic payment capabilities and/or poor integration facilities to back-end accounts receivable/accounts payable (AR/AP) systems.

8. Banks may not have the capability to deliver sufficient electronic payment and remittance information.

9. Payment systems lack a proof of payment confirmation for electronic payments.

10. Execution of trading partner agreements are time consuming and costly.[8]

One other concern that has surfaced is that the fraud prevention capability of banks appears to be better for checks than for electronic payments. Starting in September 2006, business or nonprofit checks of less than $25,000 can now be converted to electronic debits (using "point of purchase," or POP, and "accounts receivable conversion," or ARC, the same check-to-ACH conversion methods previously used for consumer checks received at point of purchase or at a lockbox, respectively).[9] Businesses and nonprofits can opt out by notifying the biller in the case of ARC (for checks sent to a biller's mailing location or dropped off to the biller's drop box) or by telling the clerk anytime a POP conversion is attempted at the point of purchase. Most businesses and nonprofits are concerned about the new conversion to ACH due to the effect it will have on their check fraud controls and accounting systems as well as the change to electronic payment regulations and rules (from check regulations and rules) that will now apply to these converted payments.[10] By using check stock with extra width beyond the normal six inches and containing an auxiliary on-us field, the organization prevents the check from being converted by the payee. (The auxiliary on-us field, or set of characters, is not seen on most checks, but may be included on the lower-left bottom of a commercial check. It normally shows the check's serial number. If it is on a check, a special symbol will precede and follow the number to indicate that this is an on-us field.)

(b) DRAFTS. Drafts are very similar to checks. The similarities and differences are profiled in Exhibit 4.6. Note especially the extra control feature associated with drafts. Two types of drafts, sight drafts and time drafts, are used extensively in international sales, as we note later in the section on international payments.

Our next two types of payments are both electronic payments, but we address them separately: card payments and other domestic electronic payments made by ACH.

Instrument	Clearing Process	Uses
Checks (Regular demand deposit account or negotiable order of withdrawal account)	Deposited by payee, cleared back to drawee bank at which point they are paid unless a stop payment has been issued or a forgery detected.	Any payment situation except when immediate transfer of value is required.
Drafts	Deposited by payee, cleared back to agent ("payable through") bank, which presents check to payor; if payor approves payment, bank pays check. Agent bank is charged for draft amount at the time of presentment and may charge for float from that point until the payor authorizes payment. Alternatively, payor allows all drafts to be paid by agent bank (from demand deposit account), with refused drafts later credited back.	When authorization control is desired over field payments (as in property and casualty insurance, when signature of agent and dollar amount need to be verified) or over off-premise purchases by an employee who cannot get the needed second signature on a check. Some federal agencies use third-party drafts to make emergency and administrative payments that cannot be made effectively electronically. Deters fraud and misuse of funds.

Source: Adapted from Terry S. Maness and John T. Zietlow, *Short-Term Financial Management*, 3rd edition (Cincinnati: South-Western, 2005), p. 380.

EXHIBIT 4.6   CHECKS AND DRAFTS

4.5 PURCHASING/PROCUREMENT CARDS

Corporate credit cards, usually called purchasing cards or procurement cards (p-cards), are quite similar to personal credit cards insofar as where they are accepted and the way in which they are used to purchase an item. They differ from personal credit cards in that they are approved based on the organization's credit rating (as opposed to the individual's credit record); they may be restricted to certain categories (office supplies and maintenance/repair items), per-charge amounts, or daily spending limits; and they may provide more detailed transaction and reconcilement services to the user.

The product opportunities you have and the number of different banks that may offer you a p-card are extensive. Nonprofits, being small in size, usually qualify for card options that are quite similar to those offered to small businesses. One bank's offerings to this market are profiled in Exhibit 4.7. Included is the bank's debit card offering.

Fifth Third Business Credit and Debit Cards

	▸ MasterCard® BusinessCard®	▸ Business Rewards MasterCard	▸ Business Debit Rewards MasterCard
Annual Fee	No annual fee	1st year free, $50 annual fee per card thereafter	No annual fee
Introductory APR on Purchases and Balance Transfers	0% for 12 months on purchases and balance transfers, then rates as low as Prime + 5.99%	0% for 12 months on purchases and balance transfers, then rates as low as Prime + 5.99%	Not applicable to this card
Business Advantage	Use as a source of capital; track business expenses	Earn rewards for necessary business spending	It's an ATM card that works like cash or a check
Why You Should Choose This Card	Manage your company's everyday expenses, cash flow, and tax preparation	Earn points that you can redeem for gift cards, travel, or merchandise. Learn More	Make purchases everywhere Debit MasterCard is accepted.
Fifth Third Rewards Program	Not available	Earn 1 point for every $1 spent. Learn more.	Available with no annual fee. Earn 1 point for every $2 spent on signature purchases. Learn more.

Source: http://www.53.com/wps/wcm/connect/FifthThirdSite/Small+Business/Credit+%26+ Debit+Cards/ Used by permission.

EXHIBIT 4.7 EXAMPLE OF BANK'S CREDIT AND DEBIT CARD OFFERINGS FOR SMALL ORGANIZATIONS

A purchasing card transaction example is provided to help you better understand the processing of these transactions (see Exhibit 4.8).

P-cards offer the most savings when they replace expensive requisition–purchase order–invoice–payment processing cycles. It costs an estimated $25 to $45 to process an ordered item from purchase order through payment, so many businesses are no longer requiring requisitions and purchase orders for all purchases; instead, they are allowing employees to use a credit card to buy small-dollar maintenance, repair, and operating supplies. Although they normally do not get as much purchase detail on their monthly statements, these organizations prefer making only one payment instead of hundreds or thousands per month for these purchases. They may keep a listing of approved suppliers on the organization's internal database, or intranet, or the organization may allow the employee to buy from any supplier accepting Visa, MasterCard, or American Express credit cards. Users in the business community are primarily large and midsize companies (those with sales of $25 million and higher). Healthcare organizations have adopted these cards widely (73 percent of surveyed organizations), as have businesses as a whole (74 percent); see "Corporate Cards" statistics in Exhibit 4.9.

The main obstacles to further usage of p-cards, according to a 2000 Phoenix-Hecht survey of corporations, are low management priority, loss of control, time commitment to implement, lack of systems resources, cost, and state sales and use tax issues. A survey by *Treasury & Risk Management* magazine finds companies use p-cards mostly for office supplies or travel and entertainment

Let's explore the use of a purchase card transaction by Jim—an employee in the Light City's Parks and Recreation Department—of four hammers, some plywood, and several boxes of nails on Friday morning. This is for a project that needs to be completed by Friday afternoon.

Jim purchases these items at the Everything in One Depot (EIOD) using his purchasing card that was issued by Bank A. When EIOD swipes Jim's card for the purchase of $75, the modem in EIOD's terminal sends the 16-digit (or 15-digit for American Express) purchasing card number, the card expiration date, the dollar amount, and the merchant number to its processor's bank—Bank B—which is located in Seattle, WA. The processing center then routes the transaction to ABC System, the purchasing card platform processor for Bank A. The authorization system determines that the purchasing card is "live" (i.e., active), has 200 available credit capacity, and fits the merchant code that has been developed by Light City's purchasing card program. The processing center then sends an "authorization code" back to EIOD's terminal display. At the end of the day, EIOD will send the day's transactions to the Bank's B processing center for posting. Payment is received within 2 or 3 days through an automated clearinghouse deposit to its bank account.

At the end of Light City's billing period, ABC System (the purchasing card platform processor) will send a bill, electronically, to Light City for all purchases by its employees for the month. There are several formats in which the electronic bill can be sent: (1) ASCII format to an electronic mailbox; (2) a standard mainframe computer file layout; (3) electronic data interchange (EIF) transmission; or (4) proprietary software from the card issuers, creating an electronic invoice that is formatted for upload to Light City's computer system. Payment of the bill is generally made within 2 to 14 days by wire transfer or by automated clearinghouse.

American Express operates its system differently from MasterCard and VISA by using a "loop" environment in which it serves as the card issuer, merchant acquirer, and the authorization and posting party. Otherwise the transactions are handled the same.

Source: "The INS and Outs of Purchasing Cards, *CPA Government & Nonprofit Report* 12 (July 2004): 1–6.

EXHIBIT 4.8 STORY OF A PURCHASING CARD TRANSACTION

purchases, with 3 in 10 having a $1,500 maximum transaction size and another 4 in 10 enforcing a maximum transaction size ranging between $2,000 and $5,000. The principal benefit seen by organizations using p-cards is fewer administrative headaches and less paperwork.

Payroll cards are not actually credit cards or p-cards, but rather a form of stored value card, much like the reloadable card you use at Starbucks. These cards are useful for providing pay to unbanked employees, bringing to your organization many of the same advantages of using direct deposit to pay employees. Your organization may use these cards to deliver funds electronically (through ACH direct deposit, covered later) to employees who do not have a checking or other "transactional" bank account. The pay amount is loaded onto the employee's card, which may be used to access these funds through ATM withdrawals, purchases using debit cards (since they are MasterCard, Visa, Discover, or American Express cards), or even "card drafts"—checks drawn against the card's funds.

4.6 OTHER ELECTRONIC PAYMENTS

Organizations are increasingly moving to making payments using ACH debits and credits. Some suppliers are slow in processing payers' check payments, primarily due to slow invoicing and/or slow check processing prior to deposit, but the float

Product Demand (2005)

Product	Healthcare Companies (%)	All Companies (%)
Cash Balance and info Reporting	91	95
Corporate Cards	73	74
ACH	97	95
Wire Transfer	94	97
Controlled Disbursement	97	93
Outsourcing Services	15	12
Wholesale Lockbox	91	77
Retail Lockbox	21	21

Source: Greenwich and Associates, "Cash Management and Short-Term Investment Practices—United States," 2005.
This research study encompassed interviews with over 760 cash management specialists and other financial professionals between May and July 2005. Used by permission.

EXHIBIT 4.9   USAGE RATES BY HEALTHCARE AND ALL COMPANIES OF CASH MANAGEMENT PRODUCTS

advantage of disbursing using checks has significantly declined in recent years. Compare the relatively small amount of remaining float to the advantages of electronic payment: lower bank charges, lower internal processing costs, and less potential for fraud or error. Paying your suppliers or another party electronically is typically accomplished through an ACH transaction, either an ACH debit or an ACH credit, depending on which party initiates the transaction.

An *ACH debit* is essentially an order to go debit someone's account and credit that amount to my account. More formally, it

> is a payment order originated by the payee, based on the prior authorization by the payer, which is routed through the payee's bank (originating depository financial institution [ODFI]). If the payee's bank (receiving depository financial institution [RDFI]) is a member of the same ACH as the originating institution, the bookkeeping entries to complete the transfer are made by that ACH's computer. Otherwise, the ACH (now called the *originating ACH*), must transmit the payment order to the receiving institution's ACH (termed the *receiving ACH*).[11]

Common uses of debits include the collection of insurance or loan payments, preauthorized distributor and dealer payments, and internal cash concentration transfers. Nonprofits are increasingly using ACH debits to collect donations, as we noted in Chapter 3.

An *ACH credit* is essentially an order to go credit someone's account and debit that amount against my account. It is originated by the payer; the originating institution is the payer's disbursement bank. The National Automated Clearing House Association has standardized computer formats that your organization will put transaction details into to initiate payments. You then transmit the transaction to the originating institution. Direct deposit of payroll, travel expense and reimbursement, pension and annuity, interest, retirement and mutual fund distributions, Social Security and other government benefits, tax refunds, dividends, and accounts payable disbursements are typical uses of ACH credits. Direct deposit continues to be the most widely used ACH payment—there were 4.4 billion direct deposit payments in 2005 (covering 71 percent of the private-sector labor force), with an average dollar amount of $1,290.[12]

There are six formats that organizations may use for ACH entries; the five primary ones, along with associated advantages and disadvantages, are profiled in Exhibit 4.10. The corporate trade exchange (CTX) format is commonly used along with electronic data interchange (EDI; structured computer-to-computer data exchange format). The most recent additions are the CBR (Corporate Cross-Border) payment, and PBR (Consumer Cross Border). CBR is used for sending business or other organizational cross-border ACH credit and debit entries. Canadian entries currently are the most common CBRs, but Mexico debits and credits on a regular basis and credits from the United States to five European nations are available: Austria, Germany, the Netherlands, Switzerland, and the United Kingdom. These payments to Europe settle on the date indicated in the ACH entry. A "gateway operator" transmits the Federal Reserve ACH (FedACH) International items to the RDFI in Europe within two days of the U.S. settlement date. These cross-border transactions are denominated at first in U.S. dollars; European credits are then sent on to the Eurogiro Network.[13] This organization then converts the entries into the Eurogiro format and forwards them to the receiving gateway operator (RGO) for the participating country. The RGO then initiates an exchange of U.S. dollars for that country's local currency on the U.S. settlement day. It will post any "on-us" items to the appropriate depositor's account(s) or route the credits through the domestic clearing system in that country. At the time of this writing, the originating bank pays a $2 per item surcharge for ACH credits going to European receivers.

There is good news and bad news on the ACH payment front. On the positive side, there were 2 billion total business-to-business ACH payments in 2005, up 11.3 percent over 2004. Furthermore, financial electronic data interchange (FEDI)— which means there was electronic exchange of payment-related information or financial-related documents in standard formats between business partners on the ACH Network—increased by about 20 percent in 2005 compared to 2004: There were 255.6 million payments with 915 million EDI-formatted remittance records accompanying the ACH payments.[14]

Format	Uses	Advantages/Disadvantages
Prearranged payments and deposits (PPD)	Direct deposit of payroll, automatic donation, or utility or loan bill paying services.	Normally settle in 2 business days; generally used only for crediting or debiting consumers' accounts.
Cash concentration or disbursements (CCD)	Movement of funds to concentration accounts or electronic payment of suppliers.	Electronic depository transfer checks (EDTCs or EDTs) created for next-day settlement. Simple data format and almost universal ability of banks to initiate or receive account for increasing utilization.
CCD plus addenda (CCD +)	The federal government uses this format in its Vendor Express payments. This format adds an addendum (up to 80 characters of computer-readable data) to the CCD format, enabling computerized relay of the remittance data into the cash application component of the company's receivables software.	Next-day settlement. Banks may not be able to capture and relay the addenda information, however.
Corporate trade exchange (CTX)	Used for intercorporate payments. May have as many as 4990 addenda records (an invoice might be one record). A standardized (ANSI X12) format that already is used by numerous companies in dealings with suppliers and customers via EDI.	Next-day settlement and standardized formats. The number of banks that can originate and receive has been an impediment to use, but that number is increasing rapidly. Companies can read and translate ANSI X12 for automatic processing and updating of payments. Encryption and authentication is feasible.
Corporate Cross-Border Payment (CBR)	Used for the transmission of corporate cross-border ACH credit and debit entries.	The CBR format is able to include detailed information unique to cross-border payments (e.g., foreign exchange conversion, origination and destination currency, country codes, etc.).

Source: Adapted from Terry S. Maness and John T. Zietlow, *Short-Term Financial Management*, 3rd ed. (Cincinnati: South-Western, 2005), p. 387. Used by permission.

EXHIBIT 4.10 ACH FORMATS FOR ORGANIZATIONS

The bad news is that nonprofits and businesses continue to resist abandonment of simple check-based disbursement systems. Many organizations continue to resist electronic payments because the supplier (trading partner) lacks the ability to receive electronic payment coupled with the associated remittance information, limited systems integration, and the additional technology costs. There is also evidence that sharing the float savings (renegotiating credit terms) has not been done to buyers' satisfaction. Another roadblock that thwarts broader usage of ACH payments is the loss of flexibility when paying electronically—especially payee-initiated ACH debits. It is simpler to stretch payables ("the check's in the mail") than to delay electronic disbursements. When the check really is mailed, the disbursement float further delays value loss. One survey done several years ago estimated that U.S. mail float averaged 3.2 days.

Organizations may also utilize ACH payments to collect funds from other organizations, governmental agencies, or businesses through a process called *Electronic Invoice Presentment and Payment* (EIPP). This process starts with an electronic invoice being transmitted, and is then followed by the payer authorizing an electronic payment. Organizations or companies can authorize ACH payment to other organizations or companies via the Internet using either the CCD or CTX formats (refer back to Exhibit 4.10). There are risk and security issues involved, so use proper risk control measures if initiating such payments. Some of the benefits to the payer of electronically transmitting the invoices and then "replying" with an electronic payment authorization include:

- streamlined segregation, routing, matching and approval of bills/invoices
- automated reporting and analysis
- automated payment scheduling and initiation
- reduced use of the seller's trade credit (valuable if up against a credit limit)
- enhanced ability to meet trade discount requirements
- reduced payment initiation, management, and posting expense
- reduced labor requirements
- facilitated dispute and adjudication
- improved cash forecasting
- related specifically to the electronic payment will be supply chain transaction integration possibilities[15]

When invoices are made available to consumers (usually via e-mail with a link to the invoice) and consumers can initiate an electronic payment after viewing the invoice online, this process is called *electronic bill presentment and payment* (EBPP). EBPP is used extensively by utilities.

4.7 COMPARISON OF ALTERNATIVE DISBURSEMENT SYSTEMS

If your organization is small, with mainly local transactions, the appropriate disbursement system is likely to be very simple. If your organization is a large

VIEW ACCOUNT INFORMATION AND INITIATE TRANSACTIONS ONLINE

Internet access to your daily account information is critical in today's fast-paced business world—for companies of every size. Use Wachovia Connection®Express to quickly access account details and perform transactions. With "real time" updates, you can effectively determine your investment, borrowing, concentration and disbursement needs, and move funds with the same Internet session.

You can also receive a comprehensive daily statement of your previous day's account activity by phone, e-mail, or fax.

MOVE FUNDS AND MAKE PAYMENTS—QUICKLY AND EASILY

Moving funds and making payments electronically is easier than ever, using **Wire Transfers** or the **Automated Clearing House (ACH)**. Both options offer convenient alternatives for timely movement of funds and payment of suppliers, taxes, vendors, and employees, depending upon your need for immediate or next-day settlement of funds

You can transfer funds and make payments electronically using our Internet service options, **Wachovia Connection Express** or **WebACHieveSM** .

PAY TAXES ELECTRONICALLY

Wachovia offers two easy ways for your company to pay its taxes:

* *TTAXplus*®an electronic tax filing and payment service, allows you to easily pay your company's federal and state taxes, 24 hours a day, seven days a week.
* *Wachovia Connection Express* offers you the ability to initiate tax payments through the convenience and ease of the Internet.

BALANCE AND MANAGE DISBURSEMENT ACCOUNTS

* With Wachovia's **Paid Only Reconcilement** service, let us help you balance your business account faster by providing check issue information via data transmission, magnetic tape, or diskette.
* **Zero Balance Accounts (ZBA)** allow you to link multiple disbursement accounts to your company's master account, giving you efficient, centralized use of available funds. Funds flow is simplified and reports provide a useful audit trail.

VIEW IMAGES OF YOUR CHECKS AND DEPOSITED ITEMS

You can quickly access images of both the front and back of your paid checks, deposit tickets and deposit items that posted to your account through our **Wachovia Connection Express** or **Image CD-ROM** services, enabling you to settle payment disputes faster than ever. As an added feature, Wachovia Connection Express allows you to view items included with your deposits, providing a quick and easy online audit trail.

GUARD YOUR COMPANY AGAINST FRAUD

Help protect your company's treasury transactions against fraudulent activity with Wachovia's **Basic Positive Pay** service. Basic Positive Pay automatically returns unauthorized checks, preventing these items from posting to your account.

Source: www.wachovia.com/small_biz/page/textonly/0,,440_1139_1142,00.html. Used by permission.

EXHIBIT 4.11 BANK PRODUCTS FOR DISBURSEMENT SYSTEMS

multinational organization, it should consider a complex system. Exhibit 4.11 profiles a typical portfolio of bank service offerings, many of which are basic and would fit any organization's disbursements system.

(a) SIMPLE DISBURSEMENT SYSTEMS. Simple disbursement systems tend to be paper-based and manual. Basic payment services, such as demand deposit accounts or NOW accounts, payroll services, and drafts, are appropriate for organizations having small daily cash flows, volunteer or only part-time financial personnel who have not been trained in specialized skills, basic IT facilities and/or skills, and local financial dealings.[16]

One bank service that this typical nonprofit should consider is some form of account reconciliation. *Account reconciliation* is a disbursement service in which the organization provides the bank with a record of checks issued, and the bank helps balance the organization's checkbook by providing the organization information regarding which checks have been paid. Not only does this relieve someone in your organization of the chore of "balancing the checkbook," but account reconciliation is also a key to rapid fraud detection. The three common types of reconciliation differ according to the degree of information provided to the nonprofit, beyond what is normally provided in the monthly statement:

1. *Paid-only reconciliation* reports all paid checks by check number, with check number, dollar amount, and date paid. The date paid can be compared with the check issue date to determine the disbursement float on an individual check. The bank will also indicate the total number of checks written and their dollar amount as well as any stopped payments or miscellaneous debits to the account. Organizations with automated payables systems may receive this information via Internet browser or PC transmission, and use it to automatically update their payables records.
2. *Range reconciliation*, also a form of partial reconciliation, provides subtotals of all checks within a range of check serial numbers. This is especially useful for identifying disbursements from the same account but from several locations.
3. *Full reconciliation* provides detailed "checks outstanding" information, along with the "checks paid" data from organization-supplied check issue detail. It generally costs $30 to $40 per month per account more than partial reconciliation.[17]

(b) DISBURSEMENTS FUNDING IN A SIMPLE SYSTEM. A simple disbursement system uses basic methods for disbursements funding: existing demand deposit account or NOW account balances, deposits of incoming daily cash receipts, or proceeds from maturing investments. Some organizations have an automated sweep account, in which any balances over and above some threshold are taken out of the account overnight and invested in one of the bank's money market accounts.[18] This threshold might be the sum of balances left in the account to compensate the bank and an average daily disbursement amount. Depending on the average balance in the disbursement account, the rate of interest earned might be 1/4 to 1/2 percent below a benchmark rate (usually the current Treasury bill yield or federal funds rate, which is the rate banks pay on overnight borrowing from each other). In low-interest-rate eras, such as in the early 2000s, many sweep accounts were turned off because the monthly fee exceeded the additional investment dollars that could be earned by sweeping monies out of the account. We return to the topic of sweep accounts in Chapter 7.

Cash-poor organizations and organizations that have disbursement accounts at the same bank that provides their credit lines—a common scenario due to the bank's desire to couple these—might simply allow excess balances to remain in the disbursement account, hoping that this buffer is replenished from each day's cash inflows. When this is insufficient to maintain the desired balance in the account, the organization taps its credit line to meet disbursement needs.

(c) ORGANIZATION CHARACTERISTICS. Organizations using a simple model for disbursements often possess four characteristics:

1. They are often small organizations providing only one or two services and doing this in one location.
2. A large percentage of their payments are local (e.g., payroll) or transfers between organization units.
3. They typically operate with a very limited treasury office—with respect to skilled personnel and information technology.
4. The businesses and nonprofits with which they transact payments may not have electronic order and remittance capabilities, or if they do, they are not applying pressure for electronic payments.

Organizations with these characteristics use paper-based payments and simple funding approaches.

(d) COMPLEX DISBURSEMENT SYSTEMS. Complex disbursement systems are typified by four things:

1. A greater reliance on electronic payments
2. Specialized disbursement accounts
3. Flexible account funding
4. Greater control and information capabilities[19]

The organization gains these facilities by having to hold higher compensating balances or incurring additional monthly account fees. The benefits of having more control, information, and additional net interest income (interest revenue from short-term investments less interest expense from short-term borrowing) outweigh the costs. Complex disbursements systems typically are tied to the organization's collection and cash positioning systems (covered in Chapter 3) to enhance the efficiency and cost-effectiveness of funds transfers. For very large organizations, these disbursements systems often are the product of elaborate disbursement studies that guide bank selection and the location of disbursement accounts.

(e) PAPER-BASED PAYMENT MECHANISMS.   Standard checking or NOW accounts play a smaller role in complex systems because of issues related to cost, control, and funding uncertainty. Larger organizations need to monitor overall system cost carefully, maintain control, and pinpoint the funding amount and timing.

For example, an organization having centralized disbursements but dispersed locations that issue paychecks and supplier payments faces a *control dilemma*. It may use specialized checks called *multiple-drawee checks* that have more than one bank listed on the face of the check; one of the banks is located in close proximity to the disbursing location (and for that bank, the check is an "on-us" item). Such accounts are popular for organizations that use a centralized disbursement system with the primary disbursement bank located in a one state but have operating units located in other states that require paychecks be drawn on an in-state bank.

The *cost dilemma* arises due to the fact that most organizations issue many small-dollar checks. This can be handled by moving more purchases to p-cards, as discussed earlier. Another approach is to attach a draft to the purchase order; the combined document is called a *purchase order with payment voucher attached*. The draft (voucher) is made out for the dollar amount of sale and then detached and deposited by the seller after the services are rendered or goods are shipped. Such drafts save payables processing expense and time for the purchaser and eliminate the need for the supplier to send an invoice and reminder letters if the payment has not been received. Consult Appendix 4A for representative bank fees for various cash management services.

Funding uncertainty comes about because banks do not generally provide same-day presentment information on regular checking or NOW accounts; this additional information is included as part of specialized checking accounts called controlled disbursement accounts. Or the bank may provide no information regarding incoming presentments, but it automatically funds the account and then the account balance returns to $0—in a setup called a zero balance account (ZBA). We offer more details on these specialized disbursement accounts later.

(f) ACCOUNT FUNDING.   Your organization may select from among several means of funding your disbursement accounts in a complex disbursement system. ZBAs typically are funded by intrabank transfers from concentration accounts (sometimes called master accounts), overnight bank loans paid off by funds transfers made the next day, or transfers in from sales of amounts held in money market funds. Controlled disbursement accounts are funded in these same ways, as well as by wire transfers, ACH debits to a funding account, or overnight investments that are becoming available as they mature (usually repurchase agreements; see Chapter 7). ACH debits take either one or two days to settle. Until same-day settlement becomes available through the U.S. ACH system, organizations will have to keep monies equivalent to one day's average disbursements in the disbursement account. ACH funding is less costly than wire transfers: It currently costs $1 or less per transaction, while a wire transfer may entail a total charge of $16 to $18 because your organization is both sender and receiver and must pay two charges. Most organizations use ACH debits for funding controlled disbursement accounts.

(g) ELECTRONIC DISBURSING MECHANISMS.   Organizations with sophisticated disbursing systems typically use electronic funds transfers to fund disbursement accounts and to the greatest degree possible pay employees and suppliers electronically using ACH transfers.

Direct deposit of payroll is by far the most prominent electronic payment application. An organization's payroll department transmits to its employees' banks, via PC or web application, a listing of employees, their Social Security or other ID numbers, bank account numbers, and that period's pay amounts. (It does this for employees who have opted for direct deposit, unless it operates in a state that allows the organization to mandate that all employees receive pay via direct deposit.) This is done at least two days prior to payday. When transmitting direct deposit information electronically, the organization simply transmits the information to that region's ACH for all employees' banks that are members of the ACH. Advantages include fewer stolen or lost checks; reduced costs for payroll processing, check printing, and check storage; and lowered disbursement bank charges. Personal computer software can quickly and automatically format your organization's employee pay data in ACH credit format.

The trend is for more ACH payments to be made for travel and entertainment reimbursement, dividends, pension payments, interest payments, and state and federal government electronic benefit transfers.

4.8   ESTABLISHING YOUR BANKING NETWORK: PRODUCTS AND SERVICES TO CONSIDER

Your organization needs to carefully consider a number of bank products to better manage your disbursements. In this section we first address the primary specialized disbursements accounts: controlled disbursement accounts and zero balance accounts.[20] We then discuss positive pay, the primary fraud detection and prevention service. Finally, we discuss the combination of EDI with electronic fund transfers.

(a) CONTROLLED DISBURSEMENT ACCOUNTS.   A *controlled disbursement account* is a checking account for which the bank provides to the cash manager early in the morning a dollar total of all checks that will clear that day.

This information may be provided using Internet access or a phone call, fax, or computer message to the cash manager. The bank's report of the total dollar amount is fairly precise because it receives only one presentment daily (or gets advance notification from the Federal Reserve of the dollar amount of any second presentment) and does not permit same-day availability for electronic or physical presentments (over-the-counter presentments or "direct sends" in which collecting banks route checks directly to the paying bank) after that time.

The big advantage of a controlled disbursement account to the disbursing organization is the ability to maintain zero or very small balances in the disbursement account. This means that the organization does not need to forecast disbursements (but it should be doing a cash forecast that would include monthly or even weekly disbursements, at a minimum), and it can then invest otherwise idle balances overnight at a higher interest yield than it would have earned if the money was auto-swept out of the account using a sweep arrangement.

The organization also receives a small clearing float increase because the controlled disbursement account is generally located near a regional check processing center or at a country bank, instead of in a Fed District Bank city, such as Cleveland. For example, Cleveland's National City Bank runs its accounts through its Ashland, Ohio, affiliate. Organizations are careful to avoid even the appearance of maximizing clearance float, however: "Remote disbursement accounts" are considered unethical and in violation of the Justice Department guidelines issued after it prosecuted stockbroker E.F. Hutton for its "check kiting" scheme of moving monies around simply to take advantage of banks' inability to track funds closely. Recently, several "add-on" services have been attached to controlled disbursement accounts, including imaging, online information access, and positive pay and other fraud control features.

Controlled disbursement accounts are used extensively by midsize and larger businesses and healthcare organizations. (We do not have data for other types of nonprofits.) A 2005 Phoenix-Hecht survey found that 92 percent of large corporations and 78 percent of midsize corporations used these accounts.[21] Greenwich Associates 2005 data (see Exhibit 4.9) shows 93 percent usage of controlled disbursement accounts by midsize and large companies (up from 81 percent in 1990 and 73 percent in 1986), and 97 percent usage by healthcare organizations. Utilization rates continue to be much lower for smaller organizations. There are economies of scale (costs per unit drop as volume increases) due to the fixed IT costs a bank incurs (such as the software annual license fees), implying that the controlled disbursement account costs should continue to decline in the future. At some point such an account will become cost-beneficial for smaller companies and nonprofits.

In some cases the organization's controlled disbursement account has a zero dollar balance. (The balance is actually negative in the amount of the day's check presentments until the point late in the day when account is funded.) This account would be defined as a type of zero balance account.

(b) ZERO BALANCE ACCOUNTS.   A *zero balance account*, when used as part of a disbursement system, is a disbursement account on which checks are written even though the balance in the account is maintained at zero. When checks and other debits are posted to the account, the total amount is covered by a transfer of funds from another account (a master account) at the same bank.

A ZBA maintains a zero dollar balance because another of the organization's accounts, usually the concentration or master account, automatically funds the total dollar amount presented against it each day. As we noted in Chapter 3, some ZBAs also have deposit amounts credited to them, so not all ZBAs are controlled disbursement accounts. One difference between ZBAs used exclusively for payroll or other types of disbursements and controlled disbursement accounts is that banks do not notify the ZBA holder of daily presentments. Rather, the bank automatically debits the master or concentration account to cover the total dollar amount of ZBA presentments. (In a controlled disbursement account, the advance notification allows your treasury personnel time to arrange a transfer or sale of securities, or to tap your credit line.)

Your organization may have several ZBAs, each of which is funded from another account at the same bank or at a correspondent bank when checks are presented. At all other times, the balance is zero, with the advantage that no idle funds are left in the non–interest-bearing account or low-interest-rate NOW account. If the ZBA also receives deposits, any positive balances will be moved at day's end to the master account. Overall, across all accounts, your organization achieves reduced deposit balances because the cash flow fluctuations can be managed in the master account instead of holding positive balances in every individual account.

Because of the risk to the bank that the accountholder may not have adequate funds for the automatic transfer into a ZBA at day's end, a pseudo-ZBA (sometimes termed a target balance account) is sometimes set up instead. This account has daily balances equal to an average day's disbursements total. Some banks require ZBA account holders to also have money market accounts or possibly a credit line at the same bank. Treasury staff should recognize that their organization will have to pass a credit approval review in order to be approved for a controlled disbursement account or disbursement ZBA. The bank is exposed to the risk that your organization will not be able to fund the account. The bank's risk exposure lasts from presentment until the time of funding.

Should an organization set up ZBAs or controlled disbursement accounts? The answer depends on many of the factors that we have mentioned in this chapter:

- Organizations with centralized disbursing can set up controlled disbursement accounts or ZBAs at each subsidiary or division, then fund these from a central master account.

- Either type of account is advisable when an organization's cash flows are unpredictable; the account should be tied to an investment account or credit line when cash receipts are volatile.
- Neither account makes sense if the organization needs only one disbursement account and receives an earnings credit rate roughly equivalent to the rate at which the organization could invest excess balances (see Chapter 5).
- ZBAs that upstream funds to a concentration account might be preferable for the organization whose divisional personnel do not have the time or expertise to determine where to invest freed-up funds.
- A controlled disbursement account generally is used instead of a ZBA when the organization has no master account at the disbursement bank, its affiliates, or correspondent banks—which implies that automatic transfers are not as easily accomplished.
- Organizations with tight cash positions might prefer the extra control afforded by the controlled disbursement account, which provides extra flexibility by giving early-morning notification of the day's disbursements.[22]

How many different accounts your organization decides to establish may depend on the number of different disbursement locations (which ties in to how decentralized your organization's disbursement system is) and your organization's desire to gain a modest amount of added clearance float.

(c) POSITIVE PAY.   In the case of *positive pay*, an organization sends its daily check issue file to its disbursing bank. (Its software should be able to produce this file automatically when printing the checks, and include the check's serial number, date, payee, and amount.) Before it honors incoming checks, the bank refers to the issue file to see if the payee and check amounts match up. If they do not (e.g., because a check issued later in the day was presented as an "on-us" check), the bank contacts the issuer to see whether the item should be honored. In addition to checks not in the check issue file, other occasions that lead to rejects are checks in excess of a specified dollar amount, duplicate check number items, and "stale-dated" checks (perhaps with a date of six months earlier or more). Think of positive pay as daily disbursements account reconciliation.

Conventional wisdom today is that a nonprofit should purchase positive pay service on every disbursement account that it has. Its liability for losses under the Uniform Commercial Code will be lower if it has the service. When a banker presents the service to your organization and suggests that you use it, and you decline, that fact alone could result in greater liability for your organization.

A very similar service that your organization may opt for is *reverse positive pay*. In this service, your disbursing bank transmits the check presentment file to your organization, and you have a few hours to let the bank know if all the items should be honored. (This system operates much like the way that drafts clear.) Banks offer browser-based or CD-based images so that your personnel can view the images of the front and back of the check before determining whether to honor the item. A number of leading cash management banks now use optical character recognition (OCR) to attempt to automatically match up presented checks to payee information provided as part of the initial check issue file data feed.

Phoenix-Hecht 2005 survey data documents that positive pay services are used with greater frequency by larger organizations: 88.5 percent of large companies (sales over $500 million) use positive pay, versus 43.4 percent of middle-market companies (sales from $40 million to $100 million). Perhaps this is due to the pricing of positive pay services: Phoenix-Hecht pricing data shows a list price of $76.20 per month (although 39.6 percent of the time this was discounted to the customer, with the discount amount being 33.8 percent, on average), along with a $0.21 per-check charge.[23] In its 2006 survey of businesses, the main reasons unearthed by Phoenix-Hecht for not using positive pay were low risk of check fraud in their business, cost (pricing), and service complexity.[24]

One weakness of first-generation positive pay services is that they could not stop payee discrepancies. Newer-generation positive pay services offer the ability to also review the Payee name on the "Pay to the Order Of" or "Payable to" portion of commercial checks. For example, KeyBank offers this service as "Payee Positive Pay." The bank compares the payee name versus the issue file that your organization submitted earlier and reports exceptions back to you in its same-day and next-day reports. Regard positive pay and other fraud prevention and detection services to be tools in your overall internal control strategy. Appendix 4B provides some of the best internal control advice available, and has been compiled by PriceWaterhouseCoopers, a preeminent accounting and auditing firm.

(d) EDI AND FEDI.   Both electronic data interchange and financial electronic data interchange offer substantial speed and accuracy advantages to the purchase-to-pay cycle.

(i) Electronic Data Interchange.   Opportunities for electronic payments are improving because more businesses, educational, and healthcare organizations are using EDI. *Electronic data interchange* (EDI) is "the electronic transmission of purchase-related data such as orders, shipping notices, invoices, credits and other adjustments, and payment notices, in standardized computer-readable format."[25] Organizations began using EDI for electronic purchase orders, then began sending invoices and shipping receipts electronically.

(ii) Financial Electronic Data Interchange.   An increasing number of companies are adopting *financial EDI*, which adds electronic disbursing using an ACH transfer to the process, but already some of this usage is migrating over to Internet transaction initiation. An estimate of the total cost to payer and payee of handling the paper documents exchange and making a single payment by check is $8.33 per payment, as compared with $3 for the handling of the same transaction using financial EDI.

Many midsize companies use the Internet instead of EDI to circumvent the message formatting and cost of EDI; Greenwich survey data indicates that 35 percent of midsize companies now initiate payments over the Internet, and the Phoenix-Hecht survey data is supportive of this trend. Electronic mail and facsimile (fax) transmissions are not considered EDIs, because they are not in structured form nor are they computer-readable.

Healthcare organizations are ahead of the curve in the nonprofit world because of Health Insurance Portability and Accountability Act (HIPAA) regulations with regard to electronic transactions. This legislation stipulated that healthcare organizations, payers, and insurers that utilize any electronic means of storing patient data and perform claims submission (including faxes) must comply with the standards contained within the "Final Rule" on electronic transactions. That rule mandates that providers, payers, and insurers send enrollments, eligibility and claims processing via EDI transactions.

(iii) Evaluated Receipt Settlement.   In a purchasing scenario involving product delivery with follow-on repeat orders, companies and a handful of nonprofits are paying using a process called *evaluated receipt settlement* (ERS). The purchaser triggers payment on receipt of goods, as opposed to the norm of awaiting invoice arrival and doing a match to purchase order and shipping receipt before releasing payment. In ERS, invoices are eliminated, and payment terms and price are determined in advance. The purchasing organization scans bar codes on merchandise packaging when receiving the shipment at the loading area. The capture of the bar code is then transmitted to the accounts payable area to initiate payment. Evaluated receipt settlement is often used in conjunction with EDI but might also be used as a separate process.

As payables management becomes more automated, EDI and financial EDI or the Internet replacement for either of these will be more commonly used.

(iv) Importance of Treasury Workstation or Bank Information System.   Online banking products are indispensable to the proper management and execution of your disbursement system. You need the capabilities of these bank portals, including access to account balances on a timely basis (you should know first thing in the morning the closing activity totals from the previous evening; many organizations now want same-day account balance information and same-day transaction details), access to check images (front and back), and other data that will help you to monitor and forecast your cash position. Furthermore, organizations now insist on the ability to initiate stop payments, wire transfers, ACH transactions, and (to a lesser degree) even investment transactions via the Internet.[26] The anytime, anywhere access afforded by the Internet is a key component of your oversight capability. Recall from Chapter 1 that your primary financial objective is maintaining a target liquidity level. You cannot manage what you cannot measure, and the web-based products available today are the key tools for maintaining oversight and control. Large organizations find it cost-effective to invest the $100,000

plus in both a full-scale treasury workstation and an enterprise resource planning (ERP) system. We return to this topic in Chapter 5.

(v) Shopping for Your Organization's Disbursement Bank(s). The primary tools for shopping for your disbursement banks are (1) networking, (2) an RFI, and (3) and RFP. Networking with organizations similar to your own is instrumental in finding out which banks are best for nonprofits in your market. A request for information (RFI) is a preliminary document you send to prospective banks to see what they might be able to offer your organization. Once you get the responses to the RFI back and study through them, you then send out a formal request for proposal (RFP; some call it a request for bid) to the short list of candidate banks. See Exhibit 4.12 for a checklist of information to include in your RFP for disbursement services. In Chapter 5 we go into more detail on banking relationship management.

4.9 FRAUD PREVENTION AND INTERNAL CONTROL

Much greater attention is being given to payables security and fraud prevention by nonprofits and businesses. Check fraud has grown explosively in recent years, with FBI estimates for the United States at about $12 billion. Banks absorb only about $1 billion of the loss, with the rest being incurred by businesses and nonprofits.

(a) INCIDENCE AND SEVERITY OF FRAUD. Survey results from the AFP's survey of fraud incidence and preventive measures are worth quoting at length to give you a better grasp of the extent of the problem:

- Fifty-five percent of survey respondents indicate that their organization was a victim of payments fraud in 2004.
    - Nearly three-quarters of organizations with annual revenues greater than $1 billion experienced fraud compared to 37 percent of smaller organizations.
    - For organizations that were victims of payments fraud in 2004, the median dollar amount of the fraud was $26,600.
- Checks are the most likely vehicle for payments fraud.
    - Among organizations that were subject to payments fraud in 2004, 94 percent indicate that they were victims of check fraud.
    - Thirty-four percent indicate that they were the victims of ACH debit fraud.
- Organizations use a variety of internal and bank-provided services to guard against payments fraud.
    - Virtually all organizations separate disbursement and reconciliation duties and use security features on their check stock.

I. Information Reporting

    A. What are the reporting times for clearing totals?

    B. Are reported amounts final?

    C. What funding alternatives are available?

    D. How soon after a check has been paid can an image of the item be reviewed via the Internet?

II. Fraud Prevention

    A. Describe how the bank's positive pay process works.

    B. Are minor encoding errors corrected by the bank or reported as positive pay suspect items?

    C. Payee verification options. Is a "payee positive pay" option available? If so, describe how it works.

    D. Will the "payee's" portion of the positive pay work if the check is converted to an image by the bank of first deposit or cleared using an Image Replacement Document (IRD)?

III. Cost

    A. Provide a complete pro forma account analysis statement reflecting all of the services requested at the volumes indicated.

    B. Over the last three years how much have prices for the services requested increased?

IV. Operational

    A. What alternatives are available for storage and retrieval of paid checks?

    B. Would you provide an analysis to compare the float results of our current bank to the site you are proposing?

    C. Provide the Phoenix-Hecht Clearing Study™ results for the disbursement site(s) being offered.

    D. Provide the bank's current Phoenix-Hecht Quality Index™ grades for all questions.

    E. Provide examples of the "full reconcilement reports" for a positive pay account.

    F. If an IRD or an image presentment is received rather than the original check, what changes are triggered in the positive pay, balance reporting, account reconcilement, and "check" archiving?

Source: Phoenix-Hecht, "The Check Book—Defining Disbursement Decisions: A Practical Guide," (January 2005), pp. 8–9. Used by permission.

EXHIBIT 4.12 ITEMS TO INCLUDE IN YOUR DISBURSEMENTS BANK RFP

- o Eighty-eight percent of organizations use positive pay or reverse positive pay.
- o Seventy-one percent of organizations use ACH debit blocks.
- o ACH debit filters are used by slightly over half of respondents.

- Seventy-nine percent of organizations indicate that they stopped at least one incident of payments fraud in 2004.

  - o Ninety-one percent of larger organizations report that they stopped at least one incident of payments fraud compared to 67 percent of smaller organizations.

- Respondents consider the use of electronic payments—specifically ACH payments—to have a significant impact on their organization's exposure to fraud.

    ○   Increasing use of ACH credits to make payments is expected to reduce fraud exposure.

    ○   Increasing permission for ACH debits to its accounts to make payments is expected to increase an organization's exposure to fraud.[27]

In contested cases of fraud, corporations typically end up being liable for the loss. Consultant Larry Marks of Marks & Associates figures that not including any losses for fraudulent checks, the cost to an organization for one occurrence of check fraud is most likely from $4,000 to $5,000.[28] This includes reconciliation time, correction (stop payment, possibly reissue), managerial time, as well as any incidental costs. If the organization decides to contest the bank's dishonoring of the check and this means getting (internal or external) legal counsel, the cost rises to about $12,000 to $15,000 per occurrence. Marks warns that the most common occurrence of check fraud is with payroll checks.

The first step for any organization regarding fraud prevention is to craft an internal control strategy. Excellent advice to guide you is found in Appendix 4B, which contains internal control guidelines compiled by PriceWaterhouseCoopers.

(b) PREVENTIVE MEASURES.   Some of the steps organizations are taking to prevent or limit fraud include positive pay or reverse positive pay services, internal controls (including bonding employees), and greater use of ACH payments and financial EDI. Since we address positive pay and EDI elsewhere in this chapter, we will address only internal controls and ACH payment fraud here.

(i) Internal Controls.   According to audit firm PriceWaterhouseCoopers, your organization's disbursements internal controls have as their objective "to ensure that cash is disbursed only upon proper authorization of management, for valid business purposes, and that all disbursements are properly recorded."[29]

Bonding (buying a fidelity bond is essentially an insurance policy against embezzlement), positive pay, and direct deposit services help deal with the *symptoms* of integrity and fraud issues. However, ethics consultants recommend that you hire employees committed to integrity as the crucial step in *prevention*.

Basic internal controls include:

- Special check stock (e.g., checks that have the word VOID showing diagonally across them when photocopied)
- Restrictions on who may access check stock and the ease with which that stock may be accessed (or use of laser-printed checks)
- Restrictions on the checks issued file

We provide two more thorough checklists for you to use: One specific to payments appears as Exhibit 4.13 and a more general internal controls checklist is provided as Exhibit 4.14.

Businesses tend to be geared more toward improving internal controls than nonprofits due to the documentation requirements brought about by the

Internal Measures in Place to Guard Against Check, ACH, and Wire Fraud
(Percentage of Respondents)

	Total (%)	Under $1 billion Sales (%)	Over $1 Billion Sales (%)
Separation of disbursement and reconciliation duties	94	95	94
Security features on check stock	91	91	92
Dual security administrators for electronic payments systems	69	61	76
Controlled access to payment processing areas	68	65	70
Daily reconciliation of electronic payment accounts	63	60	66
Daily reconciliation of checking accounts	47	44	50
Separate accounts for check and electronic payments	46	39	51
Replacement of employee pay checks with electronic pay (direct deposit or payroll cards)	45	44	46
"Post No Checks" restriction on electronic payment accounts	22	10	33
Separate accounts for ACH debits and ACH credits	11	9	14
Other	17	13	10

Source: Association for Financial Professionals, "Payments Fraud and Control Survey: Report of Survey Results," March 2005, p. 6. Used by permission.

EXHIBIT 4.13 INTERNAL MEASURES USED TO COMBAT PAYMENT FRAUD

Sarbanes-Oxley Act in 2002, as implemented in 2004. (A 2003 Treasury Strategies survey found that 80 percent of survey respondents were already at that time reviewing controls on treasury-related activities as well as documenting controls and Treasury procedures.)[30] Most banks will not enroll a new controlled disbursement account customer without a positive pay or reverse positive pay agreement.

(ii) ACH Disbursing.   Finally, numerous nonprofits and companies are moving toward ACH payments as a way of reducing the number of checks they issue—but this is triggering new concerns about unauthorized ACH debits when debits are used rather than credits for the trade payments. A Chicago Clearing House study determined that almost 40 percent of large corporations have had unauthorized ACH debits to their accounts, and even some checks returned as part of positive pay services have been converted to ACH debits and successfully charged to the account, although daily reconciliations will catch these and allow for ACH returns (which must be made available to the ODFI by the opening of business on the second banking day following the original entry's settlement date),

The following questions reflect common internal accounting controls related to paying bills. You may wish to use this list to review your own internal accounting controls and determine which areas require further action.

- Are all disbursements, except those from petty cash, made by prenumbered checks?
- Are voided checks preserved and filed after appropriate mutilation?
- Is there a written prohibition against drawing checks payable to Cash?
- Is there a written prohibition against signing checks in advance?
- Is a cash disbursement voucher prepared for each invoice or request for reimbursement that details the date of check, check number, payee, amount of check, description of expense account (and restricted fund) to be charged, authorization signature, and accompanying receipts?
- Are all expenditures approved in advance by authorized persons?
- Are signed checks mailed promptly?
- Does the check signer review the cash disbursement voucher for the proper approved authorization and supporting documentation of expenses?
- Are invoices marked Paid with the date and amount of the check?
- Are requests for reimbursement and other invoices checked for mathematical accuracy and reasonableness before approval?
- Is a cash disbursement journal prepared monthly that details the date of check, check number, payee, amount of check, and columnar description of expense account (and restricted fund) to be charged?
- Is check-signing authority vested in persons at appropriately high levels in the organization?
- Are the number of authorized signatures limited to the minimum practical number?
- Do larger checks require two signatures?
- Are bank statements and canceled checks received and reconciled by a person independent of the authorization and check signing function?
- Are unpaid invoices maintained in an unpaid invoice file?
- Is a list of unpaid invoices regularly prepared and periodically reviewed?
- Are invoices from unfamiliar or unusual vendors reviewed and approved for payment by authorized personnel who are independent of the invoice processing function?
- If the organization keeps an accounts payable register, are payments promptly recorded in the register to avoid double payment?
- If purchase orders are used, are all purchase transactions used with prenumbered purchase orders?
- Are advance payments to vendors and/or employees recorded as receivables and controlled in a manner which assures that they will be offset against invoices or expense vouchers?
- Are employees required to submit expense reports for all travel related expenses on a timely basis?

Source: Alliance for Nonprofit Management, "Frequently Asked Questions." www.alliance-online.org/FAQ/financial_management/what_internal_controls.faq. Used by permission.

EXHIBIT 4.14   CHECKLIST FOR EVALUATING ORGANIZATION'S INTERNAL CONTROLS

and organizations can use debit blocks or debit filters to thwart these attempts. A relatively new service, ACH Positive Pay, allows businesses and nonprofits to monitor and control ACH transactions more closely. It is often delivered through the bank's Internet portal. For example, Comerica Bank (Detroit) offers this service, which allows it to (1) report all ACH items, (2) give the organization the decision over which type of ACH transactions it wishes to monitor and review, and (3) have the transactions the first thing in the morning to approve or dis-approve before posting. The organization's treasury personnel or payables staff may then identify any unauthorized ACH activity, enabling the bank to return those items before they are posted to the organization's account.

4.10 INTERNATIONAL CASH DISBURSEMENTS

If your organization is making disbursements outside the United States, it will have to become aware of some important payment system differences, the additional risks involved, and some techniques for handling intraorganization funds flows. We discuss the first two issues here.

(a) **PAYMENT SYSTEM DIFFERENCES.**   One key difference in disbursement systems outside the United States is the availability of interest-bearing demand deposit accounts, typically with an automatic overdraft provision. Think of it as NOW accounts with no worries about overdrafting your account. These accounts make the minimization of disbursement account balances and control of those balances much less essential. Unsurprisingly, controlled disbursement accounts are pretty rare outside the United States. We offer one caution: Your deposit account interest rate may be relatively low, especially compared to the interest rate *charged* when the account is overdrafted.

A second difference you will find abroad is that a check's disbursement float depends heavily on what currency the check is denominated in as well as from where it is mailed. Checks must clear back to the country of the currency in which the check is denominated because there is no centralized settlement bank in most countries. If CARE's German unit sends a dollar-denominated check to a French supplier, the check must clear back to the U.S. bank on which it is written, even if the U.S. bank has a European branch. The clearing time could well exceed a week in such a case. Furthermore, when a European customer sends a euro-denominated check to a multinational organization in the United States, the mail time from a European city to New York City might also exceed a week. But *within* a given country, check clearing is typically quite rapid because both the geographic area most countries occupy and the number of banks within most foreign countries are smaller.

Third, you should be aware that there are two payment mechanisms that are much more prominent in foreign countries. The *giro system* of directly debiting consumers' accounts is popular in European countries, many of which use postal system clearing of many payments. This and other direct debit systems are very common abroad. We also note a much greater use of drafts (sight drafts and time drafts) in international purchases. Both of these mechanisms mean that you will have less discretion over disbursement float but also that having float available will be less important to you. *Value dating*, a European practice in which debits of your checking account may be back-valued to the date on which checks were issued, may further reduce your disbursement float.

(b) GUIDELINES FOR MAKING INTERNATIONAL PAYMENTS. Disbursement systems outside your organization's home country can be difficult to navigate. Here are six guidelines:

1. When your organization begins making payments internationally, look for a financial service provider that has global knowledge and international capabilities. It is often more efficient to initiate a new relationship with an international payments bank that has operations in the countries in which you anticipate doing business. This is so because using foreign currency checks for small-value payments and wire transfers through a correspondent banking network for high-value payments must pass through several banks, increasing expense and reducing speed. Furthermore, the global bank may be able to facilitate payables outsourcing as payment volumes grow.

2. Understand the payment mechanisms and the preferred payment method in each country where you have dealings. Just because a payment mechanism is available in your country does not mean it will be in every country abroad. In Germany, checks account for less than 8 percent of all payments made, both retail and wholesale, and in the Scandinavian countries, less than 1 percent of payments are by check. Banks can help in this assessment, or you can go to Web sites such as that offered by the Bank of International Settlements to get this information.

3. Seek alternative ways of providing detailed remittance information. Using in-country local banks for local currency and cross-border payments within a region provides access to less expensive, local clearing systems, but at the price of an inability to move remittance data with the payment through banks and the local clearing systems. The remittance advices may be mailed separately or conveyed via the Internet, or use a provider that automatically produces and mails this detail for you.

4. Centralize your accounts payable and consider outsourcing options for all of your payments within a region. Consider establishing a regional headquarters to centralize and control payables. Some organizations outsource payments through a shared service centrally managed by a regional network bank that operates in the same countries as the organization. The bank essentially acts as the organization's regional central hub for funds disbursement.

5. Automate your payables function. Functions may be duplicated at various local sites. One company doing a treasury review found out that its decentralized disbursement process involved more than 800 locations issuing disbursement checks, and was able to both reduce risk and cut $400,000 in administrative costs annually. When centralizing payments at a regional headquarters, efficiency is gained but the complexity of making payments in many different payment systems within central bank reporting requirements can be overwhelming. The solution is to automate payments, possibly by having a bank accept a single electronic file of both electronic

and check disbursements in one format, which is then reformatted into the various formats required by countries' clearing systems. Or the organization can use industry-standard formats or common EDI message standards for payment instructions.

6. Work toward creating a "global payments factory." A "supercenter" may be able to handle an organization's payments regardless of their destination worldwide in the not-too-distant future. Several regional centers can be tied together as part of the organization's ERP system. A bank with global payments capability and linkages to all major local clearing systems can pave the way for making the necessary country-by-country modifications of payment instructions.[31]

We close out our international disbursement section by mentioning some risks you will face when dealing abroad.

(c) INTERNATIONAL DISBURSING RISKS.   Two risks that must be monitored and managed in your organization's international disbursements are country risk and foreign exchange risk:[32]

- *Country risk* refers to the possibility of loss of assets resulting from political, economic, or regulatory instability in the nation in which operations are being conducted. Studies of country risk are usually conducted by banks or specialized consultants.
- *Foreign exchange risk* is the possibility that exchange rates will move adversely, causing results of foreign organizational activities to have a reduced value when converted into the organization's home currency. Various strategies are used to manage this risk. A simple strategy is to expedite outgoing disbursements when it is feared that a local currency will weaken (drop in value) against the dollar. The Brazilian division anticipating paying its U.S.-based parent will accelerate the disbursement if a depreciation of the cruzeiro is expected. It is hoped that this payment will be made before the depreciation occurs; if not, less dollars will be received on exchange.

4.11 IMAGING

A separate trend that may use Internet delivery and facilitate positive pay is *check imaging*. We have addressed this topic in Chapter 3 and earlier in this chapter, but it has become so important in cash management that we want to recap some of the issues regarding disbursements here.

Phoenix-Hecht survey data indicates that uses of imaging technology perceived to be the most important for businesses are for (1) long-term storage of paid items and (2) immediate retrieval of recently paid items, followed by (3) online approval of positive pay items. All three services are rated slightly more important for larger organizations than midsize ones. (Imaging is also used on the collection side, with imaging of return documents and checks slightly more important than imaging for long-term storage of paid items.)

4.12 OUTSOURCING DISBURSEMENTS OR PAYABLES

Outsourcing, or contracting with outside companies to do certain business functions, is mainly cost-motivated, but also springs from a desire by organizations to focus on their core competencies—and purchasing/payables processes are not part of those core competencies.

Comprehensive payables, also called integrated payables, involves the outsourcing of part of or all of the accounts payable and/or disbursements functions. Some organizations outsource payments; others outsource almost the entire payables function.

For example, KeyBank, a superregional bank headquartered in Cleveland, offers a "consolidated payables" service in which it receives from the organization a daily payables file in an agreed-on format, then creates paper checks or ACH, EDI, or wire payments for the organization. Remittance information can be delivered with the payment or transmitted directly to the payee via a third-party company. Advance notification may be provided to the payees. From the organization's perspective, this service may reduce the internal and external payables costs while streamlining or enhancing the organization's payables system. For example, Thrift Drug estimates that it saves $7,000 per month by having a bank handle its pharmacy payments instead of having its own employees process the payments internally. An organization may outsource more of the payables function by providing to its banks more extensive payables information, starting as early in the payment process as the original purchase order initiation. Some organizations transmit trade payables, employee reimbursement, and employee benefit payment information. The data are provided to the bank, which develops a database of the organization's payees, preferred payment methods, transit routing numbers of payees' banks, and other remittance information. The database is periodically updated with new payees or changes to existing payee profiles.

One bank employed four selling points for comprehensive payables, all from the perspective of the paying organization:

1. Increased accuracy—from eliminating paper documents and manual data entry
2. Improved cash-flow management—from using EDI and financial EDI and the certain payment timing that results from the reliable settlement of these transactions
3. Reduced administrative costs—from computer-to-computer exchange of data instead of human processing and reprocessing
4. Proactive control—since payables transmitted in EDI format include control totals, or if payables are not in EDI format, the organization faxes,

mails, or e-mails control totals to the bank, assuring file accuracy and improving the audit trail

Greenwich survey data indicates that 15 percent of companies having $500 million or more in sales are using payables outsourcing. With the renewed concern with check fraud related to Check 21 procedures, moving the liability to a third party is a great selling point for outsourcing.

One of the primary considerations for organizations contemplating outsourcing much or all of their payables function is to anticipate what strategic objectives might be pursued in the outsourcing decision, possibly including:

- Greater predictability of cash outflows
- Use of technology to create efficiencies and allow staff to redirect attention to more strategic duties
- Minimization of risk and cost
- Contingency processing and disaster recovery capabilities

These factors seem to favor outsourcing payables. But a complete analysis requires a comparison of the costs and benefits of the organization's existing internal payment process with those of the prospective bank partner's comprehensive payables service, all relative to the strategic business objectives. There are some readily apparent items, such as paper stock, postage, and printers, but also less obvious items, such as the staff required to initiate and possibly deliver payments as well as the potential risk and the cost of fraud. Another key consideration is the possibility of improved relationships with a seller or agency that could result from better meeting the other party's changing requirements and demands. All relevant issues, both quantitative and qualitative, must be evaluated in terms of the potential benefits related to cost/net revenue, cash flow, client service, or risk exposure. Conversion costs and/or sunk costs of investments in printers, real estate, or personnel may seem to outstrip the potential benefits—and this may present a roadblock impeding change. However, when looking out to a longer time horizon and within a broader context, the conversion may be seen as worthwhile.

In Chapter 5 we integrate our discussion in Chapter 3 on cash collection and positioning and our discussion in this chapter on disbursements with the managerial considerations in dealing with the parties responsible for providing many of the services we have discussed: your banks. We present usable ideas for selecting, managing, and compensating your banks.

4.13 SUMMARY

In this chapter we have demonstrated how disbursements systems work, the key products and services available for managing disbursements, detailed descriptions of fraud detection and prevention methods, some aspects of global disbursing systems, and basic coverage of the electronic disbursement methods that more and more organizations are utilizing.

Reconsider briefly your organization's primary financial objective of ensuring that financial resources are available when needed (timing), as needed (amount), and at reasonable cost (cost-effectiveness), and that once mobilized, these resources are protected from impairment and spent according to mission and donor purposes. First, note that funding payroll and payables addresses the "as needed" part of this objective. Second, evaluating the cost of your disbursements system relative to what it accomplishes for your organization points to the "reasonable cost" and cost-effectiveness subgoals. A portion of the target liquidity level that you establish for your organization is there to fund ongoing disbursements, and another portion is there to meet unexpected disbursements—such as when a collaborative venture or grant funding require immediate payments.

Appendix 4A will assist you in evaluating the cost structure of disbursement and other cash management products and services. Your internal control decision-making will be aided by a careful study of the internal control framework detailed in Appendix 4B.

We have gained a perspective on cash collections, cash positioning, and cash disbursements. In Chapter 5 we revisit these topics briefly as we find ways to effectively negotiate for banking services and manage the banking relationship.

Notes

1. Goals in Accounts Payable, 2002. Downloaded from www.recapinc.com/eap_survey_goals.htm. Accessed 9/27/06.
2. This definition is based on Terry S. Maness and John T. Zietlow, *Short-Term Financial Management,* 3rd ed. (Cincinnati: South-Western, 2005), p. 373. Our portrayal of the disbursement systems and techniques in this chapter follows the presentation in that source, and you may wish to consult it for further details and guidance.
3. Id., p. 376.
4. These principles are taken from Id., Chapter 12.
5. The breakdown was Health Net 11.2 days, UnitedHealth 3.7 days, Humana 13.2 days, Triad Hospitals 15.2 days, Tenet Healthcare 3.8 days, and Omnicare 27.6 days. Hackett-REL 2006 Working Capital Survey. Randy Myers, "How Low Can It Go?" *CFO*, September 1, 2006. Downloaded from www.cfo.com/media/pdf/TWC_survey_tables_CFOcom_091306.pdf. Accessed: 2/21/07.
6. www.recapinc.com/eap_survey_check.htm. Accessed: 9/27/06.
7. Phoenix-Hecht, *The Check Book—Defining Disbursement Decisions: A Practical Guide*, January 2005, p. 2.
8. The Clearing House, "The Remaining Barriers to ePayments and Straight-through Processing: Research Conducted October 2001–March 2002 by The Clearing House," p. 7.
9. This does not apply to business checks that have an entry in the "auxiliary on-us" field in the MICR line of the check, such as the entry to pinpoints which division

of the organization issued the check. For more specifics on this rule change, see: www.electronicpayments.org/pdfs/What_It_Means.pdf.

10. "Transformation of Treasury and Payments: Will You Survive?" Report of the AFP Payments Advisory Group, Association for Financial Professionals 24th Annual Conference, November 3, 2003 (Session # 25): 7. Downloaded from http://www.afponline.org/mbr/reg/pdf/transform_treasury_faq.pdf. Accessed: 9/27/2006.

11. Maness and Zietlow, *Short-Term Financial Management*, p. 386.

12. "NACHA Reports Nearly 14 Billion ACH Payments in 2005," May 8, 2006. Downloaded from: www.nacha.org/news/default.htm. Accessed: 9/30/2006.

13. For more on this rapidly growing system, see www.eurogiro.com. At the time of this writing, there is an excellent introduction to Eurogiro A/S at http://www.eurogiro.com/Public-docs/General_information/System_Introduction_March06.pdf.

14. Id.

15. Beth Robertson, "Electronic Invoicing and Payment: Evolution to a New Channel," *Commercial Lending Review* 17 (July 2002): 28–33.

16. This section draws on Maness and Zietlow, *Short-Term Financial Management*.

17. Maness and Zietlow, *Short-Term Financial Management*, p. 380.

18. Technically, this is not an overnight investment; it is a 24-hour investment made the next business day based on today's closing account balance. If a charge such as for ACH debits are presented against the account the next morning, many banks will not charge for an intraday overdraft, because the banks recognize that the necessary funds should be coming into the account at the close of the day. Essentially, they look at the intraday account balance as: Intraday account balance = (Collected balances + Incoming sweep funds).

19. Maness and Zietlow, *Short-Term Financial Management*, p. 381.

20. This section draws on Maness and Zietlow, *Short-Term Financial Management*.

21. Phoenix-Hecht, "2006 Cash Management Monitor," 2006.

22. Adapted from Maness and Zietlow, *Short-Term Financial Management*, p. 384. Used by permission.

23. Phoenix-Hecht, "2006–2007 Blue Book of Bank Prices: Executive Summary," 2007.

24. Phoenix-Hecht, "2006 Cash Management Monitor," 2006, p. 17.

25. Maness and Zietlow, *Short-Term Financial Management*, p. 388.

26. Phoenix-Hecht, "2006 Cash Management Monitor," p. 14.

27. Association for Financial Professionals, "Payments Fraud and Control Survey: Report of Survey Results" (Bethesda, MD: Author, March 2005): 2.

28. Quoted in John Zietlow, "8 Principles to Practical Finance: What Businesses and Not-for-Profit Managers Should Know," *AFP Exchange* (September/October 2003): 18–23.

29. Alliance for Nonprofit Management, www.allianceonline.org/FAQ/financial_management/what_internal_controls.faq. Accessed on: 10/2/2006.

30. Treasury Strategies, Inc., "The 2003 Corporate Treasury Survey," 2003, p. 9.

31. Adapted from Michael Burn, "Making International Payments—Navigating the Course," *AFP Exchange* (Winter 2000): 62–64. Used by permission.

32. These two definitions are from Maness and Zietlow, *Short-Term Financial Management*, p. 393.

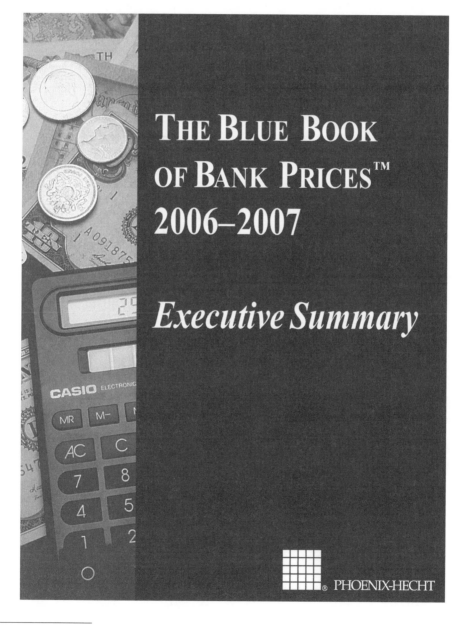

APPENDIX 4A

Prices for Bank Services[*]

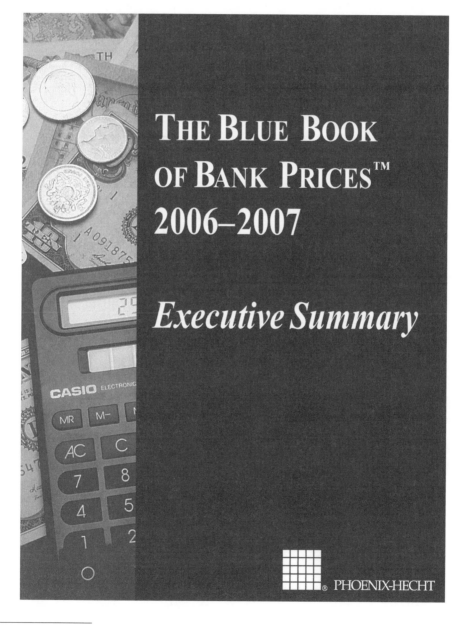

THE BLUE BOOK
OF BANK PRICES™
2006–2007

Executive Summary

PHOENIX-HECHT

2006–2007 Phoenix-Hecht Blue Book of Bank Prices™

EXECUTIVE SUMMARY

This nineteenth edition of *The Blue Book of Bank Prices™* summarizes the annual Phoenix-Hecht survey of actual prices paid for treasury management services. Over 800 companies, each with annual sales exceeding $100 million, supplied pricing data by providing account analysis statements from March 2006. Data was collected for 82 services.

List Price Increases Hold Steady With Previous Year – third year under 3%

The rate of increase for list price, the price banks would like to charge for a given service, held steady for 2006 at 2.7%. This marks the third year list price increases have been under three percent, matching a trend that last occurred 1992 – 1994. The CPI at the end of 2005 was 3.4%, a mere 0.1% increase from 2004's ending 3.3%. Historically, the previous year's Consumer Price Index has served as an excellent predictor of the rate of increase for list price. List price increases for a given year have significantly exceeded the previous year's CPI only in 2002 and 2003. For the second straight year list price increases were fractionally below the previous year ending CPI.

List Price Increase Versus Previous Year CPI Increase
— List Price Increase   —○— CPI Increase

Of the eighty services for which list price increase could be calculated, 4% had a very minor decrease, 27% had no change in list price, 32% had a modest increase (at CPI or less), 14% had a substantial increase (above CPI but below 5%), and 23% had an aggressive increase (above 5%). Thus nearly two-thirds of services (63%) increased at CPI or less. The significant set of services (more than one quarter) with no list price increase at all continues to retard the overall level of list price increases.

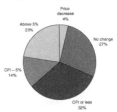

Distribution of List Price Increases

Three services had very slight decreases in average list price for 2006. All of these were electronic services with two being ACH services and one being an automated internal wire transfer.

List Price Decreases 2005-2006 (1-Year)

ACH Debit Internet Originated	(1.1)%
ACH Maintenance	(0.8)%
Internal Automated Wire Transfer	(0.4)%

Twenty-two services (27.5%) had absolutely no change in list price for 2006. Six of these services were in ACH and six were in lockbox. Last year was the first year that transmission services were analyzed in the Blue Book, and this year five of these services had no change in average list price.

No List Price Increases 2005-2006 (1-Year)

Debit Posting
ZBA Transfer
Retail Lockbox Maintenance
Lockbox Check Image Processing
Lockbox Data Capture
Lockbox Transmission Maintenance
Lockbox Data Transmission Item
Lockbox Transmission Per Transmission
Vault Issued Currency Strap
Deposit Reconciliation Maintenance
Controlled Disbursement Notification
Account Recon Input Transmission Item
Account Recon Output Transmission Item
Internet ACH General Maintenance
ACH Credit Internet Originated
ACH Debit Received
ACH Credit Received
ACH Concentration Maintenance
ACH Concentration Item
EDI Receiving
Intraday Balance Reporting
Balance Reporting - Non-specific

Twenty-two services have also averaged under a two percent per year increase since 2003. Three services have had no list price increase during the three-year period. ACH and Balance Reporting services are prominent on this list.

EXECUTIVE SUMMARY

Lowest List Price Increases 2003-2006 (3-Year)

Debit Posting	0.0%
Retail Lockbox Maintenance	0.0%
Controlled Disbursement Notification	0.0%
Intraday Reporting Transaction	1.6%
Retail Lockbox Item	2.1%
ACH Maintenance	2.3%
ACH Concentration Maintenance	2.5%
Balance Reporting - Non-specific	2.7%
ACH Credit Originated	3.1%
Lockbox Data Capture	3.1%
ACH Concentration Item	3.3%
Check Image Maintenance	3.4%
Previous Day Balance Reporting	3.5%
Intraday Balance Reporting	3.7%
Positive Pay Checks Paid	4.6%
ACH Tax Payment	4.9%
Controlled Disbursement Maintenance	5.0%
Manual Non-repetitive Wire	5.0%
Deposit Reconciliation Item	5.4%
ACH Debit Originated	5.4%
Checks Deposited - On Us	5.8%
Full Reconciliation Maintenance	5.9%

Eighteen services (22.5%) posted average list price increases above 5% this year. In somewhat of a surprise, Automated Repetitive Wire led all services with an increase just under 12%. Among expected services in this category would fall Manual Stop Payment, Coin and Currency services, Ledger Overdraft Fee, Manual Repetitive Wire, Check Sorting (to encourage truncated statements), Partial Reconciliation Item (to encourage full and positive pay). Interesting services on this list include Check Image Capture, Account Recon Input Transmission (many other transmission services had no increase), Deposits and Checks Deposited – Transit (offset temporary increases in costs as the industry transitions to image presentment), and ACH Debit Originated (despite this year's substantial increase the service is among the lowest in three-year list price increases because of no list price increase the previous two years).

Top List Price Increases 2005-2006 (1-Year)

Automated Repetitive Wire	11.7%
Manual Stop Payment	10.4%
Branch Issued Currency Strap	10.3%
ZBA Master Account	8.5%
Previous Day Reporting Transaction	7.0%
Check Image Capture	6.8%
Wholesale Lockbox Photocopy	6.7%
Vault Issued Coin Rolls	6.7%
Account Recon Input Transmission Per Transmission	6.3%
Ledger Overdraft Fee	6.2%
Manual Repetitive Wire	5.9%
Deposit	5.8%
Check Sorting	5.6%
Wholesale Lockbox Item	5.4%
Checks Deposited - Transit	5.4%
ACH Debit Originated	5.4%
Deposit Reconciliation Item	5.4%
Partial Reconciliation Item	5.3%

Only seven services have averaged greater than 5% increases per year in list price since 2003. Check Sorting and Manual Stop Payment increases reflect pricing disincentives versus less costly services. Coin and Currency increases reflect concerns over decreasing units. Automated Repetitive Wire increases seem to reflect profit enhancement. Check Image increases may reflect greater pressure for cost recovery.

Top List Price Increases 2003-2006 (3-Year)

Check Sorting	27.3%
Branch Issued Coin Rolls	26.8%
Branch Issued Currency Strap	26.4%
Check Image Capture	20.7%
Automated Repetitive Wire	19.3%
Manual Stop Payment	17.1%
Deposit	15.7%

Discount Trends

While the rate of increase in prices held steady in 2006, both discount frequency and depth rose, indicating a slightly stronger buyer's market. For 2006, average discount frequency increased three percent to 43.3%. Individual service frequencies ranged from a low of 14.6% to a high of 72.5%. Average discount depth increased 2.7 percent to 36.6%, while individual services varied from a low of 4.8% to a high of 66.7%. This acceleration in discount practices further eroded the level of list price increases, already below the CPI.

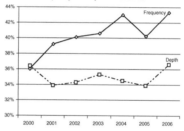

Frequency and Depth of Discounts

Frequently Discounted Services

Six services experienced substantial discount frequency, having over 60% of observations discounted. Note that tiered pricing, i.e. multiple "list" prices based upon volume processed is interpreted by *Blue Book* methodology to be discounting. There is thus some admitted bias toward higher discounting frequency within the services listed below. Account maintenance at large institutions that have undergone numerous mergers often reflects the historical pricing offered by the acquired institution. This coupled with discounting for numerous accounts explains the service's presence on this list.

Frequently Discounted Services

	Discount Frequency
Positive Pay Checks Paid	72.5%
Controlled Disbursement Checks Paid	68.6%
Retail Lockbox Item	63.3%
Account Maintenance	62.4%
ACH Credit Originated	61.9%
Credit Posting	61.6%

EXECUTIVE SUMMARY

Rarely Discounted Services

For 2006, nine services were granted discounts on fewer than 25% of observations. Although lockbox services generally receive frequent discounting, lockbox imaging, both maintenance and per check, and lockbox transmissions are rarely discounted. Otherwise, most services on this list would be expected.

Rarely Discounted Services

	Discount Frequency
Lockbox Check Image Processing	14.6%
Ledger Overdraft Fee	14.9%
ACH Concentration Maintenance	20.6%
Negative Collected Balance Rate	20.7%
ACH Tax Payment	20.7%
ACH Concentration Item	23.1%
International Incoming Wire	23.1%
Wholesale Lockbox Image Maintenance	23.2%
Lockbox Transmission Per Transmission	24.0%

Deeply Discounted Services

This year eleven services experienced a median discount percentage of at least 50%. Of those, only three exceeded a median discount of "half-off". ACH reversal and notification of change are interesting members of this list. Higher volume ACH users appear particularly sensitive to this pricing of exceptions. Interestingly, three of the eleven services are for account reconciliation transmission.

Deeply Discounted Services

	Median Discount Percentage
Account Recon Transmission Maintenance	66.7%
Previous Day Balance Reporting	55.7%
Retail Lockbox Maintenance	52.9%
Credit Posting	50.0%
Deposit Reconciliation Item	50.0%
Controlled Disbursement Notification	50.0%
Account Recon Input Transmission Item	50.0%
Account Recon Output Transmission Item	50.0%
ACH Reversal Item	50.0%
ACH Notification of Change	50.0%
Intraday Reporting Transaction	50.0%

Least Deeply Discounted Services

Only five services received a twenty percent or less median discount in 2006. Ledger Overdraft Fee and ACH Concentration Item, the two most shallowly discounted services are also on the least frequently discounted list. By contrast, wholesale lockbox items are frequently (57%), but shallowly discounted.

Least Deeply Discounted Services

	Median Discount Percentage
Account Recon Input Transmission Per Transmission	20.0%
Lockbox Transmission Per Transmission	18.4%
Wholesale Lockbox Item	17.8%
Ledger Overdraft Fee	17.4%
ACH Concentration Item	4.8%

Pricing Environment

The Phoenix-Hecht Cash Management Monitor™, a survey of corporate attitudes and quality, provides additional insight consistent with

Blue Book pricing data. In this survey of corporations with sales size of $100 million and above, the Upper-Middle Market is defined as corporations with sales from $100 – 500 million annually, and the Large Corporate Market is defined as corporations with annual sales $500 million and above.

More bank relationships are being dropped than added in these market segments. When asked what factor was most important in the decision to keep or drop a bank, corporations responded somewhat differently in 2006 than in the past, but they reiterated that competitive pricing is not a strong determinant. Quality of service has become more important relative to willingness to provide credit. In absolute terms, quality of service has become almost as important as credit availability in the large corporate market and has actually become more important in the upper-middle market. As corporations feel more comfortable in their ability to get the credit they need, they naturally shift some of their attention to the customer service supplied by their banks.

Pricing continues to be a secondary factor in determining bank selection for cash management services, well behind quality of service and credit availability. Large corporations, especially those with annual sales greater than $1 billion, pay more attention to pricing than smaller corporations and are more likely to take action based on price changes.

The Cash Management Monitor Executive Summary is available online in the publication section of PhoenixHecht.com.

Regression Analysis

The three primary factors that influence the price paid for a service are the volume purchased (most significant by far), the total monthly fees paid to the bank, and the geographic region of the customer. At the individual service level, the *Blue Book* provides the specific impact of these factors upon pricing.

Even more refined analysis of individual service pricing is available using The Pricing Calculator™, an online companion product to the *Blue Book*. The Pricing Calculator™ provides an expected range of prices for a service given the exact volume purchased, the total monthly fees paid to the provider, and the corporation's region. This price range is calculated using regression analysis performed on actual prices paid from the current *Blue Book of Bank Prices*™ publication. While the price range calculated is usually dependent upon all three of these factors, the degree of impact varies by service. The Pricing Calculator, in conjunction with the *Blue Book of Bank Prices*™, is an aid to assist corporations in benchmarking compensation for cash management services.

Conclusion

In 2004, *Blue Book* signaled the strengthening of the buyer's position in the purchase of cash management services with the return of list price increases close to CPI. 2005 suggested a further strengthening of that position with the reduction of list price increases to a rate fractionally below the CPI, albeit mitigated slightly by decreasing discount frequency. This year's *Blue Book* suggests additional leverage for the buyer as the rate of list price increase held constant below the CPI while both discount frequency and depth increased. As our Monitor research has indicated, the top four banks now command just over half the cash management revenue for companies above $100 million in annual sales. The competition for market share among these largest banks, including the next tier of large banks, certainly strengthens the position of the corporate buyer.

SERVICE PRICE SUMMARY

2006–2007 Blue Book of Bank Prices

Service Name	Average List Price	Average List Price Increase	Discount Frequency	Discount Percentage
Ledger Overdraft Fee	$38.13	6.2%	14.9%	17.4%
Account Maintenance	$34.22	4.6%	62.4%	37.1%
ZBA Master Account	$49.55	8.5%	53.4%	40.0%
ZBA Sub Account	$27.29	4.2%	55.1%	40.0%
ZBA Transfer	$0.77	0.0%	38.5%	44.9%
Credit Posting	$1.15	3.6%	61.6%	50.0%
Deposit	$1.75	5.8%	52.8%	33.3%
Checks Deposited - On Us	$0.10	1.4%	42.4%	32.9%
Checks Deposited - Transit	$0.17	5.4%	55.9%	27.3%
Return Item	$5.97	1.7%	51.8%	40.0%
Return Item Redeposit	$4.29	4.6%	47.3%	42.9%
Debit Posting	$0.43	0.0%	41.0%	40.0%
Checks Paid	$0.18	0.4%	50.1%	33.3%
Branch Issued Coin Rolls	$0.14	0.9%	52.6%	33.3%
Branch Issued Currency Strap	$0.75	10.3%	45.7%	25.0%
Vault Issued Coin Rolls	$0.12	6.7%	58.8%	48.3%
Vault Issued Currency Strap	$0.62	0.0%	34.5%	35.4%
Deposit Reconciliation Maintenance	$53.33	0.0%	26.3%	24.5%
Deposit Reconciliation Item	$0.11	5.4%	50.0%	50.0%
Wholesale Lockbox Maintenance	$127.00	2.9%	55.7%	25.5%
Wholesale Lockbox Item	$0.50	5.4%	57.3%	17.8%
Lockbox Data Capture	$0.06	0.0%	26.6%	30.0%
Lockbox Keying	$0.01	2.1%	49.5%	33.3%
Wholesale Lockbox Image Maintenance	$90.91	3.7%	23.2%	26.0%
Lockbox Check Image Processing	$0.05	0.0%	14.6%	31.7%
Lockbox Document Image Processing	$0.11	3.3%	33.5%	26.7%
Wholesale Lockbox Photocopy	$0.10	6.7%	40.4%	29.3%
Lockbox Deposit	$1.81	3.0%	46.9%	28.0%
Lockbox Transmission Maintenance	$140.00	0.0%	33.3%	33.3%
Lockbox Transmission Per Transmission	$8.40	0.0%	24.0%	18.4%
Lockbox Data Transmission Item	$0.06	0.0%	44.8%	42.9%
Retail Lockbox Maintenance	$224.38	0.0%	39.0%	52.9%
Retail Lockbox Item	$0.21	0.7%	63.3%	40.0%
Retail Lockbox Multiple Payments	$0.26		50.0%	44.5%
Controlled Disbursement Maintenance	$107.14	1.8%	58.6%	44.0%
Controlled Disbursement Checks Paid	$0.19	0.7%	68.6%	47.8%
Controlled Disbursement Notification	$65.00	0.0%	39.8%	50.0%
Positive Pay Maintenance	$76.20	0.4%	39.6%	33.8%
Positive Pay Checks Paid	$0.21	2.3%	72.5%	47.8%
Check Image Maintenance	$41.13	2.0%	39.4%	37.5%
Check Image Capture	$0.05	6.8%	52.6%	33.3%
Automated Stop Payment	$10.73	2.4%	40.7%	26.7%
Manual Stop Payment	$28.67	10.4%	44.1%	49.0%

SERVICE PRICE SUMMARY

Service Name	Average List Price	Average List Price Increase	Discount Frequency	Discount Percentage
Check Sorting	$0.07	5.6%	52.4%	40.0%
Partial Reconciliation Maintenance	$65.00	2.2%	54.3%	38.9%
Partial Reconciliation Item	$0.05	5.3%	45.1%	33.3%
Full Reconciliation Maintenance	$92.31	3.9%	57.7%	34.6%
Full Reconciliation Item	$0.06	3.5%	55.3%	38.0%
Account Recon Transmission Maintenance	$53.33	2.4%	29.0%	66.7%
Account Recon Input Transmission Per Transmission	$16.00	6.3%	34.2%	20.0%
Account Recon Input Transmission Item	$0.02	0.0%	40.8%	50.0%
Account Recon Output Transmission Per Transmission	$19.50	3.1%	30.9%	47.4%
Account Recon Output Transmission Item	$0.01	0.0%	26.3%	50.0%
ACH Maintenance	$63.85	-0.8%	48.2%	41.7%
Internet ACH General Maintenance	$41.11	0.0%	38.5%	36.0%
ACH Credit Originated	$0.14	3.6%	61.9%	45.4%
ACH Debit Originated	$0.13	5.4%	56.9%	45.0%
ACH Credit Internet Originated	$0.23	0.0%	29.5%	38.7%
ACH Debit Internet Originated	$0.24	-1.1%	39.6%	40.0%
ACH Credit Received	$0.22	0.0%	33.9%	34.7%
ACH Debit Received	$0.21	0.0%	41.5%	28.0%
ACH Return Item	$4.18	1.8%	45.6%	40.0%
ACH Notification of Change	$3.05	3.6%	44.0%	50.0%
ACH Reversal Item	$16.19	2.8%	34.0%	50.0%
ACH Concentration Maintenance	$65.83	0.0%	20.6%	21.0%
ACH Concentration Item	$0.21	0.0%	23.1%	4.8%
ACH Tax Payment	$4.39	4.0%	20.7%	33.3%
EDI Receiving	$0.40	0.0%	27.3%	25.0%
Incoming Wire	$9.12	2.7%	58.9%	30.0%
Automated Non-repetitive Wire	$8.41	2.8%	53.6%	28.3%
Automated Repetitive Wire	$8.75	11.7%	46.2%	28.1%
Manual Non-repetitive Wire	$21.00	2.2%	41.7%	41.2%
Manual Repetitive Wire	$15.50	5.9%	30.8%	33.3%
Internal Automated Wire Transfer	$5.14	-0.4%	47.6%	36.8%
International Incoming Wire	$13.13	2.6%	23.1%	23.6%
International Outgoing Wire	$22.14	4.7%	41.1%	28.6%
Previous Day Balance Reporting	$65.00	1.4%	55.0%	55.7%
Previous Day Reporting Transaction	$0.15	7.0%	55.1%	40.0%
Intraday Balance Reporting	$69.00	0.0%	55.4%	46.7%
Intraday Reporting Transaction	$0.23	0.9%	50.4%	50.0%
Balance Reporting - Non-specific	$78.75	0.0%	28.2%	22.2%

PHOENIX-HECHT

68 T.W. Alexander Drive, P.O. Box 13628, Research Triangle Park, NC 27709-3628
(919) 541-9339 • Fax (919) 541-9026 • www.phoenixhecht.com

Enhancing Internal Controls*

HOW TO ENHANCE INTERNAL CONTROLS

An institution's size affects how it assesses and enhances its internal controls. For example, smaller institutions, such as liberal arts colleges, generally have fewer officers and staff members, making an appropriate segregation of duties more of a challenge. Although control activities are likely to be informal at smaller institutions, the direct involvement of senior management often compensates for the informality.

Other factors also determine the level of effort required to assess and enhance internal controls. One is whether or not an institution's policies and procedures are well defined and documented, and another is how centrally managed an institution is. Assessing and enhancing internal controls for an institution that is centrally managed will likely take less effort. Generally speaking, the larger and more decentralized an institution is, the more important written institutional control standards, well documented policies and procedures, and formal training and communications programs will be.

Another factor is whether an institution outsources certain functions (e.g., student loan processing, investment management, payroll) to external parties. When electing to outsource certain business functions, institutions need to consider the provider's system of internal controls as though it were their own in order to ensure that the provider addresses the appropriate risks. Also, institutions must define and execute monitoring controls over the outsource provider's activities.

In summary, such factors as the following will affect how an institution assesses and enhances its internal controls:

- Its size
- Extent to which it is decentralized or centralized in its business operations

---

Source: John A. Mattie, Paul F. Hanley, and Dale L. Cassidy, Internal Controls: The Key to Accountability (Boston: PriceWaterhouseCoooopers LLP, 2005): 9-15. Used by permission.

- Degree to which policies and procedures are already well defined, documented, communicated and taught
- Whether it outsources any business functions to external providers

As institutions initiate actions to assess and enhance their internal controls, they should keep these factors in mind.

ACTIONS TO TAKE

Where should an institution begin? **Start by assessing the controls already in place.** Every institution will fall somewhere on the Internal Controls Maturity Framework illustrated in Chart 2.

Chart 2

Internal Controls Maturity Framework – Where is Your Institution?				
Unreliable Control activities are not designed or in place. The environment is unpredictable.	**Informal** Control activities are designed and in place but they are not adequately documented.	**Standardized** Control activities are designed, in place and adequately documented.	**Monitored** Controls are standardized. There is periodic testing for effective design and operation with reporting to management.	**Optimized** Controls are integrated. There is real-time monitoring by management and continuous improvement.

Our experience shows that the internal controls of most educational institutions are likely to be "informal," the second box on the left. Institutions are likely to have control activities in place, such as required approvals and verifications, but little documentation of the controls. The controls are likely to be very "people dependent" and not standardized across the institution. This poses problems when individuals change jobs or retire and do not teach their successors their procedural control responsibilities. Formal training and communications programs as well as monitoring procedures are most likely not in place. Risk assessment and management programs also may not be in place.

Sarbanes-Oxley is requiring public companies to go from the left side of the Internal Controls Maturity Framework, from "informal," for example, to "optimized" on the right in a very short period of time. It is unrealistic to expect universities and colleges to move that far that quickly—as long as it is not required. The goal for most educational institutions is to start moving "rightward" along the Internal Controls Maturity Framework.

The following provides an example of an institution that moved "rightward" along the Internal Controls Maturity Framework in response to a problem with cash management.

Example:

A large multi-campus institution has eight transaction-intensive locations on its campuses that accept cash payments. Only one of eight locations has written procedures. The other locations rely on the knowledge of long-time employees. An internal audit shows that cash at one location is not being deposited on a regular basis. Also, the employee who makes the bank deposits also counts the cash and completes the deposit slip. A key employee at that location was on long-term sick leave, and the remaining employees did not know what to do. They were aware that controls over cash were haphazard at best, and uncomfortable about the situation. This institution developed summary written procedures for all eight locations and trained the employees to help ensure accountability in the decentralized environment.

The actions that we recommend on the following pages may seem familiar. In many respects, enhancing internal controls is very much like other campus initiatives that involve significant change. The success of all such initiatives—institutional compliance programs, for example, or major systems implementation—depends on well-known factors such as good communications.

Achieve a top-down commitment to internal control. Everyone at the top, from the audit committee to the president to the chief financial officer and internal auditor to the administrative and academic department heads, should understand and support the internal control initiative. For example, the CFO of a small centralized college assigns the project's implementation to the controller, but he announces the controls enhancement project himself and makes its importance to him and the audit committee clear.

Perform a risk assessment in order to determine the most significant areas of vulnerability. Before enhancing internal controls, colleges and universities should identify their most critical risks, and then focus on enhancing the related controls. Enterprise risk management or ERM, may be a valuable new tool for colleges and universities. ERM is designed to help institutions identify potential risks (i.e., strategic, reputational, financial, compliance, and operational risks), manage them, and provide reasonable assurance regarding the achievement of the institution's objectives.

Although financial reporting is a risk-intensive area for companies with publicly traded stock—because investors must be able to rely on corporate financial reports for the financial markets to function properly—it is not usually the most significant risk for colleges and universities. The most significant risks for educational institutions are likely to also involve operational, strategic, compliance, and reputation issues. For example, student enrollment and tuition discounting may present significant operational and strategic risks for a tuition-dependent institution. Alternative investments may present significant operational risks for an institution with an endowment that is heavily invested in venture capital, hedge funds and other types of alternative investments.

Compliance risk is likely to be significant for most colleges and universities. They face numerous compliance risks related to federally funded programs, such as student financial aid and sponsored research as well as clinical billing practices in AMCs. As a condition of receiving federal funds for financial aid and sponsored research purposes, institutions must maintain internal controls that provide reasonable assurance of compliance with federal rules and regulations that could have a material effect on their federal programs. Independent auditors are required to obtain an understanding of an institution's internal controls over federal programs and perform tests of them in audits mandated by the Office of Management and Budget (OMB).

Colleges and universities have been required to undergo rigorous OMB compliance audits, including such assessments of controls over the administration of federal awards, for more than 10 years. Unless they receive federal funds, companies with publicly traded stock have not been subject to these types of audits.

It is possible that the Government Accountability Office (GAO) might impose even higher standards on recipients of federal funds in the future. The GAO establishes standards for government audits, including those mandated by OMB, and so its views are very important for institutions that receive federal funds.

The GAO's views are reflected in its December 9, 2003 comment letter to the Public Company Accounting Oversight Board (PCAOB):

> GAO strongly believes that management's assessment of the effectiveness of internal control, along with the auditor's attestation on that assessment, are critical components of monitoring the effectiveness of an organization's risk management and accountability systems. Auditors will better serve their clients and other financial statement users and will better protect the public interest by providing assurances about the effectiveness of internal control. In this regard, GAO seeks to lead by example in establishing an appropriate level of auditor reporting on internal control for federal agencies and programs, and for entities receiving significant amounts of federal funding.[1]

Evaluate the control environment, which establishes the overall tone for the institution. One component of the control environment would be how well the institution defines individual accountability and responsibility for key control activities. Another component would be how well an institution promotes ethical values. For example, activities like those in the following box would demonstrate an institution's commitment to integrity:

Demonstrating an Institution's Commitment to Integrity

A college provides ethics training. Faculty, staff, and officers at all levels are required to complete this training.

A university has a written code of conduct. All employees are held to the same standard and disciplined equally for violations.

Managers at all levels of the institution are informed about how to solicit the ethical views of potential job candidates.

The board also helps to set the appropriate tone at the top. Evidence of good governance by the audit committee, for example, would include:

- All members of the audit committee are independent (i.e., members do not have financial interests in the organization).
- At least one audit committee member has financial expertise.
- The audit committee meets as often as is necessary with the internal and external auditors to carry out its responsibilities.
- The audit committee has a written charter that is periodically reviewed and updated. The charter summarizes members' responsibilities (see Chart 3 below).

Chart 3

Audit Committee Responsibilities

The audit committee is responsible for:
All facets of the relationship with the external independent auditor, such as appointment, compensation, and retention as well as review of the audit plan, audit fieldwork, reports, and management letter, including recommendations, along with asking for the independent auditor's evaluation of management.
Oversight of financial management
Oversight of the institution's internal control structure
Reviewing financial statements and making sure that they are complete and seem reasonable based on the committee's understanding of the institution's financial health
Oversight and review of federal and state tax filings
Identifying and monitoring related party transactions
Reviewing policies for conflicts of interest, ethics, and related party disclosures
Monitoring legal matters that could affect the institution's financial health or its financial reports
Being advised regarding the adequacy of insurance coverage
Recommending improvements and remedies when problems are noted
Initiating and overseeing any special investigations that it believes are needed

Evaluate the control activities. Policies and procedures are control activities. Policies establish what should be done, and procedures are the actions that must be taken to carry out the policies. Although policies, procedures, and controls are related, the guidance in the following box helps distinguish the differences among them.

Reconciling Bank Accounts

A college's internal controls over bank accounts provide for reconciliations and reasonableness tests as well as periodic cash counts by internal audit. The internal controls also provide for the controller to maintain a complete list of open accounts along with month-end balances and for the treasurer to review it monthly.

According to the college's policy, all bank accounts with average monthly balances in excess of $10,000 and/or activity averaging $50,000 or more should be reconciled monthly. Per the policy, open accounts with balances or activity levels smaller than those outlined above should be reconciled at least quarterly.

Each month a staff member reconciles the monthly bank statement within limits of 0.1% of the average balance or $50, whichever is greater. The supervisor reviews the completed reconciliations within one week, and provides evidence of his review by initialing the work. These are the procedures.

Control activities include transaction-level controls, such as:

- Physical controls to safeguard assets, such as keeping cash in a locked safe
- Segregation of duties, so that, for example, one person counts cash and completes the deposit slip, and another deposits the cash in the bank
- An imbedded technology edit that checks the accuracy, completeness and authorization of transactions

General computer controls and application controls are also examples of control activities.

Identify and collect information that employees need to perform their jobs; develop a communications strategy to make sure the information gets to the right people. Internally, communication should flow *down* from management to staff, *across* from one department to another, and *up* from staff to management. Everyone must be clear about their roles and responsibilities, including how they relate to the work of others. Institutional policies and procedures must be widely communicated and understood.

Documentation of policies and procedures, with a specific identification of control procedures, is a best practice. We are often asked how much documentation is sufficient. It should be detailed enough that management can communicate the control throughout the institution and expect staff to understand it. It should provide answers to the following questions:

- What is the risk being controlled?
- What is the control activity?
- Why is the activity performed?
- Who (or what system) performs the control activity?
- When (how often) is the activity performed?
- What mechanism is used to perform and monitor the activity (reports and systems)?

External stakeholders, such as bondholders, lenders, donors, state and federal agencies, are becoming more interested in and aware of an institution's control environment. They want to know whether the institution effectively communicates responsibility and accountability for controls, and then whether it effectively monitors to make sure controls are working as intended.

Create workable mechanisms for monitoring compliance, reporting and operational processes to prevent or detect discrepancies and inefficiencies. It is important to monitor activities and provide for adequate follow up. If a problem is found, it must be investigated and, if indicated, corrective actions should be taken.

Monitoring has three subcomponents:

- Ongoing monitoring—Ongoing monitoring activities include regular supervisory activities that occur in the ordinary course of business.
- Periodic monitoring—Periodic monitoring activities include monthly or quarterly reviews that management performs to test the effectiveness of established procedures.
- Reporting deficiencies—There must be a process in place to report deficiencies to the appropriate level in the institution, where corrective actions can be taken.

High-level examples of monitoring controls include institutional compliance programs, internal audits, and audit committee activities. More detailed examples are presented in the following box.

Three Examples of Monitoring Controls

1. Each month, the budget director reviews a report comparing expense activity by department to its budget.
2. A senior manager reviews budgeted capital construction costs for a specific project with actual costs.
3. Directors review annually a report identifying conflicts of interest for officers.

Management's responsibility is to establish effective monitoring controls. Internal audit's role should be to assess whether management's monitoring controls are functioning as intended.

Sustain the internal control enhancement program. Enhancing controls is a continuing process—very much like the institutional compliance programs that many institutions already have in place. Ongoing enhancements to internal controls help institutions proactively respond to changes involving not only regulations, but also people, processes, and technology.

Similar to its oversight of an institutional compliance program, the effectiveness of an institution's program to enhance internal controls should be assessed annually. To ensure that the program continues to be working, the audit committee should require monitoring and periodic reporting as to the effectiveness of the institution's internal control structure.

The ongoing process to sustain and enhance internal controls should:

- Have clearly defined and documented control procedures
- Reinforce specific accountabilities at both the central and decentralized unit levels
- Include human resources mechanisms to reward the desired behaviors as part of annual performance objectives
- Be visibly supported by the institution's senior management and its audit committee
- Look for ways to streamline and simplify the processes and controls—a reduction in the number of redundant controls can lead to a more sustainable process
- Develop an adverse action policy to evaluate, report, remediate and monitor exceptions
- Communicate policy and procedure changes widely and often
- Establish training programs for employees whose roles have changed as well as for new employees

For example, the research university described in the box below established training programs for employees in decentralized units who had newly assigned accountability for controls.

Example:

When a large research university assessed its controls and defined accountability campus-wide, it found that many employees who were responsible for key controls in decentralized units did not have the necessary skills to execute newly assigned control activities. Training was needed.

Note:

1. When enhancing controls, take time to assess the competency of employees in decentralized units who are being held to new, higher levels of accountability.
2. Participation of central finance administrators should be considered in the hiring of new departmental employees with financial responsibilities to make sure they have the needed skills.
3. Training for employees in decentralized units who are responsible for key controls should be ongoing.

Notes

1. From GAO 12/9/03 comment letter to the PCAOB on proposed auditing standard, *An Audit of Internal Control over Financial Reporting Performed in Conjuction with an Audit of Financial Statements*. Comment letter can be found at: http://www.gao.gov.

CHAPTER 5

BANKING RELATIONSHIP MANAGEMENT

5.1 INTRODUCTION

Nonprofit treasurers can create value for their organizations just as do corporate treasurers. Exhibit 5.1, which we call the value pathway diagram, pictures the ways in which treasurers create value. The value of the organization, in purely

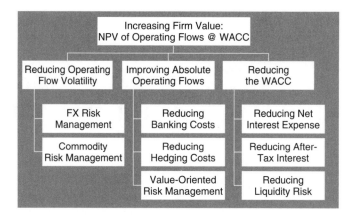

Source: Greenwich Treasury Advisors, "Treasury Performance Measurement: Metrics and Benchmarks," March 26, 2003. © 2003 by Greenwich Treasury Advisors LLC. Used by permission.

EXHIBIT 5.1   VALUE PATHWAY DIAGRAM: HOW TREASURY ADDS VALUE

financial terms, is the total of all future operating cash flows, expressed in today's money (net present value of operating flows, discounted to today's dollar value by accounting for the overall cost of your funding sources, the weighted average cost of capital [WACC]).

The value pathway diagram identifies three pathways by which you may add to the financial strength of your organization that relate directly to banking relationships: reducing hedging costs (banks are the primary hedge facilitators), reducing banking costs, and reducing net interest expense. Banking costs are explicit fees and implicit opportunity costs from lost interest on "free checking accounts" or low-interest NOW accounts that your organization may have. Net interest expense is the interest you earn on short-term investments less the interest you pay on short-term borrowing. That short-term borrowing, often obtained from banks, is one piece of the funding package that you assemble to finance your organization's property and equipment and other assets (see Chapter 6). The overall cost of your funding is termed your WACC. It accounts for all funding sources, the percentage of your financing that each represents, and the cost of each on an annual interest rate basis. In our companion volume, *Financial Management for Nonprofit Organizations* (John Wiley & Sons, 2007), we show how to compute the WACC and how to use that to discount future operating cash flows to get their value expressed in today's money.

Your organization's primary financial objective is to ensure that financial resources are available when needed (timing), as needed (amount), and at reasonable cost (cost-effectiveness), and that once mobilized, these resources are protected from impairment and spent according to mission and donor purposes.

Your banking partner(s) are instrumental in enabling your organization to carry out this objective. The top three goals for improving treasury and cash management optimization by surveyed small businesses are:

1. Reduce costs
2. Improve investment returns
3. Improve working capital[1]

These small businesses indicated that their top three action items to improve treasury and cash management are:

1. Improve cash flow forecasting
2. Automate financial transactions
3. Simplify processes in treasury and cash management[2]

Nonprofits, being small organizations, would likely agree wholeheartedly with these goals and action items. Your banks are key allies in your efforts. The link for cash forecasting is better data and more real-time data; larger organizations may also use a bank (or third party provider) treasury management system with a built-in cash forecasting module. The U.S. has almost 9,000 banks and savings institutions, as well as thousands of credit unions, giving smaller organizations many choices; larger organizations will have fewer choices due to the fact that advanced products and services are not offered by smaller financial institutions.

We begin this chapter by setting out the objectives you should aim for in your banking relationships. We note the importance of two-way communication between nonprofit treasury staff and their bankers. We then survey the services provided by banks, most of which are further developed in Chapters 3, 4, 6, and 7. How to select which banks you will work with and why you may wish to switch banks is profiled next. We follow this by explanations of the two key banking documents related to cash management: the availability schedule for your deposited checks and the account analysis statement, which is your invoice for banking services. We give the basics of your purchasing approach for contracting with banks for cash management services, normally done using requests for information and requests for proposals. We mention the emergence and growing importance of nonbank service providers next. Then we give further detail on some information services you may receive from your bank, online banking and special studies. After a brief discussion of international banking, we close the chapter by presenting bank report cards and ways in which you may evaluate your cash management activities, including those we covered in Chapters 3 and 4.

5.2   OBJECTIVES FOR YOUR BANKING RELATIONSHIP

Depending on the size of your organization, anyone from the assistant treasurer to the board treasurer could be charged with selecting the bank(s) your organization will use. This is a major purchase, and it is prudent to have the board, or at least the board finance committee, oversee the decision. If you are the chief financial officer (CFO), regardless of your title, you need to take responsibility for your organization's bank selection and the ensuing ongoing relationship management.

Your primary objective in managing the bank relationship is to ensure that all the organization's banking services are provided reliably at a reasonable cost.[3] The objective is not aimed at "minimal cost" because (1) reliability of the organization's bank relationship, and (2) reasonable compensation of the company's banks are both essential factors that supersede merely minimizing costs. You will create value for your organization by the proper selection of banks, appropriate monitoring of the banks, and rebidding and making banking service changes as necessary.

5.3 COMMUNICATING WITH YOUR BANK

Your relationship with your bank is like a relationship with any other supplier to some degree, but banks may offer you financial advice and counsel that far exceeds what other nonfinancial suppliers may offer. That happens if you work with a bank relationship manager (person assigned to your account to oversee the bank's service offering to your organization) who understands nonprofits and understands your organization. That understanding comes only when a solid relationship based on mutual respect arises.

There are steps you and your banker can take to build a strong relationship between the two organizations. Ten of the most important steps that you and your banker can take are to:

1. *Make a commitment.* While the bank should commit to efficient and affordable services, your organization should commit to loyalty and trust, giving your bank the opportunity to meet your expectations prior to ending that relationship.

2. *Communicate frequently.* Open, honest, clear, and frequent communication about service developments and policy changes on the part of the bank and about industry issues or changes in your financial health on the part of the organization help the relationship.

3. *Conduct periodic site visits/meetings.* More frequent contact strengthens relationships, and value comes from rotating those face-to-face meetings between the bank and at your organization's site.

4. *Establish multiple levels of contact.* You should know your banker's supervisor and direct reports, and your banker should know yours, as this brings a greater comfort level and builds mutual knowledge of partners.

5. *Measure quality of service.* Almost invariably, the bank's service will fall short of your expectation in some way at some time, so inform the bank immediately, not to criticize but to enable the bank to address the issue and take whatever actions may be appropriate. (Also use a bank

report card to help the bank see where to improve—see the discussion of this later in this chapter.)

6. *Set mutual objectives.* Work together to reach mutual goals, reviewing and modifying these goals in your face-to-face meetings if and when appropriate.

7. *Understand customer needs.* Your organization can facilitate your bank's understanding of your needs, realizing that as banks try harder to get to know their customers' industries, competitive environments, organizations, and operations, they can better tailor services to the customers' specific needs. (Note that your organization competes with other non-profits offering the same services in your geographic location and your organization competes for employees, volunteers, grants, and donations.)

8. *Compensate fairly and promptly.* The bank should accurately bill based on the agreed-on pricing schedule, and your organization should pay promptly. (The bank prefers that you pay with compensating balances, but discuss this and payment by fees to negotiate a payment arrangement that works well for you and your bank.)

9. *Discuss credit needs openly.* Your organization should clue the bank in regarding your current and future financing needs, and the bank should indicate its ability to provide loans if and when your organization should need them.

10. *Automate processes whenever possible.* With all the new technologies being introduced, be sure you understand the bank's offerings and the bank understands your information technology (IT) systems, and that these work in harmony and are used to gain the cost-reducing efficiencies (faster, less error, better communication) that automation should bring to both your organization and the bank.[4]

5.4 SERVICES PROVIDED BY BANKS

Banks offer five services that will assist you in your treasury management.[5] Cash management services include cash collections services (including the positioning of your cash flows), cash disbursements services, and information services. (When we use the term "bank," we are referring to any financial institution—including credit unions, savings associations, or in some cases non-bank service providers—that offers the particular service being discussed.) The other services are tied to the cash management services, as organizations that run short on cash require credit services, and organizations flush with cash may tap banks' investment services. Exhibit 5.2 summarizes the five banking services.

This chapter focuses on bank pricing and provision of cash management services. Chapter 3 covered cash collections and positioning, Chapter 4 covered cash disbursements, Chapter 6 covers short-term borrowing, and Chapter 7 covers short-term investing.

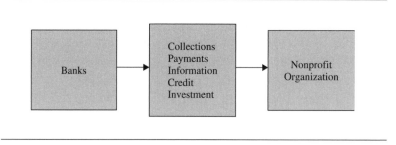

EXHIBIT 5.2   MAJOR BANKING SERVICES FOR NONPROFITS

You can better understand the context of cash management services when you see the role and location of these services in a typical bank.

(a) BANK PERSPECTIVES ON CASH MANAGEMENT SERVICES.   Banks sometimes refer to the services provided to organizational customers as "corporate" or "wholesale" services. Over 200 banks currently offer these services to businesses and nonprofits. Banks' offerings are so similar that many consider cash management services to be a commodity-type product. To stand out, banks must compete on factors such as high-quality customer service and service customization. Rather than focusing exclusively on cash management profitability, banks should be focusing on the profits coming from the overall relationship with the organization, encompassing all the services a bank provides for the organization.

(b) HOW BANKS ORGANIZE CASH MANAGEMENT.   The cash management area is typically a separate department called treasury management services in the bank's corporate services division. A bank may further divide this into three distinct areas: sales, product development/management, and customer service. The sales group generates fee-based income by selling cash management products to nonprofit and business customers; the product group spawns new products and modifies or customizes existing ones; and the customer service group hopes to accurately and quickly resolve customer inquiries and service problems. Many banks make one individual, usually called a relationship manager, responsible for an overall corporate or nonprofit customer relationship; this individual is charged with overseeing all of the services provided to the customer. Larger and more profitable accounts (clients) naturally are assigned to the best personnel.

(c) HOW BANKS VIEW NONPROFIT ORGANIZATIONS.   Banks at times complain, usually privately, that corporate and nonprofit clients are:

- Sometimes defensive
- Apt to cover up ignorance of complex products
- Unfair and tactless when having banks bid against one another
- Apt to overlook the fact that banks must make a profit on the total client relationship (and cannot accept small profit margins on all services)

- Apt to not inform the bank quickly regarding any adverse changes in the organization's financial position

Banks also consider the CFO or treasurer to be the primary source of information regarding the nonprofit and its banking needs.[6]

With the banking context in mind, we are now ready to consider the main cash management products and how to purchase and manage them.

5.5 DEPOSITORY SERVICES AND THE AVAILABILITY SCHEDULE

When a bank processes the checks you deposit, it normally follows four steps:

1. It verifies your deposit ticket, a listing of the checks and their amounts.
2. If you haven't already pre-encoded the dollar amount of the checks on the bottom right-hand side of the check, the bank then encodes the dollar amount on the MICR (magnetic ink character recognition) line.
3. It sends the checks as part of a "cash letter" (listing checks and amounts) to a correspondent bank or the nearest Federal Reserve facility to be cleared back to the bank on which the check was written.
4. The bank assigns availability on the checks, according to which of the bank's availability schedules it uses for your account.

(With Check 21, processing will increasingly be done using imaging of the check and then electronic check presentment in step 3, using "image cash letters".)

Your ledger balance is credited that day, assuming you got the checks to the bank's processing area prior to the deposit cutoff time for the day; otherwise, the ledger balance gets credited the next banking day. Even when it becomes a ledger balance in your account, not all of the deposit is available as "good funds" (usually called collected balances by the bank). Rather, the amount that is available for you to spend varies according to the bank's *availability schedule*.

(a) **EXAMPLE OF AN AVAILABILITY SCHEDULE.** Exhibit 5.3 illustrates an actual availability schedule offered by a bank on the east coast, for Baltimore-area check processing center deposits of items that are pre-encoded with the dollar amount by the depositor or a party acting on behalf of the depositor. The first part of this availability schedule has separate columns for checks deposited from Monday through Thursday and for Friday deposits (far right). The schedule shows which checks will get 0-day (same-day) availability, other than on-us checks (checks deposited at this bank and also drawn on another's account at this bank): These are checks drawn on the U.S. Treasury (such as tax refunds), postal money orders, and savings bond redemptions.

In the second column, the schedule shows each of the 12 Federal Reserve Districts' ABA routing transit (RT) numbers (which indicate which check processing location will handle certain drawee banks' checks) and what availability will be granted to those drawee banks' checks. Every bank on which checks or drafts may be drawn has its own unique routing number. ABA numbers are those assigned through the auspices of the American Bankers Association (ABA) to uniquely identify each bank to facilitate and speed the presentment of checks back to the drawee bank. At the time of this writing there are over 28,000 active routing numbers.[7]

The "Deadline" column indicates that for most deposited checks the absolute latest ledger cutoff time is 2030 military time, which is 8:30 p.m. ET (as Baltimore is in the Eastern Time zone)—this is the time by which a company must deposit a check to get the stated availability. If checks do not get to the bank's processing location by 8:30 p.m., they would be granted ledger credit the next *banking* day (normally the next business day, but there are a number of bank holidays to be aware of). Availability assignment, indicating how much longer one must wait to have "available" or spendable funds from this deposit, is not given to a check until it has been given ledger credit.

Saturday or Sunday deposits dropped off at the bank's branches are subject to Monday's cutoff. Once again, you must deposit your checks by the stated cutoff time to receive the stated availability; otherwise, you would be granted availability the next *banking* day.

How quickly deposited amounts are made available by the clearing bank is related to:

- The time of deposit
- How distant the drawee bank is
- Whether the drawee bank is in a Federal Reserve Bank city or a Regional Check Processing Center area (RCPC) area (note the word "City" and the acronym "RCPC" in the left column listings)
- Whether the drawee bank is in a check swapping agreement, electronic check presentment agreement, or local clearinghouse with either the clearing bank or one of the clearing bank's correspondents[8]
- Whether the clearing bank may use image replacement documents to speed presentment to the drawee bank

This availability float time lag may not always equate to the length of time it takes for the check to clear, but generally the two are closely linked. Notice that no check that has been pre-encoded gets more than a two-day availability assignment by our sample bank in the availability schedule in Exhibit 5.3. In other words, a check drawn on a bank in the remotest parts of the U.S. would still be treated by the bank as "available" or "spendable" funds within two days of the deposit, assuming your organization got the check to the processing center by 8:30 p.m. ET.

The availability schedule in Exhibit 5.3 is a desirable one for the depositing organization, and underscores the point that banks provide expedited check processing if you are willing to perform extra tasks or pay extra charge. Your organization or a third-party with which you contract can pre-encode checks

Description	RT Number	Monday–Thursday		Friday	
		Deadline	Availability	Deadline	Availability

First Federal Reserve District

Description	RT Number	Deadline	Availability	Deadline	Availability
Boston City	0110	2030	1	2030	1
Boston RCPC	0112	2030	1*	2030	1
Boston RCPC	0113, 0114, 0115	2030	1	2030	1
Windsor Locks RCPC	0111, 0116, 0117, 0118, 0119, 0211	2030	1	2030	1

Second Federal Reserve District

Description	RT Number	Deadline	Availability	Deadline	Availability
East Rutherford City	0210, 0260, 0280, 8000-0002, -0006, -0010, -0013	2030	1	2030	1
East Rutherford RCPC	0212, 0214, 0219	2030	1	2030	1
East Rutherford Country	0215, 0216	2030	2	2030	2
East Rutherford Country Selects	See Supplemental List	2030	1	2030	1
Utica City	0220	2030	1	2030	1
Utica RCPC	0213, 0223	2030	2	2030	1
Utica RCPC Selects	See Supplemental List	2030	1	2030	1

Third Federal Reserve District

Description	RT Number	Deadline	Availability	Deadline	Availability
Philadelphia City	0310, 0360	2030	1	2030	1
Philadelphia RCPC	0311, 0312, 0313, 0319	2030	1	2030	1
Philadelphia RCPC Selects	See Supplemental List	0730	0	0730	0

Fourth Federal Reserve District

Description	RT Number	Deadline	Availability	Deadline	Availability
Cleveland City	0410	2030	1	2030	1
Cleveland RCPC	0412	2030	1	2030	1
Cincinnati City	0420	2030	1	2030	1
Cincinnati RCPC	0421, 0422, 0423	2030	1	2030	1
Pittsburgh City	0430	2030	1	2030	1
Pittsburgh RCPC	0432, 0433, 0434	2030	2	2030	1
Columbus City	0440	2030	1	2030	1
Columbus RCPC	0441, 0442	2030	2	2030	1

(continues)

EXHIBIT 5.3 AVAILABILITY SCHEDULE

Description	RT Number	Monday–Thursday		Friday	
		Deadline	Availability	Deadline	Availability

Fifth Federal Reserve District

Description	RT Number	Deadline	Availability	Deadline	Availability
Richmond City	0510	0400	0	0400	0
Richmond City Selects	See Supplemental List	0730	0	0730	0
Richmond City On-Us Selects	See Supplemental List	2030	0	2030	0
Richmond RCPC	0514	2030	1	2030	1
Richmond RCPC Selects 1	See Supplemental List	0400	0	0400	0
Richmond RCPC Selects 2	See Supplemental List	0730	0	0730	0
Richmond RCPC On-Us Selects	See Supplemental List	2030	0	2030	0
Charleston City	0519	2030	1	2030	1
Charleston RCPC	0515	2030	1	2030	1
Baltimore City	0520	0730	0	0730	0
Baltimore City On-Us Selects	See Supplemental List	2030	0	2030	0
Baltimore RCPC	0521, 0522, 0540, 0550, 0560, 0570	2030	1	2030	1
Baltimore RCPC Selects	See Supplemental List	0730	0	0730	0
Baltimore RCPC On-Us Selects	See Supplemental List	2030	0	2030	0
Charlotte City	0530	2030	1	2030	1
Charlotte City Selects	See Supplemental List	0730	0	0730	0
Charlotte RCPC	0531	2030	1*	2030	1
Charlotte RCPC Selects	See Supplemental List	2030	1	2030	1
Charlotte RCPC On-Us Selects	See Supplemental List	2030	0	2030	0
Columbia City	0539	2030	1	2030	1
Columbia RCPC	0532	2030	1*	2030	1
Columbia RCPC On-Us Selects	See Supplemental List	2030	0	2030	0

(continues)

EXHIBIT 5.3   *(continued)*

Description	RT Number	Monday–Thursday		Friday	
		Deadline	Availability	Deadline	Availability

Sixth Federal Reserve District

Description	RT Number	Deadline	Availability	Deadline	Availability
Atlanta City	0610	2030	1	2030	1
Atlanta City On-Us Selects	See Supplemental List	2030	0	2030	0
Atlanta RCPC	0611, 0612, 0613	2030	1*	2030	1
Atlanta RCPC Selects	See Supplemental List	2030	1	2030	1
Atlanta RCPC On-Us Selects	See Supplemental List	2030	0	2030	0
Birmingham City	0620	2030	1	2030	1
Birmingham RCPC	0621, 0622	2030	1*	2030	1
Birmingham RCPC On-Us Selects	See Supplemental List	2030	0	2030	0
Jacksonville City	0630	2030	1	2030	1
Jacksonville City On-Us Selects	See Supplemental List	2030	0	2030	0
Jacksonville RCPC	0631, 0632, 8000-0008	2030	1*	2030	1
Jacksonville RCPC Selects	See Supplemental List	2030	1	2030	1
Jacksonville RCPC On-Us Selects	See Supplemental List	2030	0	2030	0
Nashville City	0640	2030	1	2030	1
Nashville City On-Us Selects	See Supplemental List	2030	0	2030	0
Nashville RCPC	0641, 0642	2030	1*	2030	1
Nashville RCPC Selects	See Supplemental List	2030	1	2030	1
Nashville RCPC On-Us Selects	See Supplemental List	2030	0	2030	0
New Orleans City	0650	2030	1	2030	1
New Orleans RCPC	0651, 0652, 0653, 0654, 0655	2030	2	2030	1
Miami City	0660	2030	1	2030	1
Miami City On-Us Selects	See Supplemental List	2030	0	2030	0
Miami RCPC	0670	2030	1*	2030	1
Miami RCPC Selects	See Supplemental List	2030	1	2030	1
Miami RCPC On-Us Selects	See Supplemental List	2030	0	2030	0

(continues)

EXHIBIT 5.3   *(continued)*

Description	RT Number	Monday–Thursday		Friday	
		Deadline	Availability	Deadline	Availability

Seventh Federal Reserve District

Description	RT Number	Deadline	Availability	Deadline	Availability
Chicago City	0710	2030	1	2030	1
Chicago RCPC	0712, 0719	2030	1	2030	1
Peoria RCPC	0711	2030	1	2030	1
Detroit City	0720	2030	1	2030	1
Detroit RCPC	0724	2030	1*	2030	1
Detroit RCPC Selects	See Supplemental List	2030	1	2030	1
Des Moines City	0730	2030	1	2030	1
Des Moines RCPC	0739	2030	2	2030	1
Indianapolis City	0740	2030	1	2030	1
Indianapolis RCPC	0749	2030	2	2030	1
Milwaukee City	0750	2030	1	2030	1
Milwaukee RCPC	0759	2030	1	2030	1

Eighth Federal Reserve District

Description	RT Number	Deadline	Availability	Deadline	Availability
St. Louis City	0810	2030	1	2030	1
St. Louis RCPC	0819	2030	2	2030	1
St. Louis Country	0812, 0815, 0865	2030	2	2030	1
Little Rock City	0820	2030	1	2030	1
Little Rock RCPC	0829	2030	2	2030	1
Louisville City	0830	2030	1	2030	1
Louisville RCPC	0813, 0839, 0863	2030	1*	2030	1
Memphis City	0840	2030	1	2030	1
Memphis City On-Us Selects	See Supplemental List	2030	0	2030	0
Memphis RCPC	0841, 0842, 0843	2030	2	2030	1
Memphis RCPC Selects	See Supplemental List	2030	1	2030	1

Ninth Federal Reserve District

Description	RT Number	Deadline	Availability	Deadline	Availability
Minneapolis City	0910, 0960	2030	1	2030	1
Minneapolis RCPC	0918, 0919	2030	2	2030	1
Minneapolis RCPC Selects	See Supplemental List	2030	1	2030	1
Minneapolis Country	0911, 0912, 0913, 0914, 0915	2030	2	2030	1

EXHIBIT 5.3 *(continued)*

Description	RT Number	Monday–Thursday		Friday	
		Deadline	Availability	Deadline	Availability
Minneapolis Country Selects	See Supplemental List	2030	1	2030	1
Helena City	0920	2030	2	2030	1
Helena City Selects	See Supplemental List	2030	1	2030	1
Helena RCPC	0929	2030	2	2030	1
Helena Country	0921	2030	2	2030	1

Tenth Federal Reserve District

Kansas City City	1010	2030	1	2030	1
Kansas City Country	1011, 1012, 1019	2030	2	2030	1
Kansas City Country Selects	See Supplemental List	2030	1	2030	1
Denver City	1020	2030	1	2030	1
Denver RCPC	1070	2030	2	2030	1
Denver RCPC Selects	See Supplemental List	2030	1	2030	1
Denver Country	1021, 1022, 1023	2030	2	2030	1
Denver Country Selects	See Supplemental List	2030	1	2030	1
Oklahoma City City	1030	2030	1	2030	1
Oklahoma City RCPC	1039	2030	2	2030	1
Oklahoma City Country	12031	2030	2	2030	1
Omaha City	1040	2030	1	2030	1
Omaha RCPC	1049	2030	2	2030	1
Omaha Country	1041	2030	2	2030	1

Eleventh Federal Reserve District

Dallas City	1110, 8000-0003	2030	1	2030	1
Dallas RCPC	1111, 1119	2030	2	2030	1
Dallas RCPC Selects	See Supplemental List	2030	1	2030	1
Dallas Country	1113	2030	2	2030	1
Dallas Country Selects	See Supplemental List	2030	1	2030	1
El Paso City	1120	2030	2	2030	1
El Paso City Selects	See Supplemental List	2030	1	2030	1

EXHIBIT 5.3 (*continued*)

Description	RT Number	Monday–Thursday		Friday	
		Deadline	Availability	Deadline	Availability
El Paso RCPC	1122, 1123, 1163	2030	2	2030	1
Houston City	1130	2030	1	2030	1
Houston RCPC	1131	2030	2	2030	1
Houston RCPC Selects	See Supplemental List	2030	1	2030	1
San Antonio City	1140	2030	1	2030	1
San Antonio RCPC	1149	2030	2	2030	1
San Antonio RCPC Selects	See Supplemental List	2030	1	2030	1

Twelfth Federal Reserve District

Description	RT Number	Monday–Thursday		Friday	
San Francisco City	1210, 8000-0001	2030	2	2030	1
San Francisco City Selects	See Supplemental List	2030	1	2030	1
San Francisco RCPC	1211, 1212, 1213	2030	2	2030	1
San Francisco RCPC Selects	See Supplemental List	2030	1	2030	1
San Francisco Country	1214	2030	2	2030	2
Los Angeles City	1220, 1223	2030	2	2030	1
Los Angeles City Selects	See Supplemental List	2030	1	2030	1
Los Angeles RCPC	1221, 1222, 1224	2030	2	2030	1
Los Angeles RCPC Selects	See Supplemental List	2030	1	2030	1
Portland City	1230	2030	1	2030	1
Portland RCPC	1231, 1232, 1233	2030	2	2030	1
Salt Lake City City	1240, 8000-0005	2030	1	2030	1
Salt Lake City RCPC	1241, 1242, 1243	2030	2	2030	1
Seattle City	1250	2030	1	2030	1
Seattle RCPC	1251, 1252	2030	2	2030	1

Government

Description	RT Number	Monday–Thursday		Friday	
U.S. Treasury Checks	0000-0050, -0051	1400	0	1400	0
U.S. Postal Money Orders	0000-0020, -0119, -0800	1400	0	1400	0
Savings Bonds	0000-9000	1400	0	1400	0

*Items less than $2,500 are deferred one additional day. See note #5 in the Notes to the Availability Schedule.

EXHIBIT 5.3   *(continued)*

Supplemental List		(partial)	

East Rutherford Country Selects

0215-0206	0216-0602	0216-0604	

Utica RCPC Selects

0213-0001	0213-0066	0213-0500	2213-7063
0213-0007	0213-0067	0213-0539	2213-7079
0213-0038	0213-0068	0213-0682	2213-7090
0213-0042	0213-0070	0213-0937	2213-7124
0213-0046	0213-0077	0213-0943	2213-7182
0213-0055	0213-0088	2213-7006	
0213-0057	0213-0262	2213-7028	

Philadelphia RCPC Selects

0313-0083	0313-0613		
0313-0153	0313-1449		
0313-0427			

Richmond City Selects

0510-0001	0510-0025	0510-0524	
0510-0010	0510-0141	0510-0677	

Richmond City On-Us Selects

0510-xxxx			

Richmond RCPC Selects 1

0514-0136	0514-0249	0514-0320	0514-0480
0514-0139	0514-0250	0514-0334	0514-0522
0514-0152	0514-0257	0514-0345	0514-0535
0514-0160	0514-0262	0514-0426	0514-0716
0514-0178	0514-0265	0514-0453	0514-0753
0514-0236	0514-0290	0514-0478	0514-0766

Richmond RCPC Selects 2

0514-0036	0514-0064	0514-0132	0514-0476
0514-0050	0514-0070	0514-0156	0514-0477
0514-0054	0514-0073	0514-0231	0514-0705

Richmond RCPC On-Us Selects

2514-xxxx			

Baltimore City On-Us Selects

2520-xxxx			

(continues)

EXHIBIT 5.3   *(continued)*

Supplemental List		(partial)		

Baltimore RCPC Selects

0521-0040	0540-0055	0550-0077	0550-0234	0560-0424
0521-0072	0540-0080	0550-0112	0550-0253	0560-0488
0521-0089	0540-0120	0550-0114	0550-0255	0560-0531
0521-0092	0540-0122	0550-0129	0550-0309	0560-0738
0521-0110	0540-0154	0550-0138	0550-0316	0560-0760
0521-0154	0550-0026	0550-0169	0550-0320	2550-7198
0521-0158	0550-0027	0550-0176	0550-0327	2550-7220
0521-0164	0550-0028	0550-0201	0550-0330	2560-7002
0540-0003	0550-0035	0550-0221	0560-0101	2560-7283
0540-0004	0550-0037	0550-0228	0560-0111	
0540-0007	0550-0050	0550-0233	0560-0408	

Baltimore RCPC On-Us Selects

0540-xxxx	0550-xxxx

Notes to the Availability Schedule

1. This availability schedule supersedes all previously published schedules. It is subject to change without prior notification.
2. Funds availability and deadlines are based upon the receipt of items at the XYZ Bank check processing facility located in Banktown, Maryland. All deadlines are stated in military time and apply to pre-encoded deposits only.
3. Availability is stated in business days from the date of ledger credit and is adjusted to reflect Federal Reserve Bank holidays and closings.
4. Items drawn on thrift institutions (RT numbers starting with a 2 or 3) receive the same availability as items drawn on banks (RT numbers starting with a 0 or 1) located in the same geographic area.
5. Items less than $2,500 drawn on selected banks located outside of the local Federal Reserve territory may be deferred one additional day. See Supplemental List of Selected Banks. In addition, items less than $2,500 drawn on selected RCPC ranges denoted with an asterisk (*) in the availability schedule will be deferred one additional day.
6. Items are processed on high speed sorting equipment. Availability on rejected items may be deferred one additional day.
7. Forward collection items that are subsequently returned for non-payment may be assessed additional float.
8. This Schedule is confidential and proprietary. You may not share, reprint or distribute the Schedule or any portion thereof without the prior express written consent of XYZ Bank.

Notes:
1. This is an actual bank availability schedule for an organizational customer in Baltimore. The bank's name has been withheld at its request, and XYZ Bank used as a pseudonym. We inserted x's in On-Us Rts for this bank.
2. Note that the schedule applies to checks that come to the bank already pre-encoded with the dollar amount on the bottom right-hand of the check.
3. The Supplemental List portion of the Availability Schedule is only partially shown due to its length.
4. Banktown, MD is a fictitious name.

EXHIBIT 5.3   *(continued)*

before depositing them as a means of reducing bank processing time, bank service charges, or both. This necessitates buying a MICR encoder, the machine used to imprint the check's dollar amount on the bottom right of the check. You would endorse the checks you receive, pre-encode them, bundle them together, total them, and then take them to the bank's processing center. Your bank should offer a later deposit cutoff time (e.g., 8:30 p.m. rather than, say, 7:00 p.m.) for ledger credit (which allows the bank to then assign the check's availability). According to William Michels at KeyBank (Cleveland, OH), doing the pre-encoding in-house makes economic sense for organizations that are depositing 4,000 or 5,000 or more checks per month.

Even if you do not perform extra tasks, it is worth checking to see if your bank offers a courier service to speed the collection of large-dollar checks. Furthermore, availability schedules are items on which you can negotiate with your bank(s). How good an availability schedule a candidate bank offers your organization is one variable you will look at as you select your depository bank(s). A good availability schedule is one that makes check deposits available to your organization within a short period of time. Having funds available more quickly enables your organization to use that money to cover payroll, pay suppliers, provide more services to clients, pay down a credit line balance, or invest in short-term investments. In other words, it enables your organization to achieve its primary financial objective and maintain its target liquidity.

(b) FEDERAL RESERVE POSTING AND A BANK'S AVAILABILITY SCHEDULE.
The Federal Reserve applies five posting times for credits and debits to banks accounts with the Federal Reserve (Fed):[9]

1. Treasury and commercial ACH credits are credited at 8:30 a.m. Eastern Time (ET; with simultaneous credit to the receiver of each automated clearinghouse [ACH] credit and debit to the originator of that ACH credit).
2. ACH debits are debited at 11 a.m. ET (with simultaneous credit to the originator of each ACH debit and debit to the receiver of that ACH debit).
3. Commercial check transactions are debited or credited, and coin and currency deposits are credited, beginning at 11 a.m. ET and then hourly, with the amounts based on proportions of the deposits drawn on the various drawee bank endpoints; debits are posted on the hour at least one hour after presentment, with any checks presented before 10:01 a.m. ET being posted at 11:00 a.m. ET
4. Wire transfers and book-entry (securities) transfers are posted as debits or credits as they occur
5. Electronic check presentments post at 1:00 p.m. local time and hourly thereafter; debits are posted to drawee depository institutions' accounts at 1:00 p.m. local time for any electronic check presentments made on or before 12:00 local time.

This Fed schedule applies to how items are posted to your bank, but since your bank will base its availability schedules on the Fed schedule, it has three important implications for your organization.

1. Funds will most likely be made available in smaller amounts throughout each banking day, instead of all at once. Your treasury staff will have to be careful to avoid intraday overdrafting of checking accounts, which could possibly incur bank charges.
2. Be careful to not disburse funds via wires or over-the-counter means until check deposits and other non-wire credits are posted and made available by your bank.
3. Because your banks are charged a fee by the Fed based on the amount of their intraday overdrafts, they will normally insist that you and other accountholders make your check presentments early enough to avoid having the Federal Reserve charge an overdraft fee to the bank's account at the Fed.

To recap this section, we urge you to carefully compare existing banks to new potential service providers so that you may ensure your organization is getting maximum value from its banking relationships. The opportunity cost of forgone interest (if you do leave extra amounts in checking accounts to compensate banks) is not the Treasury bill rate but what you could actually earn on your overnight investments: the overnight repurchase rate, the commercial paper rate, or money market mutual fund rate. Additionally, there are many "soft variables" to think about in your banking decisions, such as the length of time for which you have done business with your existing bank(s) and the other noncredit and credit services you are receiving from these bank(s). We shall return to these considerations shortly.

5.6 BANK SELECTION

(a) NONPROFIT BANK RELATIONSHIP PRACTICES.   Because there is very little information on actual nonprofit banking practices, we will report on the Lilly study findings even though this study was done in the early 1990s. The questions dealt with eight areas:

1. Use of services
   Of the surveyed organizations, 52.5 percent indicated some degree of agreement and 18.8 percent indicated some degree of disagreement with the statement that "The bank with which we do most of our cash management and depositing would say that our organization is using the most sophisticated and useful techniques appropriate for an organization of our nature and size." If this self-perception is accurate, it tells us that there was some room for improvement in the use by these faith-based nonprofits of banks' cash management service offerings.

2. How these services were paid for

    About two-thirds of these nonprofits paid for their banking services through fees, with most of the remainder paying for the services exclusively through leaving compensating balances in the account.

3. Receipt and understanding of account analysis statements

    About 55 percent stated that they received account analysis statements from their banks. Given the relatively small size of these organizations (the median annual revenue was $800,000), we suspect there was possible confusion on the part of the respondents between account analysis statements and regular monthly statements (the latter being similar to personal account monthly bank statements).

4. Adjustment of balances from bank statements

    About two-thirds of the organizations reported that they got these statements said they adjusted their bank account balances based on the statements. This was an encouraging finding, indicating some active management of cash positions. (A large portion of the organizations' cash positions was held in their bank accounts.)

5. Comparison of other banks' availability schedules to the current depository bank's availability schedule

    About one in four organizations compare other banks' availability schedules to their bank(s) availability schedule(s), with about one-half of those organizations doing so annually and the other one-half doing so less than annually. This is an area in definite need of improvement—especially with the significant decline in check clearing time now occurring due to Check 21 legislation, organizations are justified in expecting better availability to be forthcoming from their depository banks.

6. Frequency of rebidding bank services and whether competitive bids were gathered in the rebid process

    Thirty-seven percent of the surveyed organizations reevaluate their banking relationships once every year, once every two years, or once every several years. Unfortunately, fully 52 percent of the organizations said they "never" or "once every 5 or more years" made this reevaluation. Again, there is room for improvement here.

    Of those reevaluating banking, about one-half request competitive bids from more than one bank.

7. Use of outside services to assess the bank relationship

    Only 13 of the 288 organizations use an independent bank rating service or consultant to assess the organizations' bank relationships.

8. Negotiated fees or acceptance of bank fees

    When it comes to either negotiating bank fees or simply accepting the fee stipulated by the bank, 52 percent negotiate. This is good, but we would like to see that number go higher. (However, we recognize that some banks offer very attractive fee levels because of a preference to serve nonprofit clients.) Before determining your bargaining stance regarding bank services, your organization will have to decide whether to adopt a "transaction approach" or a "relationship approach" to its banking service purchases. Our earlier discussion of communication is slanted more toward the relationship approach, in which you may not negotiate as hard for individual services, but may rather accept a bundled pricing approach from the bank. In that relationship mind-set there is more loyalty on your part, and you will look to the bank to reciprocate if and when finances are sparse and you need a loan. Your transaction versus relationship stance affects your initial selection of your primary depository bank as well as your organization's subsequent decision making should you decide to change banks.

To help you draw some comparisons, we have included in Exhibit 5.4 some survey statistics of midsize and larger U.S. and European businesses so you can see (1) what percentage uses cash management services and (2) some of the other banking services that these corporations find useful. Finally, we note that small businesses are starting to select banks based on whether they offer innovative payments services such as electronic payments processing using imaging and ACH,[10] and we expect nonprofits to follow suit.

Our respondents, on average, had approximately five primary banking relationships and approximately nine secondary relationships.

The main banking services used by treasurers, regardless of size or location, were cash management services, credit facilities, and foreign exchange. The provision of credit facilities was also given as the most important criteria for treasurers when selecting a primary bank, closely followed by a full range of commercial banking services.

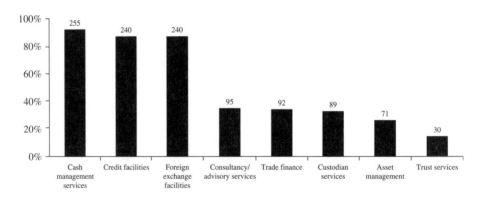

Source: JPMorgan Asset Management, "Global Cash Management Survey 2005," p. 5. There were 310 respondents, businesses predominantly located mostly in the United States and Europe. Used by permission.

EXHIBIT 5.4   BANKING SERVICES USED BY U.S. AND EUROPEAN COMPANIES

(b) INITIAL SELECTION OF A CASH MANAGEMENT BANK.   The *bank selection process* involves "assembling a system of banks to efficiently and effectively process all information and cash flows" involving the organization's short-term financial management.[11] Except for very small organizations, organizations deal with more than one bank. The larger or the more geographically widespread an organization is, the more banks it tends use. However, businesses and nonprofits continue to consolidate their banking systems toward use of fewer banks as the trend toward nationwide banking continues.

The conventional wisdom when you go to choose a bank is to select a bank that offers the services you need, reasonably priced, with convenient locations and an understanding of nonprofit organizations. As you start to grow, develop relationships with several different banks. Small, community banks may not have all the services your organization requires as it grows in its service provision and its geographical reach. You will want to develop banking relationships ahead of the actual need for those relationships. Another warning is in order: Since you may at some point have more than $100,000 in a depository account (the Federal Deposit Insurance Corporation [FDIC] guarantees only the first $100,000, although that threshold amount could change anytime with new legislation), you want to be careful to select a bank that is financially strong. One church lost $212,262 after depositing more than $312,000 in the Penn Square bank just prior to its collapse in 1982, as the FDIC only guarantees $100,000 for all accounts of one entity at a bank.

Some of the main selection criteria organizations use when first establishing which bank(s) to use for cash management and related services include:

- Location
- Bank/organization fit
- Service quality/breadth (including development of nationwide branch network)
- Bank creditworthiness
- Bank specializations
- Price[12]

(c) STAYING AWAY FROM FINANCIALLY WEAK BANKS.   Banks typically fail due to low profitability, inadequate liquidity, too-risky loan portfolios, and poor management. The trick is to anticipate when one or more of these factors will cause a bank to fail. Federal regulators use the five-component CAMELS rating system to evaluate a bank's safety and soundness: **c**apital adequacy, **a**sset quality, **m**anagement, **e**arnings, **l**iquidity, and market **s**ensitivity. If a bank has a rating of 4 or 5, it is considered a "problem bank." Four-rated banks are said to "generally exhibit unsafe or unsound practices or condition," and five-rated banks "exhibit extremely unsafe or unsound practices or condition."[13]

Federal financial regulations (specifically the Federal Deposit Insurance Corporation Improvement Act of 1991, or FDICIA) mandate yearly safety-and-soundness examinations for all banks except those banks with assets under $250 million and a composite CAMELS rating of 1 or 2.

A study of the 1,996 banks on the FDIC problem-bank list from 1990 through 2002 provides some guidance regarding what might cause a problem bank to fail (including either closure by the regulatory agency or forced merger by the regulatory agency), recover, merge, or continue as a problem. This study used these measures to determine whether one could predict, before the fact, when a bank would fail as opposed to recovering, merging, or continuing as a problem bank:

- *Capital adequacy.* Average risk-based capital and average tangible equity.
- *Earnings.* Increases in net interest income, provision for loan losses, and net noninterest income as measures of earnings.
- *Asset quality.* Poor asset quality was measured by how risky the banks' asset portfolios were, using average allowance for loan and lease losses, average loans and leases past due 30 to 89 days, average loans and leases past due 90 days or more, average nonaccrual loans and leases, and average "other real estate owned."
- *Liquidity.* Average volatile liabilities and loans and securities with maturities greater than or equal to five years.
- *Management.* Efficiency ratio (noninterest expense as a percentage of net interest income plus noninterest income), with a lower number being better.[14]

Consult Exhibit 5.5 to see how influential capital, loan quality, and noninterest expense are is in predicting whether a bank will actually fail (rightmost column) or continue, recover, or merge without failing.

(d) CHANGING BANKS. Some of the primary reasons your organization may wish to switch banks include a bank policy change (it no longer wishes to serve smaller organizations, nonprofits, or the area of the globe in which your organization operates), declining bank financial strength, you get a loan from another bank that requires your organization to switch its deposit accounts to it, or an extreme level of dissatisfaction with the present bank's performance on an ongoing basis.[15]

We offer two aids for your organization should you decide to select a bank for the first time or change banks. Exhibit 5.6 is an insightful checklist developed by consultant Cathy Rollins Gregg of Treasury Strategies. It has a prenegotiation comparison checklist, and if a new bank relationship is advisable based on that, a bidding checklist. Then, in Exhibit 5.7, the steps in a formal tender process are presented. Pay special attention to the "Implementation" phase near the end. If you are doing a preliminary prospecting for potential banks, you may wish to use a request for information (RFI). Banks that respond to the RFI with what they believe to be appropriate services for your organization may then be invited,

Mean and Standard Errors for Financial Variables, by State (Standard Errors in Parentheses)				
Variable	Recover	Merge	Remain a Problem	Fail
Number of Banks	1,326	228	2,077	116
Capital				
Tangible Equity Capital	6.68 ***	6.57 ***	6.39 ***	3.90 ***
	(0.08)	(0.20)	(0.07)	(0.29)
Capital Injections:				
From BHC	0.19 ***	0.41 ***	0.20 ***	0.14 *
	(0.02)	(0.06)	(0.02)	(0.08)
Outside	0.36 ***	0.29 ***	0.29 ***	0.42 ***
	(0.04)	(0.09)	(0.03)	(0.13)
Asset Quality				
Past-Due Loans (30–89 days)	1.88 ***	2.12 ***	2.43 ***	3.08 ***
	(0.04)	(0.10)	(0.03)	(0.14)
Past-Due Loans (90+ days)	0.59 ***	0.65 ***	0.92 ***	1.17 ***
	(0.04)	(0.09)	(0.03)	(0.13)
Nonaccrual Loans and Leases	2.17 ***	2.56 ***	2.64 ***	3.82 ***
	(0.06)	(0.14)	(0.05)	(0.20)
Other Real Estate Owned	2.00 ***	1.88 ***	2.60 ***	3.19 ***
	(0.07)	(0.17)	(0.06)	(0.23)
Allowance for Loan Loss	1.69 ***	1.97 ***	1.72 ***	2.11 ***
	(0.03)	(0.07)	(0.02)	(0.10)
Management				
Efficiency Ratio	88.32 ***	94.15 ***	94.43 ***	115.77 ***
	(0.67)	(1.62)	(0.54)	(2.28)

Significance at 1%, 5% and 10% levels are indicated by ***, **, and * asterisks, respectively.
Source: Robert Oshinsky and Virginia Olin, "Troubled Banks: Why Don't They All Fail?" FDIC Working Paper 2005-03, March 2005, p. 41.

EXHIBIT 5.5 VARIABLES PREDICTING WHETHER A TROUBLED BANK WILL FAIL

through a request for proposal (RFP) that you mail out, to submit a formal bid. After you get the bids back, you may make your final decision.

5.7 MANAGING BANK RELATIONSHIPS

Your organization should monitor its ongoing bank relations with the help of a bank relationship policy.[16] The *bank relationship policy* establishes your organization's objectives, compensation preference, and review procedures for its banking relationships. We like the policy elements devised by stock brokerage E.F. Hutton (later acquired by Shearson and now part of Lehman Brothers) after it had legal problems from its overly aggressive banking practices:

PRENEGOTIATION COMPARISON CHECKLIST

1. Is my existing service or relationship so substandard that I am unwilling to invest any more time in trying to improve it?
2. Has my current bank shown little or no interest in this aspect of our relationship?
3. Has my current bank recategorized our relationship in a way that means our importance has declined?
4. Has my current bank deemphasized products that are of particular importance to us in a way that jeopardizes our future satisfaction?
5. Are we looking for an entirely new package of services or trying to establish a new bank account structure?
6. Are these needs the result of an acquisition or major organizational change?
7. If my prices are *meaningfully* above market prices, am I satisfied that this is not the result of customization? Have I already approached my current bank about pricing improvements, to little or no benefit?
8. Have I already exhausted the capabilities or creativity of the bank(s) which have been investing in a true partnership relationship with us?

If you answer yes to any of questions 1–7 *and* yes to question 8, then you probably should bid out your services.

BIDDING CHECKLIST

In bidding, the following checklist can help guide you to a complete decision:

1. Confirm that the bank fits your bank relationship philosophy.
2. Confirm that the features you want are already available—and that you know clearly which are still being considered, planned for, or "in development."
3. Make sure you understand all financial components of the deal—all items you will be charged for, contract terms, permissible price increases, volume discount levels, and penalties for nonperformance (both yours and theirs).
4. Understand what implementation will entail, what resources the bank will commit, what resources you should expect to commit, and what (if anything) you will be charged for.
5. Know exactly who will service your account—from your calling rep to service and problem resolution people.
6. Ask what else the bank hopes to gain from this relationship over time.
7. Understand how your organization fits with the bank's strategic focus.

Source: Cathryn R. Gregg, Treasury Strategies, Inc., 309 W. Washington St., Suite 1300, Chicago, IL 60606, (312) 443-0840. Used by permission

EXHIBIT 5.6 CHECKLIST FOR CASH MANAGEMENT BANK SELECTION

- *Define bank relations ("tiering").* Rank banks in terms of importance to the company, ranging from tier-one banks used extensively in the past for credit and noncredit services to tier-four banks, which are branches and some regional depository banks that typically do not provide credit services.
- *Establish compensation ranges.* How should banks in each tier be compensated, and what is a reasonable level of compensation?
- *Establish a method for adjusting target balances.* Indicate how bank compensation would be adjusted if a bank exceeds or falls below the target,

TENDER PROCESS

When selecting a new bank, it is normal to go through a formal tender process. For that, the corporate needs to be clear about its objectives and requirements:

1. These **objectives** may include:
    - Reducing banking costs
    - Reducing liquidity requirements—squeezing unnecessary liquidity out of the system
    - Providing a good transaction banking service

2. **Analyze the requirements**
    - It is important to understand how divisions, subsidiaries, or departments—both in centralized and decentralized organizations—use all of the accounts. This needs to be clear before preparing the Request for a Proposal (RFP).

3. **Identify the potential new banks**
    - Contact them beforehand to explain your objectives and to warn them that a tender document is being sent to them, so that it will go to the correct person, who will treat it with sufficient importance, and in a timely manner.
    - Will the existing transaction bankers be included?

4. **Information**
    - Give as much information to the prospective banks as possible, including a description of the organizations needs, transaction volumes, and values.
    - Describe clearly the organization's objectives.

5. **Set a realistic timetable for the process**
    - At least 1 month for the initial response
    - The estimated time for consideration of the proposals, to reach a short-list, proposed dates for presentations, the decision, and implementation (don't be overoptimistic).

6. **Specify what the response should include**
    - Description of the service the bank is able to provide, including support and service-level agreement.
    - Details of the pricing they are offering.
    - Technical details of their electronic banking system.
    - Lending and overdraft facilities available (and interest rates).
    - Money market and other treasury lines that might be available.
    - How they would handle implementation of the transfer of the business.
    - Names of similarly sized customers, for reference.

MEETING THE SHORT-LISTED BANKS

To enable a good comparison of the short-listed banks, it is important to compare them under similar conditions, including:

- A strict timetable and agenda
- Specifying the areas which are important to the organization, such as pricing, systems, and service

It is sometimes revealing to compare whom they send to give presentations, such as existing or prospective account managers, their level of seniority and experience, and whether they bring their implementation team.

(Continues)

EXHIBIT 5.7 THE PROCESS OF BANK SELECTION AND IMPLEMENTATION

IMPLEMENTATION

Once the decision has been reached, implementation needs to be managed very carefully, involving the operational personnel who will be handling the process. The process includes:

1. Meeting with the successful bank to plan the implementation. This covers:
   - A realistic timetable
   - Regular progress reporting
   - Documentary requirements
   - Agreeing a training schedule for any new software being provided
2. Meeting with the outgoing bank to agree to a hand-over procedure

It needs to be emphasized that implementation can be a major exercise. In addition to the actions to be taken by the bank, the organization will need to consider the various issues, including changing payment instructions for existing customers if they credit your bank accounts electronically and changing internal systems that have been set up to interface with the existing bank.

Do not underestimate the potential for things to go wrong and to take longer than expected, as the sales teams from the new bank do have a tendency to promise more than their bank can deliver.

FINALLY

When the new system has been in place for 3 or 6 months, a review needs to be conducted to check that the anticipated savings and benefits are being achieved and that the new systems are working as the bank had promised, and to identify actions to be taken if that is not the case.

Brian Welch • Usercare Ltd., • "Changing Your Cash Management Bank," 23 Jun 2000
Global Treasury News (www.gtnews.com) June 23, 2000.
Source: www.gtnews.com/cash/home.html. Accessed: 10/6/06.

EXHIBIT 5.7 *(continued)*

with a goal of altering the bank's return on assets related to its business with the company.

- *Define relationship and communications responsibility.* Specify who in the corporation is responsible for managing the overall relations with banks (usually the treasurer) and the frequency and form of company-bank communications.
- *Define compensation periods.* How often will the company review compensation for each tier of banks? Compensation is negotiated and confirmed with each bank, in order to assist in the overall objective of reaching a target compensation over a certain time frame.
- *Define payment methods.* For credit services, this would normally be in fees and interest charges, while for noncredit services payment might be in fees, compensating balances, or a combination of fees and balances.
- *Define compensation agreements and contracts.* Here the company's position is articulated as a first approach toward negotiating a written agreement or contract with each bank.

- *Establish an annual review process.* The process includes an overall rating of the bank; an estimate of the bank's past and projected income and expense on the company's account; potential new business with the bank; target compensation level reestablishment; and whether a bank will remain in the same tier, move to a new tier, or be terminated.[17]

If you follow Hutton's model, you will be sure to provide your bank with a reasonable risk-adjusted return on capital (RAROC), which is a standard benchmark measure that many banks have adopted as they evaluate each of their client relationships.[18] It is considered prudent to try to negotiate and reach agreement when negotiating with a bank rather than to simply walk away from a long-standing relationship. Ongoing bank relationships create value for your organization because of the attendant predictability, streamlined and established procedures, and flexibility of the bank's response if you have new service or loan requests in the future—although the latter is less assured.

(a) ACCOUNT ANALYSIS AND THE ACCOUNT ANALYSIS STATEMENT.   Banks put larger nonprofits "on analysis" due to the number of checks they write and other services they use. Then, once a month, the bank provides an *account analysis statement*, which is an itemized monthly invoice showing:

- The services used and the fees charged to the organization
- In-depth balance information, a 12-month balance history
- A detailed listing and pricing of services used
- The degree to which the organization's actual balances offset fees charged for the services used

The statement helps your organization's finance staff determine whether excess balances are being held as well as to project ahead of time the balances that must be held, on average, in order to avoid service charges. It is a valuable cash management tool.

The month's activity charges must be shown on both a fee basis and a compensating balance basis by banks following the Association for Financial Professionals (AFP) standard presentation format, which was established in 1987 to facilitate comparisons between banks. In your evaluation of other banks that may be bidding for your account you can compare pro forma analysis statements based on the exact availability schedule to be used—which is negotiable with your bank—as most banks have two or three different availability schedules (with one applying to organizations that pre-encode checks before depositing them).

Exhibit 5.8 illustrates the main components of an actual account analysis statement used by a bank in the western region, which conforms to the standard AFP format. The name of the bank and the name of the client are disguised to preserve confidentiality. Our example statement summarizes the activity for November 2006 for a client, with the net service charge (or credit) computed in the first schedule and individual services used shown in the second schedule.

```
                                         PAGE:    1        E-STATEMENT              H
PO BOX 512999                                026-09
LOS ANGELES            CA   90051


ACCOUNT OFFICER:       JOHN SMITH
TELEPHONE NUMBER:      (858) 555-2345


ABC ENGINEERING INC
CORPORATE
1234 EL CAMINO RD  SOUTH       #209
SAN DIEGO CA   92108
                                   MASTER ACCOUNT   : DDA 011000XXXX
                                   SETTLEMENT PERIOD:  11/01/06 - 11/30/06
                                   DATE PREPARED:      DECEMBER 9, 2006



                                  BUSINESS BANK
                           ACCOUNT ANALYSIS STATEMENT
                         FOR THE MONTH OF NOVEMBER 2006
                                  AFFILIATION

                      NET  ACCOUNT  POSITION  SUMMARY




AMOUNT DUE - CURRENT SETTLEMENT PERIOD                          $470.66
AMOUNT DUE - DEFICIT CHARGED TO ACCOUNT                         $470.66-

AMOUNT DUE AND PAYABLE UPON RECEIPT                               $0.00
                                                          _____

              PLEASE SEE THE ATTACHED SUMMARY FOR COMPLETE DETAILS
```

EXHIBIT 5.8   ACCOUNT ANALYSIS STATEMENT

We begin working at the top of the exhibit, in the section entitled "Net Account Position Summary."

The "Amount Due – Current Settlement Period" of $460.66 is how much in fees the organization owes the bank for November's banking services due to not leaving enough in average balances on account during November. Put another way, the organization could have had a $0 amount due had it left significantly larger balances in its bank accounts at "Business Bank." The next line, "Amount Due – Deficit Charged to Account" simply says that the amount owed is to be charged to the organization's account (this is a direct debit, as might be done with your personal account when you order new checks; no check is written to pay this amount, normally). Later in the exhibit, you will see under "Account Position" that the bank would charge the organization's main account for this $460.66 on December 26, 2006. Banks normally have a certain business day in the month on which they charge for any amounts owed.

Under "Balance Summary," the bank shows the organization's average balances, summed for its eight accounts (which are listed later under the caption, "Clients and Accounts Included in This Analysis"). (Average balance is simply

```
                                  PAGE:     2                          H

   PO BOX 512999                      026-09
   LOS ANGELES          CA  90051


   ACCOUNT OFFICER:    JOHN SMITH
   TELEPHONE NUMBER:   (858) 555-2345


   ABC ENGINEERING INC
   CORPORATE


                         MASTER ACCOUNT   : DDA 011000XXXX

                         SETTLEMENT PERIOD:  11/01/06 - 11/30/06
                         DATE PREPARED:      DECEMBER 9, 2006


                            BUSINESS BANK
                        ACCOUNT ANALYSIS STATEMENT
                      FOR THE MONTH OF NOVEMBER 2006
                               AFFILIATION
                        BALANCE  SUMMARY

   AVERAGE BUSINESS CHECKING LEDGER BALANCE                    $749,757.46
TOTAL AVERAGE LEDGER BALANCE                                   $749,757.46
   BALANCE ADJUSTMENTS                                             174.88-
AVERAGE ADJUSTED LEDGER BALANCE                                $749,582.58
   LESS:  AVERAGE UNCOLLECTED FUNDS                              32,414.60
AVERAGE COLLECTED BALANCE                                      $717,167.98
   LESS:  RESERVE REQUIREMENT                                    71,716.76
BALANCE AVAILABLE TO SUPPORT ACTIVITY                          $645,451.22

                        ACCOUNT  POSITION

EARNINGS CREDIT RATE OF    1.7500%                                $928.39
NET EARNINGS ALLOWANCE - THIS MONTH                              $928.39
   LESS:  CHARGES FOR BALANCE COMPENSATED SERVICES             1,399.05
NET EARNINGS DEFICIT - SETTLEMENT PERIOD TO DATE                $470.66

                     ACCOUNT  POSITION  SUMMARY

YOUR ACCOUNT NUMBER 011000XXX WILL    BE  CHARGED FOR THE EARNINGS DEFICIT AMOUNT FOR THE CURRENT
SETTLEMENT PERIOD ON DECEMBER 26, 2006

FOR THE MONTH OF NOVEMBER, YOUR ACCOUNT(S) RECEIVED A $10.00
BENEFIT FROM STANDARD RATES AND PRICING.

COLLECTED BALANCE REQUIRED PER $1.00 OF SERVICE CHARGE IS $772.49

            CLIENTS  AND  ACCOUNTS  INCLUDED  IN  THIS  ANALYSIS

011000XXXX  ABC ENGINEERING INC
012000XXXX  ABC ENGINEERING INC
013000XXXX  ABC ENGINEERING INC
014000XXXX  ABC ENGINEERING INC
015000XXXX  ABC ENGINEERING LA INC
016000XXXX  ABC ENGINEERING SF INC
017000XXXX  ABC FOUNDATION
018000XXXX  ABC HOLDING CORP

            SERVICE  DETAIL
                                                                  BALANCE
                   VOLUME   UNIT PRICE       TOTAL PRICE          REQUIRED


SERVICES PROVIDED - BALANCE COMPENSATION

ACCOUNT ANALYSIS
   ACCT MAINTENANCE - WEB       8.00  $17.00             136.00   105,058.20
   FDIC INS/FICO              780.01  $.015/$1000         11.70     9,038.10
```

EXHIBIT 5.8   (*continued*)

taking each day's balance and adding them up for the whole month, then dividing by the number of days in the month.) First, you see the "Average Business Checking Ledger Balance," which includes all monies you have deposited regardless of whether the bank considers those funds available, or "spendable." The key concept here is that when you deposit checks drawn on any bank other than the bank at which you deposit them (called "on-us" checks), you will have to wait

```
                                        PAGE:      3                              H

     PO BOX 512999                      026-09
     LOS ANGELES           CA    90051


     ACCOUNT OFFICER:      JOHN SMITH
     TELEPHONE NUMBER:     (858) 555-2345


     ABC ENGINEERING INC
     CORPORATE


                               MASTER ACCOUNT    : DDA 011000XXXX

                               DATE PREPARED:    DECEMBER 9, 2006


                                  BUSINESS BANK
                            ACCOUNT ANALYSIS STATEMENT
                         FOR THE MONTH OF NOVEMBER 2006
                                   AFFILIATION

                               SERVICE  DETAIL
                                                                        BALANCE
                               VOLUME   UNIT PRICE     TOTAL PRICE      REQUIRED

BUSINESS CHECKING
  BRANCH DEPOSIT               10.00    $1.30/DEPOSIT      13.00       10,042.33
  PAID CHECK CHARGE           500.00    $.13/EACH          65.00       50,211.64
  PAID CHECK CHARGE           133.00    $.15/EACH          19.95       15,411.11
  ELECTRONIC DEBIT             13.00    $.12/EACH           1.56        1,205.08
CHECK PROCESSING
  ON US CHECKS - BRANCH DEPOSIT 4.00    $.080               0.3          247.20
  LOCAL CLR.HSE./BRANCH DEP.   18.00    $.08                1.44        1,112.38
  LOCAL FED DIST 12 - BRANCH DEP 19.00  $.10/ITEM           1.90        1,467.72
  OTHER FED - BRANCH DEPOSIT    5.00    $.125/ITEM          0.6          486.67
  ON US CHECKSERVCTR    DEPOSIT 101.00  $.05                5.0        3,901.06
  LOCAL CLR. HSE./SER. CTR     266.00   $.05               13.30       10,274.07
  LOCAL FED DIST 12-SERV CTR DEP 102.00 $.07/ITEM           7.14        5,515.56
  OTHER FED - SERV CTR DEPOSIT  24.00   $.095/ITEM          2.28        1,761.27
CUSTOMER SERVICE ACTIVITIES
  DDA AUTO-RENEWED STOP PMT    16.00    $8.00             128.00       98,878.31
INTERNET BUSINESS BANKING
  IBB ACCOUNT TRANSFER          9.00                        0.00           0.00
  IBB DDA STOP PMT              1.00    $10.00/EACH         10.00        7,724.87
  IBB CHECK IMAGE VIEW          2.00                        0.00           0.00
  IBB DEPOSIT IMAGE VIEW        2.00                        0.00           0.00
INFORMATION REPORTING
  WEB PRIOR DAY REPORT ACCOUNTS 1.00    $80.00/ACCOUNT      80.00       61,798.94
STATEMENTS
  IOD-SINGLE IMAGE (<120 DAYS)  8.00    $0.00/IMAGE          0.00           0.00
  IOD-SINGLE IMAGE(181+ DAYS)   1.00    $2.00/IMAGE          2.00        1,544.97
TELESERVICES
  ACCOUNT TRANSFER-COUNTER      1.00                        0.00           0.00
  INQUIRY & TRANSFER SERVICE    1.00    $0.00               0.00           0.00
TEAM STOP PAYMENTS
  WEB NUMBER STOP ACCOUNTS      1.00                        0.00           0.00
WHOLESALE LOCKBOX
  MONTHLY BASE CHARGE           2.00    $150.00/BOX        300.00      231,746.03
  ITEM PROCESSED-OFFLINE DEL  493.00    $.43/ITEM          211.99      163,759.47
  PHOTOCOPIES                 493.00    $.11/ITEM           54.23       41,891.96
  ACCOUNT MAINTENANCE           2.00    $0.00               0.00           0.00
  RE-ASSOCIATE INVOICE & COPIES 493.00  $.07/ITEM           34.51       26,658.52
  REJECTS / CORRESPONDENCE    109.00    $.25               27.25       21,050.26
  ADDITONAL MAILING             1.00    $45.00/MONTH        45.00       34,761.90
  PAYEE VERIFICATION (1-10)   493.00    NO CHARGE           0.00           0.00
```

EXHIBIT 5.8   (*continued*)

to be able to spend any amount other than the first $100 of the deposit. This concept of "holds" on checks shows up when we see that "Total Average Ledger Balance" is greater than the amount we can spend, which is "Average Collected Balance."

Still under "Balance Summary," the next item you see is "Balance Adjustments." These are usually corrections from something that was credited or debited the previous month. For example, perhaps a check you deposited at the end of last month was given "provisional credit," but two or three days later it "bounced"

```
                                    PAGE:     4                              H

    PO BOX 512999                         026-09
    LOS ANGELES            CA   90051


    ACCOUNT OFFICER:     JOHN SMITH
    TELEPHONE NUMBER:    (858) 555-2345


    ABC ENGINEERING INC
    CORPORATE



                         MASTER ACCOUNT   : DDA 011000XXXX


                         DATE PREPARED:     DECEMBER 9, 2006


                            BUSINESS BANK
                       ACCOUNT ANALYSIS STATEMENT
                     FOR THE MONTH OF NOVEMBER 2006
                            AFFILIATION

                          SERVICE  DETAIL
                                                                    BALANCE
                     VOLUME   UNIT PRICE      TOTAL PRICE          REQUIRED
WHOLESALE LOCKBOX
  POSTAL BOX RENTAL   145.00  COST                 145.00        112,010.58
  LOCKBOX DEPOSIT      36.00  $1.30/DEPOSIT         46.80         36,152.38
ZERO BALANCE ACCOUNTS
  SUB LEVEL 1           1.00  $35.00               35.00         27,037.04

TOTAL CHARGES: BALANCE COMPENSATED SERVICES     1,399.05      1,080,747.62

SERVICES PROVIDED - FEES WAIVED

CUSTOMER SERVICE ACTIVITIES
  NON-CUSTOMER CASH PAID ON-US   2.00  $5.00 PER CHEC    10.00

TOTAL CHARGES: WAIVED SERVICES                     10.00
```

EXHIBIT 5.8 *(continued)*

and was debited back against your account as a return item. Since last month's statement did not capture that return, it shows up on this month's statement.

The "Average Adjusted Ledger Balance" is Total Average Ledger Balance plus or minus any Balance Adjustments. Next we see a subtraction for "Average Uncollected Funds." Sometimes banks call this "Average Float." It represents checks deposited on which the bank has not yet collected funds. The Average Uncollected Funds is subtracted from the Average Adjusted Ledger Balance to arrive at "Average Collected Balance." Recapping, ledger balances are monies posted to your account but not yet spendable due to availability delays, or what we as consumers refer to as holds on the deposited checks. Float, or "Average Uncollected Funds," represents the difference between what has been deposited and what the organization may spend at that point in time.

It is important to know how banks arrive at their calculation of "Average Uncollected Funds," since this is money that you may think you have but yet you may not spend it just yet. Banks' calculation of this float amount is a function of (1) the bank's availability schedule (covered earlier in the chapter) and (2) its cutoff times. Don't assume that quicker availability implies higher collected balances, because a bank may have an earlier cutoff time for assigning ledger credit to checks. Let's say you deposit a check at 3 p.m. Availability of funds on that check deposited at 3 p.m. at bank A, which has a 1 p.m. cutoff time and assigns one-day availability, will identical to the availability of funds at bank B, which has 4 p.m. cutoff time and two-day availability. You may recall from our earlier discussion that items deposited after the cutoff time will not even be granted ledger credit until the next banking day. To make things even more complicated, there could be some retroactive adjustments: Some banks base their availability schedules on actual check clearing times for each organization's checks, whereas others use averages based on past periods for the organization or a group of similar organizations.

Restating the average ledger balance, average uncollected funds, and average collected balance relationship, the difference between collected balances and ledger balances may be represented as follows:

$$\text{Average Collected Balance} = \text{Average Ledger Balance}$$
$$- \text{Average Uncollected Funds}$$

Many banks further distinguish between collected and balances available to offset fees ("Balance Available to Support Activity") by deducting from collected balances an amount equivalent to the required reserves that the Fed mandates banks hold. This reserve requirement (by which the Federal Reserve mandates that banks set aside funds in vault cash on the bank's premises or as deposits at the bank's Federal Reserve District Bank) is 10 percent at the time of the schedule.[19] Because the bank must hold reserves in nonearning assets (vault cash does not earn interest, and the Federal Reserve does not pay banks interest as of the time of this writing), the bank will not include this part of the organization's balances in the available balance. Put another way, if your bank is not getting paid interest on part of your deposit, it will not in turn compute an earnings credit on that part of the deposit for your account. The earnings credit, also called an earnings allowance, is the amount that has been "earned" via balances left in the account that may be used to offset fees dollar-for-dollar.

The next major section is entitled "Account Position." This is where we see how the bank calculated the net fee owed for this month's banking services, or what it terms "Net Earnings Deficit." The earnings credit rate is usually based on the prevailing U.S. Treasury Bill (T-bill) rate during that period, and often significantly less than that T-bill rate. If you take the "Balance Available to Support Activity" of $645,451.22, and multiply it by the earnings credit rate expressed on a monthly basis, you will arrive at a "Net Earnings Allowance-This Month" of $928.39. November has 30 days, so 30/365 = 0.082191781; multiply this by 0.0175, which is 1.75% in decimal form, and you get 0.0014383561675. Finally, take this monthly interest rate, as expressed in decimal form, and multiply it by $645,451.22 and you arrive at $928.39. This means that the balances that the bank will calculate an earnings credit for, the "Balance Available to Support Activity," will cover $928.39 in service fees for November. Our next step is to now compare that to the fees the organization owes the bank for all the many services the bank rendered for the organization in the month of November. Those come in the "Service Detail Section." Before moving to that, let's take a final look at the concept of earnings credit and how it differs from interest.

There is a very important distinction between the law as it applies to businesses (partnerships and corporations) and the law as it pertains to sole proprietorships, government agencies, and nonprofits. Federal law prohibits a bank from paying a company interest on its demand deposit accounts balances. So banks calculate a bookkeeping credit that they will credit to the business account in order to partly or wholly offset service charges incurred by the business that month. *However, banks still will calculate that earnings credit for nonprofits that are on analysis*. The ultimate end result is still that you may be able to reduce service charges by holding account balances at the bank instead of investing those balances elsewhere or sweeping those balances out of the account on an overnight basis.

Banks' earnings credit rates are generally based on a prevailing money market rate (usually somewhat below the rate of 91-day Treasury bills from a recent auction) and your bank's business strategy, but typically they are relatively low compared with the rates at which treasurers are able to invest surplus funds. Remember that 10 percent of the account balances will not even receive the earnings credit because of the Fed's reserve requirement.

Now refer to the Service Detail in the second panel of Exhibit 5.8. You will see there that the services used by the organization during the month, the services' unit prices (how much you are getting charged for each item used, and the product of the units and their prices to get the overall amount for that service in the "Total Price" column. The rightmost column, which is called "Balance Required," converts the service charges to the equivalent amount of demand deposit balances. In other words, how much would your organization have had to have kept in average available balances to fully pay the bank for that particular service? To compute this, the bank first puts the "Earnings Credit Rate" (*ecr*) on a monthly basis by dividing it by 365, then multiplying it by the number of days in the month (which in this case is 30; we will abbreviate this as *n*). In our sample statement, we saw earlier that this was equal to 0.0014383561675 (= 0.0175 × 30/365). The bank then multiplies this rate by (1 − reserve ratio), or 0.90 (= 1 − 0.10). In our case, this is 0.00129452055075 (= 0.0014383561675 × 0.90). The bank then converts each service charge line item to the required balances necessary to exactly pay for these charges (based on this phantom interest rate, *ecr*) by applying this formula:

$$\text{Required compensating balances} = \frac{SC}{(1 - rr)\left(\dfrac{ecr}{365}\right)n}$$

Where:

$SC =$ service charge for the month

$rr =$ required reserve ratio (set by Federal Reserve, same for all banks)

$ecr =$ earnings credit rate (annual)

$n =$ number of days in month

For example, note the first line item ("ACCT MAINTENANCE – WEB"): our sample organization has eight accounts at the bank, each charged a monthly service fee of $17.00. The "Total Price," or total monthly fee owed, on these eight accounts is listed as $136.00. The $136.00 is the service charge for the month in our formula, or SC. Substituting this $136.00 into our formula, along with the denominator value of 0.00129452055075 that we already calculated above, we get Required compensating balances of $105,058.20:

$$\text{Required compensating balances} = \frac{\$136}{0.00129452055075} = \$105,058.20$$

Note that the bank has also provided a multiplier for you to use. In the section entitled "Account Position Summary," the last line says: "Collected Balance Required per $1.00 of service charge is $772.49." There will be a slight rounding difference, but if you take the $136 in service fees and multiply it by $772.49, you will get a number approximately equal to $105,058.20. This gives a quick approach to estimate what level of balances you will have to maintain to offset a specific service fee, such as the monthly account fee for these eight accounts.

Given the organization's total service charges owed of $1,399.05 for November, the "Total Charge for Services" at the bottom of the second schedule indicates a "Balance Required" of $1,080,747.62. Again, it is not mandatory that you maintain this balance, but if you wish to totally offset service fees for November, this is the amount of average balances that you would have had to have kept in these eight accounts, in total.

Return now to the "Account Position" at the top of Exhibit 5.8. Since your organization gets credit for an "Earnings Allowance" of $928.39, but owed the bank $1,399.05 for banking fees for the month, it still owes the bank $470.66 (= $1,399.05 − $928.39). This is the amount that will have to be paid to the bank, which is typically invoiced on 30-day terms and quite often directly debited to your checking account, as we see here. If your organization would rather compensate the bank by holding larger balances, a few banks have a policy by which the shortfall may make up over several months.

If your account analysis statement showed a surplus (net service credit) instead of an amount owed, in a noninterest-leaving account this amount cannot be paid out to you; thus, it is often carried over into one or more future months to offset those months when balances are inadequate to cover service charges. Settlement periods over which credits or shortfalls are cumulated might be quarterly, semiannual, or annual (calendar year). Charges would be made on the cumulative shortfall at the period's end if amounts owed were permitted to carry over.

(i) Uses of the Account Analysis Statement.   The account analysis statement is your invoice for the bank services you used; you may also use the account analysis to gain a bird's-eye view of your organization's balances and bank activity. It can also be useful when you are comparing the same service usage levels across two or more banks. There are two difficulties in doing these comparisons: (1) different banks use different formats for their statements (although this is gradually changing), and (2) banks have differing cutoff times and availability schedules that drive their float computations. The uniform account analysis format developed by AFP is being used more now, yet cash managers complain that quite a few banks have not adopted it. As a result, one must either manually adjust the different banks' statements to bring comparability or make use of Weiland software to automatically reformat them to a uniform statement.

At a minimum, do two things with each month's account analysis statement:

1. Verify the accuracy of the statement. This is an invoice, so treat it as such. Did you use all of these services in the quantities listed? Are the unit prices accurate, based on your prior negotiations and contract with the bank?
2. Consider how to improve your organization's cash management. Are there techniques listed in Chapters 2, 3, or 4 that would enable you to pay less in bank fees, yet still have adequate financial management?

Periodically, perhaps every six months, conduct one additional analysis. Should your organization continue to maintain the balances that were maintained last month? The earnings credit rate is significantly less than what you could earn on a sweep account to a money market mutual fund, so maybe the most cost-effective approach to banking is to sweep excess funds out of the account on an overnight basis. When interest rates were very low, this did not make sense. As short-term rates climbed above 3%, many organizations "turned on" their sweep accounts once again. We shall return to this analysis in more depth below.

(ii) Electronic Account Analysis Statement.   Many banks have begun making available to their institutional customers an electronic account analysis statement, called the 882 electronic analysis statement, or just "822" for short. This electronic form is a type of electronic data interchange that sends detailed account information to your organization. More quickly and accurately than with a paper form account analysis statement, the 882 helps you:

- Find errors
- Perform modeling
- Archive statements

- Make comparisons between banks, divisions, departments or regions
- Maintain strong internal control (Sarbanes-Oxley–level compliance) by examining prices and charges[20]

(b) HOW BANKS CHARGE FOR SERVICES.   Getting the most value from your organization's banking arrangements necessitates understanding how compensating balances are calculated as well as the advantages and disadvantages of paying for bank services by balances versus fees. We start by demonstrating the required compensating balance computation for bank services.

(i) Computing Compensating Balances.   Compensating balances are defined as "minimum or average deposit amounts required by banks as a means of charging for cash management or lending services."[21] Banks historically insisted that institutional customers maintain a checking account balance equal to 10 percent of amounts borrowed under a credit line or loan principal amount, but in recent years nonbank competition has forced this figure lower or led to elimination of this requirement. In fact, for large businesses, balances are a show of goodwill and not required. If they are required on lending arrangements, organizations are required both to maintain the balances and to pay interest on amounts borrowed.

It is useful to calculate the amount of balances required for each individual service you use at your bank. Once the bank will know the charges for a month's activity for a particular service, it then uses a formula to calculate the equivalent amount of balances. For example, let's say your organization is being charged $150 for wire transfers during the month. It would have to have $150/0.004438356 = $33,796.30 in compensating balances, assuming a required reserve ratio of 10 percent and an *ecr* of 6 percent (using the following formula):

$$Compensating\ balances = \frac{\$150}{(1 - 0.10)\left(\dfrac{0.06}{365}\right)30}$$

$$= \frac{\$150}{0.004438356}$$

$$= \$33,796.30$$

If a financial institution passes along this insurance charge, it will either include a line item fee on the bank's service charge schedule or it will adjust the above formula by further multiplying the denominator of that formula by $(1 - \text{FDIC assessment rate})$. The latter adjustment has the effect of pushing the compensating balance dollar amount even higher.

(ii) Should We Compensate via Balances or Fees?   More than half of all businesses pay by fees, and we noted earlier in this chapter that nonprofits responding

to the Lilly study favored fee-based compensation as well. Let's consider the different viewpoints promoted by banks and by organizations.

Banks generally favor compensating balances over fees as the method of paying them for services performed; bankers cite these advantages of compensating balances:

- Compensating balances have the effect of increasing total deposits and assets, which are traditional benchmarks of a bank's success.
- Balances can be relent to another customer, which means that in the case of compensating balances related to loans, some of the funds are actually lent twice: Compensating balances required of borrower A make up part of the loan made to borrower B.
- Balances form a cushion, so that the bank can partly recover money that would have been lost when a borrower defaults on a loan.[22]

Business and nonprofit cash managers generally prefer fees, although they may hold positive balances at the bank to meet transactions requirements and provide a liquid reserve that can be tapped on short notice in an emergency. Demand deposits (except for nonprofit organizations) are non-interest-bearing accounts, which are ideally minimized, except in the rare case in which the earnings credit rate exceeds the rate that could be earned on alternative investments available to the firm. This thinking accounts for the first among several reasons treasury professionals favor fee-based compensation:

- Earnings credit rate (*ecr*) is almost always less than the alternative investment rate.
- Fee-based compensation offers a tangible expense that can be easily monitored and included in expense budgets.
- Fees are directly comparable between banks and many times are fixed for a year (many cash management contracts are fixed for three years but allow for a capped inflation adjustment at the end of years 1 and 2), whereas the *ecr* is an unpredictable floating rate.
- Lost interest related to the balances is not a tax-deductible expense, but fees charged by the bank are (for taxable entities).[23]

One final issue to consider here is the possibility of "double-counting" of compensating balances. This can occur when a bank counts the same balances as compensation for a loan *and* as compensation for cash management services. Double-counting may steer your organization toward balance-based compensation.

(c) **OPTIMIZING YOUR BANKING SYSTEM.** Recall that your objective for bank relationship management is to ensure that all of your organization's banking services are provided reliably at a reasonable cost. Finding the best configuration of accounts and banks is difficult, given the role of qualitative criteria such as reliability that must be considered. We simply point out that you should take a "systems" or "global" view of your overall bank relationship structure. For example, often the same bank provides lending and cash collections services, although some contend that a "do-your-own" lockbox collection system is less expensive than a bank's lockbox collection system, even when taking loan considerations into account. Additionally, banks want you to invest through them, perhaps in an investment firm owned by the same bank holding company that owns the bank, but treasurers generally find that the investment services are separable from other bank services. Even sweep products can be set up to sweep your funds automatically out to a brokerage outside the bank.

5.8 NONBANK SERVICE PROVIDERS

Nonfinancial corporations are increasingly providing banking services. You may have heard about the political battles fought as traditional banks have worked to "keep Wal-Mart out of banking." Commercial and industrial conglomerates such as American Express, GE, Westinghouse, and J.C. Penney have all acquired financial institutions.

Much of the nonbank activity has taken place in lending. Banks are no longer the dominant players they once were for short-term funding: Approximately 50 percent of all consumer and business loans are now held by nonbank companies.

The nonbank penetration has also been seen in nonlending services: In information services, the primary nonbank providers are nonbank companies offering balance reporting services. In the collections area, recall how the Christian Children's Fund uses a media company's excess in-house lockbox processing capabilities. Another good example is the consulting industry, which provides nonprofits with software with which they may compare banks, mail time analyses, and bank rating services. We also see this trend in short-term investing: Look at the explosion of institutional money market mutual funds (MMMFs). Between 1987 and the begining of 2007, institutional (nonpersonal) monies held in these nonbank accounts mushroomed from $140.4 billion to $1 trillion. MMMF accounts serve as interest-bearing payment vehicles, although the minimum check amount could be as low as $500. Bankers realize these are a significant competitor to their money market deposit accounts and certificates of deposit, even though they lack the federal deposit insurance guarantee.

What does the future hold in this regard? A fascinating survey conducted in 2000, and gaining responses from 444 businesses responding, found:

- About 60 percent of businesses agree or strongly agree that "physical location of banking locations will become less important in the future."
- Almost 20 percent of businesses agree or strongly agree that "banks will play less of a role in providing my organization's financial services needs

as other types of financial services institutions offer the types of services that my firm needs."[24]

5.9 INFORMATION SERVICES

Treasurers see banks' cash management officers as individuals offering very helpful information and advice. This advice is typically geared toward placing the bank in a favorable light, however. One area that is especially important to tap bankers' expertise is that of online banking.

(a) ONLINE BANKING.   Whether you call it online banking, web-based banking, or Internet banking, this arena has exploded for nonprofits in recent years. Many bankers consider this the number-one service that nonprofits of all sizes need to have implemented. Consider these recent findings:

- Ernst & Young finds that about 30 percent of all commercial users of electronic information reporting services are receiving balance and transaction detail from their bank via the Internet.[25]
- Many banks also reported either losing clients or being left out of new relationship consideration if they lacked a specific Internet capability.
- Corporate customers found that being able to access data anywhere they could access the Internet was a major advantage of online banking, with slow response time, scaled-down product offerings, and one-size-fits-all product offerings being the main disadvantages.
- Ernst & Young finds that Internet service delivery is now offered universally to corporate (and nonprofit) clients by banks in the area of balance and information reporting; 91 percent offer between-account transfers at the bank; 75 percent offer ACH transfers and wire transfers; and 41 percent offer image delivery of issued checks (mostly for viewing exception items for a bank's fraud protection service) and lockbox items.
- A bit disconcerting is the perception on the part of 37 percent of corporate users that they could not automatically trust that security issues were taken care of by the bank once a bank launched an Internet product.
- A 2001 survey by AFP also documents that 92 percent of treasury professionals are getting information via the Internet, about four in five are using the Internet to communicate with financial service providers, 63 percent are using the Internet to transact business, and 36 percent are selecting service providers with web information.
- In Europe, large companies indicate that they are especially interested in getting account information, but over half also would like to use the web for foreign exchange or disbursement services.

(b) SPECIAL STUDIES.   Banks offer corporate and nonprofit clients various advisory services, including:

- *Lockbox studies.* The bank uses a computerized model to study the pattern of mailed checks a company receives and advises it on the best number and locations of lockboxes.
- *Disbursement studies.* Similar to lockbox studies, except the bank advises the client regarding controlled disbursement and zero balance accounts, the best locations of these accounts, and direct deposit.
- *Financial management advice.* Especially for smaller companies and non-profits, banks may give advice about basics such as cash budgeting, pro forma statements, what cash management services might be cost-effective, and the types of bank lending for which the client might be eligible.
- *International cash management studies.* Included here are analyses of foreign countries' payment systems, economies, and the best approach to pooling cash and moving cash into or out of each country.
- *Computerized treasury management IT.* In some cases, the bank will serve as a distributor under a license agreement with the developer of the computer system.[26]

5.10 BANKING GLOBALLY

Both the trend toward nationwide banking in the United States and the ongoing economic unification of Europe will spur the drift toward concentration in the banking industry and toward more globalized banking. Your organization should be aware of the impacts these trends will have as you set up your U.S. and, if operating multinationally, your global banking network.

(a) CONSOLIDATION OF BANKING RELATIONSHIPS.   Because banking networks are consolidating in the United States, your organization will at some point eliminate its use of multiple banks to operate its collection and concentration network. The Canadian payments landscape, in which there are only a handful of large banks offering most of the cash management and depository services, is helpful to see the directions in which the U.S. system is migrating. Your organization may soon have a one-bank collection center, which pools and invests or pay down borrowings, instead of having to move monies from many outlying banks to a different concentration bank. You will no longer need to actually transfer funds to position funds centrally, because the balances can be netted out within one bank's automated bookkeeping system. Refer to Chapter 3 for information on international collections and positioning products and systems and to Chapter 4 for information on international disbursement products and systems.

(b) GLOBAL ASPECTS OF BANKING RELATIONSHIPS.   One of the brightest prospects for U.S.-based banks in the coming years is the potential for selling more international cash management services. The combination of computerized treasury systems and international account balance inquiry and pooling capabilities is setting up some large U.S. banks to gain market share by aggressively serving the needs of nonprofit and business clients operating multinationally. Large U.S. banks continue to operate numerous branches abroad to service multinational customers. Several large banks have a presence in 80 to 90 different countries, and Citigroup operates in more than 100 countries and territories. Consult Appendix 5A to see the top-rated financial service providers globally, as compiled by *Global Finance Magazine*. U.S.-based multinational businesses have been free to centralize European treasury operations, often selecting London or tax-haven locales such as Dublin Docks (Ireland), Belgium, or Holland to host their finance subsidiaries. The location of a U.S. business's central treasury may be driven by tax treatment, but may also be linked to exchange rate risks or banking and other administrative costs—also key factors for a large multinational nonprofit agency to consider. Using a business illustration, chemical company DuPont concentrates its 22-country European services with Bank of America and then uses Citicorp to be its main service provider in all other areas of the world.

5.11 BANK REPORT CARDS

Continuous improvement has become an ingrained part of organization management in the United States. Implementing that concept is challenging for an organization that is understaffed and inexperienced in financial management. When evaluating your financial service provider, the best tool is a report card. We provide a usable template for your bank report card in Appendix 5B. In Exhibit 5.9 you will see how one bank uses report card information to position itself attractively.

5.12 CASH MANAGEMENT AUDITS

You will want to improve your organization's treasury management practice continuously as well. Now that we have completed our coverage of cash collections (Chapter 3), cash disbursements (Chapter 4), and banking relationship management, we can present some guidelines and checklists to assist you in doing a treasury audit. These are often called cash management audits.

(a) ASSESSING YOUR ORGANIZATION'S CASH MANAGEMENT PRACTICE.

You will want to assess these cash management areas: cash positioning/mobilization, bank relationship management, short-term investment/borrowing, and treasury systems management.[27] Each of these areas should be assessed relative to these six key elements:

1. *A high level of productivity (efficient use of organizational resources).* This includes automation of routine functions; maintaining a small clerical staff; and periodically reviewing functional techniques, strategies and systems, and integration with other functions and areas within your organization. Obviously, implementation of a complete EDI system would ensure high marks with this key element.

Balance Reporting/Internet Services

Telecash ViewPoint®, Mellon's Windows®-based information reporting and transaction initiation service, and iTelecash®, our Internet-based information reporting and transaction initiation service, provide access to timely and detailed cash management data for your Mellon and other accounts held around the world.

	Overall Mean	Mellon's Mean	Mellon's Score
Timeliness of information (Balance Reporting)	4.30	4.32	A+
Accuracy and reliability (Balance Reporting)	4.31	4.31	A+
Overall features and capabilities (Balance Reporting)	4.16	4.11	B
Ease of use (Internet Services)	4.01	4.24	A+
Overall features and capabilities (Internet Services)	3.95	4.17	A+

Source: Downloaded from www.mellon.com/cashmanagement/resourcecenter/2006ph. pdf. Used by permission.

EXHIBIT 5.9   BANK REPORT CARD EXAMPLE (PARTIAL)

2. *Utilization of advanced strategies and automation.* These include: advanced banking/third-party services, advanced cash management techniques, and fully automated and integrated treasury/financial systems. Once again, satisfaction of this key element would be evidenced by a well-integrated EDI system.

3. *Effective internal controls.* This includes regular cash management controls review performed by individuals outside the areas reviewed, adequate backup (both staff and systems), and up-to-date documented policies and procedures.

4. *Performance measurement standards.* This includes defined performance and/or quality standards, timely tracking of actual performance to performance standards/goals, integration of results with employee performance evaluations and defined and monitored standards for third-party providers (i.e., banks).

5. *Involvement in cash-related decisions organization-wide.* This includes a good working relationship with areas outside treasury, a high level of awareness of the importance of effective cash management practices, and the involvement and utilization of cash management personnel as internal consultants in decisions affecting cash.

6. *Excellent industry reputation.* This includes being known as an innovator to both peer organizations and third-party vendors and being utilized by vendors in evaluating, developing, and/or implementing new products and services.[28]

(b) METRICS FOR INTERNAL EVALUATION. Greenwich Treasury Advisors recommends that each organization use these cash management metrics for internal evaluation purposes (you may wish to modify these to fit your organization's specific practices and policies):

Cash Management Metrics—1
- Cycle time for finalizing cash position
- Cycle time for cash journal entries
- Number of wire transfer requests after 2 or 3 pm
- Number of "lost" wires
- Collections float (bank deposit to good value)
- Disbursements float
- Average end of day available balance, even if swept—Weighted average based upon overdraft rates and sweep investment rates
- Actual daily/weekly net cash flow vs. forecast—On an absolute basis

Cash Management Metrics—2
- Average number of bank accounts/unit as well as unit high and low
- Numbers of collections vs. disbursements vs. operating accounts
- Total cost of bank accounts
  - Out-of-pocket bank maintenance fees
  - Cost of transfers out to other accounts
  - Reconciliation costs
- Total banking collections costs (worldwide)
  - Soft dollar cost of availability
- Total banking disbursements costs
  - Soft dollar cost of backwards value plus float benefit
- Ratio/percentage of electronic vs. paper instruments for collections and disbursements

Cash Management Benchmarks
- Prior year results
- Multi-year trend analysis
- Total costs/headcount as a percentage of sales
- Phoenix-Hecht data
- Benchmarking group data

(c) ASSESSING THE ENTERPRISE RESOURCE PLANNING SYSTEM. Finally, for very large organizations, the treasury staff will wish to evaluate the enterprise resource planning (ERP) system.[29] A good definition of ERP systems states that they "are comprised of software programs which tie together all of an enterprise's various functions—such as finance, manufacturing, sales and human resources."[30] These systems originated in the human resource management field, then were used to tie data from the sales and customer relationship management area together with the organization's accounting system. These systems offer seamless, automatic, electronic interfacing of the organization's operations and financial data. Some of these systems produce accurate and timely flash reports (such as hourly bank statements). "End-to-end business processing" from accounts payable and accounts receivable through inventories, orders, working capital, currency, and risk forecasting are all available with a properly implemented ERP system that has the full set of modules. However, ERP systems are very expensive, and necessitate additional expenditures for proper training and to customize them to interface with treasury systems. (ERP systems can easily run $150,000 for a basic package.)

ASP, or application service provider, offerings are offering ERP functionality with a smaller up-front investment. ASP systems are either web-based or hosted. A web-based treasury information services offered through the Internet promises implementation times of only a few days and low monthly payments with no front-end license costs. "Hosted" Treasury Management Systems (TMSs) have the flexibility, integration, and cost structure of an installed ERP systems but also charge a monthly hosting cost (as the package resides on the host's computer, not on the user's computer).[31]

The biggest adopters of ASP systems are smaller and middle-market businesses. These organizations view ASP systems as having many of the advantages of ERP systems but not requiring nearly as large of an initial investment. We expect more educational and healthcare, and eventually other, nonprofits to adopt ASP systems.

5.13 SUMMARY

We have profiled the essential cash management services used by organizations: depository services and information services. The components of these services have been presented and illustrated, and relevant calculations have been demonstrated. Companies are increasingly seeking to cut banking system costs by performing more of the banking services themselves. Yet to a large degree, your organization will rely on a bank or other third-party provider to conduct these services for it.

Bank selection and relationship management are extremely important aspects of your organization's treasury management. The key factors you will want to consider as you select your bank(s) are its understanding of nonprofits, location, price, service quality, service breadth, bank/organization fit, bank creditworthiness, and bank competencies. A strong Internet services offering is becoming more important in the new millennium. Other trends coming in the future for banking are included in Exhibit 5.10.

	Average	Very Unlikely to Happen (%)	Unlikely to Happen (%)	Likely to Happen (%)	Very Likely to Happen (%)
Bank services becoming more "commoditized"	3.09	1	9	69	21
Fewer sources of credit	3.00	2	20	54	24
Banks will increasingly focus only on large organizations	2.96	1	26	50	23
Monopolistic pricing	2.88	2	26	53	19
Faster convergence of technology standards	2.86	2	25	58	15
Increase in customer risk due to concentration in banking relationships	2.74	1	35	52	12
Growth in small community banks (assets and number of banks)	2.61	8	36	42	14

Source: Association for Financial Professionals, "Financial Industry Consolidation Survey Results," 2000, p. 17. Used by permission.

EXHIBIT 5.10 LIKELY FUTURE DEVELOPMENTS IN BANKING

Finally, consider how to evaluate your bank using a report card and how to improve your internal cash management processes through treasury management audits and benchmarking. Appendix 5A provides you with a listing of the top-ranked banking institutions in global banking. Appendix 5B provides you with a sample bank report card that you may tailor to your needs as you continue to monitor your banks' service performance. In the next chapter we consider how you may tap bank and nonbank short-term credit provisions.

Notes

1. Aberdeen Group, "Setting PACE in Treasury and Cash Management: Benchmark Report." (Boston: Aberdeen Group Inc., 2006).

2. Id.

3. Based on Terry S. Maness and John T. Zietlow, *Short-Term Financial Management*, 3rd ed. (Cincinnati: South-Western, 2005): 288. This chapter draws extensively from the presentation on banking relationship management in that source.

4. Adapted from Robert W. Page, "10 Steps to a Successful Bank/Corporate Relationship," *TMA Journal* (September/October 1999): 70, 72.

5. We are consciously omitting some long-term services, such as helping your organization issue bonds, leasing, and consulting with you on a merger or acquisition.

6. Maness and Zietlow, *Short-Term Financial Management*, p. 289.

7. For more on ABA routing numbers and Acuity, the firm authorized to assign these numbers for the ABA, see http://www.aba.com/Products/PS98_Routing.htm.

8. Id., p. 290.

9. This section draws on information in Maness and Zietlow, *Short-Term Financial Management*.

10. BAI, "Research Report: Small Business Payments in 2006." (Chicago, Bank Administration Institute, 2006).

11. Id.

12. Id., p. 295.

13. Robert Oshinsky and Virginia Olin, "Troubled Banks: Why Don't They All Fail?" FDIC Working Paper 2005-03 (March 2005).

14. Id.

15. Brian Welch, "Changing Your Cash Management Bank." Posted online on June 23, 2000, at www.gtnews.com/cash/home.html.

16. This section draws on information in Maness and Zietlow, *Short-Term Financial Management*.

17. Maness and Zietlow, *Short-Term Financial Management*, p. 296.

18. For help in understanding and calculating RAROC, see http://www.erisk.com/Resource Center/Features/raroc.pdf and http://www.ing.com/cms/idc_cgi_isapi.dll?IdcService = GET_FILE&dDocName = 105462_EN&RevisionSelectionMethod = latestReleased.

19. Banks could further subtract from the average collected balance a dollar amount necessary to compensate for a loan extended to the customer, if this organization also has a credit line amount outstanding.

20. Christopher Bjorke, "Panelists: Account Analysis Key to Managing Banking Services," *AFP Online Headlines*, January 23, 2006.

21. Maness and Zietlow, *Short-Term Financial Management*, p. 302.

22. Id., p. 303.

23. Id.

24. AFP, "Financial Industry Consolidation Survey Results,"(Bethesda, MD: Author, 2000), p. 18.

25. Forman and Shafer, 2002.

26. Maness and Zietlow, *Short-Term Financial Management*, pp. 307–308.

27. Joseph J. Bonocore and Jeffrey S. Rosengard, "Managing the Effectiveness of Your Cash Management Function," *Journal of Cash Management* (January/February 1991): 32–36.

28. Quoted from Maness and Zietlow, *Short-Term Financial Management*, p. 661.

29. This section draws on information in Maness and Zietlow, *Short-Term Financial Management*.

30. WSReview.com (formerly *EDI World Magazine*). Located at www.wsreview.com/resources/glossary/default.cfm?KeywordID = E. Accessed: 1/31/04.

31. Maness and Zietlow, *Short-Term Financial Management*, p. 664.The second point is based on material in Andrew Bateman, "Is ASP a Viable Alternative in the Treasury Software Market?" 2003. Available online at www.gtnews.com. Accessed: 1/31/2004.

TOP-RATED FINANCE SERVICE PROVIDERS

Best Treasury and Cash Management Providers
Global Finance selects the leaders in a specialized area of finance that is benefiting from a surge in global trade.

Best Treasury and Cash Management Providers	
Global Winner	Citigroup

Regional Winners

North America	JPMorgan Chase
Western Europe	Deutsche Bank
Asia	HSBC
Latin America	Citigroup
Central and Eastern Europe	RZB
Middle East and Africa	National Bank of Kuwait

Best Bank For Liquidity/Working Capital Management

North America	Bank of America
Western Europe	Deutsche Bank
Asia	HSBC
Latin America	Citigroup
Central and Eastern Europe	RZB
Middle East and Africa	National Bank of Kuwait

Best Provider Of Outsourced Treasury Solutions

North America	JPMorgan Chase
Western Europe	ABN AMRO
Asia	Citigroup
Latin America	Citigroup
Central and Eastern Europe	ABN AMRO
Middle East and Africa	Standard Bank

Best Provider Of Money Market Funds

North America	Citigroup Asset Management
Western Europe	Citigroup Asset Management

Source: "Global Finance Announces Best Treasury and Cash Management Banks and Providers 2006," press release, January 25, 2006. Used by permission.

	Award Winners
Asia	HSBC
Latin America	Banco Bradesco
Central and Eastern Europe	RZB
Middle East and Africa	National Bank of Kuwait
Best Bank For Risk Management	
North America	JPMorgan Chase
Western Europe	UBS
Asia	HSBC
Latin America	Banco Bradesco
Central and Eastern Europe	RZB
Middle East and Africa	Qatar National Bank
Best Bank For Cross-Border Pooling And Netting	
North America	JPMorgan Chase
Western Europe	ABN AMRO
Asia	Citigroup
Latin America	Citigroup
Central and Eastern Europe	RZB
Middle East and Africa	Citigroup
Best Bank For Payments And Collections	
North America	Bank of America
Western Europe	Deutsche Bank
Asia	HSBC
Latin America	Citigroup
Central and Eastern Europe	RZB
Middle East and Africa	Standard Bank
Best Cls-Linked Bank Offering	
North America	Citigroup
Western Europe	ABN AMRO
Asia	Citigroup
Latin America	Banco do Brasil
Middle East and Africa	FirstRand Bank
Treasury Management Systems And Services	
Best Accounts Payable Services	Bottomline Technologies
Best Accounts Receivable Services	Getpaid
Best Electronic Bill Presentment and Payment Services	Bottomline Technologies
Best Payroll Services	Oracle
Best Corporate Card and Expense Services Provider	Visa
Best Electronic Commerce Services Provider	SSA Global
Best Loss-Prevention/Business-Continuity Services	SunGard Availability Services
Best Pension Plan Administration Services	Watson Wyatt Worldwide
Best Technology Services Provider	EDS
Best Treasury Workstations Provider	SunGard Treasury Systems
Best Treasury Management Software	XRT

SAMPLE BANK REPORT CARD

Banking Services Evaluation
For the time period:

Bank Name: ≪Company≫
Account Officer: ≪First≫ ≪Last≫

SECTION 1   CUSTOMER SERVICE

		Excellent	Very Good	Satisfactory	Poor	Unacceptable
1.	Level of Competence	5	4	3	2	1
2.	Courteous Professional Behavior	5	4	3	2	1
3.	Telephone Availability	5	4	3	2	1
4.	Back-up Coverage	5	4	3	2	1
5.	Response Correctness	5	4	3	2	1
6.	Timeliness of Response	5	4	3	2	1
7.	Follow Through on Commitments	5	4	3	2	1
8.	Overall Problem Solving	5	4	3	2	1
9.	Knowledge of Bank's Policies/Procedures	5	4	3	2	1
10.	Knowledge of Bank's Cash Mgt Products	5	4	3	2	1

COMMENTS:_____

_____

SECTION 2   DAILY BALANCE REPORTING

		Excellent	Very Good	Satisfactory	Poor	Unacceptable
1.	Availability of File	5	4	3	2	1
2.	Timeliness	5	4	3	2	1
3.	File Format	5	4	3	2	1
4.	No missing data (store #'s, proper tran codes)	5	4	3	2	1
5.	Communication of Transmission Problems	5	4	3	2	1

COMMENTS:_____

_____

SECTION 3   ACCOUNT ANALYSIS

		Excellent	Very Good	Satisfactory	Poor	Unacceptable
1.	Pricing Accuracy	5	4	3	2	1
2.	Volume Accuracy	5	4	3	2	1
3.	Timeliness	5	4	3	2	1
4.	Problem Resolution	5	4	3	2	1
5.	Format	5	4	3	2	1
6.	Overall Cost	5	4	3	2	1
7.	Value Relative to Cost	5	4	3	2	1

COMMENTS:_____

_____

SECTION 4	ACCOUNT OFFICER	Excellent	Very Good	Satisfactory	Poor	Unacceptable
1.	Knowledge of Bank's Cash Mgt Products	5	4	3	2	1
2.	Follow-up on Requests	5	4	3	2	1
3.	Provides Useful Counsel/Guidance	5	4	3	2	1
4.	Ability to Match Services To Our Needs	5	4	3	2	1
5.	Level of Competence	5	4	3	2	1
6.	Level of Preparation	5	4	3	2	1
7.	Calling Frequency	5	4	3	2	1

COMMENTS:_____

All Banks: **Avg Score**_____   **Top Score**_____   **Low Score**_____

Your Bank: **Score**_____   **Ranking**_____ **Out of**   **Banks used.**

Source: www.phoenixhecht.com. Used by permission.

CHAPTER 6

DEBT MANAGEMENT

6.1 INTRODUCTION

"D—Debt; D—Dangerous!" How many nonprofits wish they had learned that lesson before plunging into a financial crisis that was impossible to escape. Numerous nonprofits have come to financial ruin because of imprudent use of debt and either have closed their doors and been directed toward a forced marriage with another nonprofit. Many nonprofits have yet to consider their capital structures, and how they influence how much debt they might prudently carry. Before going any further, read and consider the structure of your balance sheet and the varying levels of cash and other short-term or current assets, as profiled in the material written by consultant Clara Miller (see Appendix 6A).

    Your organization's primary financial objective is to ensure that financial resources are available when needed (timing), as needed (amount), and at reasonable cost (cost-effectiveness), and that once mobilized, these resources are protected from impairment and spent according to mission and donor purposes. Since your operations are not always able to assure that these resources are available when and in the amount needed, it is wise to have back-stop sources of short-term funding. Organizations usually tap their operating reserves of cash and short-term investments first in order to meet these needs, and may try to reduce expenses or sell unneeded assets if further funds are required. Often, they become better managers of receivables (collecting more aggressively) or payables (taking the full credit period to pay rather than paying "the day the invoice hits our desk") in order to generate cash.[1] Other organizations may try to launch an emergency fundraising campaign. And yes, a few use their credit cards, despite the high interest rates they will pay on balances. However, there are other sources of short-term funding available, including banks and other financial institutions and occasionally foundations or specialized nonprofit financing entities such as the Nonprofit Finance Fund[2] or the Local Initiatives Support Corporation (LISC) for community development efforts in distressed neighborhoods.[3]

Banks may serve as providers of this funding for nonprofits, but they are often reluctant to do so because of nonprofits' uncertain operating cash flow patterns, lack of collateralizable assets, and the reputational effects were it necessary for a bank to foreclose on a nonprofit.

In this chapter, which focuses on short-term debt, we begin with the objectives of debt management, and then profile the basic aspects of an organization's debt policy. We follow this with the reasons for borrowing short-term and some survey findings depicting the use of arranged short-term debt by faith-based nonprofits and some basic aspects of healthcare and educational organizations' borrowing. Our focus then turns to how banks view lending requests coming from nonprofit organizations. To help you better monitor and measure your use of debt, we then present some debt management metrics and benchmarks. In the chapter appendixes we offer some advanced thinking on nonprofits' capital structures (Appendix 6A) and a case study applying financial ratios to an actual church loan situation (Appendix 6B). Further information on the strategic financing plan and strategic financial objectives are provided in our companion book, *Financial Management for Nonprofit Organizations: Policies and Practices* (John Wiley & Sons, 2007).

6.2 OBJECTIVES OF DEBT MANAGEMENT

Your organization should strive for these objectives as it manages its debt:

- Ensure a reliable source of backup liquidity, should revenues drop or expenses surge.
- Develop a good working relationship with your depository bank(s) and possibly establish with the bank(s) an uncommitted credit line even if you do not expect to have to use the line.
- Have a plan of action of what steps would be taken, and in what order, should the organization be thrust into a cash crunch or cash crisis.
- Avoid overreliance on arranged short-term borrowing, as evidenced by the establishment and achievement of a reasonable target liquidity level. We offered guidance on the target liquidity level in Chapters 1 and 2. (Also see

Chapter 2 of our companion book, *Financial Management for Nonprofit Organizations* [John Wiley & Sons, 2007]).

- Strive to avoid overly restrictive covenants on any borrowing arrangements.

    > Covenants may be negotiated out of loan contracts or bond indentures in some cases. *Maintenance covenants* indicate the financial ratio values or other financial requirements your organization must maintain as long the debt is outstanding. For example, your organization may need to maintain a certain level of days' cash on hand (creditworthy hospitals typically have 8 months or more of unrestricted cash on hand) and have a debt service coverage ratio of at least 1.1 times to be viewed as very creditworthy. *Incurrence covenants* indicate what events would be viewed as negatively impacting existing debtholders, and therefore your organization is pledged not to precipitate. Examples are issuance of additional debt, merging with another organization, or selling specific assets.[4]

- Target and achieve an attractive interest rate on current borrowings and a reasonable cap on potential interest expense on future potential borrowings.
- Develop a rational mix of short-term and long-term borrowing sources, together with unrestricted net assets (formerly called fund balances), based on cash flow volatility and prudent levels of tolerable interest rate risk, reinvestment risk, and funding risk.

Of course, there is some overlap between these objectives, and the chief financial officer (CFO) and treasurer will need to have multiple discussions with the board finance committee and possibly the board executive committee before dovetailing these objectives into a carefully crafted organizational debt policy.

6.3 DEBT POLICY

Your organization's debt policy should include reasonable restrictions and should address these parameters:

- Whether it may be acceptable to incur any short-term arranged debt and, if so, under what conditions (or for what uses); whether collateralization is acceptable and what might be acceptable forms of collateral; how long the debt may remain outstanding; and any ratio limitations or dollar limits on the maximum short-term debt allowable
- Whether the organization has a target short-term debt rating (e.g., if your organization is a large healthcare organization and issues asset-backed commercial paper, what rating does your organization strive for?)
- Whether and what forms of medium-term borrowing your organization may consider (e.g., leases, term loans, revolving credit agreements)
- Whether any internal interfund borrowing is allowable and, if so, under what circumstances, when must it be paid back, and whether it can be from restricted cash (and from what funds)

- To what degree internal equity (donated capital and unrestricted net assets that have accumulated from prior years operating surpluses) will be used to self-fund maintenance, improvements, and new capital outlays for building, equipment, and land
- Whether and to what degree intraorganizational borrowing may be done (e.g., between operating units or divisions or from parent to subsidiary)
- Degree of use and acceptability of arranged financing (e.g. bank loans) versus spontaneous financing (e.g., accounts payable and accrued wages)
- Debt reduction policy
- Limitations on long-term borrowing, and what constitute allowable and disallowable uses for long-term debt
- Use of swaps and other derivatives to manage the risks and cash flows related to principal and interest
- Whether the organization will act as a cosigner for another party (this is a very dubious practice that has caused great harm to those who have acted as cosigners, and as a rule should not be permitted in a nonprofit)
- Whether any loans to the chief executive officer/executive director, other senior management, or a board member are permissible and, if so, the controls (including references to pertinent aspects of your organization's conflict of interest policy) and reporting requirements on the loan and how long it may remain outstanding

No doubt you will think of other specifications unique to your organization, but the key is to devise and gain full board approval of the debt policy in the near future if you do not already have a debt policy intact.[5]

6.4 SHORT-TERM BORROWING

As this is a guidebook for cash and investment management, in this chapter we focus primarily on short-term borrowing. This borrowing bridges cash revenue–cash expenditure imbalances, helps offset seasonal downturns in cash inflows, and enables production or service delivery under contract reimbursements situations in which the government or other contractor is slow to pay.

Nonprofits are considered "unbankable" by commercial banks when early in their lifecycle.[6] We noted earlier that banks are justifiably concerned about the uncertainty of nonprofits' operating cash flows, and these flows are most uncertain at the start-up and early years of the organizations' lives. While organizations are in the start-up phase and pre-revenue stage (have plan and ideas, but no revenues), their best bet for financing is informal investors: acquaintances (spelled donors), partner organizations, local development corporations, governments offering low-interest micro-loans, foundations offering program-related investments, or credit unions that have a "small-business loan" focus. Unfortunately, many foundations still "don't get it" when it comes to unrestricted grants, not realizing the burden that their restrictions place on nonprofits.[7] Once organizations get a few years into their revenue-producing years, they are candidates for bank loans; in fact, of the roughly one-half of small businesses that received credit from market sources, about three-fourths received that financing from a commercial bank (including lines of credit, loans, and leases).[8] It is best to start with the financial institution with which you have your deposits; otherwise, have your organization's accountant or lawyer contact the bank and present your borrowing proposal.

(a) WHY BORROW SHORT TERM?   There are eight reasons why a nonprofit might borrow money.

1. *Borrowing is much faster than grants or fundraising for bringing money into the organization*, with funds made available within days or a few weeks.

2. *Borrowing can stabilize the organization's cash flow and compensate for temporary revenue shortfalls*. Meeting payroll when in a temporary cash crunch is one use that may be made of borrowed funds.

3. *Borrowing can prevent costly delays in starting new projects*. This "bridge financing" is an important role for borrowing. Government agencies at the state and local level issue bond anticipation notes for this purpose.

4. *Borrowing can increase earned income by speeding up the start of a revenue-generating project*. Getting income-producing ventures off the ground may necessitate start-up financing or financing to fund the expansion of the new venture.

5. *Borrowing can help consolidate bills*. The idea here is to enable the organization to take cash discounts or maintain good supplier relationships (by enabling your organization to pay on time).

6. *Borrowing can initiate or build on long-term relationships with financial institutions*. Individuals know the value of an established credit history, and the same holds true for a nonprofit organization.

7. *Borrowing can help improve the organization's financial management*. Financial institutions will require financial reports with a fair amount of detail and the calculation of key financial ratios. Organizations that previously managed without key financial data will be pressed to improve their financial and accountability structures.

8. *Borrowing can help the organization achieve independence*. By replacing restrictive donations or grants/contracts, the organization may be freed to pursue the mission it is called to accomplish. The flip side is that your organization may be limited via restrictive loan covenants placed on you by the financial institution. Limiting the borrowing and keeping the loan payments current will enable the organization to avoid becoming the servant to the lender.[9]

Furthermore, there is a cost to raising funds through donations and grants. Let's say that $100 is raised for every $10 spent. That amounts to a 10 percent interest rate if $10 is taken as "interest" and $100 as principal. The main difference, of course, is that the donation funding stream must be renewed every year, while the borrowed funds are there until "maturity"—which is when the organization must make the principal repayment on the borrowed funds. Our point is that there is a cost of funds, regardless of how you acquire them.

Planning for short-term borrowing must take place within the context of the organization's overall strategic planning process and long-range financial plan. Otherwise, borrowings may cost more than they should, funds will be borrowed on the wrong terms, or both.

Financial managers have two different ways with which to plan and manage an organization's debt and capital structure: (1) the *at-whatever-price theory* and (2) the *strategic planning theory*. The at-whatever-price theory is related to the traditional supply-and-demand concept and is based on the belief that any financial manager can raise enough capital to do business if there is sufficient pressure.

Under the at-whatever-price theory, capital is like any other commodity: The greater the need, the higher the cost. Unfortunately, the at-whatever-price theory suggests that the most advantageous time for an organization to borrow money is when it does not need to borrow money, the most advantageous time being when borrowing is least expensive. In some cases, such blind financing can be attractive. It can be less expensive and less restrictive than financing under more pressing circumstances—for instance, when the organization has an acquisition target in mind or has committed to a major construction project or needs to purchase a major piece of equipment. Bankers are then aware of the urgency of the need to obtain money and may be inclined to dictate stiffer terms.

The more advantageous financial approach is to make capital and debt management crucial parts of the organization's strategic planning process. In fact, capital and debt management should be accorded as important a place in strategic planning as revenue projections, cost containment programs, community marketing programs, and expansion plans. If capital and debt management is part of an organization's strategic planning process, its long-range goals and objectives can be considered under all types of financing options.

(b) LILLY STUDY FINDINGS.   About 7 in 10 nonprofits did some type of borrowing, according to a research study done in the late 1980s. More recent data compiled by Robert Yetman from the IRS Statistics of Income data indicates that about 6 in 10 nonprofits have some form of debt, and the average ratio of debt (liabilities from the balance sheet) to assets (also from the balance sheet) is about 33%.[10] However, neither of those studies identified whether any of those organizations borrowed using short-term loans.[11] A study we conducted, which we shall denote as the Lilly study, asked several questions of faith-based organizations in 1992. Here are the key findings:[12]

- Two-thirds of the organizations do no short-term borrowing
- 21 percent do short-term borrowing, but not every year
- 13 percent do borrow short-term every year

For the 34% of organizations that at least occasionally do some short-term borrowing, the primary use is:

- As a regular and constant part of its total financing, or capital structure (11 percent)
- As a cyclical part of total financing (15 percent)
- As a seasonal part of total financing (29 percent)
- To meet irregular needs (45 percent)

It is clear from these survey responses that short-term arranged borrowing is not a normal part of the financing package arranged by faith-based nonprofits.

As far as security goes, about 4 in 10 (38 percent) of those organizations that borrow are not asked to provide collateral to back their loans. About 1 in 3 (34 percent) are occasionally required to provide collateral for loan backing, and 27 percent must always provide collateral. This security provides backup repayment to the lender, who actually expects to collect the interest and principal through cash flows generated by the organization, not by having to seize and sell the pledged collateral.

Finally, 19 percent of surveyed organizations arrange leases for financing purposes. Most if not all of this would be considered long-term financing: leases are typically arranged for copies, computers, vehicles, and the like.

(c) HEALTHCARE AND EDUCATIONAL BORROWING. Healthcare organizations can borrow against their patient or third-party payer accounts receivable, and educational organizations can borrow against their student accounts receivables. These organizations are thus prime prospects for banks, assuming that their financial ratios look good. For more on the ratios that banks would look at, see Appendix 7A as well as Chapter 10 of our companion book, *Financial Management for Nonprofit Organizations* (John Wiley & Sons, 2007).

For educational organizations, financial ratios are important. However, non-financial indicators are also very useful to predict the future loan servicing ability of the organization. The future demographic and economic prospects for the school's area are important. Most important are the consistency and growth of student demand, which is a proxy for the school's reputation.[13] We will illustrate this with the information related to colleges and universities' bond ratings, even though bonds represent long-term financing. The most creditworthy institutions, which have the highest bond rating, have an acceptance rate of only 18% of applications (versus 73% for less creditworthy institutions), have a yield ratio of acceptances to admission offered of 52% (versus 38% for less creditworthy institutions), demonstrate a more diversified revenue base (they receive much less of their revenue in the form of tuition, 25%, versus 72% for less creditworthy institutions), and experience less expense related to financial aid relative to total operating costs (9.5%, versus 18.8% for less creditworthy institutions).[14] The key takeaway for all organizations: reputation and diversified revenue streams make your organization a better credit risk to bondholders and banks and other lenders.

Although banks are not yet doing this, to the best of our knowledge, bond ratings agencies are beginning to meet with boards to gain a better understanding of the would-be bond issuer. Moody's now evaluates the governance of the nonprofit as part of its credit risk assessment and ratings process. Moody's specifically assesses seven factors when evaluating hospitals and healthcare systems:

- avoidance of conflicts of interest
- development of an organization's mission
- selection and evaluation of senior management
- composition of the board and its performance
- interpretation and understanding of financial reporting
- use of performance metrics based on external benchmarks to review performance
- building and maintenance of financial resources[15]

Our focus in this chapter is on short-term debt, so we refer the interested reader to Chapter 10 of our companion book, *Financial Management for Nonprofit Organizations: Policies and Practices* (John Wiley & Sons, 2007), for more on long-term borrowing.

6.5 HOW A BANK VIEWS A NONPROFIT BORROWING REQUEST

Nonprofit financial staffers are commonly heard voicing concern that banks do not understand them, that no banks want to make short-term loans to nonprofits, or that the restrictions on any loans offered are simply too restrictive. The reality of the situation is that nonprofits are not in an enviable situation relative to businesses borrowers, especially businesses selling products rather than services.

(a) BANKS LEND BASED PRIMARILY ON CASH FLOW.   Banks are cash flow lenders, first and foremost.[16] They wish to be repaid from operating cash flows, and even more desirable is the borrower whose collateral for the short-term loan turns into cash as it is sold and the sales proceeds retire the loan amount. The collateral behind these loans is first accounts receivable and second inventories. Banks might lend 75 percent of the value of receivables and 50 percent of the value of inventories.

The catch is that few nonprofits have accounts receivable and even fewer have inventories, especially finished goods inventories. (Your office supplies or cleaning supplies don't count here.) Banks are left without their major source of security, something they could seize and sell if the borrower does not pay off the loan.

The end results of this situation are twofold: (1) Banks are understandably nervous making loans to many nonprofits, and (2) banks are forced to understand your operating cash flow sources and variability before they can approve a loan request. Couple these concerns with the perceptions, mostly factual, that (1) many nonprofits are known to have weak accounting systems and almost nonexistent cash budgeting practices, (2) soft-money grants and donations are an unreliable source of revenue, and (3) most banks are petrified by the thought by having their name splashed across a headline along with the words "forecloses on human service agency" or "forecloses on church," and you can understand the reluctance of many banks to consider short-term, nonmortgage loans to nonprofits. When short-term operating credit lines or working capital loans are made, the bank may collateralize grants receivable, contracts receivable, or even require a (or several) board member(s) to provide a personal guaranty on the loan.

(b) HELPING YOUR CHANCES WITH A BANK. Your organization's chances of winning a bank loan on favorable terms are higher if you know what information to present, the common loan structures, how banks conduct repayment evaluations, and how cash arises, or flows, from your net revenue generation.[16]

(i) Information to Present to Bank Lender. Along with three to five years of financial statements (statement of net assets, statement of activity, and statement of cash flows), you should be prepared to provide the following to a potential short-term lender:

- interim financial statements
- projected financial statements
- business plan
- aging schedules for accounts receivable (if any) and accounts payable
- listing of inventory
- articles of incorporation and bylaws
- information on any subsidiaries or holding company organization

If your organization has borrowed and repaid previous bank loans, this will be very helpful in gaining favorable consideration, assuming that your organization's financial situation is not measurably worse that it was at the time of the previous loans.

(ii) Typical Loan Structures. Assuming your organization wishes to get a working capital loan, perhaps to cover a period in which cash disbursements exceed cash receipts, it will typically request a line of credit. A *line of credit* is a structure in which the bank advances money ("principal") and your organization repays it, as needed—somewhat like a personal credit card. Your organization will pay interest on the average amount borrowed for the month on a monthly basis.

The interest rate is a variable rate, typically adjusted monthly to the prime rate plus some margin based on how risky your organization appears to be, from the bank's perspective. For example, at the time of this writing small commercial loans ($1,000–$99,000) had an average rate of 8.46%, while the prime rate was 8.25%.[17] (The prime rate is a base rate that banks may use to price commercial loans, with the London Interbank Offered Rate, or LIBOR, and the Fed funds rate also being common base rates.) The bank may require your organization to carry zero-dollar balances for a month at some point in its fiscal year, to prove that your organization is not actually depending on this loan for part of its long-term financing.

(iii) How a Bank Evaluates Your Repayment Ability.   A bank typically looks at your operating cash flow (operating cash inflows less operating cash outflows) as the source of your payment of interest, and the conversion of assets as the source of your payment of the loan principal. However, if you do not have any inventory, accounts receivable, dues receivable, or grants/contracts receivable, there are most likely only donations or product/service sales to provide principal repayment capability—meaning that both your repayment of interest and your repayment of principal must come from this operating revenue stream. To put it mildly, this makes potential lenders nervous. Donation streams are subject to spikes, as many nonprofits found out in the tough post-Katrina environment. For situations involving places of worship, much depends on the continued employment of a popular and well-respected spiritual leader. There is evidence that donation-dependent organizations have less debt overall (this includes mortgage and nonmortgage debt), possibly due to less need for large capital investments, less reliability of donations relative to fee income, and higher costs of debt relative to fundraising or using cash reserves.[18]

What if cash flow does not appear to be sufficient and there are no assets to convert? The bank may secure the loan by requiring your organization to pledge some other form of collateral (perhaps a short-term investment, such as a large-denomination certificate of deposit; the bank may lend up to 80% of the value of that investment, if it is unrestricted). This represents a secondary repayment source for the lender. The third repayment source is often "personal resources"—such as the personal guarantees by the board members of a childcare organization that had no chance to get a bank loan without that guarantee.

The bottom line here is that cash flow is the primary and most important repayment source from a bank's perspective. It may still approve a loan that is marginally acceptable from a cash-flow perspective if it sees adequate collateral and gains agreement from the nonprofit to secure the loan with that collateral, or (in rare cases) gets some sort of personal guarantee from individuals connected to the nonprofit.

(iv) How Do Our Net Revenues Generate Cash?   Operating cash flow arises from the ability of your organization to generate more cash from its operations

than its operations consume during the period. Let's say your organization is 100% donation dependent. You, as the executive director, are the only paid staff member of the organization. Your cash inflows are the donations—and in some periods your donations will be lower than in other periods. If your salary and all the other ongoing expenses of the organization are greater than the donations in a particular month, your organization has a negative operating cash flow for that month. On the other hand, in those months when donations are in excess of your salary and all other ongoing expenses, your organization achieves a positive operating cash flow. The bank will want to know how often and to what degree your organization earns positive cash flows, incurs negative cash flows, and how much of a cushion it has through unrestricted (or possibly temporarily restricted) cash reserves. Your statement of cash flows provides a record of the degree to which your operating cash flows were positive for past periods—look in the top section of that statement underneath the caption "Operating Cash Flows." Banks will normally want to see positive operating cash flows[19] that amount to at least 1.25 times the anticipated combined loan interest and principal payments (in our illustration, there is no asset conversion to consider).

You may strengthen your organization's case by documenting to the potential lender what steps your organization has planned to take in the event of deterioration risks. That is, if your operating cash flows fall unexpectedly, what steps will you take to maintain the organization's liquidity and debt repayment ability?

Plan on forwarding financial reports on a periodic basis to your bank once a loan has been made. These reporting requirements are typically quarterly on a short-term loan, but may be monthly in a situation in which the bank is wishing to monitor your organization's financial position closely.

Finally, recognize that banks do not make large profits on most loans, and often look to "ancillary services" to see if the entire relationship with your organization is profitable. How risky your organization appears to be, from the bank's perspective, plays into the interest rate charge, but so too does the overall relationship profitability of your activity with the bank. We noted in Chapter 5 the chief factors in bank selection, and simply add here that businesses choose cash management banks largely on whether those banks will also be there to extend credit to the organization. The typical business relies on five or six banks for its U.S. credit needs and another three or four banks for its international credit needs.[20] Most nonprofits would require fewer banks due to their smaller size and scope of operations.

6.6 DEBT MANAGEMENT METRICS AND BENCHMARKS

In this section we include two sets of metrics or benchmarks that you may use in your debt management. The first addresses the interest rate risk that you are taking on in your debt policy. The second set targets the rate you are paying for your borrowings as well as possible interest expense vulnerability for the future. Greenwich Treasury Advisors advocates consideration of both sets.

Metrics for Managing Interest Rate Risk[21]

As in foreign exchange, the benchmarks for these risk kinds of metrics are often per the Interest Rate Risk Policy—or in the debt covenants:

- Earnings at risk (book return basis)[22]
- Value at risk (total return basis)
- Floating rate and fixed rate debt as percent of total debt
- Weighted average maturity[23]
- Duration[24]
- Convexity
- Company's rate spread above Treasury securities for specific maturities

Metrics

- Actual weighted average interest rate
- Future value of interest expense assuming all floating rates fixed with forward rate agreements

Benchmarks

- Investment or debt indices
  - Commercial Paper (CP) benchmarks (GE Capital (GECC), Federal Reserve [Fed] rate)
  - Treasury benchmarks by maturity, and so on
- Model portfolio benchmarks
  - 50 percent fixed/50 percent floating debt portfolio as "interest rate neutral"
  - Passive maturity approach in which, say, a three-year time horizon investment portfolio is divided into three equal yearly buckets
- Spreads above Treasury securities/swaps for a given credit rating

Your organization may decide to hedge, or protect its future cash flows against, adverse movements in interest rates. In this case, your concern is with higher interest rates if you are borrowing short-term, since most short-term borrowing is done with variable interest rates that reset periodically. Most nonfinancial businesses do not hedge against interest rate risks, but there may be good reasons for a nonprofit with significant borrowings to do so.

6.7 SUMMARY

In this chapter we have briefly canvassed the short-term borrowing needs and vehicles that nonprofits should consider in meeting a one-year or partial year funding need. We emphasized the need to devise a debt policy, reported on survey findings for faith-based organizations, indicated reasons for borrowing on short-term basis, profiled the borrowing process, explained the reluctance of many banks to extend uncollateralized short-term loans to nonprofits, and provided you with some metrics for your interest rate risk and your debt management benchmarking. In Appendix 6A we include a very fine presentation on nonprofits' balance sheets, and in Appendix 6B we offer a case study on banks loans and your management philosophy. In our final two chapters we turn to the investment strategies nonprofits can pursue when they have a surplus of cash.

Notes

1. It is wise, however, to take cash discounts when offered: An invoice that offers a 2% discount if paid within 10 days, and is otherwise due in 30 days ("2/10, net 30"), implies a 37% annualized borrowing rate by your organization when the cash discount is not taken. The "Cost of forgone discount" calculation is demonstrated in John Zietlow, Jo Ann Hankin, and Alan Seidner, *Financial Management for Nonprofit Organizations: Policies and Practices* (Hoboken, NJ: John Wiley & Sons, 2007), p. 363.

2. The Nonprofit Finance Fund makes working capital loans as well as long-term facility loans, and had 500 loans totaling $130 million at year-end 2005. However, it cautions that "NFF makes loans to nonprofit organizations that are financially equipped to use debt as a strategic tool, not as an emergency stopgap measure. Our experience is that organizations that can take on debt most successfully have been in existence as 501(c)(3) tax-exempt entities for at least three years and have a minimum annual budget, which varies depending on the area we serve." (http://www.nonprofitfinancefund.org/details.asp?autoId = 12).

3. LISC "helps resident-led, community-based development organizations transform distressed communities and neighborhoods into healthy ones" (www.lisc.org). For information on their working capital loans, see http://www.lisc.org/section/products/loans/types.

4. John Zietlow, Jo Ann Hankin, and Alan Seidner, *Financial Management for Nonprofit Organizations: Policies and Practices* (Hoboken, NJ: John Wiley & Sons, 2007), Chapter 11

5. Aspects of developing a debt and hedging policy are provided in John Zietlow, Jo Ann Hankin, and Alan Seidner, *Financial Management for Nonprofit Organizations: Policies and Practices* (Wiley, 2007), pp. 385–387. Also see Judy Van Gorden, "Debt Rules," *Business Officer* (March 2006), pp. 43–46, 49.

6. "The Credit Process: A Guide for Small Business Owners." Available online at www.newyorkfed.org/education/addpub/credit.html#Info. Accessed 2/2/07.

7. For reasons given by some foundations for only making restricted grants, and a strong counter-argument against this practice, see Clara Miller, "Risk Minus Cash Equals Crisis: The Flap about General Operating Support," available online at the time of this writing at http://www.nonprofitfinancefund.org/docs/CMiller-NCRP_StateofPhilanthropy-2004-Risk%20Minus%20Cash%20Equals%20Crisis.pdf. Accessed 1/5/2007.

8. A few small organizations received funding from finance companies and leasing companies. Roger W. Ferguson, Jr., Testimony before the Small Business Committee, U.S. House of Representatives, May 17, 2001. Online at www.federalreserve.gov/Boarddocs/Testimony/2001/20010517/default.htm. Accessed 2/2/07.

9. Adapted from Edward Skloot, *Smart Borrowing: A Nonprofit's Guide to Working With Banks* (New York: New York Community Trust, n.d.), pp. 3–4.

10. Yetman's study is worthy of your careful study. See Robert J. Yetman, "Borrowing and Debt," *Financing Nonprofits: Putting Theory into Practice*, Dennis R. Young, editor (Lanham, MD: AltaMira Press, 2007), pp. 243–268.

11. Howard P. Tuckman and Cyril F. Chang, "How Well Is Debt Managed by Nonprofits?" *Nonprofit Management & Leadership* 3 (Summer 1993): 347–361.

12. John Zietlow, "Organizational Goals and Financial Management in Donative Nonprofit Organizations," (Terre Haute, IN: Indiana State University, 1992–1994). This research project was sponsored by Lilly Endowment, Indianapolis, IN.

13. FitchRatings, *Private School Credit Analysis Guidelines*. November 21, 2003. Available online at www.fitchratings.com. Accessed 12/28/06.

14. All statistics from Kathy Kurz and Jim Scannell, "Bond Rating: Beyond the Balance," *University Business* (January 2006), pp. 29–30.

15. Quoted from Paul Barr, "Moody's: Let's Size Up Boards." *Modern Healthcare* 35 (June 2005), p.10.

16. This material draws heavily on the ideas gathered from personal communication with David Wechter, Senior Vice President and, Regional Credit Officer for the Eastern Ohio Region, The Huntington National Bank.

17. All interest rates from the Federal Reserve. Current rates are available online at www.bankrate.com/brm/ratehm.asp.

18. These three hypotheses are put forward by Robert Yetman in Robert J. Yetman, "Borrowing and Debt," *Financing Nonprofits: Putting Theory into Practice*, Dennis R. Young, editor (Lanham, MD: AltaMira Press, 2007), pp. 243–268.

19. For a business, operating cash flow may be approximated by taking net profit after taxes, then adding depreciation and amortization expenses, interest expenses, and any other non-cash expenses.

20. The survey data is from personal interviews conducted by Greenwich Associates with 828 corporate finance officers, and reported on in Greenwich Associates, "Managing Banking Relationships: A Strategic Approach for Financial Executives," 2003. Available online at www.greenwich.com. Accessed: 10/6/2006.

21. Metrics are taken from Greenwich Treasury Advisors, "Treasury Performance Measurement: Metrics and Benchmarks," March 26, 2003. Used by permission.

22. Complete coverage of these risk measures is beyond our scope; consult other sources for more information, including http://www.riskglossary.com/link/corporate_risk_management.htm.

23. Weighted average maturity (WAM) is particularly revealing: Money market mutual funds' WAM is regularly reported in the financial press, and as portfolio managers buy longer-dated maturity securities the WAM increases, revealing that managers think interest rates generally will soon drop (and so they wish to lock in the higher yields that are available today, as well as possibly earn some capital gains); as WAM drops, managers are repositioning the fund's portfolio to soon replace maturity securities with then-higher yielding securities. For more on short-term investment characteristics and

short-term investment portfolio management, see Chapter 7 in this book and Chapters 14 and 15 in Terry S. Maness and John T. Zietlow, *Short-Term Financial Management*, 3rd Ed. (Cincinnati: Thomson/South-Western, 2005).

24. Duration and convexity measure how much a bond's price will change with a given change in interest rates. The calculation is shown at http://www.specialinvestor.com/terms/1933.html. Also see the calculation of modified duration at http://www.specialinvestor.com/terms/1846.html. Zero coupon securities, in which no interest is paid and the security is bought at a deep discount, have durations equal to their maturities.

LINKING MISSION AND MONEY: AN INTRODUCTION TO NONPROFIT CAPITALIZATION

An Introduction to Nonprofit Capitalization by Clara Miller*

CAPITAL STRUCTURE

Capital structure is the pattern of distribution of an organization's financial assets and liabilities. We have suggested that an organization's effectiveness in pursuing its program is critically dependent on both its organizational capacity and its capital structure. While a great deal of attention has been given to the relationship between organizational capacity, program, and mission, rather less systematic thought is generally given to the impact of financial capacity—the overall capital structure, or the third point in our triangle. This negligence of capital structure is widespread and can exert a greater drag on organizational effectiveness than any of the other points in the triangle.

The reasons for this neglect of capital structure and of building the financial capacity requisite for an organization's plans run deep. There is a belief in the nonprofit sector that energy, willpower, stamina, and enthusiasm can overcome all obstacles, and that where it does not, this is rooted in some sort of personal failing. The idea that an inappropriate capital structure can somehow subvert an organization's ability to meet its objectives can seem overly deterministic, fatalistic even. The temptation in the face of adversity is to say to oneself, "*We must work harder,*" rather than to look at the balance sheet—where money is or is not allocated—for systemic reasons for failure.

However, what works for small organizations rarely works for larger, more complicated institutions, and vice versa. In other words, "sweat equity" and an organizational culture (and capacity) driven mainly by stamina or enthusiasm does

***Nonprofit Finance Fund 70 West 36th Street Eleventh Floor New York, NY 10018.** Phone (212) 868-6710 Fax (212) 268-8653 www.nonprofitfinancefund.org © Copyright 2001, All rights reserved, Nonprofit Finance Fund.

not scale well. A major international opera company doesn't use amateur singers or a volunteer orchestra; and a small group of recent graduates who want to sing and perform experimental works does best with the least possible "infrastructure" (i.e., baggage) in the form of building, sets, costumes, orchestra, etc. Neither is better, but each implies differing capital structures and capacity requirements, and each has a differing array of artistic choices.

Along the way, organizations make implicit decisions about capital structure—because any program growth or asset acquisition decision necessarily does so—without understanding explicitly the effects of this decision. There is, alas, no healthy "natural equilibrium" in nonprofit organizations' capital structures. Left to its own devices, the balance sheet of an organization will not necessarily settle down in a form that best supports mission and enhances organizational capacity. All other things being equal, it will tend to do the opposite. Growth, in and of itself, tends to exacerbate rather than alleviate these problems. Organizations, therefore, need to analyze their current capital structure, assess the appropriateness of the structure, and then develop an explicit strategy for moving from one point to another.

The elements of an organization's capital structure are divided into assets and liabilities. Our discussion of capital structure will focus primarily on assets and the way they are allocated.

Major assets are:

- cash
- investments
- buildings and equipment
- receivables, inventory, and prepaid expenses

Cash and investments may carry a range of use restrictions imposed by the source (donors, government, or, in some cases, internally by the board or management of the organization itself). Most organizations have some cash that is unrestricted and used for ongoing operations. Sometimes this is referred to as working capital. Other cash is categorized as reserves (cash set aside for specific purposes such as building repairs) and restricted funds (cash which is meant for a specific purpose as stipulated by the donor). Investments can similarly be unrestricted or restricted. The most restrictive is endowment—funds whose corpus cannot be used, and where the use of interest earned is generally limited to a program purpose.

Receivables reflect the business cycle and are financed by cash. The most typical receivables in arts and culture organizations are capital campaign or other fundraising pledges. Other possibilities include credit card receivables for merchandise or subscriptions, and billings for services such as educational programs or classes. Inventory is similar, in that cash must be laid out with the expectation that revenue will come in as a result of sales. For both inventory and receivables, there is collection or sales risk.

Liabilities are the other side of the balance sheet equation. Liabilities include various accounts payable, short-term debt, long-term debt, etc. They also include advance ticket sales or subscriptions prior to productions. In many cases, liabilities represent the source of cash for financing assets: the mortgage on the building; a line of credit to finance inventory; or a cash flow loan against a school district contract. They are broken down into current liabilities (those requiring payment within one year) and noncurrent liabilities (those requiring payment beyond one year). Liabilities are organized on the balance sheet by increasing maturity, much as assets are listed in order of decreasing liquidity. Matching the relative liquidity and longevity of assets and liabilities is important to keeping the capital structure in balance.

The difference between assets and liabilities is the organization's net worth or net assets. The nature of the assets and liabilities dictates the varying degrees of flexibility in net assets, and donor restrictions are only part of the story. The lion's share of the "unrestricted net assets" of most performing arts organizations, for example, consists of plant and equipment (hardly a source of ready cash!). Where cash net assets are restricted by the donor for, for example, endowment, liquidity is also restricted. It bears noting, however, that it is the liquidity of an organization's net assets that has the greatest relevance to its cash flow, not simply whether or not there is a positive balance in net assets.

DEVELOPING A STRATEGY FOR COMPREHENSIVE CAPITALIZATION

How, then, does one go about developing a more comprehensive and systematic approach to the asset structure of an organization?

The *first* step in developing this strategy is to look at the underlying financial character and logic of the business(es) that you are in—your core business. What is relevant here is not that an organization is a hospital or an art gallery per se but that the outpatient services business differs from that of a mobile medical unit; building a collection is a different business from hosting only traveling temporary exhibitions. Structurally, a performing arts center has more in common with, say, a school in terms of its capital structure and balance sheet than it does with performing arts companies that don't own a performance space, and its bar business more in common with the local pub, its outreach initiatives perhaps more in common with the mobile medical unit. The underlying nature of an organization's business can best be grasped by looking at its balance sheet, and the balance sheets of a performing arts center, a school, and an airline have much in common. Even though they have widely divergent missions, they have in common the business of filling seats.

Accordingly, organizations in the same subsector often have highly diverse capital needs. An organization's core business is not the same as the particular subsector (arts, education, human services, etc.) to which it may belong. Simply identifying this important dimension of your work in a new way, and observing how other organizations or businesses that would seem to be wholly removed

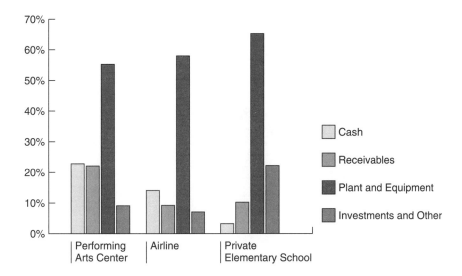

from your world—a school, walk-in clinic, church, or hotel—but are similar in their capital structures is instructive.

The *second* step is to make capital structure an explicit object of board and management attention, rather than it being merely the aggregate de facto result of other, unrelated decisions. There are explicit questions to be answered: What is your organization's capital structure? What priorities are implied by your existing capital structure? Is this an appropriate structure for your purpose and plans? What is your organization's policy for the development of an appropriate structure? How do you develop a shared understanding of the meaning of the organization's assets and liabilities? How will a growth plan affect capital structure? How will it go out of balance, or improve as a result of growth?

Third, the fact needs to be embraced that asset growth (or reallocation) of whatever kind equals risk—risk of imbalancing the capital structure and the organization itself in the process. A large, "no-strings attached" infusion of cash into an organization would seem risk free—and it is, indeed, the least risky of assets because it is the most liquid and flexible. But once new cash is converted into other goods—into funds for additional programs, or additional staff positions, or vehicles, buildings, or whatever—an explicit asset allocation decision has been made, opportunity costs have been assumed, and there are implications for the ongoing costs of servicing this growth that need to be considered.

Growth in restricted grants presents greater risk than that in unrestricted grants because they are less liquid and more likely to make demands on capacity. As noted above, additional expenses are created through restricted grants and the restricted funds themselves rarely cover them (a classic example being restricted grants for new programs, which rarely include provision for the additional staffing and operational costs that would help ensure effective delivery). These assets therefore bring greater organizational risk because of the necessary structural changes they bring to the balance sheet. *The less liquid the additional assets, the greater the inherent risk involved because of their impact on the balance sheet and the ongoing expenses required to service them*. This relationship—a fundamental one that is frequently not understood or ignored—can be represented by the following graph:

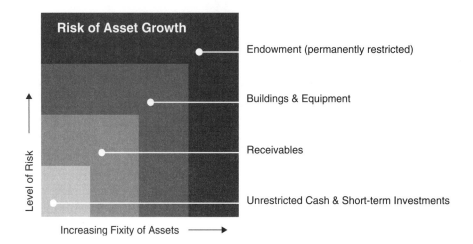

Fourth, with these principles in mind, one should work systematically through the balance sheet and address the organization's requirements under each asset category and in relation to the relevant businesses (as opposed to programs). *An understanding of the dynamics of each business and the specific market or markets that will pay for or subsidize the real costs of the business is required in order to analyze and construct a model balance sheet for an organization.* We have discussed cash/working capital. Cash reserves set aside for specific purposes are often important in smoothing out the gaps in operating cash flow, for investment in new productions or equipment, or for meeting the unpredictable outcomes of risk taking in certain specific areas. Short and long-term debt—and access to lines of credit—should also be seen in this context.

Capital invested in equipment and buildings presents another set of issues. Buildings often represent the most significant capital investment undertaken by nonprofit organizations. They represent an asset allocation decision with profound long-term implications for operations and capacity, and they are, in addition, a highly illiquid investment. All other things being equal, a balance sheet heavy in fixed assets is necessarily a higher risk balance sheet.

An endowment—cash that is restricted and only the interest of which is available for use (and use that is often restricted)—is not a "silver bullet" or *deus ex machina*. It is simply another component of the capital structure and, therefore, best understood in the context of other components. An organization's endowment requirements—and the fundraising case for them—can only be understood by analyzing the other elements of the actual and desired capital structure and then by establishing how best to close the gap between the two. Contributed income and earned income have more significant parts to play in the ongoing business dynamics of an organization than endowment—they generally make up a considerably greater percentage of the resources used for annual operations, and they are more dynamic in their responsiveness to strategic decisions the organization makes.

Endowment ties up large blocks of funding that, all other things being equal, the organization might put to use in other ways as it grows and develops. While endowment can support sustainability where mission-driven programming yields no "natural equilibrium," the opportunity costs are high. While the security of an endowment may be appealing and provide a financial cushion, it can also enable organizations to become disconnected from market realities. One example is a symphony orchestra that uses its substantial endowment to cover up cash shortfalls year after year, and—to the detriment of its long-term health—ignores a steady downward trend in membership and earned revenue.

CAPITALIZATION AND THE FUNDING SYSTEM

As we have stated, capital structure is critical to the health and effectiveness of nonprofit organizations. Unfortunately, the sector's primary source of funding for growth—contributions from funders—traditionally ignores the big picture, most explicitly the importance of capitalization.

In confining their criteria for eligible funding to the marginal costs of programs that are relevant to the pursuit of their own missions, funders may unintentionally contribute to the systemic undercapitalization of the sector—controlling rather than developing the sector and incentivizing the growth of programs without providing for the commensurate growth in capacity. Growth, as we have suggested, is inherently destabilizing, particularly when only its marginal costs are supported. Financial and organizational capacity is stretched thinner and there is systemic underinvestment in physical and organizational infrastructure.

There is, however, a growing realization among more enlightened funders that funding program costs without meeting the associated (and necessary) additional organizational costs is as shortsighted for *their* mission as is the operating nonprofit's pursuing mission-related programming without regard to long-term resource implications. It is for this reason that some have increasingly shown willingness to fund reserves and working capital funds as well as endowments and buildings. Further progress in this area, however, is critically dependent both upon the broader foundation community's recognizing the necessity of investing in the real costs of growth and, in turn, upon nonprofit organizations themselves being able to articulate the case for a more comprehensive approach to capitalization and its importance in their own context. Our work on comprehensive capitalization is designed to help organizations in that process, to educate funders about the real impact of their grantmaking practices, and to inform the nonprofit community. In this way, we hope ultimately to bolster the effectiveness and long-term health of nonprofit organizations as they make key contributions to the cultural, economic and civic health of their communities.

CHURCH LOAN CASE STUDY

A church is considering putting up a new sanctuary (worship center) to seat about 1,000 people and add some office space and classrooms as well. The church presently is running at about 90% capacity in its early service (about 450 people), and at about 10% capacity in its late service (about 45 people) on Sunday Mornings.

The church's present building, which seats about 500, is appraised at $2.2 million. The proposed new building, which would be linked to the existing building, would cost $4.4 million. The loan request that the church is preparing will be a $4 million request, in that past and present capital campaign fundraising has brought in a total of $0.4 million. The loan would be for 15 years, and the interest rate would be 7.5%. The present and proposed buildings would serve as collateral.

As of one year ago, the church attendance had grown by 90 during the previous 12 months. Since that time, there has no growth in attendance. However, the church is focusing on reaching out to bring people to Christ and expects that this emphasis will cause numerical growth in attendance and membership. The church is led by a very dynamic young pastor who is a gifted speaker and talented musician. He is well liked by the congregation.

A meeting called by the church's leadership (pastor and board of directors) including all interested members of the congregation to discuss the proposal and get congregational input has just concluded. The leadership voiced concern that the pledged monies appear not to be coming in as expected, but would like to press ahead if that is the collective view of the congregation. In the meeting, several individuals in the congregation have voiced their concerns about the timing of the proposal as well as the size of the project relative to the size of the church membership. They have turned to you for independent consulting services. What do you recommend?

Attached you will find:

1. The most recent year's balance sheet and income statement (Exhibit 6B.1). You may assume that these have been done within the past two months.

	A	B	C	D	E	F
1	**Balance Sheet**			**Income Statement**		
2	*Most Recent Year*			*Most Recent Year*		
3	***ASSETS:***			***REVENUES:***		
4	Checking Account	$ 28,172		Church Undesignated Revenue	$ 840,053	*
5	Savings Account	2,359		Daycare Revenue	364,898	
6	A/R for Daycare	18,485		TOTAL REVENUE	$1, 204, 951	
7	Receivables - Misc.	5,288				
8	Pledges Receivable	828,000		***EXPENSES:***		
9	Prepaid Expenses	7,660		Church Expenses	958,454	
10	Buildings & Improvements	1,201,482		Daycare Expenses	364,188	
11	Furniture & Equipment	213,098		TOTAL EXPENSES	$1, 322, 642	
12	Vehicles	111,486				
13	Land Improvements	48,809		NOTE: pledges in the amount of $882,000 have been made, but only $54,000 has come in during the last 9 months.		
14	Construction in Progress	413,480		The pledges have 2 years and 3 months left in which to be paid by those pledging.		
15	Accum Depreciation	914,001				
16	Net Fixed Assets	1,074,354				
17	Land	209,455		* All unrestricted offerings. These are		
18	TOTAL ASSETS	$2, 173, 773		all tithes and general offerings.		
19						
20	***LIABILITIES:***					
21	Accounts Payable	$ 58,780				
22	Lease Payable	1,731				
23	Misc. Payables	9,288				
24	Note Payable	10,979				

(continues)

EXHIBIT 6B.1   CHURCH FINANCIAL STATEMENTS

	A	B	C	D	E	F
25	Retirement Payable	5,769				
26	Mortgage	420,000				
27	TOTAL LIABILITIES	$ 506,547				
28						
29	EQUITY					
30	Budget Fund Equity	$ 517,184				
31	Stewardship Campaign Equity	1,150,042				
32	TOTAL EQUITY	$1,667,226				
33						
34	TOTAL LIABS & EQUITY	$2,173,773				
35						

EXHIBIT 6B.1   CHURCH FINANCIAL STATEMENTS (BALANCE SHEET-LIABILITIES & EQUITY) (*continued*)

2. Four of the main financial indicators that banks consider when making church loan decisions, with some of the analysis already done and some left to complete (see Exhibit 6B.2).

Questions to address:

1. The church wishes to make a decision consistent with its faith orientation. What does each of the following scriptures tell us regarding church borrowing in general and this proposal in particular?[1]

- Luke 14: 28: "Suppose one of you wants to build a tower. Will he not first sit down and estimate the cost to see if he has enough money to complete it?"
- Romans 13:8a: "Let no debt remain outstanding, except the continuing debt to love one another."
- Proverbs 22:3: "A prudent man sees danger and takes refuge, but the simple keep going and suffer for it."
- Proverbs 22:7: "The rich rule over the poor, and the borrower is servant to the lender."
- James 4:13–17: "Now listen, you who say, 'Today or tomorrow we will go to this or that city, spend a year there, carry on business and make money.' Why, you do not even know what will happen tomorrow. What is your life? You are a mist that appears for a little while and then vanishes. Instead, you ought to say, 'If it is the Lord's will, we will live and do this

	A	B	C	D	E	F	G	H
1	**Standard #1:** Church Borrowing Maximum based on 25%-35% of undesignated revenue; Using 25%, this would imply $450,000 max loan, assuming church has $200,000 annual undesignated revenue							
2	1000	denotes "per $1,000 of loan principal"						
3	7.50%	= annual interest rate						
4	15	= number of years						
5	($9.27)	= monthly payment amount for each $1,000 of loan, based on rate in cell A3 and years in cell A4						
6	($111.24)	= yearly amount, so = 12 x			($9.27)			
7	449.47	= 50000/111.24		since 50000 = 0.25 x		200000		
8	$449,472.61	= 1000 x	449.47	multiplier.				
9								
10	Note: Modify this example to fit the case study numbers.							
11								
12		= Amount may borrow based on Standard #1.						
14	**Church Borrowing Maximum based on $4,500 x Number of Reliable and Sustainable Attendees (Sunday Morning)** [NOTE: this is based on $1,500 giving per giving unit x 3 = $4,500]							
15	525	= Number of consistent givers, based on Sunday morning attendees						
16	4500	x $4,500						
17	$ 2,362,500	= Max amount of loan principal that church may support, based on Standard #2						
19	**Standard #3:** Church Borrowing Maximum based on 3x Annual Offerings (Tithes & General Fund Offerings - Restricted Gifts)							
20		= Annual Offerings, Total						
21		- Restricted Offerings						
22		= Annual Offerings, Less Restricted Offerings						
23	3	x 3						
24		= Max amount of loan principal that church may support, based on Standard #3						
26	**Standard #4:** Church Borrowing Maximum based on LTD = 29% of Total Assets							
27		= Total Assets Before Expansion						
28	4,400,000	= Total Proposed New Expansion						
29		= Total Assets Including Proposed Expansion						
30	420,000	= Total Existing Long-Term Debt						
31	29%	= 29%						
32		= Existing LTD/(TA including Expansion) Ratio						
33	0.29	= New LTD/TA Allowable [= 0.29-Existing LTD/TA Ratio]						
34		= Amount may borrow based on Standard #4.						
35								
36		**Standards #1, #2, #3, and #4 as a group:**						
37								
38		= Amount of loan supportable by Standard #1						
39								
40		= Amount of loan supportable by Standard #2					From	
41							above	
42		= Amount of loan supportable by Standard #3					calculations.	
43								
44		= Amount of loan supportable by Standard #4						
45								
46		= AVERAGE of #1, #2, #3, and #4				<= mean of 1,2,3, and 4.		
47								
48		*= OUR GROUP RECOMMENDATION FOR ACTUAL*						
49		*LOAN AMOUNT CHURCH SHOULD TAKE ON, IF ANY.*						

EXHIBIT 6B.2   LENDING RATIOS WORKSHEET

1. Deal with a lender who demonstrates an understanding of churches. Ask the lender how their church loan products, features, and covenants differ from their standard commercial loans. These subtleties can have a significant impact on future costs and your church's autonomy to effectively manage its operations.
2. Have your financing firmly in place, in writing, before starting your project. This will ensure that the project is started and completed in a timely fashion. This avoids the potential for costly delays and the inconvenience of mechanic's liens being filed.
3. Before tendering escrow dollars under an agreement to buy land or buildings, be aware of entitlement, zoning and environmental issues. An experienced church lender should be able to assist you with these matters.
4. Ask the lender and the contractor for references from other churches of comparable size. References will help you choose the right partners to make your project go as smoothly as possible.
5. You should have a banker who is knowledgeable about church operations and ministries and is experienced in lending to churches. Simply ask how many years the bank has been lending to religious organizations, how many loans have been made, and how large their full-time church lending staff is.
6. Look for an experienced church lender that can act as a consultant and be a referral source for other church industry professionals, such as fund raisers, growth planners, architects, CPAs, and contractors.
7. Avoid mortgage brokers or lenders who ask your church to sign something prior to analyzing a loan application and offering a financing commitment. You should not have to pay a fee prior to reviewing the terms and conditions of a firm offer.
8. Meet with the bank to discuss the scope of the project before you spend large sums of money on architectural designs that may be too costly to build.
9. Don't depend on the sale of your current facility or other uncertain future events to provide the funds to complete construction of your project. Circumstances beyond your control could disrupt your financial plans.
10. Deal with a bank that has demonstrated years of consistently lending to churches. Newcomers to the industry may not be there when you need to refinance or begin your next phase or project.

Source: Bank of the West Accessed: 2/22/07. Used by permission.

EXHIBIT 6B.3   DO'S AND DON'TS OF CHURCH FINANCING

or that. As it is, you boast and brag. All such boasting is evil. Anyone, then, who knows the good he ought to do and doesn't do it, sins."

2. Fill in the ratios worksheet (you may wish to access a pre-built Excel work- sheet on the Web site that supports this book, www.wiley.com/go/zietlow/).

Based on the ratios and the financial statements:

- How much do the indicators collectively suggest should be borrowed, at maximum, based on your best judgment?
      $_____

- Consider this additional information: The church leadership and two of the congregants who are not in the leadership group suggest that "faith must be exercised, regardless of what is on paper." Based on your understanding of faith, should the proposed loan amount be pursued by the church at this time? Why or why not?

3. What tools from Chapter 6 or other chapters in this book should be used before pursuing the loan with a bank or group of banks? Does the use of any of them tie back to the scriptures we looked at in Question 1? If so, how?

4. Thinking about items that may make a church more or less creditworthy, what are three important *nonfinancial* considerations that enter into the decision of a bank regarding this situation and the likelihood of the bank to approve the loan? (Consult Exhibit 6B.3 for several issues to consider, but do not limit your thoughts to these issues.)

5. What is your final recommendation for the amount of financing the church may reasonably request? Defend your recommendation.

Note

1. All scriptures from the New International Version, accessed from www.biblegateway.com.

CHAPTER 7

INVESTING PRINCIPLES AND PROCEDURES FOR OPERATING AND STRATEGIC RESERVES

7.1 INTRODUCTION

The basic principles of investing are the same, whether one is investing the liquidity or strategic reserves of an organization or its long-term endowment funds. Sound investing requires setting clear investment objectives and guidelines appropriate to each organization's situation. Prudence demands careful balancing of required return with risk, using modern portfolio theory in the long-term portfolios.

Investing opportunities occur when the institution operates with a residual of surplus cash flow or long-term capital, or when it has segregated funds earmarked for investment in longer-term assets. In order to invest appropriately, management should develop an investing strategy that recognizes both the source of the funds and their use. For example, endowment funds are invested very differently from liquidity reserves and working capital needs. The source and use of funds dictate whether surplus cash is to be invested over a short- or long-term horizon.

We will use terms such as short-term and long-term extensively in this chapter and the next chapter. Here are some definitions for investment horizons that are pretty widely accepted:

Liquidity (new cash)	Period up to 180 days
Short-term	Period up to 2 years
Intermediate-term	Period of 3 to 5 years
Long-term	Period of 5 years or longer
Endowment	A fund invested "in perpetuity" to produce a steady flow of income, both now and in the future

Our primary focus in this chapter will be liquidity and short-term investing. In the next chapter we will focus primarily on the longer time horizons, including endowment investment guidelines.

(a) OPERATING RESERVES AND CASH RESERVES.   Liquidity reserves and working capital needs are commonly called "operating reserves" or "cash reserves." To keep the distinction clear, we define "operating reserves" as funds held to meet short-term imbalances in cash receipts and disbursements as well as "money for a rainy day." These needs for cash are also termed "transactions demand" and "precautionary demand," respectively. Some operating reserves are restricted, such as those liquid funds held within the endowment fund.

"Cash reserves" denote all short-term funds and some medium-term funds held for operating reasons as well as strategic reasons. Strategic reasons include varied purposes such as to seize an unforeseen opportunity (such as an acquisition of a like organization that has run into financial difficulty), grow programs or take them to new areas, or to prefund maintenance or buildings. We further define "strategic reserves" as monies held for strategic reasons. Cash reserves thus include operating reserves as well as strategic reserves.

Endowment funds are expected to be employed permanently to augment the capital structure of the organization and are invested with growth of principal and income in mind. The first part of this section deals with investments that are part of the organization's treasury management, or short-term financial function, rather than that of long-term investing, which is discussed later. There may be situations where a portion of an endowment needs to be available to meet institutional or donor requirements in a shorter term. In these instances, the strategies for both long- and short-term investing will be employed with an endowment. Conversely, there may be situations that will allow the investment of nonendowed funds in longer-term strategies. In our final chapter, Chapter 8, we take up the investment of endowment fund and other long-term investment portfolios.

(b) IMPORTANCE OF AN INVESTMENT POLICY STATEMENT.   The investment program of the nonprofit organization is the fiduciary responsibility of the board of trustees, and it is an integral part of the board's responsibility to be good stewards of the organization's assets. In this chapter, investing objectives and guidelines are referred to as investment policy. In written form, the policy defines the allocation of investable funds across asset classes, based on short- and/or long-term objectives and risk tolerances. An institution's governing board approves the policy statement. The policy serves as a guide to the investment or finance committee in the implementation of investing programs. A comprehensive policy includes several components: return objective, time horizon, long-term asset allocation guidelines, short-term asset allocation guidelines, manager selection, and evaluation criteria. As so many nonprofits outsource investment decision-making, manager selection is one of the most important aspects of your policy. We have included the Investment Management Consultants Association (IMCA) Investment Management Questionnaire to assist you in the manager selection process (see Appendix 7D).

In the absence of a written and approved policy document, the financial or investment manager may find it difficult, if not impossible, to invest funds confidently. Without a written policy, the financial or investment manager also risks his or her job every time an investment is made, because senior officials or members of the board have the opportunity to second-guess the investment action if there are no accepted investing standards. Accordingly, in the absence of an existing written policy statement and guidelines, the financial manager should initiate the development of such a document. Consult Appendixes 7A and 7B for examples of short-term investment policies, and Appendix 8E for an example of a comprehensive investment policy.

7.2 MANAGING LIQUIDITY FUNDS AND OPTIMIZING RETURN ON EXCESS SHORT-TERM WORKING CAPITAL

(a) **CASH FLOW FORECASTING.**   The manager of a successful investing program must have an effective cash flow forecasting system in place. The forecasting system is necessary to give the manager an idea of the amount of liquidity funds available for investment and the time period that the funds will be available. Liquidity refers to the capability of an investment instrument to be converted into cash prior to maturity without the investor suffering an unacceptable loss of principal.

(b) **DEVELOPING AN INVESTING STRATEGY.**   The financial manager is ready to begin development of a strategic plan for investing liquidity funds after the necessary tools are in place for producing forecasts. These include a short-term cash flow forecast and an intermediate-term forecast for several months. A long-range forecast is also helpful in determining the amount and duration, if any, of funds available for longer-term investing. The strategic plan should be established in concert with development of the investing policy and guidelines to ensure that the guidelines are compatible with, and indeed support, the investing strategy.

At this point, the financial manager may begin to think in terms of managing two different segments of portfolios. One segment would be the liquidity portfolio containing only short-term, fixed-income securities with high-grade credit quality and liquidity. It is this portion that will be used tactically on a daily basis to absorb temporarily excess funds generated from operations and to provide liquidity to the institution when there is a shortfall of funds. The other portion of the portfolio, for longer-term strategic use, such as an endowment, could be invested in intermediate-term, fixed-income securities or stocks.

Before investing any funds, however, the financial manager will want to assess the institution's tolerance for risk. Typically, when asked about tolerance for risk, management will say that it has absolutely no tolerance for it. However, when faced with the low yields of risk-free, short-term Treasury bills (T-bills), management will frequently inquire about other securities that offer a higher yield.

7.3 CRITERIA FOR INVESTING

In evaluating the various avenues used to approach the investment of a particular pool of funds, the financial manager must consider a number of criteria and alternatives available with respect to each criterion. The criteria to be evaluated include:

- Safety of principal
- Liquidity
- Risk
- Timing of the use of funds
- Reinvestment requirements
- Management's (directors or trustees) special attitude toward such items as supporting local banks with deposits, risk sensitivity, and degree of participation in investment activities (which should be addressed in the investing guidelines)
- Particularly with liquidity funds and short-term investing, strive for "safety first," then liquidity, then yield

(a) SAFETY OF PRINCIPAL. The need for the safety of principal cannot be overemphasized. Ask a business executive or administrative manager about his or her tolerance for risk in making investments, and the response undoubtedly will be that there is no tolerance for risk. Then ask that same person whether he or she finds short-term U.S. Treasury bills to have an acceptable rate of return, and the response undoubtedly will be negative as well. Obviously, there is a conflict in these responses, because one cannot have a total absence of risk and reap high returns at the same time. The earning of a normal rate of return is related to the acceptance of a level of risk. Every investment policy must address and specify that level of risk the organization is willing to accept. The statement of risk tolerance is the number-one element in a written set of investing policy and guidelines. There are essentially two forms of risks: (1) credit risk and (2) market or interest-rate risk.

(b) LIQUIDITY. "Liquidity" refers to the capability of an investment instrument to be converted into cash prior to maturity without the investor suffering an unacceptable loss of principal. A portfolio is said to have near-perfect liquidity when it consists of extremely high-credit quality instruments and it matures entirely in one day. In that case, interest rates could change overnight but would not affect the market value of the portfolio. However, if maturity of the instruments in the portfolio extends beyond overnight, there is the possibility of the introduction of market risk and therefore the introduction of some illiquidity.

Primary goals of managing liquidity funds usually are the preservation of principal and the maintenance of liquidity (convertibility to cash). Generating a competitive yield on the funds is often a third objective. In managing an organization, whether a religious institution or a manufacturer, the maintenance of the organization's liquidity is crucial to its short- and long-term success. Even in financially successful organizations, there are periods in which disbursements exceed receipts, and the well-managed organization must be prepared for this occurrence. An entity that manages its cash properly will not maintain sufficient cash in its checking account to clear short-term hurdles. Rather, it will keep all excess cash in the form of liquid investments composed almost exclusively of short-term, fixed-income money market instruments that are convertible to cash on virtually a moment's notice with no risk to principal.

Another, perhaps more obvious dimension of liquidity relates to the depth and breadth of the market itself for the particular security involved. The good news about the huge size of the national debt is that it provides the broadest and deepest market dimensions for the debt instruments of the U.S. government. The vast breadth and depth of the market enables any investor to buy or sell virtually any amount of current actively traded U.S. Treasury securities at virtually any moment with a minimum search for buyers and sellers.

At the opposite extreme of this dimension of liquidity are debt obligations of obscure banks and corporations whose creditworthiness is not investment grade and for which there are few ready buyers or sellers in the marketplace. It would not be unusual for the holder of an instrument of an obscure company to encounter delays of days or even a week while a broker searched for a potential buyer, if one exists. It is important to note that even unusual U.S. government *agency* (not Treasury) securities can be quite illiquid, if the structure of the instrument is particularly unusual.

It is said that every asset has its price and that no matter how poor a credit risk or how long the instrument's maturity, there is always an investor somewhere in the marketplace who will buy that instrument. However, the question is, "At what price?" Even for 30-year U.S. government bonds, the market price is determined by literally thousands of active buyers and sellers at any moment. This depth of the market provides the seller the ability to convert a government obligation into cash on a moment's notice. Meanwhile, the free-flowing market mechanism of continuing transactions between buyers and sellers provides constant adjustment to the market price, based on current interest rates and expectations. This is the traditional concept of liquidity. The holder of the debt instrument of the obscure corporation may also find a willing buyer. In the absence of other potential buyers, however, the one buyer who is interested can probably dictate the price to the seller, and that price may very well represent a huge loss. Therefore, while the seller can indeed convert the security to cash, he or she may have to suffer a loss in order to do so prior to maturity.

Liquidity is also an issue when funds are placed into instruments that are legally unredeemable until maturity. These include, for example, fixed-time deposits of banks or savings and loans where the amount is small or the investor has no legal or market ability to sell or transfer the deposit to a subsequent party. In the case of certificates of deposit (CDs) of well-known and high-credit-rated institutions where the investor has the legal right to sell the instrument, liquidity is considerably improved. Interest-rate risk, however, may reduce the market value of the instrument if interest rates have risen since the instrument was acquired.

Accordingly, the financial manager who seeks to ensure a high level of liquidity for the institution's portfolio should focus on investing in instruments of the highest possible credit quality and of relatively short maturities. Where liquidity is not a large factor in the objectives of the funds, the financial manager may consider matching the maturity of the investment to a particular date when the funds are known to be needed. For example, in managing an endowment fund portfolio, the investment manager may elect to invest in an instrument maturing when a grant is expected to be made. In this case, the possibility of realized loss due to market risk would be diminished because the instrument would likely mature (at face value) in time to be used for the intended purpose. The only risk would be credit risk. Our coverage of endowment fund investing is in Chapter 8.

(c) RISK.

(i) Credit Risk.   Credit risk, also known as default risk, refers to the possibility that the obligor of a debt instrument will fail to repay principal or pay interest on a timely basis in accordance with the terms of the instrument. Credit risk can be analyzed and measured by the investor prior to investing in a particular debt instrument, or the investor can rely on a credit analysis performed for a fee, by a credit-rating agency (see Exhibit 7.1). It is generally assumed that the credit risk represented by debt of the government of the United States is the lowest available and that all other issuers' credit ratings are measured against the benchmark of the U.S. government.

Many investors mistakenly believe that the debt markets are rational and that differences in credit risk are not quickly reflected in differences of yield among similar instruments of different issuers. However, a commercial paper note due in 90 days issued by a corporation of medium creditworthiness will yield the investor a greater return than will a 90-day U.S. T-bill. Similarly, the yield on

Rating Service	Address and Phone Number
Moody's Investors Service	99 Church Street New York, NY 10007 (212) 553-0300 www.moodys.com
Standard & Poor's Corporation	55 Water Street New York, NY 10041 (212) 438-7280 www.standardandpoors.com
Fitch Investors Service, Inc.	33 Whitehall Street New York, NY 10004 (800) 89-FITCH www.fitchratings.com
Highline Banking Data Services	Highline Data LLC 807 Las Cimas Parkway, Suite 320 Austin, TX 78746
Dominion Bond Rating Service	101 North Wacker Drive, Suite 100 Chicago, IL 60606 (312) 332-3429 www.dbrs.com

Note: Duff & Phelps' rating service became part of Fitch, but Duff & Phelps continues to provide valuation of privately held businesses and equity interest (www.duffandphelps.com).

EXHIBIT 7.1 SEVERAL MAJOR CREDIT-RATING FIRMS

commercial paper issued by a very creditworthy corporation will yield somewhat less return than the rate of return on commercial paper of a medium-quality issuer.

This dilemma between no tolerance for risk and a desire for high yield should be explored and defined in the investment guidelines. If investors are unwilling to accept any risk greater than short-term U.S. T-bills, they must be willing to accept the rock-bottom yields that Treasury bills offer. If they wish to obtain higher yields, however, they must be willing to accept the reasonable credit risk of top credit-rated U.S. and foreign banks and top credit-rated industrial corporations and their captive finance company subsidiaries. This decision addresses only the question of credit risk; the issue of market risk which is determined by length of maturity still must be considered (see Exhibit 7.2 later in the chapter).

If management really wishes to have yield take a front seat, it should be willing to accept other investing possibilities. These include banks of less than top quality (although many are nevertheless sound) and commercial paper of industrial and financial companies that are rated in the second tier of credit ratings. The matter of market risk, or the risk that interest rates will rise, thereby forcing a decline in the market value of fixed-income securities, also must be considered. This is particularly important in a liquidity portfolio where safety of principal is of paramount importance. Management must be willing to accept market risk, even from T-bills, unless it is prepared to keep maturities as short as 90 days or less.

However, markets are imperfect and sometimes notably so. It is important for the financial manager to be aware of the respective "normal" relative levels of credit quality and yields among the issuers in whose securities and *instruments* the organization is investing. To do this, the financial manager must maintain current information about issuers and changes in their credit ratings.

In the management of pools of funds held for liquidity and intermediate-term purposes, investors tend to demand credit quality of the highest order; that is, they will generally invest only in instruments issued by companies of the highest-credit quality or by the U.S. government. This is to ensure the greatest degree of market "salability" or liquidity. However, the risk of such investments still must be carefully examined.

Some investors take a higher-risk approach and apply the theory of portfolio management that expects some investments in a portfolio to pay off while others actually incur capital losses. The hope, of course, is to manage a broad optimum portfolio of investments where winners will exceed the losers as to yield, with the result that the portfolio as a whole realizes a minimal amount of risk and an optimal amount of return and growth. However, this approach is suited only to highly skilled investors who can afford a higher degree of risk. Other investors use a more conservative approach and plan to have the bulk of the investments in a portfolio generate normal yields of approximately the average market rate of return.

(ii) Market Risk.   Market risk, or the risk of loss to principal due to changes in interest rates, is a subtle but very real form of risk and can be just as devastating as credit risk. Interest rates affect the market value of a debt instrument when the interest rate, or coupon, of the instrument is fixed (nonfloating or nonmarket rate adjusting). When yields in the marketplace change, either the market value of existing instruments must change or the rate of return paid on that instrument must change in order to adjust an instrument's market yield to current market yield. If a bond has a fixed-rate coupon and interest rates in the marketplace rise, then the market value of that bond must decline to a point where the fixed-rate coupon and a change in its market value combine to reflect current market yield. Likewise, when interest rates decline, the market value of the bond must rise. When this bond is purchased by an investor, the combination of the bond's coupon rate and principal cost will place the net yield, based on the price paid versus interest received, in the range where comparable instruments are now offered.

When investing in a fixed-rate coupon instrument, the investor realizes that the longer the term until maturity, the greater the possibility for fluctuation in market value due to interest rate changes and, therefore, the greater the market

1 percent rise in interest rates equals approximately this amount of dollar market value decline (Per $1 million of Par Value)

Maturity	Decline in Market Value
1 month	$ 734
3 months	2,500
6 months	4,699
1 year	8,681
2 years	23,212
5 years	43,414
10 years	70,728
20 years	113,194
30 years	129,645

EXHIBIT 7.2 HOW CHANGES IN INTEREST RATES AFFECT MARKET PRICES

risk (see Exhibit 7.2). Conversely, an instrument that matures in a relatively short period of time will be somewhat insulated from changes in market interest rates; the investor will need only to hold the instrument until maturity to receive 100 cents on the dollar.

Different types of instruments bear different levels of sensitivity to the volatility of interest rates in the marketplace. Zero coupon bonds, for example, typically carry the highest level of volatility, or market risk, because there is no current income to cushion the investor's return. Consequently, a change in market interest rate levels impacts immediately, directly, and to the fullest extent the market value of a zero coupon bond. At the other end of the volatility spectrum are floating-rate instruments, where the coupon yields are not fixed but are reset periodically to reflect changes in market interest rates. Because the coupon on these instruments changes with the market, their market value is rather stable.

High-quality credit ratings also tend to insulate a security from market volatility to some degree. It has been shown empirically that in times of stress or increasing interest rates, investors begin a "flight to quality" by buying higher-credit quality instruments. It creates a demand for the instruments, thereby further forcing their prices further up and yields down. This was amply demonstrated in the well-documented stock market crash of October 19, 1987, when equity prices went into a free fall and there was complete turmoil in both the equity and credit markets. Investors fled stocks in droves, and many placed their funds temporarily into U.S. government obligations. The yields on U.S. government securities remained inordinately low during the weeks immediately following the crash. Investors had bid up the prices as they purchased these instruments to obtain high-credit quality investments.

Loss of principal due to market risk is *realized* only when the security must be sold prior to maturity. At that time, the market value of the instrument may be above or below what the investor paid for it and also may be different from the maturity value of the instrument. Market risk does not result in a loss if the investor holds the instrument until maturity, because at that time the investor will realize the return of 100 percent of the face value of the instrument. Market risk exists not only for corporate and bank securities, but also for U.S. government securities. Therefore, it is incorrect for an investor to say that he or she demands that funds be invested only in U.S. government securities in order to avoid risk to principal. Indeed, credit risk can be avoided or at least minimized, but market risk, even for Treasury instruments, cannot be minimized unless the securities are held until maturity.

Recognition by the financial manager of the existence of market risk, in addition to credit risk, is critically important to the management of an investment portfolio, particularly a pool of funds whose use is not anticipated for several years. The temptation in managing these funds is to invest in long-term securities and collect a possibly higher income, while knowing that the securities are sufficiently liquid to be sold on very short notice. The financial manager must recognize, however, that while the liquidity and current income will remain constant, a change in interest rates may cause the market value of the portfolio to decline. Losses could be realized if it were necessary to convert the portfolio to cash prior to maturity of the instruments. Therefore, in addition to analyzing and monitoring credit risk as represented by the potential for default by issuers of securities, the investment manager also must be cognizant of market risk and its potential capability to erode the market value of a portfolio.

Because of the potentially devastating effects of both credit risk and market risk, the institution's investment policy must be clear about how these two forms of risk are to be handled. This must be done before establishing an approach to investing and before discussing the particular issues and forms of investments that are acceptable. The decisions with regard to the level of tolerance for credit risk and market risk should be made by the most senior officials in management, and ultimately by the directors or trustees themselves. The considerations should be made consciously and the results communicated in writing to the financial manager in such a way that there cancan be no mistaking the intentions of senior management.

There are two ways to protect against market risk. The customary method most companies use is simply to maintain short maturities ranging between 30 and 60 days. If interest rates rise (causing the value of the instrument to fall), the investor has to wait only a short period until maturity. The other method, which is far from perfect, is to invest in interest rate futures contracts and options as hedges. When interest rates move upward, a hedge position should generate a profit to offset the loss in the value of the investment instrument.

The use of futures, options, and swaps, however, is a very sophisticated practice. It should be used only by investors with very large portfolios, who can observe all the markets virtually on a full-time basis. Futures options and swap could be equally beneficial for investors with modest-size portfolios, but these investors typically do not have the time or expertise to become involved with the sophisticated hedging techniques that instruments represent.

Another strategy for managing short-term investment funds exists where the funds have been earmarked for a specific project, such as construction of a building. In this type of situation, market risk impact can be reduced by purchasing investment instruments with maturities that coincide with the projected need dates for the funds. For example, if construction plans call for a payment on a certain date four months from now, the financial manager can invest in an instrument maturing just prior to the payment date. The institution will be assured of receiving 100 cents on the invested dollar, plus interest, at maturity, rather than risking possible loss in a sale prior to maturity. The entire investment portfolio for the project can be assembled with maturities to coincide with estimated payment dates and amounts required for the project, thereby largely immunizing the portfolio from any market value changes due to interest rate swings. However, if construction is ahead of schedule and funds are required sooner than expected, an instrument may have to be sold prior to maturity. This may result in possible loss of principal.

(d) TIMING OF FUNDS USAGE. The financial manager must know the intended use of investment funds in order to manage maturities properly. Maturity and liquidity objectives should correspond with the purpose of the specific funds, whether it is to make a grant, repay bank debt, or meet expenses, or to be used as contributions to an employee benefit plan.

Grant payments, for example, can occur on fairly short notice and require relatively large amounts of funds. Long-term illiquid investment instruments may be inappropriate if the pool of invested funds will be used for daily expenses. Bank debt repayments are usually scheduled and known well in advance. Bank loans that are revolving credits, however, are subject to being repaid and reborrowed at the borrower's discretion. Therefore, repayments can occur virtually at any time the borrower has sufficient funds available. Most large payment requirements also are known well in advance. Employee benefit plans, such as pension plans, are subject to contributions with fairly regular and defined payment dates, but the amounts may or may not be known.

Accordingly, the financial manager must plan the maturity dates of the investment instruments in the pool to coincide with the funding dates of the various uses of the funds. The manager must also obtain the highest possible market yield on the pool of funds and attempt to schedule the maturities so as to optimize the yield along the yield curve. The challenge occurs when the investment manager must seek the optimal trade-off between safety and liquidity of principal and rate of return on the investment.

(e) REINVESTMENT REQUIREMENTS.   In order to operate an investment program properly, management must decide how to use the income earned on the pool of investments. Options include incorporating the income stream from investments with the other revenue streams of the institution or retaining the income stream in the investment pool where it is reinvested. This is a policy decision, and its implications may be relatively important if investment income is substantial and becomes a large source of "budgeted" revenue. Another consideration involves funds invested in long-term instruments where the income is not used. The financial manager may have difficulty reinvesting the income proceeds in similar long-term investments when the amount of the income stream is small.

(f) MONEY MARKET INSTRUMENTS: AN OVERVIEW.   The ideal money market investment medium is a debt instrument that does not fluctuate substantially in value, that carries no risk of default by the issuer, and that may be converted to cash at any time without loss of principal. The instrument that most closely approaches this standard is a short-maturity (90 days or less) U.S. Treasury bill, a short-term debt obligation of the U.S. government. In this imperfect world, the U.S. government is considered to carry the highest domestic credit rating, which means that the risk of default on its debt obligations is the lowest in the United States. As a result, credit ratings as well as yields of all other domestic instruments of any maturity are based on spreads (yield variations) from U.S. government securities.

Risk of loss in short-term investing is not confined to credit risk alone. Loss of principal can also occur by investing in an instrument that must be sold prior to maturity, if interest rates have risen before the instrument matures. This phenomenon is usually referred to as market risk or interest rate risk, and it can result in loss to investors, even to those who invest only in U.S. T-bills.

Because of market risk, the financial manager should purchase instruments with maturities that closely match the need for the funds. If the cash-flow forecast indicates that the funds should be available in 45 days, for example, the financial manager is well advised to purchase instruments maturing in approximately 45 days. Purchasing a six-month security under these circumstances could result in loss of principal if interest rates rise, thereby forcing value of the instrument down and having to sell the instrument to raise funds for an unexpected cash need. Of course, the opposite situation may occur. Declining interest rates during the period could result in a gain on the early sale of the instrument. However, most prudent financial managers primarily will look at avoiding risk to their liquidity funds.

Other short-term debt instruments commonly used as money market investments are the negotiable bank certificate of deposit, the time draft called a banker's acceptance (the payment of which is an obligation of a bank), and the short-term promissory note of a corporation known as commercial paper.

With the proliferation of new derivative instruments in the money markets, the typical investor is hard-pressed to discern between instruments that are truly safe and liquid and those that present hidden risks. Although there have been no major disasters in this regard yet, many investors of institutional liquidity funds remain somewhat skeptical about instruments with names such as DARTS, CATS, LYONS, and Low Floaters. Other investors, often seeking new, more unusual investments, forge ahead and usually enjoy a somewhat higher yield than their friends who remain with the traditional money market investment instruments. It is questionable, however, whether these more adventuresome investors truly understand the issues surrounding potential liquidity and credit problems, even though there is little or no documented evidence of failures in these areas to date.

If a financial manager knowingly enters into a risky investment transaction and that risk is realized with loss of principal, the loss can be much more acceptable if the manager's actions have been in accordance with board-approved policy and guidelines. Along with the variety of new instruments, the minefields also have expanded to the potential detriment of the well-being and job security of financial managers responsible for investing their institutions' liquidity funds without board direction.

(g) CASE STUDY OF RISK TAKING RESULTING IN LOSS. ABC Foundation was a large organization with more than 26 employees, serving an economically expanding middle-class (and higher) geographic area. The foundation had accumulated funds of approximately $40 million that were managed by a business manager reporting to the board of trustees. The cash flow to the foundation was more than adequate to cover expenses with no immediate need forecasted for the use of any funds; the business manager had relatively few constraints and little direction to keep cash available for immediate needs. Furthermore, no comprehensive written investment policy was in place to specifically limit ABC Foundation's investment activities.

Within this loose framework, the business manager began to purchase longer-maturity (10 through 30 years) U.S. Treasury securities for these reasons:

- The longer maturities presented a higher yield and would improve the rate of return on the organization's investment portfolio.
- There were no immediate plans to utilize the funds; therefore, short-maturity dates appeared to be inappropriate for the investment.
- Because the instruments were issued and guaranteed by the U.S. Treasury, there appeared to be no risk to principal.

As the rate of return on the foundation's portfolio was better than the yield available on shorter-term investments, such as local bank CDs, the trustees complimented the business manager on his ability to achieve an attractive rate of return. Furthermore, during this investment period, interest rates began to decline, causing the market value of the long-term securities to increase. This situation led the foundation's business manager to become more active in trading (actively buying and selling) these securities to capture a capital gain from their improvement in price. As interest rates continued to decline, the prices of these instruments continued to go up, and capital gains were realized from the transactions. Combined with their higher interest (accrual) rate, the gains substantially enhanced the foundation's investment return and brought further praise to the business manager from the trustees.

Soon the reality of interest-rate fluctuations began to set in as financial market conditions changed. Interest rates stopped going down and, in fact, began to rise quite rapidly. By this time, the foundation's bond portfolio consisted entirely of long-maturity U.S. Treasury bonds. Just as these instruments had gone up in price as interest rates were declining, they were now going down in price as interest rates were increasing. Accordingly, the business manager was no longer able to sell the instruments in his portfolio at prices higher than he had paid. Therefore, unrealized capital gains quickly turned into unrealized capital losses. Recently the government began using a single-price system in which notes are awarded at the highest yield needed to sell the securities, reducing, investor bargaining ability.

Compounding this situation was a substantial slowdown in cash flow to the foundation. Now there was a need to rely on funds from its excess cash investments, all of which were in the investment fund. This need for cash necessitated the sale of several investments, which resulted in substantial realized losses to the foundation. At this time, the losses were noted by the foundation's auditors, who discovered additional unrealized losses in the foundation's investment portfolio.

As a result of the speculation engaged in by ABC Foundation's business manager, the foundation realized approximately $2.5 million in losses. Its remaining investment portfolio, with an initial value of $40 million, had declined in value approximately 10 percent from the original principal investment.

This information contained in the audit report was made available to the trustees, who immediately demanded the situation be remedied. Unfortunately, with the losses in place and more cash needs ahead, the opportunities to remedy the situation were limited simply to establishing procedures to avoid a repetition in the future.

These procedures should have been set in place before this situation developed:

- Comprehensive investment guidelines should have been established with specific limitations on risk, including maturities.
- Maturities should have been limited to conform strictly with the estimated cash needs at that time or limited to a maximum maturity date, as stated in the guidelines, to avoid excessive interest rate or market risk.
- The business manager responsible for the investment portfolio should have been trained more thoroughly, or outside professional assistance should have been contracted.

- Frequent (quarterly) review or audit of investment activities should have been instituted to ensure that investment activities conformed with investment guidelines and to discover any unusual situations.

(h) YIELD IMPROVEMENT BY POOLING OF FUNDS. Another technique that can increase investment yields effectively for the institution is consolidation of all available funds into one pool. Many medium and large institutions, in particular, operate their cash systems in a fragmented manner with collection points and disbursement points scattered throughout their organizational structures. By centralizing cash flows and cash management, an institution can create a larger pool of investable funds (refer to Chapter 3). This gives the institution's financial manager greater bargaining power and the ability to invest more money in "round lots" in the money markets. In addition, the cash flow imbalances of various operating units in a large organization tend to average out and offset one another. The organization as a whole typically can operate on a smaller working cash balance than can the sum of its parts. The centralized liquidity pool usually can be invested for a longer duration than its separate components, which enhances the overall yield obtainable on the institution's invested funds.

Another frequent benefit of fund consolidation and a larger investment portfolio is the fact that a higher level of professionalism can be supported in the investment process. An internal professional funds manager or outside investment management firm using proper cash forecasting and cash management techniques may often bring about higher returns on available funds. The use of investment professionals also tends to reduce the institution's exposure to credit risk because they are familiar with debt issuers and instruments and can give constant attention to the market.

7.4 INVESTOR OR SPECULATOR?

Even in his prime, Babe Ruth struck out much more often than he hit home runs. The financial manager who seeks to hit home runs in managing the investment portfolio will undoubtedly find that the strikeout percentage is too high to be acceptable to senior management and the board of directors or trustees. Instead, the acceptable method of operation is to be a singles hitter with a very high batting average and probably never any home runs. After all, the financial manager who hits only singles has a certain degree of job security, while the financial manager who loses principal due to speculative investments may often be searching for a new job.

Professional institutional speculators in the investment profession are paid to risk capital in order to make considerable profits, or suffer losses, by participating continuously and aggressively in the marketplace. However, financial managers of nonprofit institutions are, in effect, part-time investors who are involved in the investment markets only occasionally. The part-time investor is at a severe disadvantage against a speculative marketplace. Even full-time investment speculators strike out with a good degree of frequency. The part-time investor, however, never can be expected to hit a prodigious home run. Yet the institution's senior management will not likely forget the strikeouts.

The cardinal rule for the small or part-time investor, therefore, is this: Be an investor and not a speculator. When the financial manager encounters an apparently attractive instrument not normally included in the institution's portfolio, he or she should seek specific management approval of the instrument before executing the transaction. Doing this requires that the financial manager thoroughly research and prepare each recommendation for senior management to review so it can determine suitability of the instrument. If management supports the investment after examining all aspects of the recommendation, the financial manager cannot be criticized later for imprudence.

7.5 STANDARD OPERATING INVESTMENT PROCEDURES

The financial manager faces credit risk and market risk daily in the management of the investment portfolio. Additional risk from other quarters certainly is not welcome. However, insidious forms of risk exist within the financial manager's own office. These include fraud, malfeasance, and repeated errors. Fraud is the intentional misrepresentation of facts for the personal benefit of the financial manager or a staff member. By contrast, malfeasance is the failure to conduct business affairs properly, resulting in poor performance. Repeated errors are usually the result of incompetence or poor training.

(a) DOCUMENTING PROCEDURES. To avoid these forms of internal risk, the financial manager is well advised to document fully all operating procedures relating to the management and operations of the investment process. Documentation of procedures is vital to the success of the internal control system. However, it is a time-consuming process, and too few firms actually get around to writing the procedure documents. A single instance of fraud or malfeasance, or repeated errors, however, can readily demonstrate the value of written procedure manuals and system documentation.

The procedure documents should include:

- A description of the operating structure
- Job descriptions and statements of responsibility
- Detailed descriptions of the processing of investment transactions, related funds transfers, and securities safekeeping requirements
- Valuation and mark to market of holdings
- A description of all forms used to execute and confirm transactions
- A description of limitations on the authority of each employee
- A clear delineation of the duties and responsibilities of each employee involved in the investing process to report any perceived impropriety or errors

(b) REVIEWING THE PORTFOLIO.   As part of the standard operating procedures in the management of an investment portfolio, senior management should review the portfolio periodically, at least quarterly or perhaps monthly, and attempt to discover any potential problems. Several elements should be examined by senior management, including an analysis of unrealized gains and losses and a trading analysis.

(i) Unrealized Gains and Losses.   An excellent way to discover potential problems in a portfolio is to analyze the gains and losses that exist on paper among the securities held in the portfolio. An accumulation of unrealized or paper losses are generally recognized in the statement of activity even though the securities may not have been sold, according to the accounting standards. Conversely, an increasing amount of unrealized gains in the portfolio may indicate success in the investing operations. Management may wish to realize these gains by selling the instruments and reinvesting the proceeds in other instruments with perhaps less future market price movement potential. Also consider the possibility that the organization's large gains seen today may reveal that the portfolio manager is engaging in speculative trading, which in the future can result in large losses.

(ii) Trading Activity.   An additional, effective way to monitor the performance of the financial manager is to review the number of transactions taking place during a one-week or one-month period. If new money is being added to the portfolio, or if there are significant numbers of maturing instruments, a higher than normal level of trading activity, particularly on the purchasing side, would be expected. If there is no unusual inflow of funds but a high level of buying and selling, the financial manager may be trading for speculative profit. The unusual activity in buying and selling should be cause to ask the financial manager to explain this action in light of the institution's investing policies.

7.6 INVESTMENT OPERATIONS: AN INTRODUCTION

Managing an investing program has many facets and considerations, but the financial manager should have three key elements in place before embarking on an investing program:

1. Written investing policy and set of guidelines
2. Safekeeping arrangements for the securities
3. Defined operating procedures

The first element is the written investing policy and guidelines (examples are provided for short-term investment accounts in Appendix 7A and Appendix 7B, for endowments and other long-term accounts in Appendix 8B, and for mixed short-term and long-term accounts in Appendix 8E). Custody arrangements for safekeeping of securities and appropriate operating procedures are explained in this chapter. A well-defined operating procedure is a key component of an institution's investment program.

(a) SELECTING A CUSTODIAN. Traditional custom and practice dictate that settlement of money market securities transactions occurs by delivery of the securities in New York City against payment to the seller of the amount due. Therefore, it behooves the investor organization to maintain a custodian account in New York for the clearance and safekeeping of its portfolio of securities. An investor organization that does not have a banking relationship in New York usually can work through a local or regional bank's New York correspondent bank to provide the custodian service. Many banks throughout the United States offer custodial and safekeeping services, but they typically act as investors' agents and make arrangements with New York City banks to handle the actual securities clearance and safekeeping operations.

It is not a good idea for delivery to occur outside of New York City. Taking delivery of securities in another city entails additional costs for delivery as well as additional costs for redelivery upon redemption or early sale. Also, it is unwise for an investor to accept physical delivery of investment instruments because of security considerations.

Selection of the securities clearance/custodian bank may be as simple as merely approving the use of the correspondent bank of the organization's principal depository bank or as complicated as an elaborate selection process that includes requests for proposals and personal visits. In any event, the investor's fundamental interest is to ensure:

- Safety of the portfolio holdings
- Integrity of the information concerning the investment instruments
- Accuracy and accountability of the custodian
- Reliability of the custodian to execute instructions concerning receipt and delivery of securities in settlement of investment transactions

Using a New York correspondent bank introduces an extra layer of administrative bureaucracy into the picture, and the financial manager should be satisfied that this extra layer provides value. The financial manager also should inquire as to where in the New York bank and the local bank the securities clearance and safekeeping services are performed. For example, many banks offer similar services out of both their trust and their investment departments. Experience has shown that securities clearance services provided by an investment department tend to be expedited because of that department's own requirement for handling transactions swiftly and accurately.

The securities clearance service offered by a trust department, however, is not often geared to the fast-paced settlements required in money market securities transactions. This difference simply reflects the nature of the business handled by the respective departments. Trust department investments are more heavily weighted toward equity securities that settle in three business days rather than same- or next-day settlements of most money market transactions. Consequently, trust departments tend not to function with the speed and cost-effectiveness required when dealing with money market instruments.

Banks that offer custody services are willing to hold in safekeeping virtually all types of fixed- or variable-income or equity securities for the customer regardless of where they were purchased. Banks usually base their charges for the service on the volume of transactions conducted in an account; however, some banks base charges on the value of the portfolio held in safekeeping or a combination of the two bases.

The concept of delivery versus payment (DVP) is fundamental to the operation of an investment portfolio because it is an important safeguard against the risk of loss for the nonprofit institution. The alternative to DVP is to pay for the purchase of securities by wire transfer and to allow the selling investment dealer to retain possession of the instruments. This presents a risk, however, that the selling dealer may fail to segregate properly the customer's securities from the dealer's own inventory of securities or fail to segregate the securities owned by each customer. Securities dealers, of course, welcome the opportunity to hold customers' securities free of charge, while banks charge fees for this service. However, an independent custodian does add value in the form of assurance that the specific asset actually exists.

The use of an independent custodian is very important in the investing process for five reasons:

1. It provides securities clearance service in New York City that makes it possible for the investing organization to deal with virtually all brokers and dealers in the country.
2. It eliminates the possible commingling of securities owned by multiple clients and the investment dealer itself.
3. It provides independent verification of the receipt and holding of securities.
4. It facilitates the investor's audit process.
5. It ensures the safety of the investing organization's funds in the event of the failure of a dealer from which the investor has purchased securities, because the DVP method of settlement involves an independent third-party safekeeping agent.

The importance of the last point is illustrated by the failure of ESM Government Securities, Inc. as well as several other securities dealers that failed during the mid-1980s. While ESM's failure was caused by a number of factors, not the least of which were alleged mismanagement and fraud, dozens of investing institutions lost hundreds of millions of dollars because they had not insisted on delivery against payment of the purchased securities to an independent custodian. Therefore, ESM was able to resell the securities, or borrow further, by using customers' securities as collateral.

One investor, a municipality, initially lost more than $14 million (it eventually recovered $10 million after spending $1 million in legal fees) when ESM failed. In the aftermath of this debacle, auditors discovered that ESM apparently had sold the same securities not only to the municipality, but to other investors as well. Had the municipality insisted that ESM deliver the securities to an independent custodian against payment, there would have been no question about the safety of the municipality's funds and the integrity of its investment portfolio. The municipality would have had either the funds or the investment securities; however, in the absence of actual delivery, the municipality had neither the funds nor the investment instruments.

(b) BEARER VERSUS REGISTERED (AND BOOK-ENTRY) FORM.   Many years ago, all securities were issued in physical form as certificates. The burden of storing and moving all of this paper became too great, however, and a number of securities markets changed their method of operation to maintenance of ownership records in electronic form. When a security changes ownership, the transaction and resulting ownership registration records are changed in the central computer. Today most markets utilize the electronic book-entry form of registration; some markets offer a combination of physical and book-entry forms. Stocks listed on the New York Stock Exchange, for example, are generally held in book entry form at a central depository, but any investor who wishes to hold a physical stock certificate may do so upon request.

The U.S. Treasury, however, has been phasing out physical certificates completely. Since 1987, all T-bills have been issued in book-entry form. The T-bill investor maintains an account with the Treasury at the Federal Reserve Bank, and all transactions involving Treasury securities are handled through this account.

To accommodate the use of book-entry delivery through independent bank custodians, settlement systems have been developed that enable the electronic delivery of a security against electronic payment. The accuracy of using an electronic system is at least as great as the accuracy of the clerk reviewing the physical characteristics of the paper certificate and authorizing the issuance of a paper check for payment. Moreover, the maintenance of inventory and transaction records is greatly enhanced by the use of the book-entry form of transactions. Finally, institutions are able to avoid the escalating costs of manually handling these transactions and can pass along savings in administrative costs to their investing clients.

The paper certificate is negotiable only when payable to "bearer" or when payable to an individual whose signature accompanies the certificate on a separate form, called a bond power, and that has been guaranteed by a bank, trust company, or stockbroker. To negotiate or transfer a certificate registered in the name of a corporation, however, requires that a certified copy of a corporate resolution authorizing the transfer of the security be attached to the certificate. This process is cumbersome and subject to legal review. Consequently, delivery of a security registered to a corporation is viewed with caution. Accordingly, corporate investors are encouraged to accept physical delivery of securities payable to "bearer" or, if registration is required for some reason, to accept delivery in negotiable form and to reregister the security in the name of a nominee of the custodian. A nominee is a fictitious name properly and appropriately registered for use by the custodian whereby the custodian is able to execute transfers without the necessity of obtaining corporate board resolutions.

(c) SECURITIES SAFEKEEPING. The prudent investor will not take delivery of securities from a dealer or bank. There is the risk of loss due to theft or damage, and it is not practical to make physical delivery upon the maturity or sale of securities.

An investor will usually select a bank to safekeep securities. Most New York City banks function as securities custodians and clearance agents for investors all over the country, either directly or through a network of correspondent banks. The investor establishes a safekeeping account either with a New York bank or one of its correspondent banks, and delivery of securities is accomplished through the account.

When the investor purchases a security from a dealer, it instructs the dealer to deliver the instrument to the safekeeping bank against payment of the amount of money due on the purchase. This ensures that the purchased instrument will be delivered exactly as ordered, because the safekeeping agent should reject the delivery if there is any discrepancy. The funds remain in the investor's account until the security is delivered. If, for some reason, the selling dealer is unable to make delivery, the funds do not leave the investor's account. The safekeeping bank renders a periodic statement showing all of the securities in the safekeeping account, which is an excellent audit tool.

Another very significant advantage of the DVP system is the investor's ability to deal with any securities dealer, wherever it may be located. The transaction is agreed to by the dealer and investor over the telephone, and the dealer then makes delivery in New York as described. The need for wire transfers of funds is eliminated because the New York agent is able to charge the investor's account directly or charge its correspondent bank, which charges the investor's account. This system eliminates the control problems associated with wire transfers and allows the investor to deal with more than just one or two investment dealers.

Bank safekeeping agents charge for their services. These charges may be based on the dollar value of the portfolio held by the agent or, more likely, on the basis of a price per transaction. Generally, all securities movements incur charges. Upon the purchase of an instrument, there is a charge for accepting it and lodging it in the inventory. At its sale prior to maturity, there is also a charge for delivering the instrument. These charges apply whether the instrument requires physical delivery of a piece of paper or only book-entry delivery.

An increasing number of securities are being made subject to book-entry delivery, including virtually all U.S. government securities. Book-entry delivery involves the maintenance of accounts with the Treasury. The Federal Reserve acts as the clearing agent for U.S. government securities and credits the delivery of securities to the investor by credit to the investor's account. Certain other securities also settle through the Federal Reserve account. Other clearing entities, such as Depository Trust Company, handle stocks and certain other corporate securities.

(d) OPERATING AN INVESTMENT PROGRAM.   Having selected a custodian to hold the portfolio of securities in safekeeping and become familiar with the registration requirements of particular securities, the nonprofit financial manager still must establish the operating procedures for the execution of transactions. In this connection, certain documentation needs to be created or borrowed from other sources. These documents are designed to do four things:

1. Record the transactions as they are made.
2. Control those transactions for research and follow-up.
3. Provide the means by which an investment manager is reminded of the maturing securities in the portfolio.
4. Provide an audit trail.

The financial manager requires a systematic approach to investing. The basic elements of the system include:

- Execution of transactions
- Verification of transactions
- Delivery and safekeeping of instruments (previously discussed in this chapter)
- Reporting of transactions, portfolio inventory, and yield earned

A properly constructed set of documentation and procedures will facilitate the swift verification of transactions and the maintenance of appropriate records for reporting and research. The discussion that follows describes many details of the procedures and documents that are used in well-designed investing programs.

(i) Executing Transactions.   It is very important for the person authorized to execute investment transactions to be fully aware of the internal rules and regulations contained in the written investing policy and guidelines. This document constitutes the "contract" between the manager who handles the investing program and the organization's senior management and board of directors or trustees.

Money market investment transactions are executed on the telephone between the financial manager (or other authorized person) of the investor organization and the salesperson of the securities dealer. The financial manager may talk with salespeople of several dealers before agreeing to buy or sell a particular instrument at a certain price. Although the aggregate dollar volume of money market transactions each day is huge, there is no central marketplace and each dealer quotes his or

Transaction no.: (1)	Name of issuer: (2)		Par value: (3)
Type: (4)	Cost: (5)	Purchase date: (6)	Settlement date: (7)
Maturity date: (8)	Coupon: (9)	Yield: (10)	Guarantor: (11)
Rating: (12)	Custodian: (13)	Delivery: (14)	Call provisions: (15)

Executed by: _____ Dealer: _____
Sales representative: _____
Glossary:
The following descriptions provide information on each of the numbered components:

1. *Transaction number:* a unique internal trace number assigned to each trade that identifies the particular transaction
2. *Name of issuer:* party whose indebtedness is evidenced by the investment security
3. *Par value:* stated value of the security; the amount that will be paid at maturity
4. *Type:* instrument, or type of security (e.g., T-bills, certificates of deposit, bankers' acceptances, commercial paper)
5. *Cost:* the amount paid by the investor to acquire the security
6. *Purchase date:* date on which the investor and dealer agree to make the transaction
7. *Settlement date:* date on which ownership of the security and payment will change hands
8. *Maturity date:* date on which the security is scheduled to be paid
9. *Coupon:* rate of interest paid on the security, as stated on the face of the security
10. *Yield:* rate of return to the investor, based on the coupon as well as the cost
11. *Guarantor (if not the issuer):* name and form of guaranty (e.g., letter of credit) attached to the security, if any
12. *Rating:* rating assigned by a credit rating agency that predicts the degree of certainty applicable to the full and timely payment of principal and interest on the security
13. *Custodian:* name of the safekeeping custodian
14. *Delivery:* description of the method of delivery (e.g., DVP, dealer hold)
15. *Call provisions:* date and price at which the security may be prepaid by the issuer, if any

EXHIBIT 7.3   TRANSACTION MEMO

her own prices to buy and sell particular securities. Therefore, financial managers should shop among several dealers for a competitive price (yield) value on their investment.

(ii) Transaction Memos.   The financial manager generally uses a form, called a transaction memo or ticket, that indicates the basic information, as depicted in Exhibit 7.3. Upon completing a transaction on the telephone, the financial manager fills out the transaction memo and sends a copy to the accounting department.

Another copy should be sent to a person responsible for independently verifying the transaction. Exhibit 7.3 presents a description of each numbered component of the transaction memo.

(iii) Maturity Ticklers. A cardinal error in managing an investment portfolio is to lose track of maturing investments and unintentionally leave the proceeds uninvested, even for a day. The financial manager, therefore, needs a foolproof system to signal maturing investments. If the portfolio inventory is maintained in a database, the database usually can be sorted by maturity date showing the earliest maturities first. As a backup procedure, the financial manager also may maintain a file of transaction memos in maturity date order and have an assistant check the file daily. It is a good idea to mark on the maturity file copy the ultimate disposition of the instrument, such as "matured" or "sold on (date) to (name of dealer)."

(iv) Transaction Log. To facilitate the tracking of inventory and the conduct of audits, each security purchase should be assigned a unique identification number. The simplest method is to assign consecutive transaction numbers by prenumbering the transaction memos in serial order. Another method is to incorporate the Gregorian or Julian date as seen in spreadsheet software of the transaction together with a one- or two-digit number that recycles each day. As transactions are executed, they are recorded in a log, either paper or electronic, to show at a glance the transactions that have been conducted. Exhibit 7.4 depicts a sample transaction log sheet.

Transaction No.	Cost	Issuer	Type	Settlement Date	Maturity	Yield	Dealer

EXHIBIT 7.4 TRANSACTION LOG

(v) Technology Tools. The financial manager responsible for investment should be knowledgeable about a number of important technology tools in the marketplace. These tools, which include the Bloomberg, and Reuters, systems, provide essential information for investors. The Internet also provides other sources of financial information, including news groups and discussion forums, as well as services that allow for the trading of stocks and bonds.

(vi) Verifying Transactions. To ensure the integrity of the investment operation, each transaction should be verified soon after execution by someone other than the person who executed the transaction. Verification takes the form of both verbal (immediately after the trade) and subsequently written confirmation from the broker or dealer and from the custodian. The verifications are matched to the transaction memo (see Exhibit 7.4) prepared by the financial manager prepared at the time of executing the transaction. If the three tickets (dealer, custodian, and the financial manager's transaction memo) match in all respects, they are then marked with the transaction number, stapled together, and filed, usually by transaction number. If there are any discrepancies, the verifier should be instructed to bring them to the attention of either the financial manager or that person's immediate superior, who should discuss the situation promptly with the financial manager. Responsibility for resolution of the discrepancy usually lies with the financial manager.

(vii) Reporting Transactions. The financial manager is responsible for reporting transactions, the inventory, and yield of the portfolio. Management should determine the frequency and extent to which reports are prepared and the distribution of these reports; however, the financial manager needs most of these reports for the internal operations and management of the portfolio.

The financial manager must have a continually updated listing of the inventory of investment instruments in order to conduct portfolio transactions. The inventory listing is often maintained in a database or spreadsheet software. It should have the capability to sort by various data fields in order to give the financial manager immediate access to the portfolio on the basis of maturity date, issuer, type of security, yield, investment dealer, or custodian (if there is more than one).

Incorporated into the inventory listing can be a program that calculates and reports the weighted average maturity and the weighted average yield of the portfolio as of any moment in time. These two characteristics, maturity and yield, can be plotted periodically to show trends in yield and maturity length. In the management of the portfolio, there should be a close correlation between changes in cash need forecasts and average maturity of the portfolio. Again, it is important to remember that maturity date decisions should not be made on the basis of anticipated changes in interest rates, since this is sheer speculation by the financial manager.

(e) OPERATIONS USING AN OUTSIDE INVESTMENT MANAGER.   Use of an outside investment manager need not compromise the security of an investor's system. Outside investment managers operate in many ways, ranging from the mutual fund approach, to investors' separate accounts under complete control of the investment manager, to investors' separate funds with no access by the investment manager. Each outside manager has its own preference for the method of operation, and the investor's management should determine for itself the degree of control, if any, that it is willing to relinquish to an outside investment manager.

If management prefers not to relinquish control over its assets, then the investor's bank account configuration can include a separate "investments" bank account. The investment manager would be authorized to operate this account for DVP transactions only. An important advantage of this method is that all investment transactions, including purchases, sales, maturing investments, and dividend and interest collections, are run through this account and can be audited easily. Further, by isolating only investment transactions in the account, the investment manager can be in control of the full balance without that balance being disturbed by other noninvestment transactions. This permits reinvestment of income as well as principal and places the burden on the investment manager to remain as fully invested as possible.

In addition, the institution authorizes the investment manager to give DVP instructions to the custodian. In this way, the investor's assets are protected; they are always in the form of either funds in the bank account or securities in the custodian account. They can never be used for other purposes.

(f) INVESTMENT OPERATIONS SUMMARY.   Initiation of an investment management program for a nonprofit institution requires careful planning well in advance of making the first investment. The institution's tolerance for investment risk must be assessed, the sources and ultimate uses for the investment funds must be examined and documented, and a written set of investing objectives and guidelines must be drafted and approved by senior management.

The financial manager should not embark on an investment program until these elements have been crafted. Otherwise the institution may incur undue risk to principal, either through unwise credit exposure or excessive exposure to the movements of interest rates; or it may unwittingly invest in maturities that do not suit the liquidity or income requirements of the institution.

A nonprofit institution typically manages several forms of investment funds. These range from a pool of liquid investments used in the daily management of its receipts and disbursements streams, to grants awaiting payment, to fixed giving programs, to endowment funds, and to employee benefit and retirement funds. Each type of fund has its unique purpose and application, which the financial manager must recognize and invest accordingly.

Operation of an investment portfolio requires careful attention to the details of executing investment transactions and monitoring the resulting inventories.

Systems and procedures must be established to ensure that all necessary information about transactions and inventories is readily available and that controls are in place to highlight promptly any errors that occur. The system also must be capable of producing reports of inventory and transactions in multiple versions to enable management to monitor compliance with guidelines and to audit the portfolio holdings.

Whether the portfolio is large or small, appropriate procedures and controls must be in place and made effective. The required procedures and controls include, but are not limited to, a system of checks and balances, reconciliation of records, written assignment of accountability to designated person(s), and written audit procedures and risk standards. Otherwise, the financial manager may jeopardize the safety and liquidity of the investment portfolio.

7.7 INTRODUCTION TO YIELD ANALYSIS

Many nonprofit organizations have a substantial commitment to fixed-income securities. This is often due to their need for a large current income to sustain ongoing expenses. Also, many elect to manage internally (i.e., not use an investment manager for) their shorter-term, liquidity funds. This section deals in depth with management of a fixed-income securities portfolio.

One enduring characteristic of investment markets is price volatility. Like any other activity within the U.S. economy, the market for fixed-income investments is subject to the laws of supply and demand. And like any other shopper, a financial manager seeks to make these laws work to the advantage of the institution. To do so, the financial manager must seek specific instruments that provide the best relative value among different securities with different maturities while meeting the institution's needs for safety and liquidity. Consequently, the financial manager must have tools and techniques with which to compare the various types of instruments and their differences in credit quality and maturity.

The financial manager can use two analytical tools to judge relative value, a yield curve analysis and yield spread analysis. By using a yield spread analysis, the financial manager can evaluate a fixed-income security in relation to others by comparing the yields of different securities having different risk characteristics but similar maturities. By using yield curve analysis, the financial manager can judge the best relative value of a maturity length in relation to other maturity lengths, because the analysis compares yields and maturities relative to market risk and reward. Combining yield spread and yield curve analyses should improve a financial manager's selection process and, therefore, the institution's overall yield.

7.8 YIELD CURVE ANALYSIS

Yield curve analysis provides a method for a financial manager to determine how changes in interest rates are likely to affect the value of the institution's investment portfolio. The yield curve shows the relationship between yield to maturity and time to maturity. It allows an investor to compare the returns of different types of fixed-income instruments, evaluate possible changes in interest rates, and gauge potential price movements. Yield curve analysis allows a financial manager to estimate the rates of return an investment will produce as interest rates change.

(a) FACTORS INFLUENCING THE YIELD CURVE.   Yield curves allow comparison if the securities they compare are identical in all respects except length of maturity. Yield data and yield curves are often published online and in the *Wall Street Journal*, most major newspapers, and publications issued by securities dealers. Each type of investment security, such as U.S. Treasurys, has a unique yield curve. The horizontal axis plots the security's maturity, expressed in months or years. The vertical axis plots yield levels. The yield curves in Exhibit 7.5 show how different economic conditions can affect the instrument's yield.

The positively sloped and the negatively sloped curves in Exhibit 7.5 illustrate an important generalization about yield curves. In periods of economic expansion, with positively sloped yield curves, investors find long-term rates more attractive. In a slow economy, with negatively sloped yield curves, investors are wary of tying up funds at low interest rates for long periods of time. One of the factors that influences the shape of the yield curve is interest rate or market risk. Investors are exposed to market risk in any investment and market risk tends to be greater as the maturity of an instrument lengthens. As a result, yield curves tend to curve upward; that is, yields are higher at longer maturities. In curve A, a relatively flat yield curve, economic expectations may be described as stable to uncertain. There is not much reward for investing in longer maturities, so most investors will remain with short-term instruments.

Curve B, however, rewards investors for taking on longer-term maturities and is more nearly like the classic positive (upward-) sloping yield curve. In

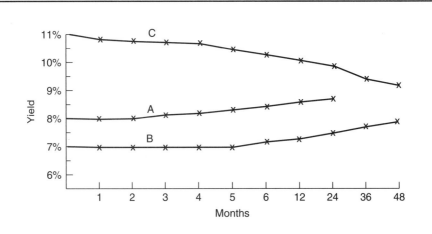

EXHIBIT 7.5   YIELD CURVES

this scenario, the yield curve rises sharply with yields increasing as maturities lengthen. Curves such as this one typically occur when business conditions are beginning to improve after a recession and interest rates are expected to increase even further. This causes investors to be reluctant to tie up their money for long periods of time. Consequently, rates for long-term securities are relatively higher to reflect the increased risk of a long-term investment under these economic conditions.

Curve C, an inverted or negative (downward) sloping yield curve, is characteristic of interest rates at the begining of a recession, where short-term interest rates are high and the market anticipates that interest rates may soon fall. As a result, borrowers are willing to pay high interest rates to cover their short-term requirements, but they will only pay lower rates for longer-term debt.

The shape of the yield curve is influenced by factors other than the present health of the economy. Such factors include the expectations of investors (affecting demand) and a heavy or light calendar of new issues (affecting supply). For instance, if investors believe that interest rates are going to rise, they will seek to keep funds invested in short-term maturities. At the same time, borrowers seek to lengthen maturities on their debt in order to lock in low interest rates before rates rise. Both responses force short-term interest rates down and long-term interest rates up. Consequently, the upward slope of the yield curve is heightened.

Conversely, if investors expect interest rates to fall, they often invest in longer-term instruments (causing demand for these maturities that forces prices to rise and yields to fall), because they want to lock in high yields for as long as possible. At the same time, borrowers are paying high short-term interest rates while they wait for interest rates to decline. As a result, the yield curve could be inverted, such as curve C in Exhibit 7.5.

Large sales of new issues also can skew the shape of a yield curve. Such sales would be reflected in the yield curve by a large upward bulge in the maturity range of the new security.

In general, then, the shape of the yield curve is influenced by the supply and demand for short-term investment maturities in relation to the supply and demand for long-term investment maturities. A pitfall to avoid when calculating the yield curve is the different methods used to measure the yield on discount securities and interest-bearing securities. For instance, interest on Treasury notes is calculated on the basis of an actual day year, while interest on CDs is calculated on the basis of a 360-day year. Consequently, a one-year Treasury note at 8 percent, using the par value of $1,000,000, produces a return of $80,000, compared with a one-year CD, where interest is calculated on a 360-day year that yields $81,111. Of course, the difference is partially offset because the CD pays interest only at maturity while the Treasury note pays interest twice a year.

(b) USING THE YIELD CURVE.   There are two basic ways a financial manager can use yield curves.

1. Yield curves allow the investor to judge whether the price of a new issue is in line with current market trends.
2. Yield curves allow a financial manager to compare securities of different maturities.

Even so, it can be difficult to predict normal spreads between securities with different maturities, because the slope and shape of yield curves vary over time.

Despite this uncertainty, yield curve analysis can be helpful in the management of an institution's investment portfolio. Yield curves are useful in determining whether yields are more attractive in short-term or long-term instruments. The duration for which an institution wants its funds invested, however, should be spelled out in a written investing policy and comprehensive set of investing guidelines and not rest primarily on yield curve analysis.

Yield curve analysis also enables a financial manager to assess market risk. The yield curve can help determine whether the potential market risk of loss on an investment is outweighed by its yield. It can also assess the effect of rising interest rates as they relate to the investor having to sell the instrument at a loss. For instance, the yield curve may shift upward as the economy heats up, with the potential increase in return outweighing the decline in value of certain securities.

(c) RIDING THE YIELD CURVE. A financial manager can receive yield on the sales of securities before they mature, and indeed in some cases the best investment strategy is to sell securities before that time. When a financial manager buys one-year T-bills at 7 percent and holds them for a year, they earn 7 percent. If the bills are sold before the date of maturity, the earned rate will, of course, depend on the market rate prevailing when the bills are sold. If that rate is higher than 7 percent, the return will be less than if the bills had been held to maturity, but the proceeds can be reinvested in higher-yield securities.

As a result, it is possible for the financial manager to use yield curve analysis to time buying and selling opportunities in order to reap unanticipated profits. Using the yield curve to help determine the timing of investments is called *riding the yield curve*. The next example, depicted in Exhibit 7.6, illustrates how financial managers can ride the yield curve to profits.

Assume that an institution has $1 million that it can invest for three months. Its financial manager observes that six-month T-bills are trading at 7.5 percent and three-month T-bills are trading at 7.1 percent. The financial manager can buy either the three-month T-bills and hold them to maturity or the six-month T-bills and sell them after three months. To determine which strategy will work best, the financial manager uses break-even analysis.

The six-month T-bill would yield an additional 80 basis points, or $2,000, compared to the three-month T-bill (over three months, one basis point is worth $25). The gain is 80 basis points because the financial manager accrues interest at 40 basis points above the three-month T-bills (7.50 − 7.10 = .40). The other

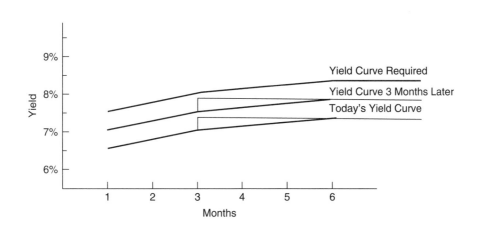

EXHIBIT 7.6 RIDING THE YIELD CURVE

40 basis points arise because, assuming the yield curve remains unchanged, the financial manager will sell the six-month bill at the 7.10 level and realize an annualized gain of 40 more basis points, bringing the total return to an annualized 80 basis points. Of course, the risk involved in this strategy lies in whether the yield curve will remain constant. If the yield curve rises during the three-month period, the investor may find that three-month T-bills yield 7.50 percent, and there would be no gain on their sale at that time.

In fact, the rate on three-month T-bills would have to rise above 7.90 percent before it would be advisable for the financial manager to buy three-month bills and hold them to maturity, assuming that interest rates remain the same. The slope of the yield curve shows that six-month T-bills should trade at 7.10 percent in three months if the yield curve remains the same. The financial manager thus has an 80 basis point cushion against increased interest rates. If he or she believes that it is unlikely that the yield curve for T-bills will rise that much, then the best bet is to buy the six-month T-bills and ride the yield curve.

7.9 YIELD SPREAD ANALYSIS

A financial manager uses yield spread analysis to ensure that the institution's investment portfolio is generating maximum profits. The yield spread is the difference between yields of various investment instruments of similar maturities. Like the yield curve, the yield spread is affected by market conditions and thus changes constantly. A financial manager should stay abreast of the spreads between different investment instruments. In fixed-income instruments, the benchmark for comparison is Treasury securities, because their liquidity and credit quality are consistently high. In general, as a security's credit risk increases and its liquidity decreases, its yield in relation to Treasury securities increases.

Type	Quality	Yield (%)
Government agencies	Discount notes	0.023–0.10
CDs	Prime quality U.S. banks	0.20 –0.55
Commercial paper	Prime rated (A1-P1)	0.15 –0.37
Euro CDs	Prime quality U.S. banks	0.25 –0.55
Time deposits, Eurodollars	Prime quality U.S. banks	0.20 –0.50
Banker's acceptances	Prime foreign banks	0.10 –0.32

EXHIBIT 7.7   APPROXIMATE YIELD SPREADS OF VARIOUS INSTRUMENTS IN RELATION TO U.S. TREASURY BILLS

Yield spreads are measured in basis points, which are equal to one one-hundredth of a percentage point. For example, if six-month Treasury bills are quoted at 6.45 percent and six-month commercial paper is quoted at 6.65 percent, the spread between the two types of instruments is 20 basis points. By studying the spreads between different types of securities with similar maturities, a financial manager can better decide whether a riskier security carries a sufficiently larger return to justify the investment, as long as the choice is consistent with investment guidelines. Exhibit 7.7 shows the yield spreads that generally exist among common investment instruments.

The yield spreads in Exhibit 7.7 are estimates as of a specific moment and under specific economic conditions. These spreads change continuously, requiring constant monitoring, and do not always follow a normal pattern. Abnormal spread relationships occur frequently, and such spreads can provide investment managers with profit-making opportunities.

The two bars on the left of the graph in Exhibit 7.8 show the normal relationship between T-bills and government agency discount notes of similar maturities. Normally, in this time period, the government agency discount notes yield 12 basis points higher than T-bills. The two bars on the right show an abnormal yield spread, where government agency discount notes are more than 100 basis points higher than T-bills. Such a difference may be possible because of a temporary oversupply in the market for government agency discount notes and a simultaneous shortage of Treasury securities. In this type of situation, a financial manager who monitors market conditions can use some of the institution's excess cash to make a short-term investment in the government agency notes, thus reaping an unexpected profit.

Time constraints and limited personnel often prevent financial managers at nonprofit institutions from checking yields on every investment vehicle suited to the institution's portfolio. They can obtain daily yield spread information easily, however, by developing strong relationships with securities dealers and bank investment departments. These organizations keep abreast of the markets and can be valuable sources of current information. Financial managers can obtain market information over the telephone or via the internet. Many organizations distribute

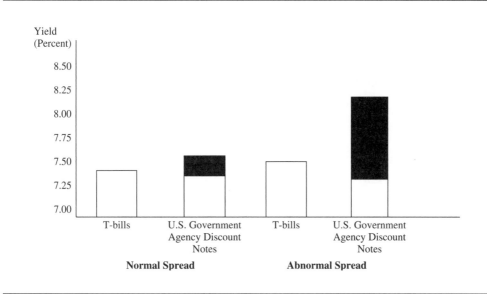

EXHIBIT 7.8 Normal and Abnormal Yield Spread Variations (Six-Month Maturities)

market information gratis through printed newsletters. By the time the newsletters reach the desks of financial managers, however, much of the information may be obsolete.

Securities dealers are happy to provide information to investors with whom they have done business before. Accordingly, it is of the utmost importance that financial managers carefully select their securities dealers, especially if they make only a limited number of transactions. (Dealers eagerly offer market information to investors with a large number of transactions.) The difference between valuable market information and market gossip is often difficult to discern, so financial managers, as buyers, must beware.

Finding an attractive value among a morning's investment opportunities requires a financial manager to obtain yield and maturity information quickly on an array of securities and to compare yield spread and yield curve data. Dealers and brokers readily provide this basic information for T-bills, government agency securities, bank instruments, and commercial paper. Rates gathered from dealers then can be plotted so that yield spreads and curves become clear. To highlight yield spreads and curves, the financial manager can use color-coded graphics to chart the yields of several instruments at various maturities. The chart should reveal the similarities and demonstrate the differences among instruments.

For instance, a financial manager may learn from yield spread analysis that T-bills currently are at yields close to those of instruments of lower credit quality. Because the lower-quality instruments are riskier than T-bills and because yield spread analysis shows that the yields are similar, the financial manager can invest the institution's money in T-bills. He or she does so knowing that T-bills have better credit quality and liquidity at a yield similar to lesser-quality instruments and therefore present a better value.

7.10 PRICE MOVEMENT OF FIXED-INCOME SECURITIES

The relationship between interest rates and the price of a fixed-income security is inverse; that is, as interest rates rise, the price of the security falls. This fact ensures that the value of the fixed-income security is brought into line with market interest rates. To compensate for fluctuating interest rates and the resulting market price risk, yields on fixed-income securities are adjusted to prevailing rates after they are issued through the market price mechanism. For that reason, it is important that a financial manager use yield curve analysis to attempt to monitor interest rate changes.

As the institution's funds are invested, the financial manager must know how the investments will introduce market risk into the portfolio. A simple approach is to examine the yield curve to predict how returns may increase as maturities are extended. In that way, the financial manager can ascertain the point on the curve where rates provide the greatest return consistent with the market risk appropriate to the portfolio. The examples that follow illustrate how changes in interest rates affect the prices of investments.

(a) RISE IN INTEREST RATES.   In the first example, the financial manager for Organization A buys a new six-month CD with a par value of $1 million, bearing interest at 10 percent. At the time the investment is made, other instruments of similar credit quality and maturity are also trading at 10 percent. One month after the purchase, however, interest rates increase. As a result, CDs maturing in five months (the term remaining on the six-month CD one month after purchase) are now yielding 11 percent. Because interest rates have increased, the value of the 10 percent CD declines so that its yield is in line with the increased market rate.

After one month, the CD has accrued interest (at 10 percent) of $8,333.33 and therefore a book value to the investor of $1,008,333.33. If the investor wants to sell the CD, the CD must fetch a price calculated to provide the new investor with a prevailing market interest rate. As a result, the financial manager must sell the CD at a loss. The buyer will pay only the amount calculated to yield an 11 percent return over the remaining five months. That amount is only $1,003,984.06, leaving the selling investor with a discount (or loss) from the accrued basis of $4,349.27. When the instrument reaches its maturity value of $1,050,000 ($1,000,000 plus interest at 10 percent for six months), the new investor will realize a return of $45,650.73 on its investment of $1,003,984.06. This results in a yield of 11 percent over the five months that the second investor owns the CD.

(b) DECLINE IN INTEREST RATES.   In the second example, the financial manager at Organization B buys a six-month CD bearing interest at 10 percent. One month later, interest rates fall to 9 percent. This increases the market value of the CD so that a new buyer must pay more than par to purchase the CD. The premium, however, will be lost at maturity when the CD is redeemed at par value plus interest; the CD thus costs the second buyer more than par. In this case, the new investor is willing to pay as much as $1,012,048.19 (compared to the first buyer's book value of $1,008,333.33) for the instrument that has a maturity value of $1,050,000 in five months. The amount of income earned, $37,951.90, represents a yield to the new investor of 9 percent over that period.

(c) CALCULATING YIELD. Financial managers can receive information that will lead to beneficial investments by analyzing and anticipating changes in yield. Calculating yield, however, can be difficult. The most widely used methods of calculating the yield of fixed-income securities are:

- Current yield
- Yield to maturity
- Yield to call
- Total realized compound yield

Each of these methods has specific uses for different investments, so financial managers must know which analysis is best suited to the instrument at hand and the available information.

(i) Current Yield. Current yield relates an investment instrument's annual interest payment to its current market price. It is the rate of return (annual interest payments) divided by the current market value of the instrument. As such, current yield does not take into account other possible sources of income, including reinvestment of interest income during the life of the security, as well as the gain or loss when an investment's market price is at either a premium or discount in relation to par. Calculation of the current yield on an instrument involves multiplying its coupon rate by its face value, then dividing that by the instrument's market price and multiplying by 100. The current yield on a note with a $1,000 face value that sells at $985.13 (a discount) and has an 8 percent coupon is thus 8.12 percent:

$$[(.08 \times \$1,000) = \$80 \div \$985.13] \times 100 = 8.12 \text{ percent}$$

On a discount note or bond, the current yield always will be less than its yield to maturity. This is because the current yield does not include the instrument's capital gain. Conversely, the current yield on a note or bond selling at a premium always will be greater than its yield to maturity. For instance, a $1,000 instrument with an 8 percent coupon selling at $1,014.73, a premium, to yield 7.5 percent has a current yield of 7.88 percent. Because current yield does not take into account capital gain (or loss in the case of instruments selling at a premium), yield to maturity or call is the most prevalent calculation of an instrument's yield.

(ii) Yield to Maturity.   The calculation of yield to maturity (YTM) takes into account the capital appreciation and depreciation of a fixed-income instrument. It also takes into account reinvestment of interest. However, the calculation assumes that the rate at which interest payments are reinvested is equal to the YTM existing at the instrument's purchase date, which may or may not be the case.

Calculation of YTM for nondiscounted format instruments includes two components.

1. The calculation includes the coupon rate, the maturity date (to determine the holding period), and any discount or premium resulting from changes in market interest rates.
2. The yield calculation includes the accrued interest that has accumulated from the time the instrument was issued.

It is important for financial managers to understand that YTM is based on total dollars invested. Because that total figure includes the premium or discount plus any accrued interest, the instrument's return at maturity is a net return based on the total dollars returned and total dollars invested in the instrument.

For example, a new six-year note with an 8 percent coupon is issued at par. Six months later the Federal Reserve tightens the money supply, causing yields on comparable securities to increase to 8.5 percent. The security must now sell at less than its par value; a new investor who buys this "seasoned," or secondary, issue will receive only the maturity value based on the 8 percent coupon and will want to be compensated for buying the instrument at a time when 8.5 percent returns are now available in other similar instruments. Consequently, the new investor will want to pay less than par value for it.

It is necessary to understand the concept of YTM as an effective yield in order to determine how much less than par the instrument should be priced. Again, there are two parts to the return an investor receives on a security that is bought at a discount and held to maturity. Return consists of the periodic interest payment plus a capital gain. The capital gain is the difference between the instrument's purchase price and its par or face value. Investors who buy instruments at a premium and hold them to maturity also receive a two-part return. In this case, the return consists of interest payments plus a capital loss, which is equal to the dollar value of the premium. An investment instrument's overall or effective yield takes into account both interest and capital gains or losses. When financial managers choose between securities of comparable risk and maturity, they do not make their decisions on the basis of coupon rate but on the basis of effective yield.

In the last example, then, once market interest rates increase to 8.5 percent, a security bearing interest at 8 percent must be priced at a discount if a buyer is to be found. The discount, of course, must be large enough to make the instrument's YTM equal to 8.5 percent. The calculations involved in putting a dollar figure to that difference are complex. Using a bond calculator, a dealer can determine that a $1,000 note with an 8 percent coupon and three and one-half years to maturity must sell at $985.32 in order to yield 8.5 percent at maturity. The dollar discount is thus $14.68.

(iii) Yield to Call. Some fixed-income investments contain provisions that allow the issuer to redeem ("call") the issue before it matures at a predetermined price. Financial managers can calculate the yields on such issues in two ways.

1. Yields can be calculated by using the yield-to-maturity method; this assumes that the instrument will remain outstanding until maturity.
2. The yield-to-call method can be used. This method assumes that the investment is called by the issuer at the earliest possible date, as specified in the bond's indenture.

Financial managers often use both methods and base their evaluation of the investment's attractiveness on the method that provides the lower yield, thus providing a measure of conservatism to the consideration.

Like YTM, the yield to call calculation assumes that all investment payments will be reinvested at a rate equal to the YTM that existed at the time the instrument was purchased. Yield to call disregards how the proceeds will be invested after the investment is called.

(iv) Total Realized Compound Yield. Total realized compound yield measures the underlying fully compounded growth or accumulation rate relating to a fixed-income instrument. The measure takes varying reinvestment rates into account. Because the rate at which coupon payments will be reinvested is uncertain, the financial manager can only estimate a range of rates. Varying assumptions on interest rates determine the range used in the calculation.

7.11 EFFECT OF CHANGING INTEREST RATES ON LONGER MATURITIES

As maturity lengthens, risk increases and long-term investments thus should be compensated for the risk. The compensation is reflected in the upward-sloping yield curve that says, in effect, that yield increases as maturity increases. Refer to Exhibit 7.2 to see how changes in interest rates affect the market value of Treasury securities.

Although a positive yield curve suggests that yields rise steadily as maturities lengthen, this is an arguable assumption when it comes to developing an investment strategy for a nonprofit institution. Financial managers who choose investments of long maturities must always assume that they are putting the institution's principal at a greater risk. They cannot assume that the additional yield will compensate for the increased risk.

7.12 SUMMARY OF YIELD CURVES

A yield curve can be used to monitor future interest rates. If the yield curve has a sharp upward slope, it often reflects the aggregate perceptions of investors that interest rates will continue to rise. As a result, investors will demand higher rates for investments with longer maturities.

The best protection against fluctuating interest rates is to distribute maturities in the institution's portfolio among short-, intermediate-, and long-term maturities perhaps using a "bond ladder." This strategy will ensure that the institution's portfolio is protected even against rates dictated by a positive yield curve.

7.13 FIXED-INCOME INVESTMENT INSTRUMENTS: AN INTRODUCTION

One of the more important jobs a financial manager performs is to ensure that the institution's cash is always working. Cash that lies in a checking account when it is not needed to pay bills is not working. Rather than leave cash in checking accounts, a financial manager invests it; the institution derives financial benefits from its cash surplus. Hundreds of investment vehicles may be used for excess cash, some with long terms and some with short terms, some extremely safe and some quite risky. A financial manager must match the yield objectives, level of risk, and liquidity tolerances of the institution, as stated in the investment guidelines, before making investments. As an aid in that decision-making process, this section describes the most common types of investment vehicles: U.S. Treasury and government agency instruments, corporate and money market instruments, and repurchase agreements. We also include Appendix 7C at the end of the chapter to provide definitions of the major fixed income instruments.

It is apparent that many of these instruments are quite similar. In many cases, the only difference is in the length of maturity. Therefore, it is important for a financial manager to understand the importance of managing maturities in an investment program. The longer the instrument's maturity, the greater the possibility that its market value will fluctuate as interest rates change. In choosing securities for investment, a financial manager must examine and be satisfied with each of these aspects of an investment instrument besides its maturity:

- Issuer's credit quality
- Instrument's liquidity
- Instrument's complexity
- Ease of obtaining an instrument's credit rating
- Instrument's sensitivity to market risk
- Flexibility of the instrument's maturity ranges
- Yield of the instrument
- Investor's potential tax exemption
- Structure of the instrument's principal and interest payments
- Financial manager's ability to actively manage a portfolio containing that particular instrument[1]

7.14 U.S. TREASURY SECURITIES

(a) BACKGROUND. The U.S. government is one of the largest economic organizations in the world; it is also one of the most indebted. In fact, the U.S. Department of the Treasury is the largest issuer of debt instruments in the world. Even so, debt instruments issued by the U.S. Treasury are considered to be the safest investments available. They are used as a means to reap investment returns from surplus cash by financial managers from all types of businesses, including nonprofit institutions that seek to put this cash to work. U.S. Treasury debt instruments meet their requirements of high liquidity and low credit risk and make perfect investments for this purpose. The strength of the U.S. economy, for instance, prompts dealers and investment analysts to grade Treasury securities as virtually free of credit or default risk.

(b) LIQUIDITY AND THE MARKET. One of the criteria for high liquidity is the existence of a large market for an investment instrument. Liquidity refers to the ability to convert a security into cash quickly and without loss of principal. Because the volume of debt issued by the Treasury is so great, the market for government securities is one of the most active and thus most liquid of investment markets. There is a tremendous amount of participation by both foreign and domestic investors in this market. Liquidity is further increased by the existence of a core of primary dealers that buy and sell huge quantities of government securities, both among themselves and with other investors. It is a highly competitive market, with prices varying between dealers by only one or two thirty-seconds of a point (on a par value of $1,000,000, 1/32 of a point is $312.50). Liquidity is also increased by the existence of a huge resale market, where dealers and investors who bought securities at issuance sell them before maturity.

Treasury securities are initially sold at auctions that are conducted through regional Federal Reserve Bank offices. Dates for those auctions are announced in newspaper notices well beforehand. There are two types of bidding at Treasury auctions:

1. Competitive bids for certain quantities of securities at a certain price
2. Noncompetitive bids submitted by an investor or institution that simply agrees to buy a certain amount of the security and pay a price equal to the weighted-average price of all competitive bids accepted by the Treasury

The difference between competitive and noncompetitive bids involves risk. When financial managers submit competitive bids, they take the risk of paying more than the average noncompetitive price or of bidding too low to obtain the desired securities. (After the auction's deadline, the Treasury reviews all bids and establishes the minimum price at which bids will be accepted.)

Individual and institutional investors may bid on Treasury securities at a Federal Reserve Bank or have major banks or securities dealers submit bids on their behalf. Institutional investors may also, of course, buy Treasury securities from the many resale markets through banks or securities dealers, or online through the Legacy Treasury Direct program.

Before considering Treasury securities as an investment, financial managers must be familiar with the different types of Treasury securities and their characteristics. Treasury securities fall into three categories: bills, notes, and bonds.

(i) Treasury Bills.   T-bills are short-term debt instruments that are issued at a discount and repaid at full value, called par value, upon maturity. The amount of interest on a T-bill is thus the difference between the purchase price and the value of the bill's par value. T-bills are issued with maturities of four weeks, three months, or six months. Also, when the Treasury needs funds to finance operations before a tax receipt date, it will issue cash management bills having odd maturities ranging from a few days to 60 days.

The advantages of T-bills for the institutional investor are the wide range of short-term maturities, their high liquidity, and an active secondary market for most denominations. The minimum denomination of a T-bill is $1,000; additional amounts are available in increments of $1,000. T-bills are sold only in book-entry form (by credit to the investor's account with the Treasury).

(ii) Treasury Notes.   Treasury notes (T-notes; also called coupon notes) are instruments that mature from more than 1 year up to 10 years and bear interest. They are issued at or near face value and are redeemed at par value upon maturity. Original maturities for T-notes are 2, 3, 4, 5, and 10 years. Notes with a 2-year, 5-year and 10-year maturity are issued each month, while notes of 3 years are issued quarterly. The Treasury issues notes of other maturities if it needs to balance its maturity schedule. Like T-bills, T-notes are issued in various denominations. The minimum denomination all notes is $1,000, and the size increases in $1,000 increments. Interest on T-notes is paid semiannually and at maturity together with par value of the notes.

T-notes, like T-bills, are initially sold to investors at auctions conducted by the Federal Reserve. Investors bid on the basis of YTM, and the Treasury accepts the bids that result in the lowest cost to the Treasury. Accordingly, the market itself generally determines the interest rate of T-notes. Also like T-bills, T-notes are highly liquid because of the existence of a vast secondary market, especially for notes in denominations of $1 million and more. The secondary market also provides a wide range of maturities and prices. T-notes, like all direct obligations of the U.S. government, carry no credit risk.

(iii) Treasury Bonds.   Treasury bonds (T-bonds) are interest-bearing debt instruments with original maturities longer than 10 years; original maturities are now 30 years. T-bonds do not have a call feature that allows the Treasury to pay off the bonds. Like T-notes, the bonds pay interest income semiannually. These long-term Treasury securities are issued in $1,000 denominations and are sold

quarterly at auctions. They have the same liquidity and credit risk characteristics as T-bills and T-notes.

(iv) Treasury Inflation-Protected Securities. Treasury Inflation-Protected Securities are not only safe from default risk but also protect the investor against purchasing power risk. Unlike a typical bond, for which the coupon rate is fixed and the par, or face value, is fixed, the TIPS have an adjustable principal amount. If prices go up, as measured by the Consumer Price Index (CPI), the TIPS principal increases. Were prices to drop, the TIPS principal amount would be adjusted downward. At maturity, the Treasury pays the original or adjusted principal, whichever is greater.

TIPS securities pay interest twice a year, and while the coupon interest is fixed, the principal amount varies with the CPI. If the CPI is positive, as it normally is, the principal amount is increased by the amount of inflation. In this way, the principal amount of one's investment, as well as the coupon interest that is calculated from that principal, keep up with inflation. This protects the investor's purchasing power.

TIPS are offered to the market in three different maturities: 5-year, 10-year, and 20-year. The 5-year securities are auctioned in April and October each year, the 10-year securities are auctioned in January, April, July, and October, while the 20-year TIPS come to market in January and July.

7.15 U.S. GOVERNMENT AGENCY SECURITIES

Most of the departments and agencies of the U.S. government, as well as organizations and corporations chartered by Congress, issue debt securities. They are referred to collectively as government agency securities. Like Treasury securities, either they are issued at a discount and redeemed at par upon maturity, or they pay a fixed rate of interest until maturity.

(a) **CREDIT QUALITY.** All agencies of the federal government are considered to be more creditworthy than private organizations. However, some government agencies are more creditworthy than others. The liquidity of government agency securities also varies by issuer. Most investors consider government agency securities to have little default risk. Even so, financial managers investing an institution's funds should keep three points in mind:

1. Not every government agency security carries the full faith and credit of the U.S. government (GNMA and VA do); many actively traded government agency securities must maintain their own financial strength and security.
2. Of the major credit-rating agencies, only Moody's rates most government agency debt. Securities that carry a direct government guarantee or are backed by collateral generally receive an AAA rating. Because the

rating agencies tend not to rate government agencies, however, it is difficult to find information on the financial strength and stability of many agencies.

3. Government agencies can experience financial difficulties, some so substantial that the agency must apply to the federal government for assistance. In 1986, for instance, earnings and assets of the Federal Farm Credit Banks (FFCB) began to suffer as a result of the deteriorating agricultural sector of the country's economy. The FFCB had to ask Congress for financial aid while the agency strengthened its financial position. While Congress was considering aid, the uncertain status of the FFCB's creditworthiness caused its debt instruments to trade at much higher yields than those of other government agencies.

(b) ADVANTAGES.   Safety, liquidity, and yield are the main advantages of government agency securities. Despite some credit concerns, these securities are still among the safest instruments available to an investor. In most instances, government agency debt is considered second only to Treasury securities in terms of safety. Although few agencies besides the Treasury are backed by the full faith and credit of the U.S. government, many experts contend that Congress has a "moral obligation" to bail out an agency that finds itself in fiscally dangerous waters. Indeed, Congress approved a form of aid for the FFCB when it was having loan problems. It ruled that the government could buy FFCB securities to provide the agency with a temporary source of funding, under the condition that the agency institute fiscal reforms.

The liquidity factor of most government agency securities, although generally not as high as Treasury securities, is still a major advantage. Many of these securities are more liquid than other types of financial instruments, because there is active secondary market trading in most government agency securities. A financial manager should look carefully at liquidity, however, as not all government agency securities have active markets. In the next section of this chapter, we do not describe those government agency securities that are not very liquid.

The differences between government agency securities and Treasury securities regarding safety and liquidity lead to yet another major advantage of agency securities: yield. Because most government agency securities are not backed by a Treasury guarantee and are slightly less liquid, they generally trade at higher yields than Treasury securities. The amount of the yield spread for any given maturity between Treasury securities and government agency securities depends on market conditions, but the yield spread is always present. This spread is usually 1/8% to 5/8% percent for maturities under one year and 1/4 percent beyond one year. For example, over a seven-year period recently, Fannie Mae discount notes have averaged 29 basis point (29/100 of 1%) spreads to Treasurys for one-month securities, 23 basis point spreads to Treasurys for three-month securities, and 19 basis point spreads to Treasurys for six-month securities.[2]

(c) METHODS OF SALE. Government agency securities are not sold at auction like Treasury securities. They are issued through an underwriting syndicate composed of a select group of securities dealers and banks. Every dealer in the group underwrites a specific portion of the total issue. Consequently, the interest rate for government agency securities is not determined in the same manner as the rate for Treasury securities, as there is generally no auction in which the market can determine the rate. Instead, the coupon yield of each issue is set by the underwriting syndicate and the agency's fiscal manager on the morning of the sale date.

Before setting the interest rate, the syndicate must obtain instructions from the agency as to the amount of money it needs and the length of maturity it prefers. If the money needs of the agency are less demanding, the security will carry a rate that is below the prevailing market rate. If the agency needs money for a particular date, however, a higher rate will be set to attract investors. Yields on government agency securities thus reflect both market conditions and the needs of the borrower, much like commercial paper rates. The public learns of the amount, maturity date, and settlement date for government agency securities through the news media. Most daily newspapers carry "pre-sale" announcements of these securities. Syndicate members then take orders from investors.

(d) "WHEN ISSUED" TRADING. Dealers begin to make markets to buy and sell new securities when an issue is announced, even if that instrument has not yet been issued. The period of time between announcement of a security issue and when it is paid for and delivered is called the when issued (WI) period. To trade in securities on a when-issued basis requires little or no principal investment during the WI period, because payment is not due until the settlement date. This enables speculation during the WI period; both Treasury and agency securities are heavily traded during this period. Conservative financial managers, however, should avoid the temptation to speculate, by committing only to securities on a WI basis when they intend to take delivery of the securities on the settlement date.

(e) TYPES OF GOVERNMENT AGENCY SECURITIES. Certain government agencies that are in the business of lending funds generally issue debt to fund lending activities. The next sections describe the more actively traded government agency debt obligations.

(i) Farm Credit System Securities. The nation's farmers require an enormous amount of credit and financial assistance. A constant supply of funds is maintained to meet farmers' credit needs through the Farm Credit Administration, which oversees the Federal Farm Credit System. The system, which contains 12 farm credit districts each having a Federal Farm Credit Bank (FFCB), raises funds to lend to farmers by selling notes and bonds to the public. The FFCB securities, called Consolidated Systemwide discount notes and bonds, are backed by the assets of the Farm Credit Banks. The securities are not guaranteed by the U.S.

government, so their market value is subject to the credit soundness of the farm loan market. In the mid-1980s, for instance, the Farm Credit Administration suffered substantial losses as a result of the collapse of the agricultural markets. Congress temporarily bailed the system out in January 1988.

Consolidated Systemwide discount notes are issued each business day and have maturities of 365 days. They are issued a discount and pay principal and interest at maturity. The system also frequently issues medium-term notes, with maturities from 3 months to 30 years with interest payable semiannually. All securities are issued in minimum denominations of $5,000, and then in $1,000 increments. All of these securities are issued in book-entry form. Longer-term securities are issued either in floating-rate or fixed-rate arrangements. However, floating-rate bonds have a minimum denomination of $100,000, then in multiples of $1,000.

(ii) Federal Home Loan Bank Securities. The Federal Home Loan Act of 1932 created the Federal Home Loan Bank (FHLB) system. The system's two primary responsibilities are to (1) oversee its member savings and loan institutions and savings banks, and (2) lend money and provide liquidity to its members. To obtain the money that the FHLB lends to its members, it borrows money from the public by issuing bonds and notes. Debt is issued by a credit system operated by the FHLB system's 12 district banks under the supervision of a central board based in Washington, D.C.

The FHLB issues three main types of securities: consolidated bonds, medium-term notes, and consolidated discount notes (mostly in the 1 to 60-day maturity range). The debt is called consolidated because it is the joint obligation of all 12 FHLBs. These banks operate under a federal charter and are supervised by the government, but their securities do not carry a government guarantee. The banks, however, are required to maintain assets at least equal to the amount of debt that has been issued. Such assets include guaranteed mortgages, U.S. government securities, and cash. Recently, FHLB has been offering master notes that are callable but have flexible maturities and rate indexes.

(iii) Federal Home Loan Mortgage Corporation. Called Freddie Mac, the Federal Home Loan Mortgage Corporation (FHLMC) is a government-sponsored enterprise. Established in 1970, the FHLMC is charged with maintaining mortgage credit for residential housing development and promoting a nationwide secondary market for conventional residential mortgages. The agency accomplishes these goals by buying mortgages from individual lenders. The mortgage purchases are financed by marketing mortgage participation certificates (PCs). Its discount notes are appealing to organizational investors.

(iv) Federal National Mortgage Association. Called Fannie Mae, the Federal National Mortgage Association (FNMA) is a public corporation owned by non-government stockholders. (It was originally a government-chartered corporation

that did not issue stock.) Its short-term securities, called "Discount Notes" (issued daily and having maturities from overnight up to 360 days, in $1,000 minimum amounts and $1,000 increments thereafter) and "Benchmark Bills" (three-month, six-month, and one-year maturities), are AAA-rated, but none of these securities has no explicit federal government backing. There is also a "reverse inquiry" program by which a securities dealer may contact FNMA on an institutional investor's behalf, and FNMA will tailor the maturity of Discount Notes or coupon-bearing short-term debt securities with either a floating rate or a fixed rate (with a 360-day maximum maturity).[3] The FNMA's primary goal is to provide funding for conventional mortgages, which it finances by selling debentures and short-term securities.

FNMA debentures have maturities of up to several years, and its short-term securities have maturities up to one year. The FNMA issues a large volume of short-term securities, thereby fueling a strong secondary market that provides a good deal of liquidity to its securities. FNMA notes are unsecured obligations of the issuer and are not backed by government guarantees. As a result, they often provide high yields in relation to Treasury securities—with one-month instrument spreads ranging from 11 to 60 basis points, as an annual average, over the past seven years.[4]

(v) Government National Mortgage Association.   Called Ginnie Mae, the Government National Mortgage Association (GNMA) supervises and sponsors support programs for mortgages that do not qualify for private mortgage insurance and therefore cannot be sold in normal nonfederally guaranteed mortgage markets. Ginnie Mae also funds and provides liquidity for conventional mortgages. GNMA securities are called PCs, and they provide a pass-through (or payout) of the interest and principal on pools of mortgages. The underlying mortgages are guaranteed by the Federal Housing Administration or the Veterans Administration. As a result, Ginnie Mae securities are considered to be backed by the full faith and credit of the U.S. government. Ginnie Mae securities are one of the few government agency securities carrying that high guarantee.

ATTRACTIVE FEATURES OF GNMA INVESTMENTS.
Because Ginnie Mae PCs have competitive yields and are backed by a government guarantee, many investors consider them to be an attractive investment in the intermediate- and long-term maturity areas. Maturities on Ginnie Mae pass-through certificates are 30 years. Homeowners whose mortgages have been sold to Ginnie Mae, however, may refinance them or sell their homes and repay the mortgage loans underlying the certificates. For that reason, Ginnie Mae mortgage pools actually have a much shorter average life than 30 years. Calculating the exact length of that average life is not easy; in fact, experts disagree over what method produces the most accurate results. Such disagreements are not academic, especially to investors who intend to hold Ginnie Mae or other mortgage-backed

securities until maturity so that they can receive a stream of cash over the security's life.

For example, if the aggregate yield for mortgages in the pool is higher than current mortgage rates, homeowners who are obligated on these mortgages will refinance the mortgages or repay the mortgages faster than scheduled. Homeowners have demonstrated a propensity to refinance mortgage loans as interest rates decline, with such refinancing representing repayment of the original mortgage and creation of a new mortgage. The new mortgage will not be part of the same Ginnie Mae pool as the original mortgage. However, mortgages in a Ginnie Mae pool with rates lower than the prevailing rate for mortgage financing will be paid off slower than the expected payment rate. Despite such uncertainties, a generally accepted estimate for the average life of a Ginnie Mae pool is about 12 years from its original creation.

ADVERSE FEATURES OF GNMA INVESTMENTS.

Mortgage-backed (MB) securities and PCs carry several potentially adverse features of which investors should be aware. Prices for these types of securities tend to be more volatile than prices of other government securities with similar maturities. GNMA prices tend to fall faster with rising interest rates than other 12-year government agency securities and T-bonds. Ginnie Maes tend to trade in a manner similar to 30-year bonds. (The stated maturity of Ginnie Mae certificates is 30 years.). As a result, an investor who sells Ginnie Maes in a market with higher interest rates than those prevailing at the time the certificates were purchased may have to take a loss.

It also can be difficult to reinvest interest proceeds on Ginnie Mae certificates (or other pass-through securities) unless the investor holds a large portfolio of Ginnie Mae securities providing several hundreds of thousands of dollars in monthly cash flow. One problem with reinvesting the proceeds of a portfolio providing less than $100,000 in monthly cash flow is the difficulty in finding instruments that have yield, portfolio compatibility, and liquidity characteristics suitable for proper investment. A financial manager may end up with a portfolio consisting of small amounts of various instruments rather than large blocks of securities. A large block of a security tends to be more liquid than a small block.

A second problem with these securities is the possibility of an accounting nightmare. Because the cash flow of the securities combines both principal and interest payments, delays and accounting errors can occur. It takes time to verify payment amounts and to file claims on incorrect amounts, both of which result in lost interest on funds received past their due dates. The yield advantage of the securities is thus diminished. Many investors think these securities are exempt from state income taxes, as Treasury securities are. In an increasing number of states, they are not tax exempt, however. It is important to have a tax advisor review state tax exemptions on government agency securities. It is also important to check into guarantees on the securities because not all of them carry a government guarantee.

Another potential problem with Ginnie Mae securities results from yield volatility. When interest rates drop and homeowners pay off mortgages faster than anticipated, the remaining life of the mortgage pool declines rapidly. An investor who bought a security with a high yield will find that the period of time the high yield continues to accrue shortens with falling interest rates. If the investor paid a premium to obtain the above-market yield, the income stream that was to amortize the premium could be prematurely eroded. Accordingly, market prices on the securities do not rise as fast as prices on other investments when interest rates fall.

(vi) **Mortgage Pass-Through Securities.**   During the past several years, financial innovations have been responsible for the creation of many types of securities based on pools of home mortgages. Mortgage pass-through securities guaranteed by GNMA have been quite popular, because they typically provide greater yields than Treasury securities. Some studies even suggest that GNMA pass-through securities provide higher returns than many other fixed-income securities, but those returns are partly the result of some investors' resistance to the complexity of the instruments.

Before investing in mortgage pass-through securities, the financial manager must study all of the characteristics of the underlying mortgage pool, especially if the securities will be sold before maturity. Again, the guarantee status of the securities is important; those issued by Freddie Mac, for instance, do not carry a government guarantee.

(vii) **Collateralized Mortgage Obligations.**   Collateralized mortgage obligations (CMOs) are bonds backed, or collateralized, by instruments such as GNMA or FHLMC pass-through securities. They were designed to improve on simple mortgage-backed securities and provide more predictable returns by taking specific characteristics of MB securities and solving the problems of receiving repayments that combine principal and interest. In essence, investment bankers have developed computer models that estimate the payback dates of a mortgage pool. Based on this analysis, specific durations, or tranches, are created. As mortgages backing the CMO pay back principal, the cash is set aside to pay off the first maturity, or tranche, on a quarterly basis. This process continues until all of the tranches are paid off. Thus a more predictable maturity duration is established.

Because the actual duration of the underlying pool is not certain, however, CMOs still suffer some of the same payment problems as other MB securities. Despite the yield advantages CMOs have over other securities of comparable credit quality, financial managers should beware of four disadvantages:

1. CMOs have very complicated payback formulas, like other mortgage-backed securities, when interest rates are volatile.

2. Accounting is difficult because flows of principal and interest are uneven.
3. Incorrect and late payments can result from problems in bank and dealer offices.
4. Market prices are more volatile on CMOs than other fixed-income securities as a result of such problems.

(viii) Asset-Backed Securities.   Asset-backed securities are instruments whose crediteworthiness is usually established by a pool of assets serving as collateral for security. Many U.S. government agencies sell securities that are asset banked (i.e., GNMA uses mortgages). However, these securities carry certain guarantees, special or implied, by the U.S. government to assure investors of their credit quality. However, many other types of asset-backed securities are not government released and have collateral pools consisting of auto loans and credit card receivables. The outstanding amount for asset-backed commercial paper (ABCP) has exploded in recent years, with over $1 trillion outstanding, comprising 53% of total commercial paper outstanding in the U.S.[5] ABCP offers about 5 basis points more in yield than similarly-rated unsecured CP in the 1-month through 3-month maturity range.[6]

The creditworthiness of asset-backed securities is evaluated by credit rating agencies agencies based on the type of loans or assets, their default history, reserves set aside for losses, and other factors. Overall, with some cautions, asset-backed securities are viable in most fixed-income securities portfolios.

7.16 MUNICIPAL DEBT INSTRUMENTS

Municipal securities are debt obligations paying a fixed or floating rate of interest as designated for a specified period of time (with principal and interest payable at maturity) that are issued by state and local governments and their agencies. Usually the interest paid on them is exempt from federal income taxes and often from state and local taxes within the state in which they are issued. However, many municipal securities pay non–tax-exempt interest and are therefore suitable for nonprofit organizations. The proceeds from municipal securities provide working capital or fulfill interim or seasonal funding needs for the issuing entity. They are grouped into two categories: general obligation (GO) securities and revenue bonds. With revenue securities, payment of interest and principal is made from revenues received, including tolls, user charges, rents paid by those who use the facilities financed by the security issue, or other revenue tied specifically to the security.

Municipal instruments are available with maturities from 7 days to 30 years, providing investors with flexibility in fulfilling their time-structured investment needs with adequate liquidity. Also, the municipal instrument market has a good overall record of safety. Municipals, in fact, are often considered second in safety only to government agency issues.

(a) MUNICIPAL BOND INSURANCE. In an attempt to provide additional security to a bond issue, some municipal investors have incorporated third-party guarantees or insured their municipal bonds. Many institutions insure municipal bonds. *However, we highly recommend that unsophisticated investors purchase only insured or pre-refunded (discussed later) municipal obligations.* The major groups, consisting of large insurance companies and banks, banks, which have formed associations to provide insurance to issuers of municipal bonds are Municipal Bond Insurance Association (MBIA), Financial Guarantee Insurance Corporation (FGIC), and the American Municipal Bond Assurance Corporation (AMBAC). These associations guarantee the timely payment of interest and principal to municipal bond investors. This type of insurance normally elicits an AAA rating from credit rating agencies, as it greatly increases the credit quality of the municipal bonds to which it is attached.

Other types of guarantees are provided by insurance companies and banks; they also bring an AAA credit rating. When selecting an instrument with a guarantee, the investor should be aware that the credit quality of the municipal issue is only as good as the credit quality of the insuring institution. Generally, AMBAC and MBIA are thought to provide better-quality insurance than banks, groups of banks, or other small institutions do.

Issuers of municipal bonds pay a fee to obtain this insurance or a letter of credit (LOC) from a major bank, either foreign or domestic, to add the element of credit quality to the municipal instruments they will issue. This LOC, depending on the creditworthiness of the bank that provides it, often gives the investor an additional assurance of safety to principal if the bank providing the guarantee is sound. However, the investor should remember that if the quality and creditworthiness of the institution that provides the LOC deteriorate, the quality of the guarantee on the municipal bond will also decline.

Furthermore, the investor should investigate whether the insurance guarantee or LOC guarantee covers natural disasters, including earthquakes. If this type of insurance is not provided, the municipal bond insurance may turn out to be inadequate in the event of a financially devastating natural disaster. Also, it is important to verify that the insurance will be in force for the life of the bond and covers the entire amount of the issue.

(b) TYPES OF MUNICIPAL BONDS. The municipal security market contains a myriad of distinct instruments, including general obligation bonds, revenue bonds, and refunding bonds.

(i) General Obligation Bonds. This type of instrument is considered one of the most credit secure of all municipal bonds, assuming that the issuing municipality is of sound credit. Payment of principal and coupon interest is secured by the state or local government's full faith and credit and the timely payment of principal and interest by the limited or unlimited taxing power of the municipality.

(ii) Revenue Bonds.   Revenue bonds are bonds issued to fund a project. When the project is completed, the revenue it produces is used to pay the principal and interest on the bond issue. It is important to be sure that completion risk is assessed and that the project will be completed. This type of financing is often used by the government entities to fund the building of bridges, tollways, and housing facilities.

(iii) Refunding Bonds.   Refunding bonds are bonds issued to replace an outstanding issue of instruments that is being called, redeemed, or refunded because more favorable interest rates are now available in the market. If an institution has bonds outstanding, it becomes economical after interest rates drop, perhaps 2 percent or more, to consider coming to market with a new bond issue and using the proceeds of that new bond issue, which would be sold at a lower interest rate cost or accrual cost factor, to pay off the older issue and therefore create a savings in future interest expense.

There are different types of refunding bond issues. Principal and interest from some issues are called or paid off immediately with the proceeds from a new bond.

(iv) Pre-Refunded Bonds.   Pre-refunded bonds are bonds that have been called and have a stipulated remaining life of one to several years. In other words, because of the initial terms of the bond indenture, the proceeds from the refunding issue are put into an escrow account and those funds are invested in a particular type of security as stipulated under the terms of the refunding. These bonds have unusually high credit ratings since the money to pay them at maturity has been placed in an escrow account and invested in a particular security that will be available to pay the interest and principal on the pre-refunded bonds on the date stipulated for their early payment. The securities purchased and held in the escrow account may vary from Treasury securities to instruments issued by a variety of institutions, including bank CDs. If the securities deposited in the escrow account are Treasuries (zero credit risk), refunded bonds possess little, if any, credit risk themselves. (Note: This type of municipal is the most appropriate type for investors who wish to avoid default risk.) Generally, such Treasury-backed refunded bonds are given AAA/Aaa ratings by Moody's and Standard & Poor's. If the escrow account contains Treasurys or government agency securities however, the investor should be careful to verify that there is no possibility the pre-refunded bonds will be called prior to their pre-refunded payment date. The investor must ascertain their specific call or maturity.

(v) Certificates of Participation.   Over the past two decades, a tax limitation mood has swept the United States, leading voters in a number of states to limit the taxing authority of their municipalities. These tax limitation initiatives require the governing bodies of their states to obtain approval by one-half to two-thirds of the voters before initiating new or higher taxes. To get around this, new

instruments, such as the certificate of participation (COP), were created to allow municipalities to meet the tax limitation initiative requirements.

COPs are bonds issued to pay for a particular project whereby a share of the revenues from the project—that is, a particular portion of the income—is used to repay the principal debt and the income expense. COPs have become particularly common in California, which was one of the first states to approve tax limitation legislation.

(vi) Zero Coupon Municipal Bonds. Zero coupon municipal bonds are issued at a large discount from their maturity value. When they mature, the difference between the investor's cost and the maturity value is their interest. However, zero coupon bonds, like longer-term notes and bonds, have call features that allow the issuer to redeem, or pay off, the bond issue before its maturity date. (This is often done if interest rates go down substantially from the date the bond was issued, enabling the bond issuer to pay off an older, high-interest bond and issue a newer one at a much lower interest cost.) Although Treasury zero coupon bonds have call features, they are not usually callable until close to maturity. Consequently, unlike many other zero coupon bonds issues, they do not present this problem. In particular, zero coupon municipal bonds with a long maturity have call provisions that, if not carefully evaluated at the time of purchase, can be extremely costly to an investor.

Specifically, many zero coupon municipal bonds are issued with a call provision stating that when the bonds are called, the call price will be equal to the initial issue price plus whatever interest they accumulate, or accrue, at the initial interest rate at time of issue until called. This is referred to as their accreted value. Let's say an investor buys a zero coupon municipal bond at a time other than its initial issue date and the bond has gone up in market price subsequent to its issue so that the investor pays investor a price greater than the bond's initial issue price. If that bond is then called at its issue price plus interest, investors may receive substantially less for it than the purchase price. The investor may have paid $400 for the bond, and receives only $350. So before buying a zero coupon municipal bond, the chief investment officer should ask these questions and be certain to have the right answers.

- How much over its original price am I paying for this bond, and how does the price relate to its accreted value?
- What are the call features of this bond?

Also, investors should be sure to have municipal zero coupon bonds registered with the issuer's paying agent. Otherwise, investors may not know when these bonds are called. For example, if investors held the bonds for 10 years to their maturity date, they might find, upon presenting them for payment that they were called eight years earlier and the investors were not notified because the paying agent, or registrar, had no record of the investors' purchases. In such cases, investors would receive invested principal and only two years' interest.

(c) MUNICIPAL NOTES. Municipal notes have a shorter maturity than municipal bonds, ranging from a few months to five years. They include tax anticipation notes, revenue anticipation notes, bond anticipation notes, tax-exempt commercial paper, and floating-rate notes.

(i) Tax Anticipation Notes. Tax anticipation notes are issued by municipalities to finance their operations in anticipation of future tax receipts. They are usually general obligations (GOs).

(ii) Revenue Anticipation Notes. Revenue anticipation notes are issued by municipalities to finance their operations, although the revenues anticipated are not always tax receipts. These are usually GOs.

(iii) Bond Anticipation Notes. Bond anticipation notes are issued by municipalities to finance projects that will later be funded by the sale of long-term bonds. These are usually GOs. Care must be used to select issues for which bonds will actually be issued to pay off the notes. Also, if a project is the purpose of this type of issue, it is important to verify that the project will be completed.

(iv) Floating-Rate Notes with Put Option Futures. The rates of a number of tax-exempt notes are set weekly or daily on the basis of an index established by the issuer. Usually an investor may redeem or put these notes at par with either one day or one week's notice, depending on their issuer format. Interest on these instruments is paid monthly. This category of municipal has become a widely accepted money market, short-term investment because of its flexibility. Although the instruments are issued with a long maturity date, the put feature of the one or seven days, which is usually secured by an LOC or other guarantee, is the critical feature.

(v) Municipal Floating-Rate Instrument Problems. Investors who buy municipal floating-rate instruments should take five steps to verify the accuracy of the documentation and to ensure proper holding procedures are followed.

1. Check the accuracy of each new reset rate and date (based on the terms of the instrument), as they can be set in error. Do not assume that they will always be set as they should be. These instruments are all a little different and must be followed closely to verify proper rates at reset dates.
2. Check the dollar amount of each interest payment. Do not assume that they will always be correct.
3. Check the date on which the interest payment is received to be sure it is on time.

4. Since these instruments mature beyond one year, they must be registered with a transfer agent and may not be held in bearer form. Therefore, investors should make sure a safekeeping agent holds these securities in their "nominee name" to facilitate the transfer if a put may occur. Furthermore, investors should recognize that any transfer of title on a security may take a few days to five weeks—or even longer. Accordingly, if investors plan to redeem or put these bonds shortly (in less than three months) after purchasing them, a problem could arise if the bonds are out for reregistration into the bank safekeeping unit's nominee name. The only way to avoid this problem is to leave the put bonds with the dealer from whom they were purchased since the dealer can easily put them on the behalf of investors. Investors should not have these instruments registered in their own name, but rather in their safekeeping agent's nominee name. Again, because paperwork to transfer ownership causes some delay, it may prevent a timely put exercise shortly after the purchase date.

5. Should investors purchase a floating-rate municipal, they should be aware that portfolio records will need to be updated regularly to reflect each new interest reset rate (i.e., each new weekly or daily reset rate). Should several issues of this type be purchased, much time and attention will be needed to keep records current.

7.17 CORPORATE DEBT INSTRUMENTS

Corporate debt is issued by industrial corporations, utility companies, finance companies, bank holding companies, domestic facilities of foreign institutions, and other private-sector organizations. All corporate debt is subject to default risk. Therefore, financial managers should examine the credit ratings of the organization issuing corporate debt instruments. In general, corporate debt falls into three categories: (1) commercial paper, (2) medium-term corporate notes, and (3) long-term bonds. The differences among these categories, of course, lie in varying maturity lengths.

(a) COMMERCIAL PAPER. Many large corporations in recent years have eschewed bank loans in favor of financing obtained from less expensive sources. For a large corporation with an excellent credit rating, the least expensive source of financing is to issue its own debt in the form of commercial paper that is sold to investors through the capital markets. Domestic and foreign manufacturing and industrial companies issue commercial paper, as do finance companies and bank holding companies. Paper issued by finance companies is called direct finance paper; it is generally sold directly to investors through banks acting as agents for the issuers. Paper issued by industrial companies is called dealer paper; it is usually sold through dealers who have purchased the paper themselves. Commercial paper is a promissory note with almost one-half of the issues unsecured, maturing on a specific date. In most cases, it is issued in bearer form in minimum denominations of $100,000. Commercial paper is liquid, because a secondary market exists. However, investors generally hold commercial paper to maturity. Issuers and dealers often will buy paper back if an investor needs cash.

Maturities on most commercial paper run from 1 to 180 days. The longest maturity that commercial paper carries is 270 days, as debt issues with longer maturities must be registered with the Securities and Exchange Commission (SEC). Registration is expensive. Commercial paper provides investors with an efficient short-term investment instrument that matures on a specific date.

The yield on commercial paper depends on the issuer's credit rating, its need for money, maturity of the paper, its face value, and general money market rates. Most companies that issue commercial paper are rated by agencies such as Moody's, Standard & Poor's, and Fitch. Commercial paper that falls into the highest rating class is called top tier. Investing in top-tier paper entails minimal credit risk, though risk is still present. Commercial paper, therefore, provides higher yields than Treasury and government agency securities of the same maturities. We noted earlier that asset-backed commercial paper, though backed, offers about 5 basis points in additional yield. Remember that an issuer would not choose to issue asset-backed paper if it could do so without the security. This implies higher default risk for asset-backed paper. The credit quality and credit status of the assets is evaluated by the rater and the investor, rather than the credit status of the issuing company. Usually a company raises funds in this market through a bank that actually issues the asset-backed commercial paper, unless the company will be issuing a significant amount of this type of paper.

(i) Issuing Formats. In addition to the flexibility and efficiency of its maturity dates, commercial paper offers a choice of two formats, interest-bearing or discounted. An investor buying $1 million in interest-bearing commercial paper pays the $1 million face value and collects interest upon maturity. Not much interest-bearing commercial paper is issued, however, except in very short maturities. Because most interest-bearing commercial paper is held to maturity, its liquidity is decreased. Discount commercial paper, which is more common, works like U.S. T-bills, where an investor buys the note at a discount and receives its face value at maturity.

(ii) Types of Commercial Paper. Commercial paper is a flexible investment vehicle available in nine types:

1. Bank holding company commercial paper is issued by the parent companies of commercial banks.
2. Industrial commercial paper is issued by major industrial companies to provide short-term working capital.
3. Finance company commercial paper is issued by captive finance companies of major industrial corporations. The finance companies use the

money generated by commercial paper programs to provide financing to buyers of the parent corporation's products. GECC and GMAC are examples.

4. Dealer commercial paper is issued by corporations through securities dealers rather than through banks or the company itself. A dealer generally underwrites an issue, which means that the dealer buys the paper and resells it to investors.

5. Direct or finance commercial paper is paper distributed by banks. Until recently, banks could not act as dealers; they could act only as agents for commercial paper issuers, generally finance companies. The bank would take orders from investors but would not invest any of its own money to maintain its own inventory of an issue.

6. Foreign commercial paper is issued in the United States by domestic subsidiaries of foreign industrial and financial organizations. The paper generally is guaranteed by the foreign parent.

7. Collateralized commercial paper is usually issued to generate funds to purchase loans from an affiliated savings and loan. The collateral often takes the form of Treasury or government agency securities pledged by the institution's parent. Many investors consider collateralized commercial paper to be a secure short-term investment.

8. LOC commercial paper (also called commercial paper LOC) is, as its name suggests, supported by a bank letter of credit (LOC). A major bank or insurance company backs the credit quality of LOC commercial paper for a fee. Companies that issue LOC commercial paper tend to be smaller, are less well known, and have less than the highest credit rating. These issuers use the LOC guarantee to enhance their credit standing to raise short-term borrowings at a lower interest cost. The credit strength behind the paper is not that of the issuing company but that of the institution that provides the LOC. LOC commercial paper comes in these varieties:

   o *Full-and-direct pay paper*. The institution backing the issue with its LOC will pay upon maturity if the issuer cannot pay the full amount directly to the investor.

   o *Standby LOC commercial paper*. This variety does not carry as strong a guarantee as full-and-direct pay LOC commercial paper. A standby LOC, for instance, may cover only partial payments and various types of delayed payments. To many investors, this is acceptable but not preferable.

   o *Irrevocable LOC commercial paper*. The LOC cannot be revoked or canceled.

9. Asset-backed commercial paper. This was discussed earlier in the chapter.

(b) LOAN PARTICIPATIONS. Major money center banks developed loan participations as a means of providing financing to bank customers in lieu of the customers issuing commercial paper. Because it had been illegal for commercial banks to underwrite commercial paper, several banks developed loan participations as a way of keeping customers from going to other institutions for financing. Under a loan participation arrangement, a bank creates a loan to one of its customers, then sells pieces of the loan to investors. It is similar to a securities dealer selling commercial paper to investors in order to provide funds for a corporate borrower.

Investors find loan participations attractive because their yields are higher than CDs and commercial paper. Yields on loan participations can be as much as 15 basis points greater than comparable investment instruments, depending on the creditworthiness of the borrower. Loan participations are attractive borrowing vehicles because they carry low administrative charges. Accordingly, finance managers look on loan participations as good investment alternatives, though they should be used selectively. Loan participations are not liquid investments. Before investing in a loan participation, an investor should examine the borrowing company's credit ratings.

(c) CORPORATE NOTES. Medium-term notes are promissory notes that pay either a fixed or variable rate of interest, with principal payable at maturity. As the name suggests, these instruments lie in the middle ranges of the yield curve. Corporate notes carry maturities ranging between 9 months and 10 years; their maturities thus begin where commercial paper maturities end. Issued in much the same way as commercial paper, corporate notes are available either through underwriting or ongoing issuance programs called medium-term notes or shelf registrations. Under a shelf registration, an issuer maintains a continuing registration statement with the SEC and posts rates daily for a range of maturities. This allows the issuer to control both maturity length and the overall distribution of securities. The ability to offer medium-term notes whose rates fluctuate for different maturity periods allows large corporations to plan borrowing better based on corporate needs and market rates. (Shelf registrations were made possible by changes to SEC Rule 415 that allow corporations to make certain types of amendments to debt documents without SEC review)

For investors, however, medium-term notes allow financial managers to choose the exact maturities they need and to base investment decisions on the yield curve. Medium-term notes offer four basic advantages to institutional investors:

1. Medium-term notes are issued with a range of maturities. By choosing any maturity date within that range, financial managers can tailor the instruments somewhat to fit into a portfolio.

2. The primary and secondary market availability of medium-term notes allows investment managers to satisfy maturity, yield, and duration needs of a portfolio.

3. Yield spreads on medium-term notes are relatively stable under most market conditions, because many different issuers and maturities are available on any given day.

4. Growth in the medium-term market, has resulted in excellent liquidity for the instruments. This allows financial managers to use active investment management techniques.

(d) CORPORATE BONDS. Corporations seeking to borrow large sums of money over a period of time longer than 10 years issue corporate bonds. A corporate bond is essentially an IOU under which the borrower (bond issuer) agrees to pay the investor a fixed amount of interest in return for the use of the investor's money over the period of the loan (the bond's maturity). There is an active secondary market for the corporate bonds of a few large companies, and this enhances their liquidity. When an investor wants to sell bonds before maturity, the bond's value becomes critical, especially because the long-term bond market can fluctuate widely. Bonds offer the important advantage of high return to financial managers who can invest in longer maturities. Because an investor takes on more risk when investing in instruments with long maturities, fixed returns are greater. Bond investors also stand to gain if interest rates decline, though bonds often have call features, allowing the issuer to redeem them prior to maturity without penalty.

(e) HIGH-YIELD (JUNK) BONDS. High-yield bonds, commonly called junk bonds, are bonds that have a high default risk. They are issued by unrated borrowers or borrowers with low credit ratings. Because bonds issued by these borrowers have low perceived credit quality that portends a high default risk, they offer a high yield. In terms of credit ratings, junk bonds carry a rating of Ba and below when rated by Moody's Investors Service and BB or less when rated by Standard & Poor's, assuming they are rated at all. According to Moody's, "Obligations rated Ba are judged to have speculative elements and are subject to substantial credit risk."[7]

(f) MASTER NOTES. Master notes are variable-rate demand notes that are used in ongoing borrowing programs of large companies. Master notes are made available to investors through bank trust departments by some of the same companies that issue commercial paper and medium-term notes. Master notes are generally issued in denominations of between $5 million and $10 million. They are flexible instruments that allow an investor to determine the terms under which funds are invested. Investors can stipulate such requirements as:

- The amount of money they want to invest initially and the ability to add or withdraw from that investment on short notice
- The length of maturity that they want, as investors can withdraw funds on short notice
- The times at which they want to receive interest payments, whether monthly, quarterly, or semiannually

Accordingly, each master note has its own terms and conditions that can be discussed and set through negotiations with the dealer. The ability to deposit and withdraw funds on short notice is the primary advantage of a master note.

A master note is generally issued in two parts: (1) A Note, a variable-term note, and (2) B Note, a fixed-term note. The note is divided because master note investors usually keep their balances at a certain level. The bottom half of the master note (the B Note) is the half in which funds are maintained. Investors often are required to give notice of up to 12 to 15 months to withdraw funds from the B Note. Investors can withdraw funds from the top half of the master note (the A Note) on demand. A master note structured in two parts should pay a higher yield than a regular master note because the borrower is able to lock up a portion of the funds for a fixed term.

Yields on master notes are generally set in relation to a well-established base rate. For instance, daily floating yields may be set on the basis of the Federal Reserve's daily Fed funds rate. Yields on master notes are about the same or slightly less than those of other money market instruments. The reason for the lower rate is that master note investments are highly liquid and flexible, as they essentially allow financial managers to determine maturities and investment amounts.

7.18 MONEY MARKET INSTRUMENTS ISSUED BY BANKS AND INVESTMENT COMPANIES

The term "money market," as distinguished from the term "capital market," refers to borrowing and lending for periods of a year or less. Organizations issue money market instruments for a variety of reasons, one of the most common of which is the mismatched timing of their cash receipts and cash disbursements. They need financing in the short run and can obtain it by borrowing from a lender or issuing short-term, or money market, instruments. From the investor's point of view, the money market affords a way to earn interest on excess capital without tying it up for long periods of time. The more common money market instruments used by financial managers for short-term investing are discussed next.

(a) BANKER'S ACCEPTANCES. Banker's acceptances (BAs) are short-term drafts whose drawee bank has accepted the obligation to pay the instrument at maturity. BAs are used primarily to finance trade transactions, frequently in international trade, and are similar to commercial paper except they entail less risk to investors. A BA is drawn on and accepted by a domestic bank and sold to an investor at a discount. The bank agrees to redeem the note at maturity for full face value. Most BAs have maturities of three months, though they can be as long as six months, and are sold in denominations of $500,000, $1 million, and multiples of $1 million. BA investments offer these advantages:

- Yield spread advantage ranging between 10 and 33 basis points higher than T-bills
- Smaller capital investments that produce yields similar to CDs
- Full negotiability
- Active secondary market for BAs of $500,000 or more

The next example illustrates how BAs work to finance international trade transactions. Company A, a U.S. company, plans to import optical lenses from Company B, a German company. Company A wants to pay for the lenses six months after shipment, hoping that the lenses will have been sold and the proceeds collected by that time. Company A is too small to issue debt in the open market, so it seeks financing from its bank. The company uses BA financing, because it is less expensive than a normal business loan. For its part, the bank issues a LOC to Company B on behalf of Company A for the purpose of importing and paying for the lenses. When the lenses are shipped, Company B draws a time draft due in six months on Company A's bank that issued that LOC, discounts the draft at its own German bank, and receives payment. The German bank then sends the time draft to Company A's bank, which "accepts" the draft, indicating acceptance of the liability to pay the instrument when it matures.

Company A's bank is obliged to pay the draft at maturity. Meanwhile, Company B's bank may hold the draft until maturity or sell it in the money market to investors as a BA. Ultimately, it is the responsibility of Company A's bank to pay off the acceptance at maturity even if Company A cannot. As a result, BAs are direct obligations of both the accepting bank and issuing company, and usually the goods underlying the transaction are pledged to secure the obligation. Investors have very little risk if the draft is accepted by a bank with a top credit rating. Very large banks long have been active in BA financing. In 90 years, no investor has lost principal except on counterfeit BAs.

(b) NEGOTIABLE CERTIFICATES OF DEPOSIT AND TIME DEPOSITS. The removal by the Federal Reserve System of interest rate restrictions on time deposits during the early 1980s has led to increased competition among banks. Banks now attract deposits by offering higher interest rates than their competitors, especially for deposits of more than $100,000. The result has been an active resale market for CDs in amounts exceeding $1 million.

Corporations and other investors with large sums to invest did not use fixed time deposits because they lacked liquidity. Consequently, negotiable time CDs were introduced in 1961. Negotiable CDs provide institutional financial managers with the advantages of flexible maturities, an active secondary market, and some collateralization of deposits.

Marketable CDs are generally sold in units of $1 million or more. They are issued at face value and generally pay interest semiannually if issued for maturities of one year or more. Maturities on CDs range between a few days and several years, but most are less than a year. Yields on CDs are greater than Treasury and government agency securities, as investors are exposed to some credit risk. Liquidity depends on the credit quality of the issuing bank and the size of the instrument. An excellent secondary market for CDs issued by major banks does exist.

There are four sources for negotiable CDs: (1) domestic banks (Domestic CDs); (2) U.S. branches of foreign banks (Yankee CDs); (3) thrift institutions (Thrift CDs); and (4) foreign-issued CDs, denominated in U.S dollars (Eurodollar CDs). Thrift institutions include savings banks and savings and loan associations. There is an active secondary market for Domestic CDs and, to a somewhat lesser degree, Yankee CDs. Domestic and Yankee CDs are sold directly to investors by banks or through dealers. These dealers also contribute to the activity of secondary CD markets. Since CDs have federal deposit insurance (Federal Deposit Insurance Corporation [FDIC] only up to $100,000, an investor must check the credit quality of the issuing entity for amounts over $100,000.

(i) Variable-Rate CDs. Variable-rate CDs are a relatively new type of negotiable CD. Two types of variable-rate CDs dominate the market: (1) six-month CDs with a 30-day roll, and (2) one-and-a-half-year or longer CDs with a three-month roll. Interest is paid on each roll and a new coupon set. Coupons established at issue, as well as those set on roll dates, are set at some increment above a benchmark interest rate that often is the average rate banks pay on new CDs with similar maturities. Rates range from 12.5 to 30 basis points above the benchmark, depending on the credit of the issuer and the maturity of the note. Benchmark rates are published by the Federal Reserve System. Financial managers must examine variable-rate CDs closely because of their unique features. Variable-rate CDs provide investors with some rate protection against increasing interest rates. They tend to be less liquid than other CDs, however, until their last roll period, when they trade like regular CDs of similar maturity.

(ii) Eurodollar Time Deposits. Eurodollar time deposits are nonnegotiable U.S. dollar-denominated deposits made in an offshore branch of a foreign or domestic bank. They have all the protection afforded to any domestic deposit except FDIC insurance. As their name suggests, Eurodollar time deposits are deposits; hence, no financial instrument is created. Because the deposits are not traded, they are illiquid. Some banks, however, will allow depositors to withdraw their money early with no interest penalty, although investors interested in liquidity should use Eurodollar time deposits only as short-term investments (1 to 90 days).

A unique risk element of Eurodollar time deposits is sovereign or country risk. This refers to an investor's exposure when money falls under the control of the country in which it is deposited. If the foreign government decides that funds will not be transferred out of the country, investors may find their money tied up for longer periods than they had planned. Investors can minimize sovereign risk by selecting offshore sites carefully. Professional investors consider the branches of major banks in London, the Cayman Islands, and Nassau to be relatively safe locations for depositing investment dollars.

(iii) Eurodollar CDs. Because eurodollar time deposits are not liquid and many investors desire liquidity, banks that had accepted Eurodollar time deposits in London and Nassau began to issue Eurodollar CDs. A Eurodollar CD is similar to a domestic CD, except that the liability resides with the bank's offshore branch rather than its domestic branch. Any domestic or foreign bank can issue Eurodollar CDs, though Eurodollar CDs issued in London and Nassau are the most common.

The primary advantage of eurodollar CDs to a financial manager is their rate of return, which is higher than for most domestic CDs. However, they are also susceptible to sovereign risk and are slightly less liquid than domestic CDs. These CDs do not have FDIC deposit insurance coverage. Many Eurodollar CDs are issued through dealers that maintain an active secondary market in the instruments. If the instrument is denominated in U.S. dollars, domestic investors have no foreign exchange exposure.

(iv) Yankee CDs. When foreign banks issue U.S. dollar-denominated CDs through their domestic U.S. branches, the instruments are called Yankee CDs, in contrast to Eurodollar CDs, which are issued by banks through offshore (non-U.S.) branches. Yankee CDs are not as liquid as domestic CDs, so their rates are closer to those of Eurodollar CDs and a little higher than domestic CDs but not substantially. Most of the institutional investors that buy Yankee CDs are interested primarily in yield. Federal Reserve regulations that make it more expensive for foreign banks to raise money by issuing Yankee CDs account for less attractive rates on Yankee CDs.

(c) MONEY MARKET MUTUAL FUNDS. Pools of money invested in particular categories of instruments (i.e., stocks, bonds, and short-term money market instruments) and managed by professionals are called mutual funds. Money market funds, of course, are a type of mutual fund that invests solely in short-term, fixed-income instruments. In return for investing money in a mutual fund, an investor receives shares and becomes a part owner of the mutual fund. The original purpose behind mutual funds was to allow individual investors to earn the same returns as large institutional investors. However, large institutional investors are now investing in mutual funds because they are easier to manage than some other forms of investment: total institutional investment total over $1.3 trillion.

In fact, a money market mutual fund can occasionally provide higher yields than direct investments made by experienced money market investors. When interest rates are falling, for instance, yields on money market mutual funds are slow to fall, because of the time it takes for instruments to mature and be replaced with new instruments that carry the lower rate. Money market mutual funds generally invest in instruments with maturities of 60 days or less dollar weighted average portfolio maturity must be 90 days or less, and they generally do not penalize investors for early withdrawal.

There are other advantages to money market mutual funds as well. Some funds allow investors to write checks or otherwise transfer money invested in the fund. Many money market mutual funds invest in municipal instruments that provide tax-exempt returns to investors in high tax brackets. These funds also may limit market risk, as most instruments carry maturities of less than 60 days and do not tend to fluctuate in price. Many newspapers carry listings of current yields and weighted average maturities on a variety of money market mutual funds. It is easy to compare yields and lengths of maturity, because most funds use standard formulas in reporting them.

However, there are also risks associated with money market mutual funds. The primary risk is mismanagement, although the investment manager is required to keep any promises made in the prospectus. The other risk is poor investing. The fund must invest in instruments that have risk characteristics acceptable to the institution and that have performed well over time. Be careful to avoid funds with high expense ratios (which in this case means more than 30 basis points), as the low-rate environment of the early 2000s taught us. Some funds provided returns close to 0% (implying inflation-adjusted, or real returns that were negative) due to their expense ratios.

(d) BOND FUNDS.   During recent years, bond funds have grown in relation to the number of funds offered and the number of investors attracted to them. Marketing of all types of bond funds, from those investing in municipal bonds to those investing in government securities, has been heavy. The major advantages of bond funds are (1) reduced administrative expenses, (2) reduced research and management costs, and (3) yields equal to a broad market index for government, corporate mortgage, or municipal securities.

However, it is recommended that institutional financial managers take particular care when investing in bond funds for the five reasons:

1. Until recent federal regulations were imposed, advertisements often did not state fund income accurately. The advertised yield was the current yield of the items in the fund, not the fund's total return. The total return may have been substantially lower because of the effect of market prices on yields. Investors should make sure that fund yields, as advertised, comply with the new standards for accurate comparison.

2. Bond funds, in order to present more attractive yields to investors, often buy bonds with the longest maturities available, and these usually have the highest yields. At the same time, however, long-term bonds decline in price faster than other instruments when interest rates increase, and they are difficult to sell in unsettled markets. Bond funds, therefore, can decline in value relatively fast.

3. Investors are often under the impression that no-load funds allow them to buy shares without paying a sales charge (called a load). Fund managers can, however, charge a redemption fee that reduces an investor's total yield.

4. Bond funds sometimes have difficulty changing investment strategies to reflect changes in the bond market. This is especially true of funds that specialize in municipal bonds, Ginnie Mae securities, and junk corporate bonds. Their markets may not be highly liquid or stable; indeed, in the highly unstable markets of May and October 1987, for example, massive redemptions by municipal bond funds contributed to market instability.

5. A bond fund can receive permission from the U.S. SEC to stop redeeming its shares in situations such as panic selling, a fact not many investors know. Such situations are rare, however.

When these five factors are considered, along with sales charges and management fees, it is often less expensive to retain a professional fixed-income investment advisor than to buy into a bond fund. This decision, however, depends on the amount of money the institution has invested in fixed-income securities.

Of particular interest to organizations investing for the short-term, say for six months up to three years, is the availability of "ultra-short bond funds." One of these that you may have heard about is the Strong Ultra Short-Term Income Fund (formerly the Strong Advantage Fund). This fund was marketed by Strong as an investment vehicle on which individual and institutional investors could earn a higher yield than on a money fund, retain the liquidity, diversification, and professional management advantages of a money fund, and yet take only a slightly higher risk. From its inception in 1988 until the late 1990s, the Ultra Short-Term Income (STADX hereafter) Fund was able to meet its stated objective. However, the fund's price (net asset value) declined in the latter part of the 1999-2002 period, and its yields were either inferior to or only slightly superior to lower-risk money funds. Yield advantages relative to money funds are tough to maintain for ultra-short bond funds, except in a declining interest rate environment.[8]

7.19 REPURCHASE AGREEMENTS

(a) INTRODUCTION.   For many institutional financial managers, repurchase agreements, or repos, are one of the most common fixed-income investment media. Repos are short-term investments, often for one day only, that supplement a cash management or liquidity portfolio. Securities dealers use repos to

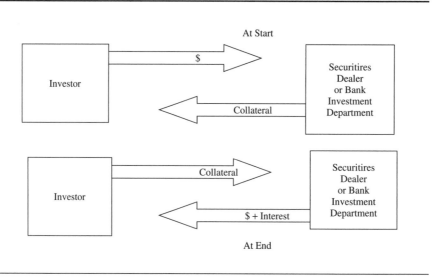

EXHIBIT 7.9 Repurchase Agreements

finance their inventories of U.S. Treasury, government agency, and other securities. The dealer puts its inventory of securities up as collateral (see Exhibit 7.9). The repos allow the dealer to finance its inventory at a lower interest rate than other sources of short-term capital. The Federal Reserve System also uses repos to manage the nation's money supply. It initiates repos to add money and reverses repos to decrease the money supply. For investors, repos can be exceptionally sound investments. Before financial managers use repos, they must understand the nature of their investment and financing uses so that funds are not lost. The legal aspects of these agreements are important, and your organization should get proper counsel in establishing its agreements.[9]

Repurchase agreements became particularly popular in the late 1970s, when interest rates reached new heights. Interest rates were so high that banks were barred from paying interest on short-term deposits by regulations limiting interest rates. By investing in an overnight repo, however, financial managers could effectively create demand deposits that paid interest. Financial managers were able to use repos to earn high yields but retain liquidity.

Repos can be somewhat expensive in terms of paperwork and complexity, especially overnight repos. Other instruments, such as overnight commercial paper, can provide better returns with less administration. When funds arrive late in the day, however, there is often no other investment vehicle available for the funds. Delivery transactions generally must be made before noon Eastern Time. However, a repo that is executed with a local bank often can be executed later.

(b) DEFINITIONS. The term "repurchase agreement" refers to the basic feature of the instrument. A repo involves the temporary sale of a security that is repurchased at a later time. To a securities dealer, the repo represents a borrowing at a fixed interest rate for a specific period of time. (Interest is payable upon maturity and rates are generally lower than those on federal funds loans or deposits because the transaction is backed by collateral.) By nature, therefore, a repo involves two simultaneous agreements, one under which the security is sold at a specified price and another under which the security is repurchased at a higher specified price on a date that can be anywhere from one to 360 days later. The interest, of course, is the difference between the sale and repurchase price. What happens, in essence, is that investors give funds to the dealer and receive collateral (the security) in return. When the funds are returned, investors receive interest.

When entering into a repo transaction, financial managers should seek to receive securities with a slightly higher market value than the funds they are lending, especially if the agreements last for more than a few days. This is to protect the investor (lender) if the seller defaults. It also protects the investor in the event that the market value of the securities declines before the conclusion of the agreement. A repo agreement may also include a provision requiring the investor to return a portion of the securities to the borrower if they increase in market value. Some financial managers seek to limit risk further by limiting repo activities to banks that have high credit ratings and to primary dealers monitored by the New York Federal Reserve Bank.

(i) Reverse Repurchase Agreements. A reverse repo is one viewed from the side of the counterparty, or dealer. A borrower puts up Treasury, government agency, or other securities as collateral and borrows funds against them for a specified period of time. A reverse repo, therefore, is not an investment but a loan with securities used as collateral. To a financial manager, reverse repo is a means of borrowing funds, while a repo is a means of lending them. In fact, because it involves two agreements, every repurchase agreement consists of a repo on one side and a reverse repo on the other. When a transaction is viewed from the dealer's point of view, it is a reverse repurchase agreement when the customer delivers the securities to the dealer. An investor that needs funds for a short period of time should consider a reverse repo instead of an outright sale of a security.

An institution's financial manager can derive two benefits from reverse repos.

1. Reverse repos provide a relatively low-cost source of short-term debt.
2. The funds obtained through a reverse repo often can be used to make investments that will pay a higher return than the rate at which they were borrowed. (The difference between the cost of borrowing the funds and the yields received from reinvesting them is a form of interest arbitrage.)

In considering a reverse repo, a financial manager must determine the credit quality of the dealer with which the securities are placed. If it is insufficient, the dealer may not be able to return the securities upon conclusion of the agreement, even when the securities appreciate during the agreement. The amount of the loan is generally 85 percent of the value of the securities used as collateral in a reverse repo; the lender is thus protected against a decline in their value.

(ii) ***Brokered or Matched Repurchase Agreements.*** Brokered repos are tied to reverse repurchase agreements. Rather than placing collateral directly with the lender, the borrower places the collateral with a third party, a dealer or a bank. The collateral is placed with an investor by the third party. In exchange for this service, it receives a "spread," the difference between the cost the third party charges the borrower and the return it pays the lender.

(c) RISKS OF REPO TRANSACTIONS. Repurchase agreements contain three sources of risk. The first involves control over the securities that are being used as collateral. The investor should seek to obtain control by using one of the custodial arrangements discussed in a later section or by taking physical possession of the securities. In that way, there will be no misunderstanding of whether there are liens on the securities. Even when an investor has control over the securities, however, questions over the ability of the investor to see these securities in the event of a default by the borrower may still arise.

The second source of risk in repo agreements involves changes in market conditions. If the value of the securities used as collateral in the agreement falls, the collateral may not be of sufficient value to compensate the investor in the event of a default. The seriousness of market risk, of course, depends on the length of the agreement; an overnight repo contains very little market risk. In recognition of this risk, many repo agreements contain margin requirements. An investor lending $10 million, for instance, generally will require that the securities dealer put up securities having a market value of $10.1 million to $10.5 million, depending on their volatility. Such agreements can also include provisions that the borrower put up additional cash if market conditions threaten the value of the securities during the agreement.

The third source of risk is the possibility that the securities dealer or bank may fail during the term of the repo. This risk was reported extensively during the early 1980s, when several securities dealers and banks failed for reasons unrelated to repos. Unless steps are taken to safeguard capital, such failures can subject an investor to losses. Examining the capital position of the securities dealer is one step an investor can take. However, often such examinations are difficult to make because many dealers are not regulated, which means they are not subject to examination by an independent agency.

The possibility that a dealer may fail should not be taken lightly. Although dealer failures have been rare in recent years, the early 1980s provide some good history lessons on the importance of knowing your counter-party.

A string of failures and near failures ended with losses suffered by clients of E.S.M. Government Securities, Inc. Other failures include the 1982 failure of

Lombard-Wall, the 1983 bankruptcies of RTD Securities and Lion Capital Corporation, and the collapse of Drysdale Government Securities in 1984. Drysdale, for instance, got into trouble because it used a quirk in the repo market to assemble a massive securities portfolio without having much cash. When bonds are bought or sold, the amount of accrued interest is added to their price. Drysdale ignored that accrued interest in its repo transactions. When it sold the securities, the firm profited from both the sale price and the accrued interest. The practice caught up with the company when the interest payments came due and it did not have the cash to pay them. As a result, investors no longer ignore accrued interest in repo transactions.

When Lombard-Wall filed for bankruptcy in 1982, its repo customers were left without recourse. The investors had made repo agreements with Lombard-Wall because they believed they were not really loaning money to an unstable firm but rather were purchasing government securities. The bankruptcy court ruled, however, that a repo was not a separate purchase-and-sale transaction. It ruled instead that a repo was a collateralized loan, and Lombard-Wall's collateral was millions of dollars less than it needed to cover outstanding repo loans. Even after the 1984 Drysdale failure, investors still did not examine the creditworthiness of their counterparty dealers closely enough. Congress has since amended the Bankruptcy Code so that repurchase agreements are exempt from a provision freezing a bankrupt corporation's assets; now lenders can liquidate the securities immediately.

The question of collateral takes on extreme importance in light of past failures. A financial manager should realize that the institution's collateral is likely to be used by the dealer or bank as collateral on a repo with another client. The dealer will lend an organization money against its collateral at one rate and then use the same collateral to borrow in another repo transaction. The dealer thus makes interest on the spread (the difference in rates between the two transactions). Dealers are required to provide investors with written notice of the possibility that their collateral may be used in other transactions. These agreements are called substitution agreements, as the dealer is effectively substituting one group of securities for another.

(d) REDUCING REPO RISK. Because of the repurchase agreement market's history of dealer failure, it is of utmost importance that investors do not rely solely on collateral when examining the quality of a repo dealer. The dealer's creditworthiness should be the foremost consideration. Investors should also take seven steps to guard against the risk of exposure in a repo transaction:

1. Verify that the dealer, even if it is a bank, is a creditworthy institution; it should have a high credit rating from a major investment-rating service.
2. Confirm that the repo's collateral is delivered to a safekeeping agent if the repo term is seven days or longer (see the next subsection).

3. Monitor the collateral's market value to ensure that it is always greater than the amount invested in the repo.
4. Make certain when entering into the transaction that the collateral meets the organization's investment guidelines for credit quality.
5. Sign a written repurchase agreement before executing the transaction.
6. Ensure that the repo rate is in accord with the quality of the securities used as collateral.
7. Ascertain the dealer's substitution policy, and obtain a higher rate if the dealer retains the right to substitute collateral.

(e) CUSTODIAL ARRANGEMENTS. Custodial and contractual arrangements can lessen the risks of repos. The custodian is a third-party institution that takes delivery and control over the securities used as collateral in a repo transaction. Financial managers can choose among three types of custodial arrangements: (1) delivery repo, (2) tri-party repo, and (3) letter repo.

DELIVERY REPO.
The delivery repo is generally considered to be the most secure arrangement. The securities used as collateral in the transaction are physically delivered to the investor. In the case of book-entry instruments, the dealer wires the collateral securities into the custodian bank's Federal Reserve account. If the securities are in physical form, they are physically delivered to the investor or its custodian against payment. Despite the security of delivery repos, however, they are expensive; delivery costs can erode the investor's return on the repo unless the transaction is large or lasts more than a week.

TRI-PARTY REPO.
In the tri-party repo, the original custodian of the securities retains physical possession, but it acknowledges that it is holding the securities of a three-party repo in the investor's own safekeeping account, rather than that of the securities dealer. The entity that retains custody of the securities is the dealer's clearing bank, not the investor's. The contract among the investor, dealer, and bank stipulates that the bank must transfer securities into the investor's safekeeping account against payment to the dealer. The bank then polices the repo by monitoring the value of the securities. It will also calculate the margin to ensure that the securities meet the collateral conditions of the transaction. The advantage of a three-party repo is its lower costs, because no external transfer of securities is involved. (Both the investor and dealer use the same custodian.) In addition, the custodian makes sure that no securities are transferred until funds are transferred as well. Tri-party repo is by far the most common form of custodial arrangement, in large part due to the ambiguity regarding who controls the borrowing party's securities that was inherent in the "letter repo" arrangement.

LETTER REPO.

Under a letter repo, the securities dealer sends a letter of confirmation to the investor that it is holding the securities in the investor's account. These are risky deals, and letter repos have been nicknamed "trust-me repos." Many repo transactions with no transfer of securities by the dealer's clearing bank from the dealer's account to the investing customer's account use letter repos, however, because no transfers are involved, which means costs are minimized.[10] Before entering into a letter repo, a financial manager must verify that the dealer's integrity is impeccable. Legal counsel should also approve such transactions.

(f) ALTERNATIVES TO REPOS. Repurchase agreements are not the only alternative to flexible short-term investing; other instruments provide a similar degree of credit quality and flexibility for investments of between 1 and 30 days. In fact, it is wise for financial managers to diversify investment exposure by investing funds in other instruments. The instruments, discussed in previous sections that are alternatives to repos include government agency discount notes, commercial paper, master notes, Eurodollar time deposits, and money market funds.

7.20 SUMMARY

One of the jobs of investment bankers and securities underwriters is to devise new and different investment instruments that will strike investors' fancies and cause them to part with their funds. In many cases, the creativity of investment bankers has worked to the benefit of institutional investors. At the same time, however, many innovative instruments have caused more problems than they have solved. CMOs, for example, were designed to solve the problems inherent in the repayment of principal and interest in mortgage-backed securities. However, CMOs have disadvantages distinctively their own.

Accordingly, financial managers must weigh all of the possible problems of new and unusual securities. Such securities often have yield advantages over other types, but such yield advantages may be eroded or even eliminated for three reasons:

1. The accounting effort to maintain the securities in an investment portfolio is costly.
2. Interest income is diminised because principal is not paid on time.
3. Most new instrument types have limited initial market activity. A weak market can destroy the liquidity and further adversely affect the market price of the instruments, thus lessening the additional return earned by the investor should they have to be sold.

Financial managers should examine all the consequences of investing in new and exotic instruments, estimate any yield problems, and evaluate the problems against the benefits before buying the instruments.

Finally, an organization's size makes a big difference in what instruments it might invest in. One survey found that 56% of large companies but only 35% of small companies invested in Eurodollar deposits, 54% of large companies but only 37% of small companies invested in municipal notes, 44% of large companies but only 34% of small companies invested in asset-backed securities, and 19% of large companies but only 5% of small companies invested in "enhanced cash total return vehicles" offered by outside investment advisors.[11] It is worthwhile checking around with organizations of your same size and type to see what types of investments they find most attractive. Not surprisingly, the same survey finds that more than two-thirds of organizations place over half of their liquidity funds and short-term funds in bank deposits, money funds, government agency securities, and T-bills.[12] These will continue to be the "bread and butter" investments for the shorter-term portfolios.

We include four appendixes to this chapter to further assist you in understanding fixed income instruments, crafting investment policy, and selecting investment managers. Appendix 7A and Appendix 7B address policy components that you may consider for your short-term policy. Appendix 7C defines the major fixed-income instruments, and may prove helpful as a resource as you meet with senior management and board members. Appendix 7D is IMCA's excellent standardized Investment Management Questionnaire.

Notes

1. For a listing of current market news and newsletters, see http://www.bondmarkets.com/gateway.asp?31.

2. Source: Fannie Mae, "Historic Discount Notes Rates Compared to Treasury Bills." Accessed online at: http://www.fanniemae.com/markets/debt/pdf/historicdiscountnotes.pdf. Accessed: January 11, 2007. Rate comparisons are for 1999–2005, inclusive.

3. About 1% of all FNMA Discount Notes are held by nonprofits. For more on FNMA debt securities from an investor's perspective, see Fannie Mae, "A Primer for Local Government Authorities Investing in Fannie Mae Debt Securities," *Funding Notes*, (April 2006). Accessed online at: http://www.fanniemae.com/markets/debt/pdf/fundingnotes_4_06.pdf. Accessed: January 11, 2007.

4. Id.

5. Credit Suisse, "Asset Backed Commercial Paper Weekly Newsletter," (December 15, 2006), p. 2.

6. Id.

7. Moody's Investor Service, Ratings Definitions: Long-Term Obligation Ratings. Accessed online at: http://www.moodys.com/moodys/cust/aboutmoodys/AboutMoodys.aspx?topic=rdef&subtopic=moodys%20credit%20ratings&title=Long+Term+Obligation+Ratings.htm. Accessed: January 11, 2007.

8. This conclusion is drawn from our own original research. Our study is presented in John Zietlow, "The Relative Advantage of Using a Short-Term Bond Fund for Savings Purposes," Paper Presented to the 2002 Annual Meeting of the Academy of Financial

Services (San Antonio, TX: October 16, 2002). The full paper is available upon request from the author.

9. See the example of a "Master Repurchase Agreement" at http://www.bondmarkets.com/agrees/master_repo_agreement.pdf.

10. Lumpkin notes: "Letter repo arrangements are used most often in overnight arrangements involving small par amounts or in transactions with nonwireable securities. Compared with most other common repo arrangements, letter repo arrangements give a dealer greater control over the underlying collateral, enabling the dealer to make last-minute substitutions at low cost if specific securities previously designated as collateral are needed to satisfy other commitments. A common letter repo arrangement is the "hold-in-custody" repo in which the borrower retains possession of the repo securities but either transfers them internally to a customer account or delivers them to a bulk segregation account or a bulk repo custody account at its clearing bank. The extent to which the investor's interest in the pledged securities is protected depends on the type of custody arrangement. If the borrower acts as both custodian and principal in the transaction, the lender again relies mostly on the borrower's integrity and creditworthiness. Even when a clearing bank is involved, if the securities are held in a bulk segregation account, the bank has no direct obligations to the dealer's individual repo customers; the dealer's customers are identified only in the dealer's own accounting records and not in those of its clearing bank. This contrasts with a bulk repo custody arrangement in which the bank performs some policing functions and also provides some form of direct confirmation to the repo customers." Stephen A. Lumpkin, "Chapter 6—Repurchase and Reverse Purchase Agreements," *Instruments of the Money Market* (Richmond, VA: Federal Reserve Bank of Richmond, 1993). Accessed online at: http://www.richmondfed.org/publications/economic_research/instruments_of_the_money_market/ch06.cfm. Accessed: January 11, 2007.

11. Based on a 2006 study conducted by the Association for Financial Professionals in conjunction with Credit Suisse Asset Management, and reported in Kevin Roth, Jeff Glenzer, and Nicholas Jon Wood, "Excess Currency is Unexpectedly Burning Holes in Company Pockets," *AFP Exchange* 26 (July/August 2006), 50–53.

12. Id.

SAMPLE OF SHORT-TERM INVESTMENT POLICY AND GUIDELINES

This example may be best suited for a large organization and may be compared and used in the development of organizational policies.

INVESTMENT COMMITTEE

Within the spectrum of activities of this organization, it is necessary to provide a framework for the regular and continuous management of investment funds. Because there is currently no formal investment committee, the directors will assume this responsibility.

INVESTMENT POLICY

The policy shall be to invest excess cash in short-term and intermediate-term fixed-income instruments, earning a market rate of interest without assuming undue risk to principal. The primary objectives of such investments in order of importance shall be preservation of capital, maintenance of liquidity, and yield.

INVESTMENT RESPONSIBILITY

Investments are the responsibility of the vice president of finance, as authorized by the board of directors. This responsibility includes the authority to select an investment advisor, open three accounts with brokers, establish safekeeping accounts or other arrangements for the custody of securities, and execute such documents as necessary.

Those authorized to execute transactions include: (1) vice president of finance, (2) director of accounting, and (3) cash manager. The vice president of finance shall ensure that one qualified individual is always available to execute the organization's investments.

REPORTING

The treasurer shall be responsible for reporting the status of investments to the directors on a quarterly basis. Those reports should include a complete listing of securities held, verified (audited) by parties either inside or outside this organization who have no connection with the investment activities.

INVESTMENTS

OBLIGATIONS OF THE U.S. GOVERNMENT OR ITS AGENCIES   Specifically, these obligations refer to the U.S. Treasury, Federal Home Loan Bank, Federal Home Loan Mortgage Corporation, Federal National Mortgage Association, Federal Farm Credit Bank, and Government National Mortgage Association. Note: When-issued items must be paid for *before* they may be sold.

BANKS: DOMESTIC   The organization may invest in negotiable certificates of deposit (CDs) (including Eurodollar-denominated deposits), Eurodollar time deposits (with branches domiciled in Cayman, Nassau, or London), and BAs of the 50 largest U.S. banks ranked by deposit size. Thrift institutions whose parent has long-term debt rated A by Moody's or Standard & Poor's are acceptable. Exceptions may be local banks or thrift institutions that have lent the corporation money or that would be appropriate to use for some other reason. (These banks and institutions should be listed, along with the maximum dollar amount of exposure allowable for each.)

BANKS: FOREIGN   The organization may invest in negotiable CDs (including Eurodollar-denominated deposits), Eurodollar time deposits (with branches domiciled in Cayman, Nassau, or London), and BAs of the 50 largest foreign banks ranked by deposit size. However, the issuing institution's parent must have a Moody's or Standard & Poor's rating of at least A.

LIMITATIONS

1. The organization's aggregate investments with foreign entities shall not exceed 50 percent of total investments.
2. No more than 10 percent of total investments shall be exposed to any one foreign country's obligations, or $X million per country, whichever is greater.

COMMERCIAL PAPER   All commercial paper must be prime quality by both Standard & Poor's and Moody's standards (i.e., A-1 by Standard & Poor's and P-1 by Moody's).

CORPORATE NOTES AND BONDS   Instruments of this type are acceptable if rated at least A by both Moody's and Standard & Poor's credit rating services.

MUNICIPAL   Municipal instruments are suitable only if they are taxable. Only municipal notes with a Moody's Investment Grade One rating, or bonds that are rated by both Moody's Investor Service, Inc., and Standard & Poor's as A, may be purchased. Not more than 15 percent of the total issue size should be purchased, and issues of at least $20 million in total size must be selected.

REPURCHASE AGREEMENTS Repurchase agreements (repos) are acceptable, using any of the securities just listed, as long as such instruments are negotiable/marketable and do not exceed other limitations as to exposure per issuer. The firm with which the repo is executed must be a credit-acceptable bank or a primary dealer (reporting to the Federal Reserve). Collateral must equal 102 percent of the dollars invested, and the collateral must be delivered to the organization's safekeeping bank and priced to market weekly (to ensure correct collateral value coverage) if the repo has longer than a seven-day maturity.

MONEY MARKET FUNDS Acceptable funds are those whose asset size place them among the 30 largest according to the *Morningstar Analyst Report* having a four-star or five-star rating, and that are in the top rating for Standard & Poor's Corporation.

SAFEKEEPING ACCOUNTS Securities purchased should be delivered against or held in a custodian safekeeping account at the organization's safekeeping bank. An exception shall be: (1) repos made with approved (see above) banks or dealers for one week or less, and (2) Eurodollar time deposits, for which no instruments are created. This safekeeping account will be audited quarterly by an entity that is not related to the investment function of this organization and the results of that audit shall be provided to the vice president of finance.

DENOMINATION All investments shall be in U.S. dollars.

DIVERSIFICATION OF INVESTMENTS In no case shall more than 15 percent of the total portfolio be invested in obligations of any particular issuer except the U.S. Treasury.

MATURITY LIMITATIONS

Overall, maximum weighted average maturity shall be three years. However, on "put" instruments, which may be redeemed (or put) at par, the put date shall be the maturity date.

REVIEW AND/OR MODIFICATION

The vice president of finance shall be responsible for reviewing and modifying investment guidelines as conditions warrant, subject to approval by the directors at least on an annual basis. However, the vice president of finance may at any time further restrict the items approved for purchase when appropriate.

Source: Alan Seidner.

ABC FOUNDATION UNENDOWED
SHORT-TERM INVESTMENT POOL POLICY

This example might be more easily adaptable to small- or medium-sized organizations.

GENERAL POLICY

The basic objective of the Unendowed Investment Pool is to maximize returns consistent with safety of principal, liquidity, and cash flow requirements. The maximum maturity shall be five years except for mortgage notes related to ABC Foundation property transactions, the XYZ Department Loan Program, and mortgage-backed securities with an average life not to exceed five years. The portfolio shall be invested at no less than 20 percent for under one year. The Vice President-Finance is responsible for arranging the actual investments pursuant to this policy. All investment activity shall be under the general jurisdiction of the Investment Committee.

AUTHORIZED INVESTMENTS

The following categories of investments shall be authorized as indicated:

A. Commercial Paper—Rated A-1 (Standard & Poor's) and P-1 (Moody's)
B. Bankers Acceptances—Any bank rated A or better by Standard & Poor's or Moody's
C. Eurodollars—An amount not to exceed 10 percent in banks or subsidiaries of banks below top investment grade. (No Eurodollars shall be purchased with a term greater than one year.)
D. Certificates of Deposits—Not to exceed 10 percent in any bank whose parent rated A or better by Standard & Poor's or Moody's. (For banks not rated, investments shall be limited to amounts within FDIC's insurance limit.)
E. U.S. Treasury Bills, Notes, and Bonds—No limitation on amount invested

   F. U.S. Government Agencies—No limitation on amount invested

   G. Repurchase Agreements—There shall be no limitation on the amount invested, provided the vehicle is collateralized by U.S. government securities

   H. Corporate Bonds and Medium Term Notes—Rated investment grade BBB/Baa by Standard & Poor's Corporation or Moody's Investor Services

   I. Master Participation Notes—Notes of issuer shall be rated Al /P1 for its commercial paper or BBB/Baa or better for its long-term debt

   J. Mortgage-Backed Pass-Through Securities—Rated AAA and an average life not to exceed five years

   K. Floating Rate Securities—Debt of issuers with maturities not to exceed five years, provided interest rates reset at least every 90 days to reflect changing market conditions

   L. Bargain Sale Investments—Not to exceed $500,000 per individual transaction, as authorized by the Planned Gifts Committee unless approved by the Board of Directors

   M. Mortgage Notes—Related to ABC Foundation property transactions and second trust-deed program for the Athletic Department and Coaches Loans

   N. Mutual Funds—Domestic or global funds invested in a portfolio of high quality debt securities. (Funds must have a reasonable performance record and net asset value in excess of $100 million.)

   O. Equity Securities—Limited to financially stable issuers, high yielding equities. (When such equities are in a managed portfolio, a proven hedging strategy must be in place to significantly reduce exposure to principal erosion caused by changing market conditions.)

   P. Other Investments—Between meetings of the Investment Committee, if deemed advisable, other investments not specifically authorized by this policy may be made if approved by both the Vice President-Finance and Investment Committee Chairman. (Any such action shall be taken to the Investment Committee at its next meeting for approval.)

INVESTMENT PROCEDURES:

Selection of the appropriate investment from among the approved alternatives shall be determined by relative availability and maturities required. All other things being equal, the investment providing the highest return will be preferred.

DIVERSIFICATION:

Securities purchased shall be diversified in terms of industry concentration as well as type of investment instrument.

QUALITY RATINGS:

Quality rating is defined in terms of the underlying credit of an issuer in a particular transaction. For maturities over one year, the minimum acceptable rating is BBB or Baa based on Standard & Poor's and Moody's ratings. For short-term securities, the equivalent commercial paper rating of A-1/P-1 is the minimum acceptable. If a security has a Letter of Credit (LOC)/guarantee supporting it, then the issuer is the entity providing the LOC/guarantee.

The quality rating guidelines to be used shall be the ratings as of the date of purchase of the security. If a rating change occurs which disqualifies a security that is already held in the Pool, the security must be reviewed for determination of possible sale.

Ratings on securities purchased shall be, as indicated in this policy or in its absence, an equivalent rating as appropriate in keeping with ABC Foundation guidelines on quality.

MARKETABILITY:

Securities purchased should be readily marketable and should meet the quality guidelines of this policy.

SAFEKEEPING:

Securities purchased shall be held in the ABC Foundation safekeeping account at its principal banks except for Repurchase Agreements and Branch Certificates of Deposit, which shall be held by the branch bank.

DEFINITIONS OF FIXED-INCOME INSTRUMENTS

U.S. TREASURY SECURITIES

The U.S. Treasury finances federal deficits by issuing debt instruments called Treasury bills, notes, and bonds. The credit standing of each is the same, and the sole difference is the length of maturity. Treasury bills are issued for periods of 1 year or less, notes are issued to mature from more than 1 year to 10 years, and bonds are issued to mature from more than 10 years up to 30 years. Because of the credit quality of U.S. Treasury securities, investors from all over the world with all forms of investment needs are attracted to these instruments. As a result, the market for these securities enjoys a depth that provides for substantial liquidity.

U.S. GOVERNMENT AGENCY OBLIGATIONS

Various agencies of the U.S. government issue debt securities to finance various types of public operations. The agencies that issue the most popular securities, and probably issue the largest volume of government agency securities, are the Government National Mortgage Association (GNMA, commonly referred to as Ginnie Mae), Federal National Mortgage Association (FNMA, commonly known as Fannie Mae), Federal Home Loan Mortgage Corporation (FHLMC, commonly known as Freddie Mac), and Federal Farm Credit Banks (FFCB).

Both FNMA and FFCB are privately owned organizations that perform specific functions in the public interest. They have strong ties to the federal government; however, there is only implied federal responsibility for the financial health of the institutions and protection of investors in the debt instruments issued by these institutions.

When an investor is considering a debt obligation of a federal agency, the investor should make a diligent investigation into the adequacy of the instrument for its purposes. In some cases, the cash flow emanating from these securities is very good; they provide current income and repayment of principal to the investor. At the same time, however, accounting considerations are complicated because of the combination of both principal and interest in the cash stream. Moreover, before making the investment, the investor should understand the nature and long maturity of the mortgages or other debt contained in the investment pool.

For example, a GNMA pool of FHA mortgages may have an average maturity of 17 years, but in a period of declining interest rates, many of these loans in the pool may be prepaid by their respective homeowners/obligors as they refinance their home mortgages at lower interest rates. As a result, the investor in the GNMA pool will realize a more rapid return of capital and a smaller total income figure than had been anticipated. This situation may not fit into the investor's plans for providing cash flow over a budgeted period, or the heavier than anticipated stream of cash flow may cause the investor problems in reinvesting the excess funds.

MUNICIPAL SECURITIES

These are instruments issued by various nonfederal government political entities, such as states, counties, water districts, and so on. They provide, in most cases, tax-exempt income to investors who pay taxes. However, increasingly, they are appropriate for investors who have no tax liability. Municipal securities come in a variety of types and maturities, often providing a yield advantage over government securities or corporate instruments of similar credit ratings.

BANK OBLIGATIONS

Bank obligations are evidenced either in the form of deposits in the bank or instruments that have been guaranteed or endorsed by a bank and offered in the secondary (resale) markets, such as banker's acceptances.

There are two basic forms of interest-bearing bank deposits: (1) negotiable time certificates of deposit, known as certificates of deposit (CDs), and (2) fixed-time deposits.

CERTIFICATES OF DEPOSIT CDs maturing in a year or less are payable to the "bearer." Therefore, if properly held by a New York custodian, they are liquid in the hands of the holder, if the CD is issued for at least $1 million. Many banks and investment dealers establish markets in CDs of the leading banks of the world and offer to buy and sell CDs for their own account. This is known as the secondary market. An investor can purchase a CD from one of these banks or dealers in the secondary market. Alternatively, an investor may initiate the bank deposit directly, in which case the CD is known as a primary certificate of deposit. If the investor chooses to sell the primary CD prior to maturity to recoup its cash funds early, it may sell it in the secondary market to another bank or dealer. A bank is not permitted to repurchase its own CDs; this would be tantamount to early redemption of the deposit and subject to penalties. It is critical to note that a secondary market exists only for CDs issued by better-known banks and savings and loan institutions. Also, the instrument itself must be in correct negotiable form and available for prompt delivery in New York. A CD issued by a bank located offshore—usually London, Cayman Islands, Nassau—is called a Eurodollar CD.

FIXED-TIME DEPOSITS   Fixed-time deposits are similar to negotiable CDs except that a bearer certificate is not issued. Fixed-time deposits often are issued domestically for amounts a bank wishes to accept. However, amounts of $1 million and more are usually required in London branches of major banks located in London, Nassau, the Bahamas, and the Cayman Islands. These are called Eurodollar time deposits since they are placed in offshore branches. Because these deposits are not represented by negotiable certificates, they are not liquid. Therefore, they often carry a higher yield to the investor than CDs.

BANKER'S ACCEPTANCES   Banker's acceptances (BAs) are drafts drawn by a bank customer against the bank; the instrument is then "accepted" by the bank for the purpose of extending financing to the customer. The bank's acceptance of the draft means that the bank plans to sell the instrument in the secondary market, and it also indicates the bank's unconditional willingness to pay the instrument at maturity. A BA often originates as the result of a merchandise transaction (often in international trade) when an importer requires financing.

   As an investment instrument, a BA of a particular bank carries higher credit quality than the same bank's CD, because it is not only a direct obligation of the bank, like a CD, but is also an obligation of an importer and usually collateralized by the merchandise itself. However, BAs are not deposits and do not carry the $100,000 insurance coverage of the Federal Deposit Insurance Corporation. Often BAs can be purchased at a few basis points' higher yield than a CD from the same issuing bank, because many investors are not as familiar with BAs as they are with CDs.

ASSET-BACKED SECURITIES

These are securities where some type of collateral, or pool of assets, serves as the basis for the creditworthiness of the security. These include, for example, Government National Mortgage Association Securities whose underlying collateral are a "pool" of mortgages. Also, many other nongovernment securities are issued with collateral, such as auto loans or credit-card loan receivables.

COMMERCIAL PAPER

Commercial paper is an unsecured promissory note issued by a corporation. The issuer may be an industrial corporation, the holding company parent of a bank, or a finance company that is often a captive finance company owned by an industrial corporation. Commercial paper is issued to mature for periods ranging from 1 to 270 days. Corporate obligations issued for longer than 270 days must be registered with the Securities and Exchange Commission; therefore, companies needing short-term financing typically restrict the maturities of this debt to 270 days or less. Commercial paper is available to the investor through many major banks that issue the bank's holding company commercial paper or act as an agent for other issuers, and through investment bankers and dealers who may underwrite the commercial paper for their clients. A newer form of commercial paper, asset-backed commercial paper, has some type of asset backing up the commercial paper. This collateral provides security to the investor should the issuer face financial problems.

LOAN PARTICIPATIONS

A loan participation as an investment medium is attractive to an investor, because it presents an opportunity to invest in a corporate obligation that is similar to commercial paper but normally carries a somewhat higher yield. Banks have invested in loan participations of other banks for decades as a means of diversifying loan portfolios. However, the use of loan participations as an investment medium for corporations began in the late 1980s.

The loan participation investment medium begins when a bank makes a loan to a corporation using standardized loan documentation. After the loan has been made, the bank seeks investors to buy "participations" in the loan. The investor in the loan participation has the obligation to investigate the credit of the obligor, since the bank selling the participation offers no guarantee or endorsement, implied or otherwise. Many companies that are obligors of these loans are rated by the commercial paper rating agencies, such as Standard & Poor's and Moody's Investors Service. In some cases, the entire short-term debt of the issuer is rated, while in other cases, only the commercial paper of the company is rated. However, if the short-term debt or commercial paper is unrated and an investor must rely on his or her own credit analysis, the investor must use extreme caution due to the difficulty in ascertaining the credit soundness of the investment. Loan participations may have maturities ranging from one day to several months. Occasionally the investor may be able to obtain a loan participation to suit its precise maturity requirements, particularly when large amounts (in excess of $1 million) are available for investment.

The investor should be aware that a loan participation is not a negotiable instrument and, therefore, is not a liquid investment. It does not constitute good collateral for the investor who needs to pledge part or all of his or her investment portfolio to secure certain obligations. A loan participation, however, may be a good investment from the standpoint of yield, subject to appropriate credit investigation by the investor.

CORPORATE NOTES AND BONDS

Corporate debt instruments with maturities longer than 270 days are considered notes if they mature within 10 years from their original issue date. The instruments are considered bonds if they mature more then 10 years from the original issue date. Notes with maturities up to approximately 3 to 5 years can play an important role in portfolios where the objective is to increase yield over what is available from strictly short-term portfolios and where nearly perfect liquidity is not necessarily required. Because they have a longer maturity than money market instruments, corporate notes are subject to greater market risk due to changes in interest rates. However, because the maturities may be only 3 to 5 years, the instruments are not subject to swings in market values as much as bonds.

Corporate bonds are often included in investment portfolios in which the time horizon is much longer than liquidity portfolios. Bonds are seldom included in liquidity portfolios unless they will mature in 1 year or less.

REPURCHASE AGREEMENTS

A repurchase agreement is an investment transaction between an investor and a bank or securities dealer, in which the bank or dealer agrees to sell a particular instrument to the investor and simultaneously agrees to repurchase that instrument at a certain date in the future. The repurchase price is designed to give the investor a yield equivalent to a rate of interest that both parties negotiate at the time the transaction is initiated.

On its face, a repurchase agreement transaction, commonly referred to as a repo, appears to place full and complete ownership of the underlying securities in the hands of the investor. However, a number of incidents of default by dealers occurred during the 1980s, resulting in court rulings that brought the fundamental nature of repos into question. Those rulings implied very strongly that a repo was not, in fact, a purchase with a simultaneous agreement to repurchase the underlying securities, but rather a loan made by the investor to the dealer secured by the pledge of the underlying instruments as collateral to the loan. This viewpoint was bolstered by the fact that in the repo business, the underlying instruments always have been called collateral. Investors who were previously authorized to invest instruments subject to repurchase were now faced with making secured loans to banks and brokers.

Because repos traditionally have been a fundamental investment medium used by institutions to invest temporarily surplus funds overnight and for periods of approximately one week, the court rulings seriously undermined the viability of the repo for this important purpose. It was not until Congress adopted the Government Securities Act of 1986 (as supplemented by regulations issued by the Treasury Department early in 1988) that the investment community regained confidence in the repo as an investment medium. That act, laid out very clearly the rights, duties, and obligations of the dealer in a repurchase agreement as long as the dealer is not a bank. However, if left hanging in the wind the relationship of the dealer if the dealer is a bank.

In order to fill the void, the investor should enter into an underlying written agreement with the dealer or bank as the counterparty to the transaction.

The agreement should spell out very clearly the rights, duties, and obligations of each of the parties, particularly in the event of the default of one of them. The agreement should also state clearly that the transaction is intended to be a purchase/repurchase transaction and explicitly is not a loan by the investor to the dealer or bank. The agreement should further provide that in the event of the default of the dealer, the investor has the right to take possession of the collateral, if the investor does not already have such possession, and to dispose of that collateral in order to recover its investment.

The Public Securities Association, an organization of securities dealers, prepared a model agreement in 1986 that many banks and securities dealers have adopted and which they require their repo customers to execute. This model agreement appears to have been drafted in an even-handed manner and supports the interests of both counterparties in the repurchase transaction. Therefore, if the bank or securities dealer does not offer such an agreement, the investor should ask for the agreement from the bank or dealer. A 1996 version of a repo model agreement is available online (see the Chapter 7 discussion of repurchase agreements).

Because of past history involving the collapse of some investment houses that were heavily involved in repos, an investor should be forewarned that the real risk in entering into a repo is the risk of failure of the counterparty (i.e., either a dealer or a bank) to perform under the agreement. Before the spate of failures during the 1980s, the investor typically looked only to the collateral for safety of principal. The investor, however, should recognize that the success of the transaction actually depends on the viability and willingness of the dealer or bank to repurchase the securities at maturity of the transaction. Accordingly, the investor must be diligent to investigate the credit standing of the counterparty to the transaction.

As an additional protection, the investor should specify to the dealer or bank those securities that are acceptable as underlying collateral. Investing guidelines should specify that such underlying collateral may consist of only investment instruments permitted by the guidelines. Moreover, the guidelines should require that in a repo transaction, the value of the underlying collateral should exceed the amount of the investment transaction by some small increment, usually stated in terms of 102 percent of the amount of the transaction. This should be monitored by the investor on a regular basis to keep current on the market value of securities used as collateral. One final point to be considered is whether the collateral is set aside for the investor and does actually exist.

MONEY MARKET MUTUAL FUNDS

A money market mutual fund is itself a portfolio of money market instruments. It provides a reasonable vehicle for investing modest sums where the amount may be too small to manage an effective investing program. For example, in managing amounts of less than $3 million, an investor is hard-pressed to meet the objectives of preservation of capital, maintenance of liquidity, and yield because money market instruments normally trade in $1 million pieces. The portfolio loses some diversification because of the large size required. If diversification is necessary, it forces the size of any one investment to be less than $1 million, and the company will sacrifice liquidity.

One solution to this dilemma is to invest in a money market mutual fund where the amounts invested may range from a minimum of perhaps $1,000 (in a retail oriented money market fund) to many millions of dollars. Various kinds of money market mutual funds exist. The more popular funds cater to consumers and businesses with modest amounts available; others serve institutional investors with large amounts of investable funds. Generally, both categories of funds operate similarly, with the institutional funds requiring larger minimum investments and often taking smaller management fees.

The mutual fund affords the investor the opportunity to meet its investment objectives of safety of principal, maintenance of liquidity, and yield provided that the investor carefully selects the particular fund. Fund selection should be based on a thorough review of the prospectus, with particular attention paid to the investment objectives of the fund, the experience and investment record of the fund's management, and the quality and liquidity of the investment instruments that the fund maintains in its portfolio.

The investor should inquire about redemption privileges and requirements of the fund and the fund's "pain threshold" for withdrawals. Most money market mutual funds allow withdrawal virtually on demand either by check (which is actually a draft drawn against the fund) or by electronic funds transfer to the investor's bank account. Electronic funds transfer may be either a wire transfer for value the same day as the withdrawal or an automated clearinghouse transfer with settlement the following day. The pain threshold refers to the size of withdrawal that the fund can tolerate without incurring its own liquidity problems. For some of the very large money market mutual funds, an immediate withdrawal of $50 million can be tolerated with little pain because of the fund's size. A small fund of less than $500 million, however, may have a problem meeting a withdrawal request for $5 million. The size factor should be seriously considered when selecting a money market mutual fund.

IMCA STANDARDIZED INVESTMENT MANAGER QUESTIONNAIRE

Please read the following instructions before completing this questionnaire:

1. All questions must be completed.
2. Type or select answers to each question.
3. If any questions are not applicable or the answer is not available, please answer as N/A.
4. If any answer is larger than the space available, please include it in an attachment that references the page and section number. Answer only the question asked. Any additional information required will be requested.

Investment Management Consultants Association

5619 DTC Parkway, Suite 500

Greenwood Village, CO 80111

(303)770–3377. www.imca.org

IMCA® Standardized Investment Manager Questionnaire

This questionnaire is in compliance with IMCA *Performance Reporting Standards*.

I.   BACKGROUND INFORMATION

A.   Firm Name & Address

Firm Name
Address
City, State ZIP
Telephone Number Fax Number
Email address

B.   Contacts

Questionnaire completed by: Your name	Title: Your title
Primary client contact: Client contact name	Title: Primary client contact title
Backup client contact: Backup client contact name	Title: Backup client contact title

C.   Ownership & Affiliates

Your firm is organized as a:
List ALL owners of your firm:
Explain owners' relationship to firm:
List ALL related companies:
Explain related companies' relationship to firm:

D.   Other offices

List the locations where the firm has other offices.

E.   History

List names, positions held, and dates of all professional-level personnel hires in the past five years.

List names, positions held, and dates of all professional-level personnel departures in the past five years.

Provide information pertaining to any organizational changes that have occurred during the past 10 years that a prudent investment professional would consider significant.

F.   Important Dates

Date assets were first managed (MM/DD/YY):
Date current investment process initiated:
Date present firm was operative
Exact date of SEC filing, if applicable   . SEC file #:

G.   Personnel

1.   Number of employees

Portfolio managers

Analysts (NOT included above)

Client service/marketing (NOT included above)

Administrators (NOT included above)

Other professionals (NOT included above)

Other full-time employees (NOT included above)

Total Employees

2. **Provide an organizational flow chart.**

3. **Indicate the number of portfolio managers and analyst specialists for equity, fixed income, and other assets:**

	Equity	Fixed Income	Other Assets
Portfolio Managers			
Analysts			

H. **Indicate the name of your insurance carrier and the dollar amount of your coverage:**

Errors & Omissions: Name of carrier	Coverage: $
Fiduciary Liability: Name of carrier	Coverage: $

II.   ASSETS AND BREAKDOWN

A. **Assets managed and number of portfolios.**

1. **Employee Benefit Plans (tax exempt)**

	Discretionary	*Non-Discretionary*
Corporate:	Assets: $0.00 / Portfolios:	Assets: $0.00 / Portfolios:
Taft-Hartley:	Assets: $0.00 / Portfolios:	Assets: $0.00 / Portfolios:
Public:	Assets: $0.00 / Portfolios:	Assets: $0.00 / Portfolios:
Other:	Assets: $0.00 / Portfolios:	Assets: $0.00 / Portfolios:
Describe "other"		
Total (1):	Assets: $0.00 / Portfolios:	Assets: $0.00 / Portfolios:

2. **Other Tax Exempt**

	Discretionary	*Non-Discretionary*
Endowment/Foundation:	Assets: $0.00 / Portfolios:	Assets: $0.00 / Portfolios:
Insurance:	Assets: $0.00 / Portfolios:	Assets: $0.00 / Portfolios:
Other:	Assets: $0.00 / Portfolios:	Assets: $0.00 / Portfolios:
Describe "other"		
Total (2):	Assets: $0.00 / Portfolios:	Assets: $0.00 / Portfolios:
Total Tax Exempt (1 & 2):	Assets: $0.00 / Portfolios:	Assets: $0.00 / Portfolios:
Total Taxable:	Assets: $0.00 / Portfolios:	Assets: $0.00 / Portfolios:
Total Collective Trusts	Assets: $0.00 / Portfolios:	Assets: $0.00 / Portfolios:
Mutual Funds:	Assets: $0.00 / Portfolios:	Assets: $0.00 / Portfolios:

B.   Largest, median, and smallest discretionary accounts currently being managed.

	Tax-Exempt	Taxable
Largest	$0.00	$0.00
Median	$0.00	$0.00
Smallest	$0.00	$0.00

Balanced Assets

C.   Assets managed and numbers of portfolios by asset size.

Balanced Assets

Size	Market Value	# of Portfolios
Under $1 MM		
$1 MM–$10 MM		
$10 MM–$25 MM		
$25 MM–$50 MM		
$50 MM–$100 MM		
Over $100 MM		
Totals		

Equity

Size	Market Value	# of Portfolios
Under $1 MM		
$1 MM–$10 MM		
$10 MM–$25 MM		
$25 MM–$50 MM		
$50 MM–$100 MM		
Over $100 MM		
Totals		

Fixed Income

Size	Market Value	# of Portfolios
Under $1 MM		
$1 MM–$10 MM		
$10 MM–$25 MM		
$25 MM–$50 MM		
$50 MM–$100 MM		
Over $100 MM		
Totals		

Other Assets

Size	Market Value	# of Portfolios
Under $1 MM		
$1 MM–$10 MM		
$10 MM–$25 MM		
$25 MM–$50 MM		
$50 MM–$100 MM		
Over $100 MM		
Totals		

Describe other assets:

D.   List the market value at time of addition and the number of accounts gained in each of the last 5 calendar years:

Year	Market Value	# of Portfolios

E.   List the market value at time of departure and the number of accounts lost in each of the last 5 calendar years:

Year	Market Value	# of Portfolios

F.   Explanation of account departures and additions:

III.   INVESTMENT PROCESS

A.   Describe your firm's overall investment philosophy for both equity and fixed income securities.

B. Methodology

Indicate all styles which describe your equity management. Place an X in the appropriate box.

	Most Applicable	Partially Applicable	Not Applicable
Top-Down	☐	☐	☐
Bottom-Up	☐	☐	☐
Value Oriented	☐	☐	☐
Defensive/High Yield	☐	☐	☐
Contrarian	☐	☐	☐
Theme Selection	☐	☐	☐
Sector Rotation	☐	☐	☐
Growth	☐	☐	☐
Emerging Growth	☐	☐	☐
Tactical Asset Allocation	☐	☐	☐
Market Timing	☐	☐	☐
Quantitative	☐	☐	☐
Large Capitalization	☐	☐	☐
Medium Capitalization	☐	☐	☐
Small Capitalization	☐	☐	☐
Core Equity	☐	☐	☐
Hedged Equity	☐	☐	☐
Socially Responsible	☐	☐	☐
Non-Diversified	☐	☐	☐
Other:	☐	☐	☐

Explain "other":

Indicate all styles which describe your fixed income management.

	Most Applicable	Partially Applicable	Not Applicable
Passive	☐	☐	☐
Active	☐	☐	☐
Maturity Ladder (Buy-Hold)	☐	☐	☐

	Most Applicable	Partially Applicable	Not Applicable
Immunization	☐	☐	☐
Credit Analysis	☐	☐	☐
Duration	☐	☐	☐
Interest Rate Anticipation	☐	☐	☐
Sector Swapping	☐	☐	☐
Maturity Swapping	☐	☐	☐
Other:	☐	☐	☐

Explain "other":

C. Investment Strategy

Within your investment process, rank the order of importance (1 being highest):

Asset Mix   Diversification/Concentration
Sector/Industry   Other (explain in addendum page)
Individual Security

List the relative importance of each of the following decisions (each column should add to 100%

	Asset Mix	Sector/Industry	Security	Diversification/ Concentration	Other
Single Decision Maker					
Portfolio Manager					
Investment Policy					
Committee					
Research					
Other (explain below)	____	____	____	____	____
Totals	100	100	100	100	100

D. Asset Allocation

List the end of quarter asset allocation percentages for the past 5 calendar years, for equity, balanced, fixed income and any other accounts.

Year	Equity (Equity/Cash)	Balanced (Equity/Fixed /Cash)	Fixed (Fixed/Cash)	Other Accounts (Describe)
1Q	/	/ /	/	/
2Q	/	/ /	/	/
3Q	/	/ /	/	/
4Q	/	/ /	/	/

Year	Equity (Equity/Cash)	Balanced (Equity/Fixed /Cash)	Fixed (Fixed/Cash)	Other Accounts (Describe)
1Q	/	/ /	/	/
2Q	/	/ /	/	/
3Q	/	/ /	/	/
4Q	/	/ /	/	/
1Q	/	/ /	/	/
2Q	/	/ /	/	/
3Q	/	/ /	/	/
4Q	/	/ /	/	/
1Q	/	/ /	/	/
2Q	/	/ /	/	/
3Q	/	/ /	/	/
4Q	/	/ /	/	/
1Q	/	/ /	/	/
2Q	/	/ /	/	/
3Q	/	/ /	/	/
4Q	/	/ /	/	/

E.   Investment Decision Process

Describe the process by which an investment idea is originated and implemented.

Provide the names and titles for all members of the investment policy or strategy committee:

What individual discretion does each portfolio manager have in structuring portfolios? %

What is the frequency of regularly scheduled investment policy or strategy meetings?

F.   Research

Provide name and title of the most senior employee charged with your research activities:

   Name: Title:

What is the frequency of regularly scheduled research meetings?
What is the approximate number of securities generally followed?

What is the average number of securities on your "buy" list?

And what is the maximum number?

Indicate how you measure risk (i.e., Standard Deviation, Beta, Quality) in choosing individual securities and structuring portfolios:

What percentage of the investment process is based on technical analysis? (0 to 100%):

      Overall Market   Individual Securities

List your ten largest equity positions as of the end of the last 5 calendar years (no symbols) and the % allocation to a typical portfolio.

	Year:	Year:	Year:	Year:	Year:
1					
2					
3					
4					
5					
6					
7					
8					
9					
10					

What percentage of the research effort comes from various sources (must add up to 100%)?

Wall Street Research	Research Vendors (i.e., Value Line)
Regional Brokerage Research	Internal Original Research
Annual Reports 10K, etc.	Company Visits

Other:

Explain "other" percentage:

What percentage of your brokerage transactions are allocated to purchase research?.

G. Disciplines

Describe any "sell discipline" or "watch list" designed to realize profits and cut losses, reduce risk, or provide quality control. Explain when such a discipline will be enacted:

Indicate the average number   , the largest number   , and the smallest number of issues in a fully invested equity account.

If a client does not provide you with objectives and guidelines, how do you establish guidelines?

Provide the average or typical portfolio characteristics for:

Dividend Yield   Price/Book Value   PE Multiple

Average Market Capitalization

Are your portfolios managed by one manager, separate equity and fixed managers, or by teams?

What is the average number and the maximum number of portfolios managed by one portfolio manager?

Describe your policy regarding diversification:

Describe how you control portfolio risk:

When you purchase a security, what is your time horizon?

H.   Trading

Provide the name and title of the most senior employee charged with your trading activities:

     Name: Title:

How many employees are involved with trading your portfolios?
How many broker-dealers have you regularly traded with over the last calendar year?
Describe any restrictions you may have on client directed transactions:
List the average annual turnover per account (the minimum of purchases and sales):

Equity   Balanced   Fixed   Other

Complete in detail your policy regarding commission discounts for stocks and bonds:
Discount from current posted rates (   ) Bonds usually done @/   credit per bond
Discount from May 1, 1975 rates (   ) Option Contracts @   each
Trades usually done @ $ /share   Other (explain:)

I.   Fees

Please list or attach your fee schedule.
What is the minimum tax-exempt account your firm will accept?
What is the minimum taxable account your firm will accept?
What is the minimum annual fee?
Under what circumstances are your fees negotiable?
What is your billing frequency?
If you have a different fee schedule for eleemosynary (nonprofit) or public fund clients, explain:

IV   CLIENT SERVICES

A.   Provide name and title of the most senior employee charged with client service:

     Name: Title:

B.   How many employees are involved with client services?

C.   **Provide a breakdown for a portfolio manager's allocation of time (must add to 100%):**

Client Contact

Portfolio Management

Administrative Duties

Trading

Investment Research

Marketing (new business)

D.   **Indicate the minimum frequency for various forms of communication for all clients:**

Telephone Calls: Periodic Portfolio Reviews:

Market Letters: Individual Issue Reviews:

Attach samples of market letters, portfolio and individual issue reviews.

E.   **Describe your policy regarding client meetings at both the client's offices and your offices:**

V.   **BUSINESS PLANS**

A.   **Indicate what your future plans may be involving both investment management or other business activities:**

B.   **Indicate the details of any new investment services you plan to introduce:**

C.   **Do you have any plans to cap or limit your growth in terms of total assets $, and total number of portfolios ?**

Describe:

D.   **What emphasis are you placing in the following areas regarding future business (must add to 100%)?**

Corporate: IRA & 401K:

Public Funds: Taxable:

Taft-Hartley: Other:

Describe "Other":

E.   **Describe any past or pending regulatory action or litigation. Please attach formal filings.**

MANDATORY AND RECOMMENDED REQUIREMENTS AND DISCLOSURES

Mandatory Requirements and Disclosures—Manager Search and Analysis

Listed below are the mandatory requirements and disclosures regarding manager search and analysis for compliance with the IMCA *Performance Reporting Standards.*

1. Performance composites presented to clients must be obtained from firms which state they are in compliance with the AIMR *Performance Presentation Standards.*
2. The investment manager must provide individual performance composites that have been prepared in accordance with the AIMR *Performance Presentation Standards.* The consultant must present AIMR compliant performance composites to clients.
3. Supplemental performance information must be identified and disclosed. At least one AIMR compliant performance composite must accompany the supplemental information.
4. Model portfolio results must not be linked with performance composites of actual accounts for presentation to a client.
5. A statement must be included that because a performance composite is an average of two or more accounts it does not represent the performance of an actual portfolio.
6. When a performance composite has been compiled by the investment manager, this must be disclosed.
7. Cumulative returns for each manager for the longest common term must be shown.
8. Annual returns for each year presented must be shown for every manager presented.
9. Rates of return for periods longer than one year must be presented on an annualized basis. Returns for periods shorter than one year must not be annualized.
10. If only gross return information is presented to the client, information must be provided to enable the client to determine the impact of the manager's fee.
11. The manager's fees must be presented.
12. At least one appropriate risk measure must be presented.
13. At least one appropriate market index must be presented as a basis for comparison.
14. The consultant must disclose potential conflicts of interest, relevant business relationships or other pertinent information that the consultant may have that may result in a conflict of interest.

Mandatory Requirements and Disclosures—Client Performance Reporting
Listed below are the mandatory requirements and disclosures regarding client performance reporting for compliance with the IMCA *Performance Reporting Standards.*

1. Time-weighted total rates of return must be calculated on at least a quarterly basis using quarterly asset valuations and monthly transactions.
2. If the source of the portfolio accounting data is the investment manager this must be disclosed to the client.

3. Annual rates of return for each year must be presented for ten years or inception, whichever is shorter.

4. A cumulative return from inception to date must be shown.

5. Rates of return for periods longer than one year must be presented on an annualized basis. Returns for periods less than one year must not be annualized.

6. Information must be provided to enable the client to determine the impact of the manager's fees.

7. At least one appropriate risk measure must be presented.

8. At least one appropriate market index must be presented as a basis for comparison.

9. The consultant must disclose potential conflicts of interest, relevant business relationships or other pertinent information that the consultant may have that may result in a conflict of interest.

Recommended Requirements and Disclosures—Manager Search and Analysis

Listed below are the recommended requirements and disclosures regarding manager search and analysis for compliance with the IMCA *Performance Reporting Standards*.

1. If sufficient history exists, one-, five- and ten-year cumulative returns must be presented.

2. Cumulative returns for each manager from inception of the firm, the inception of the investment product or ten years, whichever is shorter, must be shown.

3. Performance composites presented to clients should be shown on both a gross (before the deduction of the investment manager's fee) and a net (after the deduction of the investment manager's fee) basis.

Recommended Requirements and Disclosures—Client Performance Reporting

Listed below are the recommended requirements and disclosures regarding client performance reporting for compliance with the IMCA *Performance Reporting Standards*.

1. Time-weighted total rates of return should be calculated on at least a monthly basis using monthly asset valuations and daily transactions.

2. When a cash flow in excess of 10% of the portfolio or segment occurs, and the interim market value is available or can be obtained, interim time-weighted calculations should be performed.

3. Trade-date accounting using accrued interest should be used to calculate returns and valuations.

4. If sufficient history exists, one-, five- and ten-year cumulative returns should be presented.

5. An internal or dollar-weighted rate of return should be shown for at least inception to date.

VI. PERFORMANCE DATA STANDARDS

NOTE: The following information is extracted from the IMCA *Performance Reporting Standards*, **Section 2 - I. Consult the full standards document for further explanation.**

MANAGER SEARCH AND ANALYSIS

This section details standards to be followed by the consultant when assisting clients in the selection of investment managers.

I. SOURCES OF DATA

A. Typically, the data used in providing manager search and analysis information is an investment manager's performance composite(s). These composites are usually prepared by the investment managers. When this is the case, the consultant must disclose that the data was prepared by the investment manager and does not represent the performance of an actual portfolio. In other cases the source and definition of the data must be disclosed.

B. The consultant should obtain performance composites from investment managers which best represent the investment performance the client might have experienced had it been a client of the investment manager during the period being evaluated. For each investment manager to be reviewed, the consultant should review all composites within a firm or product group before selecting the appropriate composite(s) to be presented to a client. The intent is to ensure that a "select" composite is not presented to the client.

C. The consultant should obtain information from the investment manager that supports the performance composite calculations to ensure that the performance results presented accurately reflect a particular investment firm or product. Requested information could include the aggregate market values and cash flows of the performance composite, the returns for individual portfolios in the performance composites, or the underlying individual portfolio performance accounting data.

II. COMPOSITE CONSTRUCTION

A. Investment management consultants should use composites from firms that are in compliance with the AIMR *Performance Presentation Standards.* If a consultant chooses to use a firm which is not in compliance with AIMR, the noncompliance must be disclosed to the client. The individual composites presented must also be prepared in compliance with the AIMR *Performance Presentation Standards,* and noncompliance disclosed. Supplemental information should not be presented on a stand-alone basis.

B. Consultants, at a minimum, must use quarterly rate-of-return data in calculations. Monthly rate-of-return data is preferable.

C. Consultants are encouraged to obtain additional quantitative information about the performance composite such as equal-weighted results, the median, range, standard deviation, and other information necessary to effectively assess that a composite is representative of the investment product.

D. Model (Simulated) Portfolio: The consultant may present model portfolio results to a client as supplemental information, subject to the constraints listed below:

1. The consultant should provide the client with full disclosure concerning the methodology used and assumptions made. A statement that no assets were actually managed using the model must be included.

2. Model portfolio results should not be linked with actual results.

3. The investment manager should be encouraged to continue to calculate model portfolio results after the actual implementation of the investment product to facilitate analysis and comparison by the consultant.

E. Hypothetical Portfolio: The consultant may use hypothetical portfolio results to analyze an investment product and process, subject to the constraints listed below:

1. The consultant should provide the client with full disclosure concerning the weighting methodology used and assumptions made.

2. The firm must be in compliance with the AIMR *Performance Presentation Standards,* and the underlying composites used to construct the hypothetical portfolio must be constructed according to the AIMR *Performance Presentation Standards.*

3. Disclosures for all underlying composites must be presented in accordance with the IMCA *Performance Reporting Standards.*

F. Transferability of Historical Record

1. Past investment results belong to the investment firm (as defined by AIMR) which achieved those results, not to any single individual(s), and should not be altered to reflect personnel or other organizational changes. The consultant should disclose any significant changes in personnel or organizational structure of the investment management firm which, in the consultant's opinion, may affect future performance.

2. Performance results achieved by key investment personnel while employed with another investment firm may be used by the new firm if the consultant determines those professionals are implementing the same investment process with similar resources and disciplines at the new firm. The prior historical record may be linked with results achieved at the new firm to provide a long-term investment record. Disclosure of these circumstances to the client is mandatory.

G. Special Cases: In the absence of IMCA or AIMR *Standards* for an investment product, the manager and/or consultant should prepare performance results in accordance with appropriate, recognized industry standard (e.g., the AICPA standards for GICs). The goal should always be to have an accurate representation of the product's performance.

H. Additional Information: The consultant should review the following information for each performance composite being presented (from the inception of the firm, the inception date of the product, or ten years-whichever is shorter).

1. AIMR disclosure(s).
2. The total number and market value of portfolios included in the performance composite.
3. The total number and market value of discretionary portfolios managed in a similar manner but not included in the composite.
4. The total number and market value of nondiscretionary portfolios managed in a similar manner not included in the composite.
5. The average, median, smallest, and largest portfolios in the performance composite.
6. The average asset allocation of the performance composite.
7. An explanation of the criteria by which portfolios are excluded, deleted, or added to the performance composite.
8. The standard deviation of individual portfolio returns around the performance composite return.
9. The range of returns (and median) within the performance composite.
10. Quarterly, annual and cumulative returns, and the risk of the composite returns.

I. IMCA *Standards* encourage investment management firms to obtain third party verification that the performance composite is in compliance with the AIMR *Performance Presentation Standards*.

III. Client Disclosure and Presentation of Composite Results

A. Sources of data and definitions relating to that data must be disclosed.

B. Whenever investment results containing leverage are presented to a client, the details regarding the leverage must be disclosed.

C. The consultant should present the performance composite on both a gross (before the deduction of the investment management fee) basis for comparative purposes, and a net (after the deduction of the investment management fee) basis. If only gross return information is presented to the client, additional information should be provided to enable the client to determine the impact of the manager's fee. The consultant must be consistent when using gross or net data. The manager's fee must also be presented.

D. The consultant should use "best efforts" to ensure that any rate-of-return comparisons are reasonable and appropriate.

E. Annual and cumulative returns for each performance composite should be presented by the consultant to clients in the format that facilitates the objective comparison of one manager with another. At a minimum, each year and longest common time period should be included in the report. Returns for client-requested time periods, market cycles or other time periods should be presented when needed. At a minimum, the returns for each composite should be presented from the inception of the firm, the inception of the investment product, or ten years, whichever is shorter.

F. Rates of return for periods longer than one year should be presented in annualized form. Returns for periods shorter than one year should never be annualized.

G. Statistical Measures of Risk

1. Measures of risk should be presented in addition to rates of return to give the client a more complete picture of the investment manager's results. The consultant should determine the number of observations that are sufficient for risk calculations.

2. At a minimum, portfolio risk should be measured by calculation of an annualized standard deviation derived from monthly or quarterly total rates of returns for a meaningful reporting period (as determined by the consultant).

3. Measures of beta, residual standard deviation, correlation, covariance, semivariance, or other measures may be presented when appropriate.

4. Presentation of fundamental portfolio characteristics such as P/E ratio, duration, yield, or quality is encouraged.

H. Benchmarks

1. The intent of including benchmark comparisons is to provide the client with a means of making comparisons of the investment managers being analyzed.
2. The consultant should ensure benchmarks are appropriate.
3. Comparisons should be made for any time periods for which performance composite results are being shown. At a minimum, comparison of annual and cumulative returns should be made. The inclusion of other time periods (e.g., quarterly, market cycles) is encouraged.
4. Comparisons must include the presentation of appropriate measures of risk over time, which might include standard deviation of return and beta.

I. Sample Comparisons

1. The consultant should determine the appropriate investment product sample or grouping based on information analyzed by the consultant.
2. The consultant should disclose to the client the composition of any investment product sample used, including the treatment of fees.

J. Information provided to the client directly by the investment manager(s) should be in compliance with the AIMR *Performance Presentation Standards.*

K. The consultant is responsible for providing the client with appropriate disclosures regarding potential conflicts of interest, relevant business relationships, and other pertinent items.

IV. NONTRADITIONAL ASSET CLASSES

A. Types of Assets: These asset classes would include, but not be limited to, derivative securities, municipal bonds, private investments, and real estate.
B. Treatment: Nontraditional assets should be generally handled in accordance with the AIMR *Performance Presentation Standards.*
C. Disclosure: Since many nontraditional asset classes involve complex investment strategies, complete disclosure of the nature and consequences of the investment strategies being used is essential.

CHAPTER 8

INVESTING PRINCIPLES AND PROCEDURES FOR ENDOWMENT, SELF-INSURANCE, AND PENSIONS

8.1 INTRODUCTION

Your organization's primary financial objective is to ensure that financial resources are available when needed (timing), as needed (amount), and at reasonable cost (cost-effectiveness), and that once mobilized, these resources are protected from impairment and spent according to mission and donor purposes. Financial management includes devising and managing the portfolio of revenue streams that is best suited for your organization's financial stability and for resourcing your organization's mission. For established nonprofits, that revenue stream typically includes an income stream coming from long-term investments.

Long-term investments held by nonprofits are primarily made for one of three reasons: as part of an endowment fund, to self-insure against one or more risks or future expenses, or as part of a pension fund. By far the most common purpose is the endowment fund. We include here investments held in trust for gift annuities, as the intent of such deferred gifts is largely the same as the intent of a donor providing an endowment gift.

8.2 ENDOWMENT MANAGEMENT

(a) WHAT IS ENDOWMENT?   As typically established, an endowment is a fund donated to a tax-exempt (nonprofit) organization with a donor-imposed restriction that the funds not be expended but rather invested for the purpose of producing income. The earnings on the fund(s) can be used to advance its charitable, religious, or educational mission as long as the organization exists. It allows donors to transfer private dollars to the ongoing support of public purposes.

The function and purpose of an endowed fund is to provide monies through investment to be spent for a specific purpose today while ensuring that the fund will exist in perpetuity. The overall management of an endowment must assure that adequate monies exist today to fund the named activity as well as maintenance of comparable purchasing power in the future. An endowment investment policy that provides inadequate income for current needs while emphasizing long-term fund growth is as inflexible and constraining as a policy that spends too much on current programs and erodes the purchasing power of the endowment in the future.

There are three types of endowment; our discussion to this point has focused on a "true endowment" and a "term endowment", but many organizations have also set aside funds in the form of a "quasi-endowment":

1. *True endowment.* Contains donor provisions prohibiting the spending of principal, and the "permanently restricted" nature of the principal may not be altered by the board of directors unless expressly authorized to in writing by the donor or by a court order[1]
2. *Quasi-endowment.* Does not carry legal prohibition against spending principal; these funds are considered "unrestricted" from an accounting standpoint, and are sometimes referred to as "funds functioning as endowment" or "board-designated endowment"
3. *Term endowment.* Allows the principal to be spent at a prespecified date; the funds are handled as "temporarily restricted" for accounting purposes

The quasi-endowment is relevant for the short-term cash reserves and the strategic reserves that your organization establishes (see Chapter 7). Especially for those donors who do not understand the absolute necessity of holding significant cash reserves as part of the liquidity target that your organization establishes, the establishment of a "board-designated endowment" is a helpful management and communication device. True, the funds in this type of endowment will show up on your statement of financial position as "unrestricted net assets," but at least a careful observer of your financial statements will gain some understanding of why you hold significant cash reserves. It also lends credibility to your discussions with donors and grantors when you point to the fact that much of your cash reserves are already dedicated as shown in the amount set aside as a "quasi-endowment."

(b) WHY IS ENDOWMENT IMPORTANT TO NONPROFIT ORGANIZATIONS?
Endowment is important to nonprofit organizations because it:

- Provides stability
- Provides the ability to plan
- Reduces pressures on the public for funds
- Provides independence from economic and political forces
- Subsidizes the organization's operating budget
- Underscores the importance of the programs that the nonprofits support
- Provides flexibility
- Guarantees a long-term relationship between the donor and the institution

All of these factors improve the nonprofit organization's ability to carry out its mission. In today's world of reduced funding and competition for financial resources, most nonprofit organizations are looking more and more toward

National Association of College and University Business Officers (NACUBO) conducts annual surveys of colleges and universities on many facets of their endowment management. Commonfund is a nonprofit membership organization dedicated to educational institutions. The mission of Commonfund is "to enhance substantially the financial resources of educational institutions through superior fund management and investment advice." Commonfund has helped shape endowment management for more than 25 years." These two organizations offer some of the best information available for gaining a better understanding of endowment management best practices. Further information is available online at: www.nacubo.org (then select research) and at www.commonfund.org.

EXHIBIT 8.1   COLLEGE AND UNIVERSITY ENDOWMENT RESOURCES

building their endowment so that endowment income is increased to support the annual spending for their programs. Exhibit 8.1 explains why we feature so prominently college and university sector endowment management in this chapter. Colleges and universities serve as models within the nonprofit sector when it comes to endowment establishment and management. Investment practices of large endowments such as that held by Harvard University are worthy of your careful study, especially with regard to their inclusion of alternative investments such as hedge funds, emerging foreign markets securities, timber, and real estate to reach aggressive total return objectives.

(i) Stability.   Endowment provides stability to an organization because the principal of the endowment is not spent and generates earnings year after year to support the programs of the institution (for some background information on college and university endowments, see Exhibit 8.1). This financial stability is important for all programs, especially those that cannot be easily stopped and restarted. Fluctuations in support can be costly and debilitating to programs.

(ii) Ability to Plan.   Endowment facilitates organizational financial planning because a consistent portion of the earnings that it generates, along with capital gains, may be used on a consistent basis for funding operations.

(iii) Reduced Pressure on Public.   An endowment allows an organization to provide a higher level of service at a lower cost. Without endowments and other private gifts, nonprofit organizations would be forced to charge for or reduce their programs and services to the public and/or obtain additional public funding for their programs.

(iv) Independence from Economic and Political Forces.   To the degree that endowment-generated funds enable the organization to depend less on private donations, corporate gifts, or government grants, these funds reduce funding pressure on the organization and enable it to stabilize its revenue stream. The organization is then less subject to changes in corporate leadership or party-in-power giving patterns.

(v) Subsidy for Organization's Operating Budget.   Fees and contracts, as well as sales revenue, may not bring in enough operating revenue to cover expenses in

some years. The payout from your endowment may be set at some fixed percent, such as five percent of a fund's average assets for the year, providing a consistent subsidy of investment portfolio returns to cover some of your operating expenses in those lean years.

(vi) Endowed Program Importance Underscored. The importance of programs that are supported by endowed funds is clearly stated by virtue of the endowment. People give to endowments because they believe in the importance of those programs and want to resource them for years to come.

(vii) Flexibility. Endowed funds provide important flexibility to the nonprofit organization. Unrestricted endowed funds established by your board of directors create additional flexibility because their use is unrestricted and can be determined by the organization's leadership to help meet its unfunded needs.

(viii) Long-Term Relationship. A long-term relationship between the donor and the recipient of endowed funds is guaranteed because the endowed gift continues to give year after year in perpetuity. This continued giving encourages the ongoing relationship between the donor and the nonprofit organization. A donor who creates an endowment is assured that the gift will continue to support his or her vision in the future.

(c) HOW IS AN ENDOWMENT CREATED? As provided for in-state trust and probate law, an endowment is created by donated funds where the donor stipulates that the income, but not the principal, may be spent. The income generated from the gift is used to support the program designated by the donor.

A quasi-endowment is set up by vote of the board of directors. (See a sample quasi-endowment resolution in Appendix F-1 of Robert P. Fry, Nonprofit Investment Policies, Wiley, 1998.)

(d) HOW CAN ENDOWMENTS BE DIRECTED? Nonprofit organizations usually have many opportunities for endowed gifts. The nature of the opportunities depends on the mission of the organization and the organization's unmet needs. In general, endowed funds can be earmarked for a special purpose, program, or area of interest. The direction of endowed gifts varies among nonprofit organizations and depends on the mission of the organization.

Examples of directed endowments in a college or university include endowed professorships in specific academic discipline, undergraduate scholarships, graduate fellowships, faculty research, teaching support, or community service.

Endowments can also be undesignated or unrestricted by the donor, so that the board of directors or president of the organization can use the income from the endowments to meet the high-priority needs, as determined by the institutions.

At a large university, some examples of how some endowments are directed include:

- *Faculty chair.* Provides the resources to award a distinguished faculty member for academic achievement; income from the endowment provides funds for the chairholder to pursue new research, teaching, and other scholarly initiatives
- *Faculty research fund.* Supports the vital research of a renowned faculty member
- *Graduate student fellowship.* Enables the university to attract the best advanced degree candidates (helping to support future scholars and leaders in their special area of expertise)
- *Undergraduate scholarships.* Provides support to exceptionally talented students
- *Endowed lecture series.* Allows the university to bring distinguished speakers to share their research with the campus and community at large

(e) WHO IS RESPONSIBLE FOR THE ENDOWMENT?

(i) Board of Trustees.   The board of trustees of the nonprofit organization has ultimate management and oversight responsibility for the endowment management functions of the organization. The board is charged with the fiduciary responsibility of preserving and augmenting the value of the endowment. It is one of the board's responsibilities to set the investment policy for the organization. Through its investment policy, investment objectives for the institution are spelled out to maximize total return. In organizations where size and resources allow, the board often delegates responsibility for implementation of the investment objectives to a board committee.

An investment policy set by the board of trustees will address these objectives:

- Support the current needs of the institution
- Preserve or enhance the purchasing power of the endowment
- Strike the appropriate balance between current and future interests

In larger nonprofit organizations, the board committee structure includes an investment committee that is charged with managing the organization's investments, including endowment.

(ii) Investment Committee.   The investment committee of the board has fiduciary responsibility for the management of endowment assets. The investment committee may include members who are not on the board of trustees—in fact this almost a necessity for nonprofits with small boards—although the investment committee chair should be a trustee.

In today's environment, the investment committee should be a small group that seeks professional investment advice from consultants and external investment managers. It is critical that the advice sought is relative to the needs of the organization and the size of its portfolio.

It is unusual in today's world for an investment committee to make its own direct investments, although the committee can reserve the right to do so in certain circumstances. Today's role for members of the investment committee requires good judgment and the ability to work with other investment committee members and external money managers. It does not require the technical knowledge necessary to buy and sell securities.

The investment committee is responsible for developing the strategies and guidelines required by the nonprofit organization to meet the investment objectives set by the board of trustees.

Responsibilities of the investment committee, some of which it will normally delegate to an investment advisor, include:

- Determining how to manage the investments of the organization
- Making asset allocation decisions (the investment policy statement sets the parameters)
- Setting endowment spending rate targets
- Defining permitted and excluded investments (again, the investment policy statement communicates this)
- Selecting, reviewing, and/or replacing investment managers
- Reviewing the performance of the endowment portfolio (how this will be done and which benchmarks may be used should be in the investment policy statement)
- Monitoring compliance with endowment investment and management guidelines
- Providing periodic reports of investment operations and results to the board of trustees

(f) HOW ARE ENDOWMENTS MANAGED?   Each nonprofit organization determines its own strategies and rules for the management of its endowment funds. These strategies and rules are meant to maximize the endowment's ability to support both current spending and future needs without using principal.

Some institutions manage their endowment with internal staff; others rely on trustees, external investment counselors, or some combination (multi-manager) of all these approaches. Some organizations manage their endowment investments to maximize annual income stream (interest and dividends); others manage to achieve total return (income plus capital appreciation) and set an annual spending rate to determine the amount of annual return devoted to programs. As a general rule, the latter "total return" approach is preferred.

(g) WHAT IS UMIFA?   The Uniform Management of Institutional Funds Act (UMIFA) is a Federal law introduced in 1972 and immediately adopted by approximately 25 states, followed by a number of others up to the 48 states and the District of Columbia that have now adopted it in whole or in part.[2] UMIFA changed the focus of endowment management away from the simple practice of collecting and spending income from a portfolio assembled from donated funds and toward selecting from many investment alternatives and spending options regulated by trust and corporation law. UMIFA opened up a number of investment opportunities to endowment managers, who formerly were focused on generating high current income rather than managing on a total return basis.

UMIFA established five provisions:

1. Endowment funds can be pooled for purposes of investment, as in a mutual fund.
2. The "prudent man" standard can be applied to the endowment as a whole, and not necessarily to each separate investment. The "prudent man" requirement is rooted in trust law, which holds that trustees can be held personally liable for investment losses if they do not act according to appropriate standards. Further, the "prudent man" might be described as an individual who makes investments in a way that maximizes income and protects principal. The "prudent man" is not a speculator; he—or she—is prudent and discrete.
3. Endowment funds can be invested in the full range of investment vehicles, including newly-developed ones.
4. Capital appreciation may, under general circumstances, be spent without violating the prohibition against spending principal. Put another way, a year's spending (payout from the endowment) may be taken not only from investment income but also from net realized (appreciated assets sold that year) and unrealized ("paper gains," but assets still being held in the portfolio) investment gains
5. Trustees may delegate investment-management responsibilities.

A digest version of the original UMIFA legislation is provided in Appendix 8A. The actual law text is quite lengthy and cannot be included in this publication. Additional information may be found in your local law library or university or at various sites on the Internet.[3]

(h) WHAT IS UPMIFA?   UMIFA was modified and updated in 2006 in the form of the Uniform Prudent Management of Institutional Funds Act (UPMIFA). The model legislation was passed by the National Conference Of Commissioners On Uniform State Laws, but each state must independently pass a law enacting this model legislation or some modified version of it.

The primary thrust of the act was to change the standard of care that the board of directors and the nonprofit's investment committee must meet. Formerly, that standard was limited to "ordinary business care and prudence." The new language requires the board and the investment committee to "manage and invest the institutional fund in good faith, with the care that an ordinarily prudent person in a like position would exercise under similar circumstances." This means that a portfolio approach must be followed in evaluating the risk and return targets and trade-off, as well as in selecting and disposing of investments. The Modern

Portfolio Theory approach we profile in the next section and Appendix 8F is the framework for this portfolio approach. In fact, the new act expressly encourages whole portfolio management through investment diversification, pooling of assets, and total return investment.[4] Only when there are verifiable special situations may the portfolio not be diversified. All of the institution's funds, not just gifted funds or restricted funds, are to be invested in this manner. Below is the official description of the legislation.

> The is an update of the Uniform Management of Institutional Funds Act (UMIFA) which dates back to 1972. UPMIFA applies to funds held for charitable purposes by nonprofit, charitable institutions. The three principal issues addressed are scope of coverage, investment obligations and expenditure of funds. The earlier UMIFA did not include charitable trusts or necessarily nonprofit corporations. UPMIFA applies its rules to charitable institutions no matter how organized. That is its scope. Investment obligations are governed by prudent investment rules derived from the Uniform Prudent Investor Act. They sharply refine the investment obligations in the 1972 UMIFA. An express rule for prudent expenditure of appreciation as well as income replaces the older rule in the 1972 Act. Abolished is the concept of historic dollar value as a floor beneath which an endowment cannot be spent. The new rule allows a prudent use of total return expenditure. An optional provision allows a state to flag a total return expenditure of more than 7% of total return measured by a three year average as presumed imprudent. UPMIFA also provides a better, modern rule for exercise of *cy pres* — that is, changing an obsolete charitable purpose. Changing a charitable purpose will require notice to the appropriate regulator in a state.[5]

(i) MODERN PORTFOLIO THEORY. Modern portfolio theory (MPT), developed by Harry Markowitz during the 1950s, brings probability theory to investment management. Based on statistical analysis, MPT projects investment performance based on investments of different types in order to achieve optimal investment results. Harry Markowitz and William Sharpe, who extended the usefulness of MPT in the area of asset pricing theory, received the Nobel Prize in 1990 for their work in this field. All large endowment, pension, and foundation funds use these MPT models to make their investment decisions.

The primary insights from MPT that investment managers act on are:

1. Diversify — do not put "all of your eggs in one basket," but rather "divide your portion to seven, even to eight"[6] (or more), spreading assets across asset classes (such as bonds, stocks, real estate, and alternative investments), across countries, across industries, and across issuing companies
2. Pay Attention to Correlation — risk for individual assets is not the same as risk for a portfolio, or collection of assets, and the latter is based on the riskiness of individual assets as well as how these individual assets' returns correlate with the returns of other assets held in the portfolio (low correlation means the return patterns are very different over time, and bad

years for some assets are offset by good years by other assets held in the portfolio)

Detailed coverage of MPT is beyond our scope, but Appendix 8F provides a compact and readable introduction to the theory and how it applies to mutual fund selection. Many nonprofits now outsource their investments, either investing in mutual funds directly or upon the advice of a professional investment advisor.

8.3 CHARACTERISTICS OF ENDOWMENT

The next sections provide the characteristics of endowment, according to information provided by the National Association of College and University Business Officers (NACUBO). There were 753 colleges and universities surveyed for the endowment study, and the response rates were very good for many of the items that were included in the survey.

(a) SPENDING RATE FROM ENDOWMENT.   On average, the spending rate from endowment ranged from 4.4% to a high of 5.1% from in the ten years included in this study of 715 organizations. In 2005, the most recent year included, the average spending rate was 4.7% (if done on a dollar-weighted average, in which large endowments such as Harvard's count more than small endowments, the spending rate was 4.2% on average).

(b) ENDOWMENT ASSET ALLOCATION.   Endowment holdings are classified into eight broad asset categories: equity, fixed income (bonds and notes), real estate, cash, hedge funds, private equity (such as LBO funds), venture capital, and natural resources (see Exhibits 8.3 and 8.4).

Exhibit 8.3 shows how endowment funds are invested, on average. As of fiscal 2005, 58.5% of assets were invested in equity, 21.5% in fixed income, 3.1% in real estate, 8.7% in hedge funds, 1.6% in private equity, 0.8% in venture

Annual Reported Spending Rate, 2005–1996

	2005 %	2004 %	2003 %	2002 %	2001 %	2000 %	1999 %	1998 %	1997 %	1996 %
N	715	712	702	681	676	659	621	592	569	550
Equal-Weighted Average	4.7	5.0	5.1	5.0	4.8	4.6	4.5	4.6	4.5	4.4
Dollar-Weighted Average	4.2	4.8	4.9	4.5	4.2	4.0	4.0	3.9	4.0	4.3

Source: *2005 NACUBO Endowment Study.* Copyright 2006 by National Association of College and University Business Officers. Used by permission.

EXHIBIT 8.2   ENDOWMENT SPENDING RATE (PERCENT)

Average Asset Class Allocation of Total Assets

Investment Pool Assets	Equity %	Fixed Income %	Real Estate %	Cash %	Hedge Funds %	Private Equity %	Veature Capital %	Natural Resources %	Other %
Greater Than $1.0 Billion	44.9	14.2	4.0	2.0	21.7	5.7	3.6	3.4	0.4
> $500 Million to ≤ $1.0 Billion	53.7	16.0	3.7	1.7	15.8	4.7	2.0	1.9	0.4
> $100 Million to ≤ $100 Million	57.8	18.9	3.0	3.5	11.4	2.3	1.1	1.3	1.7
> $50 Million to ≤ $100 Million	60.6	22.1	3.2	3.8	7.0	0.7	0.4	0.5	1.7
> $25 Million to ≤ $50 Million	61.2	23.3	3.8	3.3	5.8	0.3	0.3	0.6	1.5
Less Than or Equal to $25 Million	60.7	27.8	1.7	6.1	2.4	0.2	0.0	0.1	1.0
Public	58.4	23.5	2.7	4.2	7.1	1.3	0.6	0.9	1.2
Independent	58.5	20.6	3.2	3.1	9.5	1.7	0.9	1.0	1.5
Equal-weighted Average	58.5	21.5	3.1	3.5	8.7	1.6	0.8	0.9	1.4
Dollar-weighted Average	48.3	17.2	4.5	1.7	16.6	3.9	3.2	3.6	1.0

738 institutions provided investment pool asset class data in 2005. Table data are equal-weighted unless otherwise noted. Natural resources include: Timber + Oil and Gas Partnerships + Commodities.

Source: *2005 NACUBO Endowment Study.* Copyright 2006 by National Association of College and University Business Officers. Used by permission.

EXHIBIT 8.3 ENDOWMENT ASSET ALLOCATION (PERCENT)

Ten-Year Comparisons of Asset Class Allocation

Asset Class	2005 %	2004 %	2003 %	2002 %	2001 %	2000 %	1999 %	1998 %	1997 %	1996 %
Equity	58.5	59.9	57.1	57.4	59.4	62.1	64.3	63.5	63.4	60.9
Fixed Income	31.5	22.1	25.9	26.9	24.9	23.3	23.6	25.6	26.1	28.5
Real Estate	3.1	2.8	2.8	2.7	2.4	2.0	2.0	2.1	1.9	1.9
Cash	3.5	3.7	4.0	3.9	4.1	4.1	4.0	4.3	4.7	5.3
Hedge Funds	8.7	7.3	6.1	5.1	4.2	3.0	3.1	2.8	2.2	1.8
Private Equity	1.6	1.3	1.3	0.9	0.9	1.0	0.8	0.4	0.3	0.2
Venture Capital	0.8	0.8	0.8	1.1	1.5	2.4	1.4	0.7	0.7	0.7
Natural Resources	0.9	0.6	0.4	0.4	0.4	0.4	0.2	0.2	0.3	0.2
Other	1.4	1.6	1.6	1.6	2.1	1.7	0.5	0.4	0.4	0.5

738 institutions provided investment pool asset class data in 2005. Data for 1996 to 2004 are from past studies. Tables data are equal-weighted. Natural resources include: Timber + Oil and Gas Partnerships + Commodities.

Source: *2005 NACUBO Endowment Study.* Copyright 2006 by National Association of College and University Business Officers. Used by permission.

EXHIBIT 8.4 ENDOWMENT ASSET ALLOCATION TRENDS (PERCENT)

Average Rate of Return by Asset Class

Investment Pool Assets	Greater Than $1.0 Billion %	> $600 Million to ≤ $1.0 Billion %	> $100 Million to ≤ $600 Million %	> $50 Million to ≤ $100 Million %	> $25 Million to ≤ $550 Million %	Less Than or Equal to $25 Million %
Equity—US	9.3	9.3	9.2	8.8	8.7	7.9
Equity—Non-US	18.7	15.2	16.1	15.5	15.0	13.6
Fixed Income—US	9.8	7.3	7.1	6.5	6.1	5.4
Fixed Income—Non-US	18.9*	11.9*	9.3	8.6	7.0	6.9*
Real Estate—Public	36.4*	35.2	28.7	27.2	22.3	23.9*
Real Estate—Private	18.1	17.8	12.7	13.9	13.3	11.4*
Cash—US	2.1	2.4	2.3	2.5	1.9	2.4
Cash—Non-US	—	−0.4*	4.5*	—	—	—
Hedge Funds	10.4	8.4	9.2	8.0	6.6	5.6
Private Equity	23.9	18.1	15.4	15.3	6.1*	4.0*
Venture Capital	20.3	17.1	16.7	9.3	6.0*	−37.9*
Natural Resources	32.4	21.9	33.7	34.3*	30.5*	14.2*

544 institutions completed same information regarding asset class returns. Table data are equal-weighed.

*Fewer than 10 institutions responding.

Source: *2005 NACUBO Endowment Study.* Copyright 2006 by National Association of College and University Business Officers. Used by permission.

EXHIBIT 8.5 AVERAGE ASSET CLASS RATE OF RETURN BY ENDOWMENT SIZE

capital, 0.9% in natural resources, and 3.5% in cash. The dollar-weighted averages reveal that the larger endowments put relatively more money in alternative assets such as hedge funds, private equity, venture capital, and natural resources.

Exhibit 8.4 reveals the ten-year trend in average asset allocations. This chart is equally weighted, meaning that the size of the endowment has no bearing on the average—each college's percent allocations counts the same. Note once again the decline in the more traditional asset classes—equity, fixed income, and cash—and increased allocation to alternative investments. It will be interesting to see if allocations return to a more traditional allocation posture after some bad years in the alternative asset classes.

(c) ENDOWMENT ASSETS. In the most recent NACUBO Endowment Study (NES), the 753 institutions participating reported endowment assets totaling $298.9 billion. The median endowment asset amount was $76.3 million, and $43,804 in endowment assets was held per full time equivalent (FTE) student. The median rate of returned in 2005 was 9.1%, compared to benchmark returns that same year of 8.1% for the Russell 3000 index, 6.3% for the Standard & Poors 500, 6.8% for the Lehman Brothers Aggegate, and an inflation rate of 2.5% (as measured by the CPI-Urban index of prices). This study also determined:

- Larger endowments tended to achieve higher rates of return across almost all asset classes (see Exhibit 8.5); notice especially the results in the "more than $1 billion" category (56 institutions were included in this category)
- In the largest endowments and in the third-largest endowments, as well as in private colleges as as whole, at least half as much was held in quasi-endowments as in true endowments;

We reiterate the comment made earlier about quasi-endowment: If your organization, regardless of whether it is a college, does not have a board-designated endowment ("quasi-endowment"), make that a priority in the near future.

8.4 ENDOWMENT INVESTMENT

(a) ENDOWMENT INVESTMENT POLICY. Investment policy sets in writing the investment objectives of the endowed fund. Endowment investment policy is made up of two major components:

1. Investment strategy
2. Spending and accumulation policy

(b) INVESTMENT PHILOSOPHY. The key elements of any investment philosophy and objectives for endowment investing are:

- Maximization of real long-term total return within prudent levels of risk
- Safety of principal and liquidity

Average Values of Endowment Components

Endowment Assets		True Endowment ($000)	Term Endowment ($000)	Quasi- Endowment ($000)	Funds Held in Trust by Others ($000)
Greater Than $1.0 Billion	$	1,746, 833	165, 573	1,037,562	173,592
	%	55.9	5.3	33.2	5.6
> $500 Million to ≤ $1.0 Billion	$	430,560	23,694	188,745	50,883
	%	62.1	3.4	27.2	7.3
> $100 Million to ≤ $500 Million	$	139,180	5,373	72,874	10,568
	%	61.0	2.4	32.0	4.6
> $50 Million to ≤ $100 Million	$	46,752	1,480	17,473	2,886
	%	68.2	2.2	25.5	4.2
> $25 Million to ≤ $50 Million	$	24,237	1,272	9,820	1,507
	%	65.8	3.5	26.7	4.1
Less Than or Equal to $25 Million	$	9,718	707	3,277	362
	%	69.1	5.0	23.3	2.6
Public	$	165,228	6,409	80,698	33,785
	%	57.7	2.2	28.2	11.8
Independent	$	201,417	16,876	111,521	10,658
	%	59.2	5.0	32.8	3.1
Full Sample Average	$	190,179	13,625	101,949	17,840
	%	58.8	4.2	31.5	5.5

702 institutions provided data on their endowment components. Table data are dollar-weighted.
Source: *2005 NACUBO Endowment Study.* Copyright 2006 by National Association of College and University Business Officers. Used by permission.

EXHIBIT 8.6 TYPES OF ENDOWMENTS AND DOLLAR AMOUNTS IN EACH

- Preservation of purchasing power by achieving returns that are equal or greater than the rate of inflation
- Increased income to support designated activities

Chapter 7 provides a more detailed discussion on investment policy and guidelines. In Appendix 8B we provide a sample investment policy for a long-term endowment pool. In Appendix 8 C we include investment policy aspects of an ERISA-compliant pension plan. Finally in Appendix 8E we give an example of an actual nonprofit's comprehensive investment policy statement so you can see how one organization coupled its short-term and long-term investment policies.

(c) ENDOWMENT GROWTH. Three factors contribute to endowment growth:

1. Gift contributions
2. Investment return
3. Spending rate

Of these three factors, this chapter discusses investment return and spending policy (which determine spending rates) in some detail. Gift contributions are not discussed in detail. However, the combination of good management, accountability, investment returns, policies and procedures, performance review, and communication of all the factors with donors and prospective donors will enhance the potential gift contributions for the future.

(d) ENDOWMENT INVESTMENT RETURN. Investment return is a key component of successful endowment management. Coupled with the endowment spending rate, it determines whether the endowment requirements of preserving principal, maintaining purchasing power, and funding the current program supported by the endowment can be achieved. An endowment investment strategy must be developed, implemented, monitored, and rebalanced in order to achieve the investment returns required to meet the endowment goal.

8.5 PRINCIPLES OF ENDOWMENT MANAGEMENT

The principles of endowment management include:

- Asset allocation
- Spending rate
- Bond investments
- Equity investments
- Diversification
- Investment horizon
- Managing risk
- Monitoring performance

(a) ASSET ALLOCATION. Asset allocation decisions result in the mix of investments made with endowed funds. Asset allocation determines which assets are held and in what proportions, and it is a significant determinant of investment performance for the endowment. Many studies validate that asset allocation (in combination with spending decisions) far outweighs the contribution to return that investment managers make through selection of securities. Two landmark studies have confirmed this:

- "93 percent of long-term portfolio return is the result of asset allocation"[7]
- "90 percent of equity portfolio return is the result of equity style (growth versus value) selection"[8]

Typically, endowments are invested in a mix of asset classes such as domestic equities, fixed-income securities, foreign equities, real estate, and private equities. Refer to the *NACUBO Endowment Study* to see how colleges and universities are investing in alternative asset classes to an increasing degree each year.

Once the organization sets its investment goals, the next and most important step is to make the asset allocation and spending policy decisions. These policy decisions determine whether an endowment accomplishes its goals.

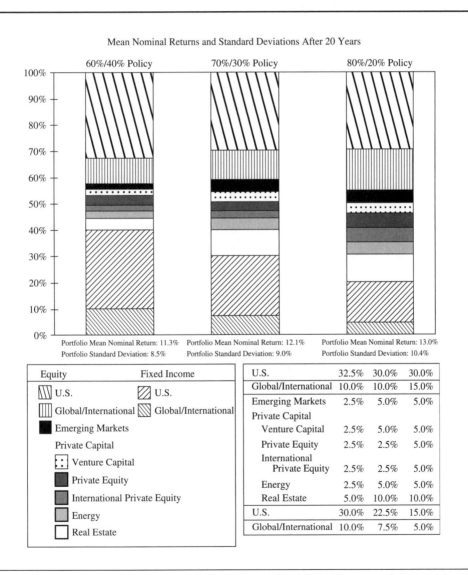

Mean Nominal Returns and Standard Deviations After 20 Years

	60%/40% Policy	70%/30% Policy	80%/20% Policy
U.S.	32.5%	30.0%	30.0%
Global/International	10.0%	10.0%	15.0%
Emerging Markets	2.5%	5.0%	5.0%
Private Capital			
Venture Capital	2.5%	5.0%	5.0%
Private Equity	2.5%	2.5%	5.0%
International Private Equity	2.5%	2.5%	5.0%
Energy	2.5%	5.0%	5.0%
Real Estate	5.0%	10.0%	10.0%
U.S.	30.0%	22.5%	15.0%
Global/International	10.0%	7.5%	5.0%

Portfolio Mean Nominal Return: 11.3% Portfolio Mean Nominal Return: 12.1% Portfolio Mean Nominal Return: 13.0%
Portfolio Standard Deviation: 8.5% Portfolio Standard Deviation: 9.0% Portfolio Standard Deviation: 10.4%

Equity: U.S., Global/International, Emerging Markets, Private Capital (Venture Capital, Private Equity, International Private Equity, Energy, Real Estate)
Fixed Income: U.S., Global/International

Source: Reprinted, with permission, from Commonfund's *Endowment Planning Model.*

EXHIBIT 8.7 THREE ASSET ALLOCATION ALTERNATIVES

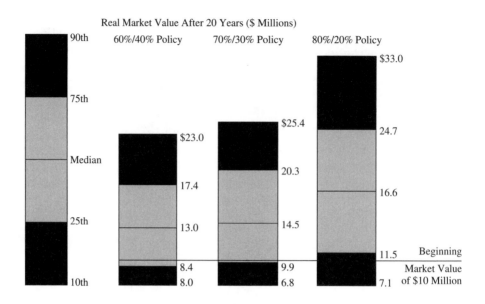

This chart represents the Endowment Planning Model results from three asset allocation alternatives based on a beginning market value of $10 million and a spending policy of 5 percent of a three-year moving average of market value. It shows graphically that by increasing the endowment's exposure to equities, there is a greater probability of exceeding the original market value and experiencing real (net of inflation) growth in the endowment. Source: Reprinted, with permission, from Commonfund's *Endowment Planning Model.*

EXHIBIT 8.8 ENDOWMENT PLANNING RESULTS FROM THREE ASSET ALLOCATION ALTERNATIVES

Exhibits 8.7 and 8.8 display three asset allocation alternatives and the results.

(b) SPENDING RATE. The spending rate is inextricably linked to achieving the investment objectives of endowment investing. This is the case because endowment growth is significantly affected by the amount of endowment funds spent to support the ongoing program on an annual basis. As described by Commonfund, trustees should attempt to "maintain generational neutrality" (or, preserve intergenerational equity) to protect the purchasing power of the endowment in perpetuity. In order to accomplish this objective and achieve stability over time, spending must remain steady (net of inflation), and the principal must not be eroded. Commonfund says that these requirements "should lead trustees to a specific investment objective, which is to earn a total return equal to the sum of inflation plus the spending rate and the costs associated with investing." Stated another way, a sustainable spending rate is total investment return minus inflation. Because asset allocation is the chief determinant of total return, asset allocation and spending are inexorably linked. Exhibit 8.9 shows the

Asset Class	Geometric Mean (compounded return, %)
Large company stocks (S&P 500)	13.33%
Corporate bonds (Lehman Brothers)	10.07%
30-day Treasury bill	5.23
Memo: U.S. inflation rate	*3.01*

Source: Figures compiled cover the period 1984–2003 and come from Frank K. Reilly and Edgar A. Norton, *Investments*, 7th Ed. (Cincinnati: Thomson/South-Western, 2006), p. 27.

EXHIBIT 8.9 AVERAGE ANNUAL COMPOUND RATES OF RETURN FOR THREE ASSET CLASSES

fairly dramatic differences in average yearly returns across the three major asset classes.

Since asset allocation and spending rates are inexorably linked, Exhibit 8.10 provides some useful calculations to help choose asset mixes and compatible spending rates.

Institutions have adopted a wide variety of spending policies, rates, rules, and practices. Exhibits 8.11 and 8.12 show hypothetical spending profiles in the college and university setting.

Stock prices fluctuate widely, so different stock allocations are appropriate for different investors. Past stock performance is not a guarantee of similar future returns.

(c) BOND INVESTMENTS. Bonds can provide income and the potential for capital appreciation to your portfolio. Complementing a stock portfolio with bonds helps diversify the total investment because bonds often do well when stocks do not. Inflation-protected bonds, such as TIPS, are especially attractive.

Bond prices depend on several factors, the most important of which is the level of interest rates. In general, bond prices appreciate as interest rates fall, and vice versa. Generally, when the economy is improving, inflation tends to rise and interest rates tend to follow. As a result, bonds often do not appreciate in price during economic good times, and will probably fall. Conversely, when the economy is not doing well, rates tend to fall and prices tend to rise.

A bond's income or yield changes with interest rates and is also affected by many other factors. Bonds are issued by many countries, states, localities, corporations, and increasingly, nonprofit organizations such as churches. They come in various qualities (for example, church bonds are mostly unrated) and have different maturity periods that may be 30 years or longer. Bond selection should be determined by your investing time frame, risk tolerance, and need for current income.

(d) EQUITIES INVESTMENT (STOCKS). History shows that, over time, stocks have a greater return than bonds and short-term securities (see Exhibit 8.13).

A quick calculation can help you match various asset mixes and spending levels:

- Total Return − Inflation = Real Return
- Real Return = Spending
- Assume Real Return: Stocks = 7.3% and Bonds = 0.9%

In order to determine the asset mix consistent with a 5 percent spending rate, solve this equation:

$$7.3x + 0.9(1 - x) = 5$$

where

$x =$ proportion invested in stocks, $1 - x =$ proportion invested in bonds.

Answer: 64 percent stocks/36 percent bonds.

How much can you spend without depleting the purchasing power of the endowment?

Equity/Fixed-Income Asset Mix %	Spending %
80/20	6.0
70/30	5.5
60/40	5.0
50/50	4.0
40/60	3.5

Source: Used with permission. © 1997 Ibbotson Associates, Inc. All rights reserved. (Certain portions of this work were derived from copyrighted works of Roger G. Ibbotson and Rex Sinquefield.)

EXHIBIT 8.10   Calculating Compatible Asset Mixes and Spending Rates

A stock's return on investment is determined by many factors including the company's management, industry, country or region, and the economy. Stocks of small, cutting-edge companies (small-cap stocks), for example, do not perform the same during various market cycles as the stocks of large, well-established companies (large-cap stocks). The style of investing in equities is also a significant determinant of portfolio performance. Two well-known styles of stock investing are value and growth. Each style is successful at various times. Value managers seek stocks of established companies that are currently undervalued. These stocks pay high dividends and feature low selling prices compared to their earnings and book values. Growth managers focus on the future and buy stocks of fast-growing companies exhibiting accelerated earnings and increasing market share. Growth managers believe that rapidly growing sales and earnings will benefit stockholders. The stock of growth companies can be very volatile.

(e) DIVERSIFICATION.   After asset allocation decisions are made for the organization, these assets can be spread to achieve greater investment diversity. The

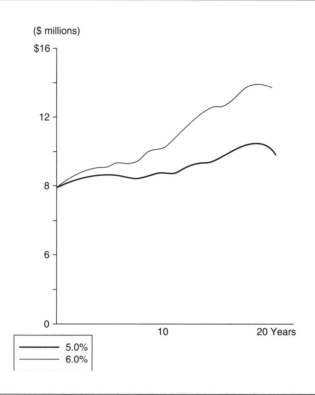

(\$ millions)

Source: Reprinted, with permission, from Commonfund's *Endowment Planning Model*.

EXHIBIT 8.11   MEDIAN EXPECTED REAL ENDOWMENT VALUE ASSUMING 80 PERCENT/20 PERCENT POLICY AND DIFFERENT SPENDING RATES

goal of diversification is to increase the probability that your investment portfolio will achieve or exceed the earning goals.

Many techniques are used to diversify, and the list grows each day. Some of the ways in which an investment portfolio can be diversified are by:

- Investment type
- Asset class
- Manager style
- Single versus multi-manager
- Type of issuer
- Industry sector
- Geography
- Time
- Domestic versus global
- Small cap versus large cap
- Emerging markets

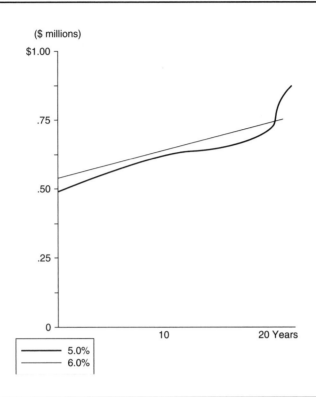

These graphs show that spending a lower percentage of market value results in a higher dollar level of spending over the long term. After 20 years, schools spending 5 percent will be able to spend more than those spending 6 percent.

Source: Reprinted, with permission, from Commonfund's *Endowment Planning Model*.

EXHIBIT 8.12 MEDIAN EXPECTED REAL SPENDING FROM ENDOWMENT ASSUMING 80 PERCENT/20 PERCENT POLICY AND DIFFERENT SPENDING RATES

We shall elaborate on all but the last two of these diversification approaches in the following sections.

(i) Diversification by Investment Type or Asset Class. Diversification by type or asset class in simplest terms refers to investing in stocks, bonds, and short-term securities. Investment managers choose to invest in assets from different classes, based on their style. Examples of asset class categories relevant to long-term investors are: cash (even endowment funds hold some cash, including proceeds from recent sales awaiting reinvestment), equities, bonds, real estate, and venture capital.

The latter two ways that we listed for diversifying portfolios, small cap versus large cap and emerging markets, are variants on this same theme. Some analysts consider small cap and large cap (and even mid cap) as different invest-

Asset Class	1926–2005	1966–2005
Treasury bills	3.75%	5.98%
Treasury bonds	5.68	8.17
World bonds	6.14	9.40
U.S. large stocks	12.15	11.64
U.S. small stocks	17.95	14.98
World large stocks	11.46	12.12
Inflation (CPI)	3.13	4.70

Source: Figures compiled from data presented in Zvi
Bodie, Alex Kane, and Alan J. Marcus, *Investments*, 7th Ed.
(Boston, McGraw-Hill Irwin, 2008), pp. 132, 146.

EXHIBIT 8.13 HISTORICAL RETURN BY ASSET CLASS

ment types, and other analysts see this as another way to split out manager style (which we shall address shortly). Many analysts consider emerging markets to be a separate asset class, or perhaps consider emerging markets stock or emerging markets bonds to be one of the important alternative assets from which to select.

It is important for the financial manager in the nonprofit organization to be aware that these various aspects of the professional investment discipline exist and are considered in the development and implementation of an investment program for the nonprofit organization.

(ii) Diversification by Manager Styles and Single versus Multiple Manager. As mentioned, professional investment managers have different styles. In this context, "style" refers to the approach used by the investment manager to select securities for investment. "Style" refers to the stocks that an investor picks and the process by which he or she decides to choose specific stocks. Two important but different styles of management are value and growth. Each style is successful at various times and tends to move in and out of favor. Subcategories of these two major styles further describe how the manager makes investment choices.

The investment policy and guidelines should spell out who will manage the investment portfolio. Will the portfolio be managed in house, by external professional money managers, or by a combination of both? If external money managers are engaged, will there be one or more than one? Generally, the multiple-manager approach is the most effective because it provides a number of investment-style options. However, too many managers and duplication of styles should be avoided because they are difficult to administer and expensive. One advantage of a single manager is that the investment committee can delegate asset allocation decisions. The multiple-manager approach is more demanding on the investment committee. If more than one professional manager is hired, it must be determined what style of manager is to be hired. Consultants are available to assist in identifying styles and to report historical performance of the manager.

(iii) Diversification by Type of Issuer. Four basic forms of debt issuers are: (1) governments, (2) banks, (3) industrial companies, and (4) finance companies. Presumably, the banking industry could become severely stressed, with all banks as a group suffering in credit quality. This condition probably would affect other companies functioning in the economy, but it can be assumed that the other companies would not be as directly affected as the banks. Industrial companies as a group could be impacted by a recession; the finance companies that support their sales would not be as affected, because their portfolios of receivables are very broadly based. These examples indicate that diversification by type of issuer makes sense. However, some investors erroneously believe in diversification by type of instrument. The instruments are irrelevant if they are all guaranteed by the same type of issuer.

(iv) Diversification by Industry Sector. Industry is divided into sectors, such as utilities, technology, and manufacturing. There is some overlap possible here with issuer type diversification, as financial services are a key industry sector for many investors. During periods when interest rates are trending up or down, financial services stocks and bonds become a key component to add or avoid.

(v) Diversification by Geography. Most investors attempt to maintain a geographical dimension to their portfolio diversification. Many factors influence the world's economies, including economic policies and differentials in interest rates between countries. Investments of nonprofit institutions in debt instruments issued by both U.S. and foreign companies and banks should not present a problem. However, quite often, debt instruments issued by a particular bank or company will offer both higher yields and very good credit quality. The institution should exercise care in preventing its portfolio from being dominated by instruments of one country or one industry, or of several countries closely related to each other. Events could occur within a country or industry that would adversely affect investments. Civil war, severe inflation resulting in economic chaos, a natural disaster, or sudden political instability can wreak havoc on an institution's portfolio that is not well diversified. Investing guidelines should place a dollar or percentage limit, or both, on the portion of a portfolio that may be invested in the securities of any one country, region, or industry.

(vi) Diversification by Time. The idea when diversifying by time is to spread the investment portfolio across various maturity sectors. This is particularly applicable to fixed income (debt) portfolios. Some money will be held as "cash" (probably in a money fund), some in one-year or two-year notes, and some in longer maturities.

The concept of "laddering" a portfolio to hedge against interest rate risk is one implementation of time diversification. If one ladders with one-year, two-year, three-year, four-year, and five-year securities, as each year passes the one-year securities mature and each other maturity "bucket" is now one year shorter in current, or remaining, maturity. The investor would replace the maturing one-year securities with new five-year maturities.

(vii) Diversification by Global (Foreign) Investing. Global investing for the U.S. investor means adding foreign stocks to a domestic-only portfolio. We are living in an increasingly global society, and new markets are rapidly evolving around the world. In 1980, the U.S. stock market represented more than one-half of the world's stock market value; now it represents less than 40 percent as foreign stocks outperform U.S. stocks and as new markets emerge around the world. The U.S. stock market value of $17.4 trillion is still easily the largest in the world. However, with Japan's market value of $4.8 trillion, Hong Kong's $2.1 trillion market value, and China's market value now over $1 trillion, just the latter three countries alone now have market values that are almost half of that of the U.S. market.[9] Clearly, the U.S. dominance of worldwide markets is less significant than in past years.

Global investing allows access to these growth and income prospects. When the U.S. economy is struggling, the foreign markets in England, Japan, Germany, and other countries may provide good investment opportunities. Foreign stocks and bonds provide a way to further diversify your investment portfolio. Portfolio studies indicate that the investor including non-U.S. stocks outperforms the domestic-only investor in return-risk terms: Either a higher return may be earned with the same risk, or less risk need be borne for the same return.

(f) INVESTMENT TIME HORIZON. A long-term investment perspective tends to reduce investment risk. This is especially so for equity investments: The chance of losing money in any given year is relatively high, but for a twenty-year period the chance of losing money in the stock market is extremely low. Volatility is reduced when assets are held over longer time periods and yet returns can be enhanced.

(i) Risk Tolerance. Risk management involves assessing the potential for loss under any circumstances. Risk is managed by implementing sound internal controls and procedures as well as monitoring external managers' controls, monitoring compliance with the investment guidelines for the organization, engaging in due diligence and manager oversight, and reviewing performance.

Controlling the risk of an investment portfolio involves allocating the investment among small and large company stock and domestic and foreign company stock to participate in both the growth and value styles of investing. Many investment managers now calculate "Value at Risk" (VaR) for a portfolio. The VaR is the amount that we should expect to lose at a minimum 5% of the time. In other words, it gives us a dollar amount that we might reasonably expect to lose in a scenario that should only happen 1/20 of the periods over which we invest money in this portfolio.

Asset quality can be determined by consulting asset quality ratings assigned by well-respected agencies such as Standard & Poor's, Moody's, and others. A list of generally accepted rating agencies is provided in Exhibit 7.1. Two measures of risk are volatility and duration.

(ii) Volatility. Volatility is the characteristic of a security or market to rise or fall sharply in price within a short period of time. Volatility is typically measured by standard deviation, which gives a greater weight to large changes up or down. As just noted, portfolio managers and analysts are beginning to look more at VaR as a supplemental risk measure. A major reason for this is that returns are not normally distributed, that is, they do not follow the symmetrical bell-shaped curve. VaR accounts for the lack of symmetry in the return distributions.

(iii) Duration. Duration is a concept that measures bond price volatility by the length or time period of a bond. Longer-maturity bonds have more price volatility when market interest rates move up or down, but bonds with higher coupon rates move less than those with lower coupon rates. Duration brings a bond's maturity and payment timing together in one measure of risk that works well for small changes in market interest rates.

(g) MANAGING RISK. Managing risk means assessing the loss under any circumstances, in light of the investor's risk tolerance. Managing risk is a critical factor in endowment management programs. A number of risk elements are involved in any endowment management program. Some key areas of internal and external risk to be managed and monitored include:

- People
- Partnership
- Financial
- Manager oversight
- Compliance with investment and guidelines
- Performance review
- Due diligence
- Communications risk
- Technology operations
- Policy and procedures
- Credit
- Interest rate
- Volatility
- Currency
- Legal
- Liquidity
- Accounting
- Concentration
- Capital

The successful nonprofit organization will perform a risk assessment survey in its own endowment management program to identify and reduce those risks before significant losses are incurred.

(h) MONITORING PERFORMANCE. Monitoring performance of the organization's endowment management program is essential. The next list will be useful in the development of such a performance monitoring program.

Your investment performance review program should:

- Compare the performance of your investment portfolio to comparable, acceptable benchmarks. See Exhibit 8.14.
- Compare investment returns with inflation rates.
- Compare investment returns with investment returns of the market in general.
- Compare investment returns with investment returns of similar investments.
- Compare investment returns with investment returns of competing investments.
- Compare investment returns with historical comparisons (see earlier Exhibit 8.13).
- Compare the cost of your investing to industry standards.
- Obtain an independent analysis of your program's investment performance.
- Quantify level of risk assumed relative to return.

8.6 ENDOWMENT SPENDING POLICY

Endowment spending policy is a unique component of endowment management that does not come into play in the nonprofit organization's other long-term investing programs. Endowment spending policy should not be confused with endowment investment policy. However, endowment investment policy includes endowment spending policy since the two are integrally related and must be compatible.

Endowment investment policy deals with issues related to how the investments are made, and spending policy addresses how much of the endowment income or return can be spent to support programs on an annual basis. Spending policy deals with issues such as:

- How should the current needs of the institution be weighed against its future needs?
- How much of the return from endowment funds should be spent and how much saved?

Examples of spending policy rates are:

- *Spend income only.* Spend only the current income (dividends and interest) earned on the endowed investment.
- *Spend total return.* The total return of a portfolio is the combination of interest, dividends, and other current earnings, plus capital appreciation

(or less capital depreciation) for the period. Thus, a fund utilizing the total-return approach may spend not only current investment income but also may use a portion of capital appreciation over time as part of its spending rate.

(a) ENDOWMENT INVESTMENT STRATEGY: A DISCUSSION.

The determination of investment strategy for endowment funds can be viewed as the resolution of creative tension existing between the demand for immediate income and the need for a growing stream of income to meet future needs.

Investment policy deals with issues such as: How to diversify? What level of risk is to be assumed in the investment portfolio? How can the investment

---

Equity

- DJIA
- DJ Global-U.S.
- DJ Global-World
- S&P 500
- NASDAQ Comp.
- London (FT 100)
- Tokyo (Nikkei 225)
- Small-Co: Index Fund
- Lipper Index: Europe
- Barra
- Russell 1000, 2000, 3000
- Morgan Stanley World Index
- MSCI EAFE (Europe, Asia, and the Far East)

Fixed Income

- Lehman Brothers Universal Bond Index, Aggregate Bond Index
- Salomon Mortgage-Backed
- Bond Buyer Municipal (tax-exempt clients)
- Merrill Lynch Corporate and Government Bond Indices
- Lipper L-T Government
- iMoneyNet's First-Tier Institutional-Only Rated Money Fund Report Averages-Index (MFR Index)
- Consumer Price Index (Inflation measure to compare or measure objective of preserving purchasing power)

Others

- Commodity Research Bureau (CRB) Index
- Goldman Sachs Commodity Index

Source: Reproduced, with permission, *1996 NES Executive Summary*, © 1996 by National Association of College and University Business Officers.

EXHIBIT 8.14 INDICES USED AS BENCHMARKS FOR COMPARING INVESTMENT PERFORMANCE EQUITY

focus change from income to total return? How can the focus be shifted from the performance of the individual investment to the performance of the total portfolio? How can new investment opportunities, such as venture capital and emerging markets, be incorporated into the portfolio? How can new delegations of authority and responsibility be used in managing the endowment investment portfolio?

Spending policy deals with issues such as: How should the current needs of the nonprofit organization be weighed against its needs in the future? How much of the return from endowment funds should be spent and how much saved?

(b) INVESTMENT POLICY. The current investment policy of some nonprofit organizations is one of total return; specifically, to maximize real, long-term total return and to preserve capital and the purchasing power of endowed projects. The spending policy, however, is to spend income only. Thus, the investment policy is to invest for total return (income plus capital appreciation), with the spending policy being to pay only current income earned (excluding any realized capital gain) during the period.

The investment management world has changed dramatically in the past few decades. The UMIFA and UPMIFA allow governing boards to operate according to principles that take full advantage of available investment vehicles. Important developments in the field include expansion of the "prudent man" rule, introduction of portfolio theory, new investment opportunities, and delegation of investment decisions.

Current investment strategy generally indicates that diversification pays, risk should be judged in the context of the total portfolio, and investment performance should be judged over the long term, not the short term.

Increasingly diverse asset classes are emerging that pay few or no dividends. The prospect for lower yields on fixed-income investments remains for the foreseeable future. Both of these trends mean that it will be difficult to maintain the income streams at their historic or current levels without changing asset mix or putting unnecessary constraints on investment selection.

This points to the need for endowment funds to have highly qualified and skilled professional managers who are not overly constrained. It is likewise important to develop a clearly defined plan of long-term investment strategy and to retain it despite other variable factors as long as the fundamental assumptions on which it is based can be shown to have continuing validity.

(c) SPENDING POLICY. Existing endowment funds are invested to return current income or yield (interest, dividends, and rents) and, usually, capital gains. A critical question is whether an institution contributes only its endowment yield, or a combination of its yield and gain, to the operating budget.

If the decision is to contribute only endowment yield, spendable income becomes a by-product of the investment policy. If an institution opts for the latter, it must adopt a "spending rule" that determines how yield and gain totals are allocated between the operating budget and endowment. The "spending rule" approach requires a considered choice between spending and saving.

Adoption of a total-return spending policy with a spending rule decouples investment decisions from spendable income decisions. Spending rules, however, add complexity and require strong discipline.

(d) TOTAL-RETURN SPENDING.   Many endowments have adopted a total-return approach to their spending policies. The total return of a portfolio is the combination of interest, dividends, and other current earnings, plus capital appreciation (or less capital depreciation) for the period. Thus, a fund utilizing the total-return approach may not only spend current investment income, but also may use a portion of capital appreciation over time as a part of its spending rate.

The investment community is aware of the Ford Foundation study on the total return spending approach during the late 1960s and the fact that many concepts introduced in that study have proven to be sound over time. This is evidenced by the results of the 1995 NACUBO study of trends in endowment management spending rules in colleges and universities, as cited in Exhibit 8.15.

Today many endowment governing boards use various approaches to set investment policies and establish a meaningful spending rate, and use a variety of formulas to incorporate these factors into a total rate of return approach. Funds using these techniques have benefited from the achievement of consistently above-average returns over time. In terms of the real objectives (inflation adjusted) of these funds, risk has been modified rather than significantly increased.

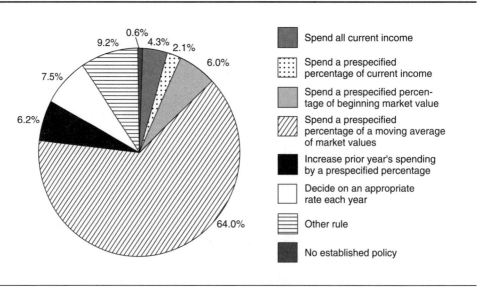

Source: Reproduced, with permission, *1995 NACUBO Endowment Study,* © 1995 by National Association of College and University Business Officers.

EXHIBIT 8.15   ENDOWMENT SPENDING RULES

(e) SPENDING RATES.   A number of formulas have been developed by different endowments to establish their total return objective, generally inclusive of the rate of inflation and a compatible maximum spending rate. Such formulas indicate how much of the total return may be used for the endowment's current needs as opposed to being reinvested. The spending rate can be viewed as a specific portion of the total return (e.g., 5 percentage points) applied to a moving average of asset values over any period desired (e.g., the past three years or five years).

The desired rate of return and spending rate require careful consideration and thought, although many endowments tend to pick these rates somewhat arbitrarily and to set them at levels too high to be justified by historical experience (see Exhibit 8.16). Over long periods of time, spending rates exceeding 5 percent ultimately result in erosion of the purchasing power of the principal, as the spending rate plus inflation begins to exceed actual rates of return.

Endowments with higher proportions invested in common stock have less risk in this regard because equities have historically provided higher returns than fixed-income securities over longer periods of time, but they also pay less current income.

(f) EFFECT OF INFLATION.   One problem facing all endowment fund managers is the requirement that funds must grow to compensate for inflation. Endowment funds depend on their returns on an ongoing, continuous basis. As seen in Exhibit 8.17, in endowment funds, asset classes do not always move together, and real estate can help protect returns against inflation.

Spending Rule	Participating Institutions Number	Percentage
Spend all current income	20	4.3
Spend a prespecified percentage of current income	10	2.1
Spend a prespecified percentage of beginning market value	28	6.0
Spend a prespecified percentage of a moving average of market values	299	64.0
Increase prior year's spending by a prespecified percentage	29	6.2
Decide on an appropriate rate each year	35	7.5
Other rule	43	9.2
No established policy	3	0.6
Total	467	100.0

Source: Reproduced, with permission, *1995 NACUBO Endowment Study*, © 1995 by National Association of College and University Business Officers.

EXHIBIT 8.16   SPENDING RULES FOR 1996

	S&P	U.S. Small Cap	Venture Capital	International Equity	Real Estate	U.S. Treasuries 1 yr.	U.S. Treasuries 5 yr.	U.S. Treasuries 20 yr.	International Bonds
S&P 500	1.00								
U.S. Small Cap	0.76	1.00							
Venture Capital	0.28	0.22	1.00						
International Equity	0.55	0.43	0.19	1.00					
Real Estate	0.24	-0.20	-0.04	-0.12	1.00				
1-Year U.S. Treasuries	0.07	-0.09	0.02	-0.01	0.38	1.00			
5-Year U.S. Treasuries	0.13	0.12	0.04	0.06	-0.23	-0.14	1.00		
20-Year U.S. Treasuries	0.06	0.06	0.00	0.01	-0.25	-0.32	0.88	1.00	
International Bonds	0.09	0.07	0.05	0.42	-0.12	-0.07	0.50	0.45	1.00
Inflation	-0.32	-0.26	-0.07	-0.19	0.52	0.42	-0.06	-0.02	-0.05

Source: Reprinted, with permission, from Commonfund's *Endowment Planning Model.*

EXHIBIT 8.17 CORRELATIONS AMONG SELECTED ASSET CLASSES AND INFLATION

(g) IMPLEMENTATION ISSUES WHEN SPENDING POLICY IS SET OR CHANGED.
If your nonprofit organization changes its spending policy from income only to total return, the next list below will help ensure that all related changes are also part of the implementation. This change presents a number of other challenges including:

- Review individual fund terms for all true endowments to determine spending requirements.
- Determine how much to spend, and establish a formula.
- Evaluate economic conditions, levels of risk, price-level trends, expected total return.
- Invest in more than just fixed-income securities.
- Set spending rules and rates.
- Make related policy changes.
- Review and respond to all legal and accounting issues.
- Change related procedures.
- Attend to detail of ongoing processing.
- Track the addition of new funds and contributions to existing funds to determine the base to be used for calculating total return.
- Increase levels of education, communication, and training for everyone involved.

(h) ENDOWMENT SPENDING POLICY SUMMARY. Endowment funds are a critical source of funding for nonprofit organizations. They are given by donors for a specific purpose and invested by the nonprofit organization through prudent investment policy to ensure that the purchasing power of the funds will exist in perpetuity. This responsibility is achieved by setting comprehensive investment strategy to govern the investment of endowment for the institution.

Two of the most important components of this investment strategy are investment policy and spending policy. Investment policy deals with issues such as diversification, level of risk, and investment focus. Spending policy deals with weighing present needs against future needs and determining how much endowment return should be spent and how much saved.

Some nonprofit organizations have a total-return investment policy and an income-only spending policy. This means that investments are made with a total-return objective (the sum of income earned, and realized and unrealized appreciation), while spending is limited to income only.

The policy to spend income only has been acceptable for some organizations, but like all policies, it should be periodically reviewed to make sure it is the best policy for the future. In the university setting, about three-fourths of institutions target their spending at approximately 5% of the most-recent three-year average of their endowment value. Illustrating, if a college had an endowment value of $150 million, $165 million, and $171 million for the most recent three years, the three-year average (called a three-year moving average) would be ($150

+ $165 + $171)/3 = $162 million. Multiply this by 0.05, and you find that this year's "payout" from the endowment fund would be $8.1 millon. Today many endowment boards use a total return investment approach and a preset spendable income target. Many of these funds have achieved consistently above-average rates of return over time and are well positioned for the future.

Some organizations have adopted a total-return spending policy with a spending rule to mitigate the effects of short-term market volatility on spending from endowment.

This policy change should be considered by nonprofit organizations, in part, to make it easier to fulfill their investment strategy for the endowment pool of total return through principal growth and consistent growth in income. With increasingly diverse asset classes developing in the market, it is more difficult to obtain both objectives. Equity investments that often have the best potential for principal growth may pay few or no dividends, making income growth difficult. In a falling or stable interest rate environment, fixed income instruments may not provide any significant level of income growth. Illustrating with an actual example, in an endowment that had 2.3 percent of the pool invested in emerging-market equities and venture-capital partnerships, two areas where the potential for significant principal growth was and continues to be very high, the current income generated was only 0.18 percent of market value (as compared to 2.66 percent of market value for domestic equities in that same period). A spendable income policy that spends a preset amount from income or capital appreciation should eliminate any potential conflict and not impede the investment strategy for the endowment pool.

Adoption of a total-return spending policy will increase flexibility for the nonprofit organization through the provision of:

- A stable and easily predictable source of funds to support its mission and programs
- Flexibility for the investment committee to consider a variety of investment vehicles without considering current yields or interest rates

A key consideration in setting the endowment spending policy is to determine the primary objective of your organization's endowment. Ultimately, the objective is a subset of your primary financial objective: Your organization's primary financial objective is to ensure that financial resources are available when needed (timing), as needed (amount), and at reasonable cost (cost-effectiveness), and that once mobilized, these resources are protected from impairment and spent according to mission and donor purposes. The focus of your endowment, and your endowment spending plan, should be to maximize the benefit of the endowment to the organization—not merely to do whatever necessary to maintain its value or even its inflation-adjusted value. There may be times when you are forced to dig into the corpus to help fund a building, meet a cash flow crunch, or another nonfinancial investment in your organization. For example, Stanford University increased its payout for two consecutive years to 6.75% (versus the normal 4.75%) because it faced temporary deficits linked to its research grants revenue stream. This increased payout allowed the operating budget to be reduced gradually to better match that revenue stream, rather than taking severe and disruptive spending cuts. More than one-half of colleges surveyed by Commonfund in its 2004 Benchmarks Study gave as their primary concern in managing endowments "provide a consistent and growing stream of income."[10]

(i) DEFINITIONS OF TERMS USED IN ENDOWMENT MANAGEMENT.   There are a number of key terms to master when it comes to endowments and long-term investment management. Below are some of the key terms.

- *Alternative equities.* Investments in emerging markets and venture capital partnerships, which are included in equity holdings
- *Asset allocation.* The distribution of endowment or investment pool assets among various asset classes (e.g., cash, equities, bonds, real estate, venture capital)
- *Average annual total return.* A hypothetical rate of return that, if achieved annually, would have produced the same cumulative total return if performance had been constant over the entire period (also called geometric return)
- *Diversification.* Participation in different asset classes in domestic and global financial markets
- *Efficient markets.* A theory that states that the market prices reflect the knowledge and expectation of all investors, and that prices and required returns adjust almost immediately to any new information that is relevant to the risk and return of securities
- *Endowment pool.* A group of endowment funds consolidated into one pool for purposes of investment
- *Hedging.* Strategy used to offset an investment risk; a perfect hedge is one eliminating the possibility of a gain or loss
- *Inflation rate.* Measured in terms of the Consumer Price Index (CPI) to reflect changes in the price of goods and services (the rate of inflation affects the purchasing power of endowments)[11]
- *Investment management fees.* Charges incurred for the external or internal management of assets
- *Investment policy.* The goal set by the board of trustees for its organization's investment return, as well as investment parameters
- *Large-cap stocks (large-capitalization stocks).* Usually have a market capitalization of $5 billion or more
- *Liquidity.* Ability to buy or sell an asset quickly, and in large volume, without affecting the asset's price (for an organization, refers to ability to meet ongoing needs for cash without undue cost)

- *Maintain purchasing power.* To maintain the purchasing power of endowment funds, the long-term total return of the invested endowment portfolio must be equal to, or greater than, the rate of inflation
- *Mid-cap stocks (middle-capitalization stocks).* Usually have a market capitalization (number of shares outstanding multiplied by the stock price) of from $500 million to $5 billion (although, for portfolio and account analysis, typically the "mid-cap" category is for stocks from $1 billion to $5 billion in market capitalization)
- *Quasi-endowment.* A type of endowment treated as permanent capital that functions like a true endowment and permits spending of principal and income as provided in the gift agreement or board designation
- *Small-cap stocks (small-capitalization stocks).* Usually have a market capitalization (number of shares outstanding multiplied by the stock price) of $500 million or less (and "micro-cap" might refer to stocks with a capitalization of $100 million or less)
- *Specialty-managers approach.* Use of multiple specialized investment managers to access different investment styles and varied investment strategies
- *Spending policy.* The guideline used by an institution to determine annual distributions from its endowment
- *Spending rate.* Expressed as a percentage of market value, it represents amounts withdrawn from an investment pool or endowment; distribution calculated as an annual rate; and may include earned income as well as net realized or unrealized gains
- *Total return.* Gain or loss plus income generated
- *True endowment.* Assets donated to provide permanent financial support to designated activities of the nonprofit organization; consists of permanent capital and an ongoing stream of current cash; intended to support a program or activity in perpetuity
- *Yield.* The rate of income earned on invested assets calculated as a percentage of total market value; consists of interest and dividend income earned from cash, money market, bond, stock, or mutual fund holdings

8.7 SELF-INSURANCE AND PENSIONS

(a) SELF-INSURANCE. Whether it is for self-insuring health or employee life insurance, or some other possible financial commitment in the future, some nonprofits invest funds long-term to provide coverage for these obligations. The principles of investing are the same as for endowments, but the annual draws are not usually an issue. Rather, one must be careful to match investment cash flows (amount and timing) to the sometimes uncertain future liability. It is for this reason that many nonprofits prefer to outsource these obligations through employee purchase of insurance policies (with possible organizational provision of part of the premiums).

(b) PENSIONS.   Only the largest nonprofits would consider doing the retirement account set-up and investing for employee retirement accounts. Most businesses have moved away from traditional pension plans, in which a defined benefit was promised to employees who remained with the firms for a set number of years. Most organizations now contribute, perhaps on a matching basis, to the employee's 401k (or for a charity, 403b) plan, and the defined contribution keeps the organization from having to guarantee a set dollar amount benefit to the retiree.

(c) INVESTMENT POLICY STATEMENT FOR PENSIONS.   Because of the rarity of traditional pensions, we offer minimal coverage of pension investing and the differences in investment policy occasioned by this type of investment account. In Appendix 8 C we include an investment policy statement checklist for ERISA Section 404(c) plans that has been compiled by Benefit Resources, Inc.

(d) UNIFORM PRUDENT INVESTOR ACT (UPIA).   While UMIFA governs the management of investment assets held by charitable organizations, the Uniform Prudent Investors Act (UPIA) provides the state standard of care that applies to most charitable trusts. The trustee must invest and manage trust assets as a prudent investor would—meaning that the trustee must exercise reasonable caution, skill, and care. We include as Appendix 8D a brief synopsis of this act. The entire text of UPIA is available online.[12]

8.8 INVESTMENT ADVISORS

(a) PROFESSIONAL INVESTMENT ADVISORS.   Because of other duties, the non-profit organization's financial manager may find the operation, supervision, and management of the institution's investment portfolio unduly burdensome. Proper investment management requires hands-on experience in the securities market-place. It is also necessary to maintain complete records that account for portfolio transactions, provide reports, stay abreast of changes and trends in the securities markets, and continually remain within the bounds prescribed by the organization's investing guidelines and the overall context of an investing strategy.

These responsibilities may be impossible for the nonprofit organization's financial manager to handle along with other duties. Therefore, many financial managers turn to outside professional investment advisors for assistance in managing their organizations' investment portfolios. Professional advisors with the necessary qualifications and investment expertise constitute a useful resource for the institution.

(b) REASONS FOR USING OUTSIDE INVESTMENT ADVISORS.   Outside investment advisors are used by organizations with portfolios of all sizes. One major reason for employing an outside investment advisor is the organization's lack of a sufficiently large portfolio to support a full-time, in-house investment manager and the research and information services needed for an in-house investment manager to function properly. Often institutions with small portfolios are in the greatest need of outside advisors. With the small portfolio, the financial manager probably is not attuned to the fast-paced securities markets. Consequently, the overall knowledge of markets and investment securities is at a relatively low level, and the financial manager can easily make a mistake that would cost the organization dearly.

Another occasion for using an outside investment advisor is a large portfolio that is not permanent. This impermanence effectively prevents the investor from hiring permanent staff to manage the portfolio and makes it desirable to retain outside professional investment management. When the investment funds are no longer available, the relationship with the investment advisor can be terminated.

Professional investment advisors outside the institution can be particularly helpful in monitoring investment changes and trends in the marketplace. Competent advisors usually can enhance the profitability of the institution's portfolio sufficiently to offset their fee. The advisor provides an additional service by reducing the risk of loss due to inadequate evaluation of risk, as well as reducing the risk of loss of employment by the financial manager when principal losses occur. The financial manager also has more time available for other responsibilities.

(c) TYPES OF OUTSIDE INVESTMENT ADVISORS.   Two types of outside professional investment advisors work with financial managers in handling investment portfolios: investment managers and investment consultants. Investment manager services range from simple advisory consultation (with no authority to manage investments) to full management control over investment activities. The latter use their own discretion in the selection of particular instruments within client-approved guidelines. Investment managers often specialize in one investment area, such as stocks or fixed-income instruments, as well as other specifics, such as in equities emerging growth-type issues, global, and capitalization (see Exhibits 8.18 and 8.19). Within the fixed-income arena, they may

Equity	*Balanced*
• Capital Appreciation	• Stock/Bond Blend
• Growth	*Fixed Income*
• Small Company	• Short-Term Debt
• Mid-Cap Stock	• Intermediate Corporation Debt
• Growth and Income	• Intermediate Government
• Equity Income	• Long-Term Corporation
• Global (including U.S.)	• High-Yield Taxable
• International (non-U.S.)	• Mortgage Bond
	• World Income

EXHIBIT 8.18   TRADITIONAL ASSET CLASSES—EXAMPLES OF VARIOUS GENERAL INVESTMENT MANAGER SPECIALTIES BY INVESTMENT OBJECTIVE

Market Neutral

- U.S. Convertible/Warrant Hedging
- Japanese Convertible/Warrant Hedging
- European Convertible/Marrant Hedging
- Statistical Arbitrage—Global
- Fixed-Income Arbitrage—Global
- Long/Short
- Long/Short Japan
- Long/Short Utilities
- Closed-End Fund Arbitrage
- Pairs Trading
- Emerging Market Debt

Event Drivers

- Distressed Debt
- Capital Structure Arbitrage
- Merger Arbitrage
- Distressed Mortgages
- Niche Financing
- Mezzanine
- Bank Debt

Hedge Funds

- Global Long/Short
- Regional and Country Funds
- Sector Funds
  - Technology
  - Energy
  - Banking
  - Healthcare
  - Natural Resources
- Macro Trading
- Day Trading
- Commodities
- Emerging-Market Equities
- Emerging-Market Debt

Private Investments

- Venture Capital
- Buyout Funds
- Real Estate
- Distressed
- Sector Funds
- Emerging Markets
- International
- Regulation D
- SBIC/Mezzanine

EXHIBIT 8.19 Nontraditional Asset Classes

Callan Associates Inc 101 California Street, Suite 3500 San Francisco, CA 94111 4159745060	**UBS*** 1 North Wacker Drive Chicago IL 60606 3125255000
Cambridge Associates 2001 Ross Avenue, Suite 3155 Dallas, Texas 75201 2144682800	**SEI Investments*** SEI Investments Co. 1 Freedom Valley Drive Oaks, PA 19456
Canterbury Consulting 660 Newport Center Drive, Suite 300 Newport Beach, CA 92660 8008884551	6106761000 **Watson Wyatt Investment Consulting** One Ravinia Drive Suite 1300
Federated Investors, Inc.* The Federated Funds ATTN: FTR Financial P.O. Box 8602 Boston, MA 02266-8602 8002454270	Atlanta, GA 30346-2128 7702908500 **Wilshire Asociates** 1299 Ocean Avenue, Suite 700 Santa Monica, CA 90401 3104513051
Frank Russell Company 909 A Street Tacoma, WA 98402 2535729500	**Wurts and Associates** 999 Third Avenue, Suite 3650 Seattle, Washington 98104 2066223700
Hewitt Associates 100 Half Day Road Lincolnshire, IL 60069 8472955000	**Yanni Bilkey** 310 Grant Street, Suite 3000 Pittsburgh, PA 15219 4122321000
* Also invests client funds.	

EXHIBIT 8.20 REPRESENTATIVE LIST OF INVESTMENT CONSULTING FIRMS

specialize in short-, intermediate-, or long-term maturities. Generally, institutions seek investment managers who specialize in short- to intermediate-term maturities of fixed-income securities for their working cash investments and stock and long-term bond managers for their endowment or growth-type portfolios.

Investment consultants (see Exhibit 8.20), however, do not manage funds; rather, they assist the financial manager by reviewing the institution's investment objectives and other investment needs and searching for a suitable investment advisor/manager in the marketplace who appears qualified to fill those needs. Investment consultants are not only instrumental in selecting an outside investment manager, but they also may help to develop the investing guidelines, monitor the investment advisor's performance, periodically review current strategies, and make recommendations for adjustments in any of these areas.

(d) SELECTING AN OUTSIDE INVESTMENT MANAGER.   The selection process for an investment manager should include careful attention to all appropriate details. Frequently, an investment consultant is enlisted to assist in the selection, as already mentioned. The process begins with the consultant's review of existing guidelines to ensure that they adequately address the client's investing objectives and provide the necessary amount of flexibility. For example, it hardly would be worthwhile to retain an investment manager if the guidelines restricted the portfolio to U.S. Treasury bills maturing in 90 days or less.

When a well-crafted set of investing guidelines is in hand, the consultant searches a proprietary database of investment managers to identify those who appear to meet the criteria for the type of investments, credit quality, and maturity required by the investor. After reviewing the results of the initial search, the consultant identifies three to five of the most attractive candidates. If a consultant is not used, the institution's financial manager prepares a request for proposal (RFP) describing the nature and size of the portfolio, the investment objectives and existing guidelines, and the requirements for the investment manager. The RFP should also describe any unusual features or requirements pertaining to operation of the portfolio. Refer to Appendix 7D for help in crafting a questionaire. Investment managers have widely varying approaches to the management of funds; the institution's financial manager will want assurance that the investment manager will use compatible methods of operation, goals, and objectives. These candidates are then brought to the investor's designated representative to make the final selection. These representatives are usually a committee of the board of trustees, such as the investment subcommittee or the finance committee.

After receiving written proposals from the top candidates, the consultant and the financial manager, as representatives of the investor, conduct in-person interviews. Each candidate is given an opportunity to discuss past performance and method of operation and to respond directly to the investor's questions. The interview process should include discussion of investing goals and differing assumptions and criteria on which they are based. There usually is more than one way to state an investing goal; experienced investment managers often provide guidance in this area. In any event, the investment manager must fully understand and accept the investor's goals before a meeting of the minds can occur.

Other important considerations are brought to the surface through the candidates' formal proposals and the interviews:

- The candidate's willingness to engage in discussion, to demonstrate flexibility regarding the client's investing program, and to use the client's own investing guidelines
- Other clients of the investment manager with similar investing goals and guidelines
- The investor's portfolio size in comparison with the portfolios of the investment manager's other clients

- The registration of the investment manager with the U.S. Securities and Exchange Commission (SEC), under the Investment Advisors Act of 1940, and with the state of the investment manager's domicile
- Performance history of the manager, calculated in compliance with Association for Investment Management and Research (AIMR) rules (now administered by the CFA Institute, as AIMR has changed its name recently to CFA Institute; see www.cfainstitute.org), over at least the past three years, which should then be compared to a benchmark, such as an index (see Exhibit 8.14), for a comparable period
- Any past censures by the SEC or other regulatory authority of the investment management firm or its principals for misconduct
- The turnover rate among the investment management firm's portfolio managers, key support staff, and supervisory personnel
- The experience and background of the investment management firm's principals and portfolio managers
- The ease with which the client may communicate directly with the investment management firm's portfolio manager
- The use of a written investment management contract and the inclusion of these four elements:

  1. Clear description of how fees are calculated
  2. Additional charges above the basic fee
  3. Reasons for termination of the contract by either the client or the investment manager
  4. Capabilities of the investment manager to handle the type of portfolio involved

- Computerized information and analytical resources, and the specific credit review services that are used
- The format and frequency of reports, and the investment manager's ability to customize reports to meet the investor's particular needs

When the investment manager is selected, the institution may retain the consultant to provide assistance in reviewing the manager's performance.

(e) COMPENSATING OUTSIDE INVESTMENT ADVISORS.   Investment managers usually receive compensation based on the size of the portfolio that they manage. Investment advisors typically are compensated with a flat fee, which may be made in either soft dollars or hard dollars.

Soft-dollar compensation is when the investment advisor directs the commissions generated by the execution of investment transactions to the consultant. Payment via soft dollars superficially saves the investor from paying the additional consultant's fee; however, the use of soft-dollar compensation can discourage the investment manager from seeking the most competitive prices on the execution of transactions. Instead, the investment manager may seek to execute transactions where soft-dollar compensation is available rather than where the best prices are obtainable. The investor may wish to confirm the investment manager is obtaining a competitive execution, thereby minimizing transaction costs.

There are two principal aspects to the evaluation of an investment manager's fee:

1. The fee should be competitive with those of other qualified investment managers dealing with similar investment instruments and maturities.
2. The fee should not exceed the cost of establishing the investment management function internally with an acceptable level of sophistication and quality.

Summary of Criteria for Reviewing Investment Managers

Organization

- Experience of firm
- Assets under management
- Ownership
- Number of professionals; turnover
- Fee and minimum account size

Performance

- One-, three-, or five-year comparisons
- Up/down market comparisons
- Risk/return graphs

Skill set analysis

- Sector diversification
- Security selection
- Security consideration
- Market timing

Securities Summary

- Equities
- Bonds
- Other

(f) WORKING WITH AN INVESTMENT MANAGER. The investment manager should become familiar with the objectives, liquidity requirements, and relative risk-aversion tendencies of the institution's financial and administrative managers. After meeting with the institution's managers, the investment manager should review the existing investing guidelines. If they do not appear adequate or sufficiently comprehensive, the investment manager should propose revisions.

In addition to refining the investing guidelines, the investment manager should assist in developing operating arrangements necessary to execute investment transactions and facilitate delivery of investment management and advisory services to the client. In this process, the investment custodian must be selected for the safekeeping of securities, and appropriate documentation must be executed authorizing the investment manager to conduct business with securities dealers and the custodian. Finally, regular contacts with the client institution's financial staff must be established, including a meeting schedule for regular review of the investment manager's performance, usually quarterly.

With all these details handled, the nonprofit organization's financial manager will be able to use a structured, methodical, full-time, and professional approach to the task of managing the institution's investment portfolio. The financial manager thereby assumes the role of overseeing the investment manager and becomes insulated from the minutiae of daily investment tasks.

(g) INVESTMENT ADVISORS SUMMARY.   Developing an investment program for the short- and long-term portfolios of an institution has many facets, including managing the funds to meet their respective objectives and purposes and providing a meaningful forecast of receipts and disbursements of funds. The latter enables estimations regarding the size of the remaining pool of funds and the time horizon for its availability. When the physical aspects of the investment portfolio are determined, management can begin to develop a strategy for investing the funds to meet goals and maintain appropriate levels of liquidity and risk/return. Finally, the organization must develop an operating plan for executing, verifying, and settling transactions and ensuring the safety of instruments held in the portfolio.

Unfortunately, many financial managers begin investing surplus funds without giving conscious thought to each of these elements. Too often the absence of a well-thought-out and structured program leads to losses caused by either acute sloppiness or by working with unscrupulous investment dealers who take advantage of an unsuspecting investor.

Many sources of investment advice, advisors, and managers are available to assist financial managers in developing an informed approach to investing. Operation of an investment portfolio requires careful attention to the details of executing investment transactions and monitoring the resulting inventories. A feasible approach may use the services of an outside professional investment advisor to guide the institution through the thicket of details or to manage the investments according to the institution's investing policy and guidelines. After a review of the investment information, the financial manager will be better able to decide whether to manage funds internally or to seek the assistance of an outside professional.

One of the jobs performed by investment bankers and securities underwriters is devising new and different investment instruments in response to changing investor needs and demands. In many cases, the creativity of investment bankers has worked to the benefit of institutional investors. At the same time, however, many innovative instruments have caused more problems than they have solved. Collateralized mortgage obligations (CMOs), for example, were designed to solve the problems inherent in the repayment of principal and interest in mortgage-backed securities. However, CMOs have their own set of disadvantages. A well-informed, educated investor should be aware of the characteristics and risks of an instrument before a purchase is made.

Accordingly, financial managers must weigh all the possible problems of new and unusual securities. Such securities often have yield advantages over other types, but frequently the yield advantages are compromised for three reasons:

1. The accounting effort to maintain the securities in an investment portfolio is costly.
2. Interest income is lost because principal is not repaid on time.
3. Most new instrument types have limited initial market activity. Therefore, a weak market can destroy the liquidity and further adversely affect the market price of the instruments, reducing the additional income paid if they must be sold.

Financial managers should examine all the consequences of investing in new and exotic instruments, estimate any yield problems, and weigh the problems against the benefits before buying the instruments.

8.9 SUMMARY

In this chapter we covered the basics of endowment fund investing, using that as our template for all long-term investing that your organization might engage in. We noted the importance of an investment policy statement, the rarity of in-house endowment management, the increasing use of alternative asset classes, the importance of diversification and modern portfolio theory, and some recent statistics on college and university endowment management.

In our chapter appendixes we include coverage of UMIFA (Appendix 8A), three sample investment policies (8B, 8C, and 8E), coverage of UPIA (8D), and a primer on Modern Portfolio Theory (8F). We believe that Chapter 7 and Chapter 8, taken together, will provide you with a sound underpinning for your understanding of nonprofit investment management.

Notes

1. Dan Busby, "Endowment Gifts: How to Effectively Handle Them," *Faithful Finances* (September 2002), p. 5.
2. As of the time of this writing, the only states that have not adopted UMIFA in whole or in part are Alaska and Pennsylvania.
3. The entire UMIFA text is available online at: http://www.law.upenn.edu/bll/ulc/fnact99/1970s/umifa72.pdf.

4. Richard T. Cassidy, Esq., "National Law Conference of Commissioners on Uniform State Laws Concludes 115th Annual Meeting," *The Vermont Bar Journal* (Fall 2006), 1-2.

5. From National Conference Of Commissioners On Uniform State Laws, "Uniform Prudent Management Of Institutional Funds Act," 2006. Accessed online at: http://www.nccusl.org/Update/Docs/Finals_NC/UPMIFA_Final_NC.doc. Accessed on 1/13/2007.

6. Ecclesiastes 11:2 (New American Standard Bible) from the wisdom literature of the Bible.

7. Gary P. Brinson, Randolph L. Hood, and Gilbert L. Beebower, "Determinants of Portfolio Performance," *Financial Analysts Journal* (July–August 1986).

8. William F. Sharpe, "Asset Allocation: Management Style and Performance Measurement," *Journal of Portfolio Management* (Winter 1992).

9. Data is from www.bloomberg.com (Emerging Markets page). Accessed: 1/13/2007.

10. A persuasive advocate for this approach to endowment spending is Paul Goldstein, director of financial and strategic studies at Stanford University. See his thoughts in Perry Mehrling, Paul Goldstein, and Verne Sedlacek, "Endowment Spending: Goals, Rates, and Rules," in Maureen E. Devlin, ed., *Forum Futures 2005, Exploring the Future of Higher Education* (Boulder, CO: Educause Forum for the Future of Higher Education, 2005), 27–32.

11. For more on the CPI and other inflation measures, see http://www.federalreserve.gov/generalinfo/faq/faqei.htm. For the most current level as well as historical CPI data, see http://www.bls.gov/news.release/cpi.toc.htm.

12. The entire text of UPIA is available online at: http://www.law.upenn.edu/bll/ulc/fnact99/1990s/upia94.pdf.

UNIFORM MANAGEMENT OF INSTITUTIONAL FUNDS ACT

Bill Summary & Status for the 93rd Congress
H.R. 12196
SPONSOR: Rep Fauntroy, (introduced 1/22/74)

- SHORT TITLE(S) AS INTRODUCED:
  Uniform Management of Institutional Funds Act

- OFFICAL TITLE AS INTRODUCED:
  A bill to adopt for the District of Columbia the Uniform Management of Institutional Funds Act, and for other purposes.

- STATUS: Floor Actions
  1/22/74 Referred to House Committee on the District of Columbia

- COMMITTEE(S) OF REFERRAL:
  House District of Columbia

- INDEX TERMS:
  District of Columbia

DIGEST:
(AS INTRODUCED)

Uniform Management of Institutional Funds Act—States that the governing board may appropriate for expenditure for the uses and purposes for which an endowment fund is established so much of the net appreciation, realized and unrealized, in the fair value of the assets of an endowment fund over the historic dollar value of the fund as is prudent under the standard established by this Act/except when the applicable gift instrument indicates the donor's intention that net appreciation shall not be expended.

Provides that the governing board, subject to any specific limitations set forth in the applicable gift instrument or low, may (1) invest and re-invest an institutional fund in any real or personal property deemed advisable by the governing board; (2) retain property contributed by a donor to an institutional kind for as long as the governing board deems advisable; (3) include all or any part of an institutional fund in any pooled or common fund maintained by the institution; and (4) invest all or any part of an institutional fund in any other pooled or common fund available for investment.

States that, with the written consent of the donor, the governing board may release, in whole or in part, a restriction imposed by the applicable gift instrument on the use or investment of an institutional fund.

SAMPLE INVESTMENT POLICY STATEMENT FOR THE ABC FOUNDATION'S LONG-TERM ENDOWMENT POOL

The purpose of the ABC Foundation's endowment is to support the educational mission of the ABC University by providing a reliable source of funds for current and future use. Investment of the endowment is the responsibility of the Investment Committee (Committee). The Committee establishes investment objectives, defines policies, sets asset allocation, selects managers, and monitors the implementation and performance of the Foundation's investment program. The Committee is supported by the office of the vice president–finance, which analyzes investment policies and management strategies, makes recommendations to the Investment Committee, and supervises day-to-day operations and investment activities.

STATEMENT OF INVESTMENT OBJECTIVES

The endowment will seek to maximize long-term total returns consistent with prudent levels of risk. Investment returns are expected to preserve or enhance the real value of the endowment to provide adequate funds to sufficiently support designated university activities. The endowment's portfolio is expected to generate a total annualized rate of return, net of fees, and 5 percent greater than the rate of inflation over a rolling five-year period.

The foundation's spending policy governs the rate at which funds are released to fund holders for their current spending. The foundation's spending policy will be based on a target rate set as a percentage of market value. This rate will be reviewed annually by the Investment Committee. The spending target rate is 5 percent for Fiscal Year 2007–2008.

ASSET ALLOCATION

To ensure real returns sufficient to meet the investment objectives, the endowment portfolio will be invested with these target allocations in either domestic or global securities:

	Minimum	Target	Maximum
	(%)	(%)	(%)
Fixed income	30	35	40
Equities	60	65	70

The Investment Committee may appoint equity and fixed-income managers, or select pooled investments, when appropriate. It is the overall objective to be 100 percent invested in equities and fixed income. If at any time the equity manager determines it is prudent to be invested at less than 80 percent, the Committee shall be notified. Equity managers may invest cash positions in marketable, fixed-income securities with maturities not to exceed one year. Quality rating should be prime or investment grade, as rated by Standard & Poor's and Moody's for commercial paper, and for certificates of deposit, an A or higher rating by Standard & Poor's. The managers are expected to reasonably diversify holdings consistent with prudent levels of risk.

At the discretion of the Committee, the endowment portfolio will be rebalanced annually to target allocations as opportunities permit.

GUIDELINES FOR THE SELECTION OF FIXED-INCOME SECURITIES

DIVERSIFICATION.   Except for the U.S. government, its agencies or instrumentalities, no more than 5 percent of the fixed-income portfolio at cost, or 8 percent at market value, shall be invested in any one single guarantor, issuer, or pool of assets. In addition, managers are expected to exercise prudence in diversifying by sector or industry.

QUALITY.   All bonds must be rated investment grade (BBB/Baa or better) by at least one of these rating services: Standard & Poor's or Moody's. Bonds not receiving a rating may be purchased under these circumstances:

- The issue is guaranteed by the U.S. government, its agencies or instrumentalities.
- Other comparable debt of the issuer is rated investment grade by Standard & Poor's or Moody's.

The average quality rating of the total fixed-income portfolio must be A or better. Securities downgraded in credit-quality rating subsequent to purchase, resulting in the violation of the policy guidelines, may be held at the manager's discretion. This is subject to immediate notification to the Investment Committee of such a change in rating.

DURATION At the time of purchase, the average duration of the bond pool should be no longer than the average duration of the current Merrill Lynch 3–5-Year Treasury Index plus one year.

GUIDELINES FOR SELECTION OF EQUITIES

DIVERSIFICATION FOR EACH MANAGER. No more than 5 percent at cost, and 10 percent at market value, shall be invested in any one company. In addition, managers are expected to exercise prudence in diversifying by sector or industry.

PERFORMANCE

Performance of the endowment and its component asset classes will be measured against benchmark returns of comparable portfolios in this way:

Total Endowment	SEI Balanced Median Plan; Merrill Lynch Balanced Universe
Domestic Equities	S&P 500 Index; Russell 2000 Index;
Global Equities	MSCI World Index
Fixed Income	Merrill Lynch 3–5-Year Treasury Index

At least annually, the Investment Committee will conduct performance evaluations at the total endowment, asset class, and individual manager levels. At the total endowment level, the Committee will analyze results relative to the objectives, the real rate of return, and composite indices. Further, investment results will be reviewed relative to the effects of policy decisions and the impact of deviations from policy allocations.

On the asset class and individual manager levels, results will be evaluated relative to benchmarks assigned to investment managers or pooled investments selected. These benchmarks are a vital element in the evaluation of individual and aggregate manager performance within each asset class.

The Committee may utilize the services of performance measurement consultants to evaluate investment results, examine performance attribution relative to target asset classes, and other functions as it deems necessary.

PERMISSIBLE AND NONPERMISSIBLE ASSETS

All assets selected for the endowment must have a readily ascertainable market value and must be readily marketable. These types of assets are permitted:

Equities	Fixed Income
Common stock	U.S. Treasury and agency obligations
Convertible securities	Mortgage-backed securities of U.S. government
Preferred stock	Money market funds
Warrants	Short-term investment fund accounts
Rights (corporate action)	Certificates of deposit
Rule 144a stock	Bankers acceptances
American Depositary Receipts (ADRs)	Commercial paper
Collateralized mortgage obligations	Repurchase agreements
ABC Shared Appreciation Mortgage Program	Asset-backed securities/ collateralized bond obligations
First trust deeds of gift properties	
Index funds and Exchange-Traded Funds (ETFs)	

Within the mortgage-backed securities and collateralized mortgage obligations sector, investments in CMO tranches with reasonably predictable average lives are permitted, provided at time of purchase the security does not exceed the average duration of the current Merrill Lynch 3–5 Treasury Index plus one year. Interest-only (IO) and principal-only (PO) securities—or other derivatives based on them—are prohibited, as are securities with very limited liquidity.

Emerging market investments are permitted within the global equity manager's portfolio, subject to a maximum of 10 percent. Likewise, currency hedging as a defensive strategy is permitted in the global portfolio.

These types of assets or transactions are expressly prohibited without prior written approval from the Investment Committee:

Equities	Fixed Income
Commodities	Unregistered securities, except rule futures 144-A securities
Margin purchases	
Short selling	Tax-exempt securities
Put and call options	Any asset not specifically permitted
Direct oil and gas participations	
Direct investments in real estate	

SELECTION OF INVESTMENT MANAGERS

The Investment Committee may choose to select and appoint managers for a specific investment style or strategy, provided that the overall objectives of the endowment are satisfied.

RESPONSIBILITIES OF THE INVESTMENT MANAGER
ADHERENCE TO STATEMENT OF INVESTMENT OBJECTIVES AND POLICY GUIDELINES

1. The manager is expected to observe the specific limitations, guidelines, and philosophies stated herein or as expressed in any written amendments or instructions.

2. The manager's acceptance of the responsibility of managing these funds will constitute a ratification of this statement, affirming his or her belief that it is realistically capable of achieving the endowment's investment objectives within the guidelines and limitations stated herein.

DISCRETIONARY AUTHORITY The manager will be responsible for making all investment decisions for all assets placed under its management and will be held accountable for achieving the investment objectives stated herein. Such "discretion" includes decisions to buy, hold, and sell securities (including cash and equivalents) in amounts and proportions that are reflective of the manager's current investment strategy and that are compatible with the endowment's investment guidelines.

INVESTMENT POLICY STRATEGY FOR ERISA SECTION 404(C) PLANS

This checklist is designed to provoke discussion about how the plan's investment committee and/or trustees select and monitor investments available to participants in the plan. From that discussion, an Investment Policy Statement for the plan can be generated.

Evaluate plan and participant needs
    Age ranges
    Death/disability assumptions
    Longevity in retirement
    Role/responsibility of fiduciaries and consultants

State the investment objectives and goals
    Long-term growth
    Aggressive growth
    Preservation of principal
    Overall annual performance goal

Develop criteria for selection process
    Investment managers
    Mutual funds
    Other investments

Standards/benchmarks of investment performance
    Lipper ratings (peer comparisons)
    Morningstar reports (star ratings)
    Stock indexes (DJIA, S&P, NASDAQ, Wilshire, Russell)
    Volatility (beta factors)

Classes/styles of authorized investments
    Core funds:
        Stable value (money market or GIC)
        Fixed assets (bonds)
        Stocks (large U.S. blend)

    Recommended alternatives—stock funds:
        Large U.S. value
        Small U.S. blend
        Small U.S. value
        Large international
    Other options:
        Short-term bonds
        High-yield bonds
        Global bonds
        Large U.S. growth stocks
        Small U.S. growth stocks
        Mid-cap U.S. stocks
        Real estate
        Small International stocks
        Value International stocks
        Emerging market stocks

Diversification within and among investment classes/styles
    Growth/value/blend stocks
    Large/small/blend stocks
    Short-/mid-/long-term bonds

Investment restrictions
    Trading/transfer timing
    Outside brokerage options
    Distribution timing

Reporting procedures/timing
    Participant reports
    Investment performance updates

Procedures for monitoring investment performance
    Timing for investment committee reviews (quarterly/semiannual/annual)
    Comparison against benchmarks
    Minimum acceptable investment returns
    Policy with respect to fund manager changes
    Criteria/process for making changes

Source: Benefit Resources, Inc. Used by permission.

UNIFORM PRUDENT INVESTOR ACT

WEST'S ANNOTATED CALIFORNIA CODES
**PROBATE CODE DIVISION 9. Trust Law Part 4. Trust Administration Chapter 1. Duties of Trustees
Article 2.5—Uniform Prudent Investor Act**

Current through end of 1995–1996 Regular Session and lst–4th Executive Session. Section 16047.
Standard of Care: Investments and management; considerations

(a)   A trustee shall invest and manage trust assets as a prudent investor would, by considering the purposes, terms, distribution requirements, and other circumstances of the trust. In satisfying this standard, the trustee shall exercise reasonable care, skill, and caution.

(b)   A trustee's investment and management decisions respecting individual assets and courses of action must be evaluated not in isolation, but in the context of the trust portfolio as a whole and as a part of an overall investment strategy having risk and return objectives reasonably suited to the trust.

(c)   Among circumstances that are appropriate to consider in investing and managing trust assets are the following, to the extent relevant to the trust or its beneficiaries:

    (1)   General economic conditions.

    (2)   The possible effect of inflation or deflation.

    (3)   The expected tax consequences of investment decisions or strategies.

    (4)   The role that each investment or course of action plays within the overall trust portfolio.

    (5)   The expected total return from income and the appreciation of capital.

    (6)   Other resources of the beneficiaries known to the trustee as determined from information provided by the beneficiaries.

    (7)   Needs for liquidity, regularity of income, and preservation or appreciation of capital.

    (8)   An asset's special relationship or special value, if any, to the purposes of the trust or to one or more of the beneficiaries.

(d)   A trustee shall make a reasonable effort to ascertain facts relevant to the investment and management of trust assets.

(e)   A trustee may invest in any kind of property or type of investment or engage in any course of action or investment strategy consistent with the standards of this chapter.

Note: This information is also available publicly at: www.clrc.ca.gov/pub/Printed-Reports/sRPT-UPIA-1995.pdf.

Reprinted from West's Annotated California Codes, 1997 Electronic update, with permission of Thomson West.

COMPREHENSIVE INVESTMENT POLICY: GENERIC FAITH-BASED ORGANIZATION

INTRODUCTION

It is the policy of the Board of Directors to treat all assets of the Generic Faith-Based Organization (GFBO), including funds that are legally unrestricted, as if held by GBFO in a fiduciary capacity for the sake of accomplishing its mission and purposes. The following investment objectives and directions are to be judged and understood in light of that overall sense of stewardship. In that regard, the basic investment standards shall be those of a prudent investor as articulated in applicable state laws.

INVESTMENT ASSETS

For purposes of these policies, "investment assets" are those assets of GFBO which are available for investment in the public securities markets and as accounts at financial institutions: common stock, preferred stock, bonds, cash, or cash equivalents. These assets may be purchased directly or through intermediate structures such as a brokerage or bank investments subsidiary.

Within its holdings of investment assets, GFBO holds both operating reserves and excess reserves.

"Operating reserves" are monies held for emergency needs and cash inflow and outflow timing differences. GFBO anticipates the amount of operating reserves to generally approximate two–three months' of operating expenses, depending on the ministry fund.

"Excess reserves" are monies not normally needed within the next 12 months.

"Illiquid assets" are described elsewhere in GFBO's Gift Acceptance Policies and Guidelines document, and are governed by those rules and not by these investment policies unless and until such assets are converted to cash.

PURPOSE OF THE INVESTMENT POLICY

In general, the purpose of this statement is to outline a philosophy and attitude which will guide the investment management of investment assets toward the desired results. It is intended to be sufficiently specific to be meaningful yet flexible enough to be practical. This statement of investment policy is set forth by the Board of Directors of GFBO in order to:

1. Define and assign the responsibilities of all involved parties
2. Offer guidance and limitations to the investment manager(s), the individual(s) selected to manage the investment assets, regarding the investment of operating reserves and excess reserves
3. Establish a basis for performance measurement and evaluating investment results

DELEGATION OF AUTHORITY

The Board of Directors of GFBO in adopting these policies and forming an Investment Committee has delegated authority to the Investment Committee to supervise GFBO investments. The Board reserves to itself the exclusive right to amend or revise these policies, based on input from the Investment Committee.

The Investment Committee of GFBO is a fiduciary, and is responsible for directing and monitoring the investment management of assets. As such, the Investment Committee is authorized to delegate certain responsibilities to professional experts in various fields. These include, but are not limited to investment management consultants, investment managers, custodians, attorneys, auditors, and others deemed appropriate in fulfilling the fiduciary responsibility of the Board of Directors.

The investment manager(s) will be held responsible and accountable to achieve the objectives stated in this policy. While it is not believed that the limitations will hamper the investment manager(s), the manager(s) should communicate to the Investment Committee any modifications which they deem appropriate.

RESPONSIBILITIES OF THE INVESTMENT COMMITTEE

The Investment Committee is charged with the responsibility for the management of the assets of GFBO. The Investment Committee may be comprised of the Executive Director, Finance Director, at least one Board member who would chair the Committee, up to three total Board members, and up to three nonboard members, who serve at the pleasure of the Board. It shall be the responsibility of the Committee to:

1. Prudently and diligently select and hire qualified investment professionals, including investment manager(s) and custodian(s).
2. Establish an investment strategy within 30 days of hiring an investment manager(s).

3. Supervise the overall implementation of GFBO's investment policies by GFBO's executive staff and outside investment manager(s).

4. Communicate GFBO's financial needs to the investment manager(s) on a timely basis.

5. Determine GFBO's risk tolerance and investment horizon, and communicate these to the investment manager(s).

6. Establish reasonable and consistent investment objectives and allocations which will direct the investment of the assets.

7. Monitor and evaluate the investment performance of GFBO's Funds at least quarterly.

8. Meet two times each year with the investment manager(s) to review the performance of the portfolio, evaluate the results, and report back to the Board of Directors.

9. Monitor and evaluate the performance of the investment manager(s) at least annually to assure adherence to policy guidelines and to monitor investment objective progress.

10. Review all costs associated with the management of GFBO's portfolio, manager fees, trading expenses, custodial charges, and so on.

11. Enact proper control procedures to replace investment manager(s) if necessary due to professional turnover, underperformance, or failure to comply with investment policy guidelines.

12. Grant exceptions as permitted in these policies, as required by cash flow needs or market conditions.

13. Recommend changes in approved policy, guidelines, and objectives as needed.

14. Execute such other duties as may be delegated by the Board of Directors.

Whenever these policies assign specific tasks to the Committee, the Committee may in turn delegate certain tasks to the Finance Director or other designated staff, with the Committee maintaining full oversight responsibility.

In discharging its authority, the Investment Committee can act in the place and stead of the Board and may receive reports from, pay compensation to, enter into agreements with, and delegate discretionary investment authority to such investment manager(s). When delegating discretionary investment authority to one or more manager(s), the Committee will establish and follow appropriate procedures for selecting such manager(s) and for conveying to each the scope of their authority, the organization's expectations, and the requirement of full compliance with these policies.

The Investment Committee will establish such custodial and brokerage relationships as are necessary for the efficient management of GFBO's Funds. Whenever the Committee has not designated a brokerage relationship, then GFBO Investment Manager(s) may execute transactions wherever they can obtain best price and execution.

RESPONSIBILITIES OF THE INVESTMENT MANAGER

Each investment manager must be a registered investment advisor under the Investment Advisors Act of 1940, or a bank or insurance company, and must acknowledge in writing its acceptance of responsibility as a fiduciary. Each investment manager will have full discretion to make all investment decisions for the assets placed under its jurisdiction, while observing and operating within all policies, guidelines, constraints, and philosophies as outlined in this statement and others issued by the Investment Committee. Specific responsibilities of the investment manager(s) include:

1. Holding discretionary investment management responsibility, including decisions to buy, sell, or hold individual securities, and to alter allocation within the strategic asset allocation and investment asset quality and diversification guidelines established in this statement.
2. Reporting to GFBO management on a timely basis: Monthly for investment activity.
3. Reporting on a timely basis to both the Investment Committee and GFBO management: Quarterly for investment performance results, with the reporting to include assistance in interpreting the results.
4. Communicating to the Investment Committee any major changes to the following: Economic outlook, investment strategy, legal or regulatory environment, or any other significant factors which affect implementation of the investment process or the investment progress of GFBO's investment portfolio.
5. Informing the Investment Committee regarding any qualitative change to investment management organization, including changes in portfolio management personnel, ownership structure, investment philosophy, and so on.
6. Reviewing portfolios and recommending actions, as needed, to maintain proper strategic asset allocations and investment strategies for the objectives of each fund type.
7. Executing such other duties as may be mutually agreed.

RESPONSIBILITIES OF THE CUSTODIAN

The Custodian will be a registered broker/dealer who is a member of the Securities Investor Protection Corporation (SIPC) established by Congress under the Securities Investor Protection Act of 1970. This custodian will provide the first $500,000 of coverage subject to Federal requirements. The remaining coverage to be provided by the custodian through Lloyd's of London. This membership is understood to insure against impropriety rather than market risk.

The custodian will physically maintain possession of securities owned by GFBO, collect dividend and interest payments, redeem maturing securities, and effect receipt and delivery following purchases and sales. The custodian may also perform regular accounting of all assets owned, purchased or sold, as well as movement of assets into and out of the accounts.

CASH FLOW REQUIREMENTS

GFBO will be responsible for advising the investment manager(s) in a timely manner and at least annually of GFBO's cash distribution requirements from any managed portfolio or Fund. Each investment manager is responsible for providing adequate liquidity to meet such distribution requirements.

GENERAL INVESTMENT PRINCIPLES/ASSUMPTIONS

1. Investments shall be made solely in the interest of GFBO.
2. The assets shall be invested with the care, skill, prudence, and diligence under the circumstances then prevailing that a prudent person acting in like capacity and familiar with such matters would use in the investments of a fund of like character and with like aims.
3. Investment of the assets shall be so diversified as to minimize the risk of large losses, unless under the circumstances it is clearly prudent not to do so.
4. The Investment Committee may employ one or more investment managers of varying styles and philosophies to attain GFBO's objectives.
5. Cash in operating reserves accounts and cash balances in excess reserves accounts and portfolios is to be employed productively at all times, by investment in short-term cash equivalents to provide safety, liquidity, and maximum return. Safety and liquidity take precedence over return in the investment of cash balances.
6. All purchases of securities will be for cash and there will be no margin transactions, short selling, or commodity transactions.
7. Investments in limited partnerships or derivatives (including futures, forwards, options, and swaps) may not be utilized without the prior permission of the Committee.
8. Investment asset class allocations that fall outside the permissible strategic asset allocation range shall be rebalanced as frequently as each year, and cannot go longer than every two years before being rebalanced.
9. GFBO's investment philosophy is predicated on the recognition that inflation will continue and will also contribute to the loss of purchasing power of the dollar.
10. Over the long term, equity investments will grow faster than fixed income investments and inflation, and will provide the best protection of the real value of principal and the preservation of purchasing power.

ASSET DIVERSIFICATION

The investment manager(s) will maintain reasonable diversification at all times in the investment of excess reserves. The equity securities of any one company should not exceed 5 percent of the overall GFBO excess reserves portfolio at the time of purchase and the combined debt and equity securities of any one company should not exceed 10 percent of the overall GFBO excess reserves portfolio at any time.

Also, a sizable stock gift to the ministry may cause a short-term imbalance and that such an imbalance will be allowed for the prudent timely reproportioning as the market allows.

ASSET QUALITY

1. **Common stocks.** The investment manager(s) may invest in any unrestricted, publicly traded common stock that is listed on a major exchange or a national, over-the-counter market, and that is appropriate for the portfolio objectives, asset class, and/or investment style of the fund type that is to hold such shares.
2. **Preferred stock and convertible bonds** The investment manager(s) may select high-quality standard preferred stocks, convertible preferred stock, or convertible bonds as equity investments. The quality rating of all preferred stock and convertible bonds must be "investment grade," which is BBB or better, as rated by Standard & Poor's, or Baa or better, as rated by Moody's.

   The investment manager is given discretion regarding evaluating quality in any case in which the preferred stock or convertible bond security has a split rating. The common stock into which either may be converted must satisfy the standard of Section XI (1), above.
3. **Bonds and notes (fixed income).** The quality rating of bonds and notes must be "investment grade," which is BBB or better, as rated by Standard & Poor's, or Baa or better, as rated by Moody's. The portfolio may consist of only traditional principal and interest obligations with current maturities of 7 years or less.

   Any bond or note security that is downgraded to below *both* a BBB S&P rating *and* Baa Moody's rating, must be sold immediately. In the case where only one of the ratings falls below "investment grade," the investment manager is given discretion regarding retention of the bond or note security.

   The average quality of any bond mutual fund shall be BBB or better, as rated by S&P's, or Baa or better, as rated by Moody's. Any bond mutual fund whose average quality drops below *both* of these ratings, must be sold immediately.

4. Operating Reserves and cash equivalents in the Excess Reserves portfolios:

Certificates of deposit. CDs may be purchased from financial institutions if they are insured by the FDIC and only in amounts of $100,000 or less.

Commercial paper. The quality rating of commercial paper must be:

- A-1, as rated by Standard & Poor's;
- P-1, as rated by Moody's, or
- F-1 as rated by Fitch.

No split-rating commercial paper may be held. Any commercial paper that is downgraded below either A-1, P-1, or F-1 must be sold immediately.

Money market mutual fund. The assets of any money market mutual funds must comply with the quality provisions for bonds and notes securities and those listed for Operating Reserves above.

5. Other securities. The investment manager(s) may invest in real estate investment securities (REITs), REIT mutual funds, and any other publicly traded investments that the Committee determines to be appropriate. The investment manager(s) may not utilize derivatives without the prior permission of the Committee.

INVESTMENT OBJECTIVES

GFBO's primary investment objective is to preserve and protect its assets by earning a total return for each category of assets (a "fund type"), which is appropriate for each fund type's time horizon, distribution requirements, and risk tolerance.

GFBO currently maintains three fund types:

1. Operating Reserves
2. Excess Reserves
3. Endowments

In the future, additional fund types may include:

- Charitable Trust Funds
- Annuity Reserves and may add other fund types in the future

These policies apply to all GFBO Funds, although the specific objectives, risk parameters, and asset allocation will vary, as appropriate, from Fund type (i.e. operating reserves versus excess reserves) and with the possible future Fund types, from Fund to Fund.

OPERATING RESERVES INVESTMENT OBJECTIVES   The Operating Reserves investment objective emphasizes preservation of capital and income (with an emphasis on security of principal and liquidity). Over the investment time horizon, these assets are to be protected (i.e. willing to sacrifice some positive return in order to protect from loss of existing assets).

EXCESS RESERVES INVESTMENT OBJECTIVES   The Excess Reserves investment objective emphasizes total return. This is the aggregate return from capital appreciation and interest and dividends. Specifically, the primary objective of the management of the overall Excess Reserves portfolios is the attainment on an average *annual real return rate* of *3.0 percent* over every trailing five-year period. *Real return rate* is the actual return minus the inflation rate. Asset growth, exclusive or contributions and withdrawals, should exceed the rate of inflation in order to preserve purchasing power of the assets.

For example, if the average annual inflation rate for most recent five years was 3.5 percent, the Excess Reserves portfolios would be expected to have earned at least 6.5 percent per year. Short-term volatility will be tolerated in as much as it is consistent with the volatility of a comparable market index.

This investment objective applies to the aggregate return for all Excess Reserves portfolios taken as a group, and is not meant to be imposed on each investment account (if more than one account is used).

EXCESS RESERVES CALCULATION   Excess Reserves will be calculated by this formula:

> Begin with: Total Net Assets Averaged over the last 12 months
>
>> (excluding December)
>
> Less: 3 month General and Administrative reserve
>
> Less: 3 month Campus Region Account reserve
>
> Less: 2 month Staff MTD accounts reserve based on average over last
>
>> 12 months (excluding December)
>
> Less: 2 month Medical, Dental, and Employment Insurance Account
>
>> reserves
>
> Less: Added safety cushion as determined by Investment Committee
>
> Equals = Excess Reserves available for investing

This calculation will be updated annually.

ASSET ALLOCATIONS

Actual asset allocations for each fund type will be established and maintained by GFBO on the advice of its investment manager(s), within the ranges provided in this table:

Fund Type	Equities	Asset Classes: Fixed Income	Cash & Cash Equivalents
Operating Reserves	0%	0–25%	75%–100%
Excess Reserves	0–15%	0–90%	0%–25%
Endowments	50–100%	0–50%	0–20%

SOCIAL RESPONSIBILITY

GFBO desires to benefit society generally, and the Investment Committee has placed restrictions on the portfolio. Specifically, investment in the securities of companies that manufacture or market alcoholic beverages, tobacco products, gaming products and/or facilities, pornographic, lewd or obscene materials are prohibited.

PERFORMANCE EVALUATION AND REPORTING REQUIREMENTS

1. **Monthly.** Management will obtain written monthly custodial statements. Such statements should contain all pertinent transaction details for each account that holds all or a portion of any GFBO investment fund types. Each monthly statement should include:
   - Description of each security holding as of month-end
   - Percentage of the total portfolio
   - Current price
   - Quantity
   - Current market value
   - Income summary
   - Name and quantity of each security purchased or sold, with the price and transaction date

   In addition, if not included in the custodial reports, the investment manager(s) should provide a report for each fund type or portfolio that shows the month-end allocation of assets between equities, fixed-income securities, and cash.

   The monthly review of custodial statements will also be done by a management position within GFBO that is independent of the cash management and investment process.

2. **Quarterly.** The Committee should obtain from its investment manager(s), a detailed review of GFBO's investment performance for the preceding quarter. Such reports should be provided as to each fund type and for GFBO investment assets in the aggregate. Each quarterly report should include:
   - Description of each security holding as of month-end

- Percentage of the total portfolio
- Current price
- Quantity
- Average cost basis
- Current market value
- Unrealized gain or (loss)
- Indicated annual yield at market
- Estimated annual income derived from security
- Consolidated portfolio summary showing total percentage by security type (e.g., common stock, bond funds, corporate bonds, government bonds, money market, etc.)
- Distribution of fixed income portfolio by maturity, Moody rating, S&P rating
- Management fees charged against account

As to each account or fund type, the Committee should establish with its investment manager(s) the specific criteria for monitoring each account's or fund type's performance, including the index or blend of indices that are appropriate for the objectives of each fund type and for the investment style or asset class of each portfolio within a fund type.

The quarterly review of the investment manager's report will also be done by a management position within GFBO that is independent of the cash management and investment process.

3. **Annually.** The Committee should meet with its investment consultant at least annually to completely review all aspects of GFBO's investment assets. Such a review should include:

- Strategic asset allocation as it compares to the actual asset allocation
- Manager and investment entity performance
- Anticipated additions to or withdrawals from fund types
- Future investment strategies
- Any other matters of interest to the Committee

This Investment Policy is formally adopted by vote of the GFBO Board of Directors on _____/_____/_____.

_____   _____

GFBO Board Secretary   Date

USING MODERN PORTFOLIO THEORY TO IMPLEMENT STRATEGIC ASSET ALLOCATION

Modern Portfolio Theory (MPT) is an investment philosophy representing a quantitative approach to portfolio construction that strives to identify optimal levels of risk and expected returns. MPT's quantitative statistics, which include R-squared, Beta, and Alpha, serve as tools for conducting security selection, portfolio construction and performance analysis.

MODERN PORTFOLIO THEORY—THE INVESTMENT PHILOSOPHY

MPT was pioneered by Harry Markowitz in his paper *Portfolio Selection,* published in 1952 by the *Journal of Finance.* Before MPT, investors gave little consideration to quantifying the concept of risk, although they had known intuitively for many years about the prudence of diversification—that is, spreading risk across more than one security or one type of security. Markowitz was the first to formalize the concept of portfolio diversification. He showed quantitatively how portfolio diversification works to reduce portfolio risk for an investor.

Source: UBS, "Fundamental: Using Modern Portfolio theory to Implement Strategic Asset Allocation," (Author: February, 2005) at http://financialservices.ubs.com. Accessed: 12/02/06.

Fundamentals is a series of white papers addressing a range of topics related to constructing and implementing an investment portfolio. This educational series has been created to help Financial Advisors and their clients discuss relevant investment strategies and vehicles. To learn more about how Modern Portfolio Theory can help you pursue your investment goals, please contact your UBS Financial Advisor.

Markowitz posed the question, "Is the risk of a portfolio equal to the average of the risks of the individuals securities comprising?" MPT demonstrates that the risk of a diversified portfolio is not necessarily equal to the average of the risks of its individual securities and, as a result, some combinations of securities can offer superior combinations of risk and reward than other combinations. The key to finding these combinations is correlation—a measure of the degree to which two securities move in similar patterns.

Diversifying a portfolio among securities with lower correlation can reduce overall portfolio volatility, since the independent price movements of the different securities can be offsetting. This key insight in Markowitz's paper indicates that investors should measure, monitor and control risk at the portolio level rather than the individual security level. A potential investment can be evaluated on the basis of how it fits into an investor's entire portfolio rather than on its individual risk and reward characteristics in isolation.

By combining investments with lower or negative correlations, investors may be able to increase the "efficiency" of their portfolios. One portfolio is more efficient than another if it has higher expected return but the same or less expected risk, or if it has lower expected risk but the same or more expected return. The set of portfolios that has the maximum expected return for every given level of risk is called the "efficient frontier."

The graph below provides a hypothetical illustration of how an efficient frontier is developed from three securities with differing risks and returns.[1] The curved line represents only those portfolio combinations that provide optimal levels of risk for a range of specified target returns. This graph has some important features:

- The efficient frontier built from these three securities consists of points on the curve. Each of these points provides the highest expected return for a given level of risk. Neither Security 1 nor Security 2 is on the efficient frontier.
- Security 2 is suboptimal but can be used in combination with Securities 1 and 3 to derive more optimal portfolios, such as the one represented by the point labeled "An Efficient Frontier Portfolio," which has a higher expected return and less expected risk than a portfolio consisting only of Security 2 (or some other less optimal mix). This is because Security 2 has a high negative correlation with Security 1 and a less than perfect correlation with Security 3.

- A portfolio consisting only of Security 3 is on the efficient frontier because it offers the highest return for a given level of risk.

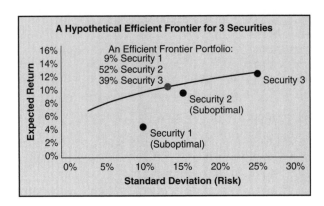

Markowitz showed that increasing the number of lower correlation securities or asset classes in a portfolio can lead to an increasingly optimal efficient frontier (shifting the curve up and/or to the left). At its limit, this exercise yields an efficient frontier containing the "market portfolio," a theoretical portfolio contianing the optimal mix of all risky assets in the market. Markowitz and William Sharpe proposed that all rational investors would hold mixes of this market portfolio and a risk-free asset such as cash. The appropriate mix of the market portfolio and the risk-free asset depends on each investor's risk tolerance and return objectives.

MODERN PORTFOLIO THEORY—CONSTRUCTING A PORTFOLIO OF MUTUAL FUNDS

ESTABLISHING A POLICY PORTFOLIO   Modern Portfolio Theory and the benefits of diversification justify the strategic combination of asset classes in an asset allocation strategy. To determine an appropriate combination, investors often rely upon asset class proxies—or benchmarks—that are an extension of Markowitz's market portfolio concept. These benchmarks represent the risk, return and cross-correlation characteristics of different asset classes. They can be used to form a set of capital market assumptions,[2] which can then be used in conjunction with the investor's profile in an optimization tool. The optimization tool will choose the weight of each asset class in the portfolio that maximizes expected return for a desired level of expected risk or, conversely, minimizes expected risk for a desired level of expected return.[3] This exercise results in a strategic asset allocation plan—sometimes called a policy portfolio[4]—that guides the selection and allocation of investments and the maintenance of the portfolio over time.

Once a policy portfolio has been created, investors are charged with the task of implementing it. Because the optimized policy portfolio is intended to adequately reflect the investor's unique profile,[5] an important goal is to select investments that conform to the policy portfolio. When implementing a portfolio with mutual funds, the corresponding consideration is to identify mutual funds that fulfill the investment mandates for which they are being chosen. A useful approach is to use the MPT statistic *R-squared* to identify funds that have higher correlation to the benchmarks used during optimization.

THE R-SQUARED STATISTIC FOR BENCHMARKING MUTUAL FUNDS

R-squared can be used to compare the historical returns of a mutual fund with the historical returns of a specified benchmark. R-squared ranges between 0% and 100% and can measure the similarity between the return pattern of the benchmark and that of the mutual fund; the closer the R-squared statistic is to 100%, the greater the similarity in return patterns. In more technical terms, R-squared can be used to measure the percent of a mutual fund's return variance that is explained by the variance of the benchmark's returns. It is the correlation coefficient squared.

R-squared has two important and related uses for benchmarking mutual funds:

- *Measuring the degree of correlation between a mutual fund and its benchmark*—R-squared helps determine whether a fund provides consistent exposure to the desired asset class, which helps determine whether it is appropriate for implementing the policy portfolio.
- *Assessing performance*—When a mutual fund has a higher R-squared with a benchmark, a reasonable comparison can be made between the performance of the fund and that of the benchmark. When a mutual fund has a lower R-squared with the benchmark, such comparisons are not likely to be valid, and selecting mutual funds for the portfolio on the basis of those comparisons could result in decisions that are inconsistent with the policy portfolio.

R-Squared	Interpretation
100%	Perfectly correlated to benchmark (e.g., index fund)
80% – 100%	Reasonably correlated to benchmark; benchmark may be used to assess manager's performance
<80%	Fund and benchmark perform less similarly. The benchmark may not be appropriate to assess performance.

ACTIVELY MANAGED MUTUAL FUNDS AND R-SQUARED

Benchmarks used during the optimization process are sometimes thought of as passive representations of asset classes. "Passive" benchmarks can be contrasted with "active" investment management. An important objective of active fund management is to make investment decisions that provide returns superior to those of a passive benchmark. Such investment decisions are often based upon the fund manager's unique strategy or research insights and are reflected in differences between the portfolio holdings of the investment manager and those of the benchmark.

Index funds make no active investment management decisions; they hold all of the benchmark securities at the benchmark's weight.[6] Thus, it is likely that an index fund's return experience will be nearly identical to the benchmark's and that its R-squared will be very close to 100%. In contrast, an active fund manager's investment decisions will differentiate the mutual fund's portfolio holdings from those of the benchmark, which provides the potential for the mutual fund's return experience to deviate from that of the benchmark. Thus, it is highly unlikely that an actively managed mutual fund would have an R-squared with the benchmark of 100%.

Since portfolio managers must make some active decisions in order to outperform the benchmark, an R-squared less than 100% is desirable for active managers. At the same time, when R-squared is too low, it becomes doubtful that the fund is an appropriate vehicle for fulfilling the investment mandate.[7] Choosing a fund with an R-squared of at least 80%[8] should provide the investor with an opportunity to balance these seemingly competing goals: consistent exposure to the desired asset class or investment style and the possibility of achieving returns that exceed the asset class benchmark.

THE BETA STATISTIC FOR RELATIVE RISK ASSESSMENT

Modern Portfolio Theory measures risk with a statistic called *beta*. Beta refers to the sensitivity of a security to changes in the broader market. Investors commonly use beta to measure a mutual fund's expected return and volatility relative to the broader market. For example, if a mutual fund has a beta of .9 and the index return is 3%, we would expect the fund to return 2.7% (= .9 × 3%) for that period. The interpretation of beta is quite straightforward. A beta of 1.0 indicates that a mutual fund has been equally as volatile as the benchmark. A beta less than 1.0 indicates a mutual fund has been less volatile than the benchmark, and a beta greater than 1.0 indicates a mutual fund has been more volatile than the benchmark.

Beta	Interpretation
> 1	The mutual fund has realized more risk than the benchmark.
1	The mutual fund has realized benchmarklike risk.
< 1	The mutual fund has realized less risk than the benchmark.

Since investors can eliminate nearly all security-specific risk through diversification, only market risk, or beta, compensates investors with additional expected return. Thus, an investor can lower a portfolio's sensitivity to market risk (in other words, decrease the beta of the portfolio) but only at the expense of less expected return.

Investors implementing an asset allocation strategy might choose a mutual fund with a beta between approximately. 0.8 and 1.2.[9] This increases the likelihood that the selected mutual fund will properly contribute to the desired portfolio risk level, which is used as an input to determine the investor's optimal asset allocation strategy.

It is important to point out that beta is not a meaningful measure unless the fund is being compared to an appropriate benchmark. As discussed earlier, benchmark appropriateness can be measured with R-squared. A high R-squared figure facilitates an apples-to-apples comparison of risk between the fund and the benchmark index and indicates that the fund's beta is reliable.

Using Beta to Compare Two Mutual Funds

Relative to the S&P 500 Index, Acme Fund has a beta of .75, whereas Top Fund has a beta of 1.50. If the S&P 500 Index rose 10%, investors would expect 50% more return from Top Fund than from Acme Fund (15%) and 25% less return from Acme Fund than from Top Fund (7.5%). If on the other hand, the S&P 500 Index fell 10%, investors would expect Top Fund to fall 15% and Acme Fund to fall 7.5%.

THE ALPHA STATISTIC FOR MEASURING RISK-ADJUSTED PERFORMANCE

In making active investment decision, fund managers rely upon proprietary investment strategies, investment analysis and trading expertise. These activities provide an opportunity to outperform the index, but they also increase the costs of managing a fund. Thus, mutual fund investors who select actively managed funds generally incur larger expense ratios[10] for the chance to achieve superior risk-adjusted returns. *Alpha* provides an indication of whether a fund manager has added value relative to the index on a risk-adjusted basis, after fees and expenses. Simply put, it indicates whether investors have gotten what they've paid for.

Alpha	Interpretation
+	The fund has returned more than predicted by its beta. The fund is delivering higher returns than expected, given the amount of risk assumed.
0	The fund has met return expectations predicted by its beta.
−	The fund has returned less than predicted by its beta. The fund is delivering lower returns than expected, given the amount of risk assumed.

Alpha is a risk-adjusted measure of excess return over the benchmark. It measures the differences between a mutual fund's actual returns and its expected returns, given the fund's beta (risk relative to the benchmark). When these differences are consistently positive, the manager has positive alpha. When these differences are consistently negative, the manager has negative alpha. As with beta, alpha statistics are not meaningful unless a mutual fund has a high R-squared with its benchmark.

Calculating a Mutual Fund's Alpha

Fund's return − Return of 90– day Treasury bill (risk free investment) = Excess return

Excess return − Fund's expected excess return based on its beta = Alpha

Alpha is the difference between a fund's expected returns based on its beta and actual returns.

ASSESSING ALPHA QUALITY

Alpha is a summary statistic that can mask the underlying character of a manager's relative returns. Thus, alpha must be interpreted carefully, and investors should not rely solely upon the absolute level of alpha when making investment decisions.

Unfortunately, there are no rules for ascertaining an appropriate level of alpha, except that for active managers, alpha should be greater than zero. Although higher alpha is generally more desirable, the level of alpha that is "good" depends largely on the asset class to which the fund belongs. An alpha of 1% per year might not be significant for a stock fund but could be very significant for a U.S. Government bond fund. For this reason, when using alpha to compare mutual funds, the mutual funds being compared should correlate highly with the same benchmark index. A positive alpha statistic provides evidence that the manager has generated positive risk-adjusted returns relative to its benchmark historically, but it says very little—if anything—about the manager's ability to generate alpha in the future. Even so, not every fund's historical alpha is created equally! An important consideration is whether historical alpha has been generated by the fund manager's investing skills or by luck. Although it is impossible to conclude skill with absolute certainty, dissecting the fund's returns can provide some insight. For example, extreme outperformance—perhaps related to a single timely investment—generated during one or two monthly periods can result in positive alpha for the entire measurement period. In such cases it may be less likely that alpha is indicative of manager skill. If, on the other hand, the manager's alpha has been generated by consistently outperforming the benchmark, it may be more likely that the manager's alpha is attributable to investing skill—skill that may be more relevant to future periods.

Ultimately, quantitative measures will only reveal so much about the quality of a fund's alpha. Such measures provide evidence of past success, but investors should carefully evaluate the sources of that success. This requires qualitative analysis to determine whether those sources are repeatable and have the potential to lead to future alpha generation.

APPLYING MODERN PORTFOLIO THEORY

Modern Portfolio Theory offers investors a strategic way to implement and maintain their asset allocation plans. MPT is both the philosophical foundation guiding the formulation of an asset allocation plan and the quantitative tool that helps select investments that conform to the plan.

SUMMARIZING MODERN PORTFOLIO THEORY PRINCIPLES   Modern Portfolio Theory extends the concept of diversification and attempts to quantify its benefits. The key takeaways include:

- Investors should build portfolios that maximize expected return for a given level of desired risk.
- The risk of a portfolio is not necessarily equal to the sum of the risks of the individual securities comprising it.
- Diversification across securities that have low correlations to one another can reduce a portfolio's overall risk and volatility level.
- An efficient portfolio is a portfolio that has the smallest portfolio risk for a given level of expected return, or the largest expected return for a given level of risk.
- Investors must examine their own risk tolerances and return objectives to determine their optimal balance between risk and expected return.

DEVELOPING A SHORT LIST   An efficient and cost-effective means of implementing a portfolio is to use mutual funds. But with thousands of mutual funds from which to choose, selecting appropriate mutual funds for an investment policy can be complicated and time consuming. MPT statistics are published by many mutual fund data reporting services and can facilitate the decision-making process. For each asset category in the asset allocation plan, an investor may use the following process to narrow mutual fund choices to a "short list":

- Choose benchmarks that appropriately reflect the desired asset category exposure.
- Choose mutual funds with an R-squared of 80% or greater to this benchmark.
- Further limit choices to mutual funds that have a beta between .80 and 1.2.
- Choose mutual funds that have generated positive alpha, with a preference for funds that have generated alpha consistently.

CONDUCTING DUE DILIGENCE Once a short list for each asset class has been obtained, the investor should conduct further due diligence to discern which fund(s) are most likely to fulfill the investment objectives, as outlined in the investment plan. MPT statistics are not the only factors that should be considered when choosing a mutual fund. However, they offer a good starting point for identifying funds on which to conduct further research. Investors should also consider:

- Management fees and sales charges
- The tenure of the manager/management team
- Any other considerations that indicate whether the investment meets an investor's unique set of financial needs and preferences

GLOSSARY OF MODERN PORTFOLIO THEORY TERMS

Correlation is the complementary or parallel relationship between two securities. For example, the performance of two stocks within the same industry will likely be strongly correlated.

Diversification is a widely embraced investment strategy that helps counteract the unpredictability of the markets. Spreading risk across several types of investments can help smooth out the ups and downs in a portfolio's value. Should one investment be out of favor, another investment might be in favor, helping to offset price declines.

Efficient Portfolio is a portfolio that has the smallest portfolio risk for a given level of expected return, or the largest expected return for a given level of risk.

Efficient Frontier represents a set of portfolios that have the maximum rate of return for every given level of risk.

Standard Deviation is a measure of the dispersion of outcomes around the mean (or expected value), used to measure total risk. It is the square root of the variance.

IMPORTANT INFORMATION TO CONSIDER WHEN INVESTING IN MUTUAL FUNDS

Mutual funds involve investment risk, including the possible loss of principal. Unlike bank deposits, mutual funds are not insured or guaranteed by the FDIC or any other government agency.

Additionally, each type of mutual fund has different types of risk. For example, a fixed income fund is exposed to interest rate risk, because as interest rates increase, the prices of the bonds in the fund may decrease. Equity funds are affected by changes in interest rates, general market conditions and other political, social and economic developments, as well as specific matters relating to the companies in the portfolio. Investing in international securities is subject to risks associated with changes in currency values, economic, political and social conditions, the regulatory environment of the countries in which the fund invests, and the difficulties of receiving current and accurate information.

Each mutual fund's prospectus includes information about the investment objectives, risks, charges and expenses associated with the fund. You should obtain a prospectus from your Financial Advisor and read and consider this information carefully before investing.

Notes

1. This graph is intended to illustrate the math of building a hypothetical efficient frontier, assuming we limit the investment options to these three securities. A portfolio of three securities is concentrated and is thus not likely to offer an optimal level of risk and return.

2. Capital market assumptions generally include the risk (measured by standard deviation), cross-correlation and return estimates for each asset class. Many practitioners use historical estimates of risk and correlation, since research indicates that these measures have some predictive power. However, for return estimates many practitioners use forecasted returns rather than historical returns, since historical returns have tended to be poor predictors of future returns.

3. There is some disagreement in the academic and investment communities about the value of optimizers. Some have criticized them on the basis that they maximize estimation errors. However, Mark Kritzman, Research Director of the Research Foundation of the CFA Institute, has argued that for a given level of estimate quality, an optimizer will converge to the best solution.

4. "Policy portfolio" and "strategic asset allocation plan" are used interchangeably in this appendix.

5. An important assumption here is that the benchmarks were carefully chosen to reflect the asset classes being optimized.

6. Some index funds use quantitative methods to replicate the return experience of the index without holding all of its constituents.

7. This problem, sometimes called "benchmark mismatch," cuts both ways: Perhaps the fund doesn't provide the desired asset class exposure, but it is also possible that the benchmark is improperly specified. The investor should be aware of the limitations of certain benchmarks in order to determine whether deviations from the benchmark might be justifiable.

8. Eighty percent is a general rule of thumb. More or less R-squared may be appropriate depending on an investor's tolerance for achieving returns that deviate from those of the benchmark returns. The characteristics of the underlying benchmark are one factor in determining that tolerance.

9. A wider range takes into account the considerable effect that outlier observations can have on the regression slope (beta). Those wanting to assess the statistical confidence of beta may examine the standard error of the beta coefficient. Generally, funds with a high R-squared will also have a statistically significant beta coefficient.

10. The expense ratio is periodically deducted from a fund's NAV to compensate the manager for managing, administering, and distributing the fund.

INDEX